THINKING
LOGICALLY

THINKING LOGICALLY
Basic Concepts for Reasoning

JAMES B. FREEMAN

Hunter College
The City University of New York

PRENTICE HALL
Englewood Cliffs, New Jersey 07632

Library of Congress Cataloging-in-Publication Data

FREEMAN, JAMES B.
    Thinking logically.

    Bibliography.
    Includes index.
    1. Logic. 2. Thought and thinking. I. Title.
BC71.F74 1987   160   87-12572
ISBN 0-13-917733-7

Editorial/production supervision and
    interior design: Mary A. Bardoni
Cover design: Lundgren Graphics, Ltd.
Cover photo: Key Photo/FPG
Manufacturing buyer: Harry P. Baisley and Margaret Rizzi

 © 1988 by Prentice Hall
A Division of Simon & Schuster
Englewood Cliffs, New Jersey 07632

Printed in the United States of America

10 9 8 7 6 5 4 3 2 1

ISBN   0-13-917733-7   01

PRENTICE-HALL INTERNATIONAL (UK) LIMITED, *London*
PRENTICE-HALL OF AUSTRALIA PTY. LIMITED, *Sydney*
PRENTICE-HALL CANADA INC., *Toronto*
PRENTICE-HALL HISPANOAMERICANA, S.A., *Mexico*
PRENTICE-HALL OF INDIA PRIVATE LIMITED, *New Delhi*
PRENTICE-HALL OF JAPAN, INC., *Tokyo*
SIMON & SCHUSTER ASIA PTE. LTD., *Singapore*
EDITORA PRENTICE-HALL DO BRASIL, LTDA., *Rio de Janeiro*

This book is dedicated to my mother
and to the memory of my father

CONTENTS

PREFACE

No one can tell another person in any definite way how he *should* think, any more than how he ought to breathe or to have his blood circulate. But the various ways in which men *do* think can be told and can be described in their general features. Some of these ways are better than others; the reasons why they are better can be set forth. The person who understands what the better ways of thinking are and why they are better can, if he will, change his own personal ways until they become more effective; until, that is to say, they do better the work that thinking can do and that other mental operations cannot do so well.
— John Dewey, *How We Think*
Logic is not everything. But it *is* something—something which can be taught, something which can be learned, something which can help us in some degree to think more sensibly about the dangerous world in which we live.
— David Hackett Fischer, *Historians' Fallacies*

There is a lot of healthy discussion about what texts and courses in informal logic and critical thinking should contain. What formal tools, in particular how much formal deductive logic, should be included? Should we emphasize inductive logic applied to everyday contexts and problems? Does a course in scientific method suit our purposes well? Should the primary focus be on the fallacies, learning to identify particular mistaken patterns of reasoning which nonetheless may be very persuasive? Or, rather, should it be on general criteria for evaluating reasoning, any piece of reasoning we might encounter? To what extent should we concentrate on argument and to what extent should we look at other topics related to logic and critical thinking—language analysis, advertising, decision making, and problem solving? Should we discuss composing arguments of our own besides evaluating those we encounter? Finally, to what extent should we address broader issues impinging on critical thinking—our image systems which have a profound effect on what we believe and the strength of our confidence in our beliefs, our egocentric and sociocentric prejudices which may block critical thinking?

These are live questions. It is not surprising, then, that there is a great diversity among texts currently available in the field and in the agendas and expectations people have for courses in informal logic and critical thinking. If one tried to include all the items on everyone's agenda in one text, I fear the book would become a mountainous tome, prohibitive in size and cost. Hence I feel I must make an honest statement right at the beginning concerning what this text is and is not about.

I distinguish informal logic from critical thinking. As I see it, informal logic includes the generic analysis and evaluation of arguments—How does an argument hang together? What factors make an argument logically convincing? Why does an argument fail to be logically convincing?—and the study, through analysis of language, of factors which may lead us to feel convinced when we have not been given good reasons. By generic analysis and evaluation, I mean a method applicable to any type of argument, not based primarily on assessing just deductive validity or inductive correctness. There is something reactive in this. We are confronted with a message which we subject to challenge. Critical thinking, on the other hand, is more pro-active. Here the emphasis should shift to constructing arguments of one's own, to employing inquiry and scientific method in making decisions and solving problems, to developing self-scrutiny in identifying blocks to critical thinking. Logical thinking involves both informal logic and critical thinking. However, I see informal logic as prerequisite to critical thinking. If we are to construct good arguments, if we are to discover explanations, make decisions, arrive at solutions which can be justified by good argument, shouldn't we be able to recognize what makes an argument good? There is enough here for a semester's work. Hence, in this text we concentrate on informal logic exclusively.

The book falls into two parts. In the first, we develop when a logical thinker should challenge a message—when no argument has been given for it but should have or when the argument is bad. This presupposes being able to recognize types of messages—informative, expressive, directive—to distinguish arguments from nonarguments, and to know the distinguishing marks of good arguments. It also involves recognizing where lies the burden of proof. Properly included here in addition are recognizing obviously fallacious patterns of reasoning—emotional appeals and fallacies involving problems of meaning—and recognizing persuasive techniques. In Part II, we turn to the analysis and evaluation of arguments proper, in effect giving the logical thinker special tools for making challenges. Argument analysis involves being able to display argument structure via the circle and arrow method introduced by Monroe C. Beardsley in *Practical Logic* and *Thinking Straight* and developed by others, especially Stephen N. Thomas in *Practical Reasoning in Natural Language*. A special feature of our approach is to incorporate aspects of Stephen Toulmin's very different method presented in *The Uses of Argument*. Argument evaluation involves asking three critical questions: Are the premises believable? Do they adequately support the conclusion? Are they relevant to the conclusion?

The core of this book consists of Chapters 1 through 4 and 6 through 9. These present the basics of logical challenge and generic argument analysis and evaluation. The remaining chapters offer additional material nice to include in the informal logic course. In particular, Chapters 10 and 11 relate our general method of appraising argument strength to families of inductive and deductive arguments. Chapter 5 includes an exposé of advertising techniques.

We want to acknowledge our debt to other works and workers in the field of informal logic, whose contributions have influenced this book. Specific acknowledgments occur in the "For Further Reading" sections at the end of each chapter. We have already mentioned the Beardsley and Thomas texts. These and Irving M. Copi's *Introduction to Logic* and J. Michael Sproule's *Argument: Language and Its Influence* have been central to our work. Ralph H. Johnson and J. Anthony Blair's discussion of three basic fallacies in *Logical Self-Defense* has suggested the three basic general questions for argument evaluation. Our distinction of informal logic and critical thinking parallels Richard Paul's weak and strong sense for critical thinking. The title of Carl Wellman's book, *Challenge and Response*, has proved seminal in developing our concept of what logical thinking is all about. We want to thank the contributors to the *Informal Logic Newsletter* for supplying much illustrative material in informal logic, to which we owe a number of examples. We also want to thank the editors of the *Sunday Star-Ledger* (Newark, N.J.) for allowing us to use much material from the Readers' Forum section. We are also indebted to many of our colleagues at Hunter College for suggestions and encouragement. To all these, we express our appreciation.

J.B.F.

THINKING
LOGICALLY

INTRODUCTION: LOGICAL THINKING—WHAT IS IT?

What on earth does it mean to think logically? What is logical thinking? Let's approach this question by asking under what circumstances may logical thinking arise. Suppose I am having a conversation with you. I might say many things which you accept without question or comment. But suppose suddenly I say something which you find distinctly questionable. "There is life in outer space." You ask me to defend my claim. "Why should we believe that is true?" I now have a challenge which I did not have before. How should I respond? Suppose I present evidence based on scientific investigation. Wouldn't there be something logical in that?

Here is another illustration. Suppose I go to the movies. The movie itself is just plain entertainment—nothing to challenge me here. But suppose a fire breaks out in the theater. I am definitely challenged. What am I going to do? We can think of various responses—panic or just mindlessly following everyone else. The philosopher John Dewey suggests another: first, I locate the available exits; then, I estimate which one would get me out of the theater most quickly and safely; finally, I proceed to that exit. Clearly, the first two courses of action do not involve logical thinking while Dewey's suggestion exemplifies it. But why? Situations that challenge us, either because some person has called one of our claims into question or because the situation is somehow problematic, are situations which call for logical thinking. That at least is one possible response, and the situation demands a response. To understand what makes a response logical, when a response involves logical thinking, let's look at a further, more detailed, example.[1]

1

On November 1, 1955, Flight 629 crashed within 11 minutes of takeoff from Denver. All forty-four persons on board were killed. Officials of the Civil Aeronautics Board (CAB) and the Federal Bureau of Investigation were called to investigate. Here again we have a problematic, challenging situation. By calling for an inquiry, the problem was recognized and defined. One CAB inspector proceeded to entertain certain possible explanations:

1. A storm caused the crash.
2. Engine failure was responsible.
3. Structural failure in the plane precipitated the accident.

Now if any of these three explanations were correct, we would expect certain consequences to be true, which we could check by making appropriate observations. If observation showed that these consequences held, that would be evidence for the explanation. If observation showed them false, that would constitute damaging evidence against the explanation. By elaborating the consequences, the investigators could devise tests.

Consider:

If (1) is the explanation, weather reports should show bad flying conditions in the Denver area at the time of the crash.

If (2) is correct, the flight recorder might show that one or more engines had been running badly at takeoff or the pilot would have reported engine problems shortly before the crash.

If (3) were true, we would expect evidence of structural failure could be found in the wreckage of the plane.

The investigators carried out these tests. All were negative. Flying conditions were good. All engines were functioning normally at takeoff. In addition, debris from the plane was widely scattered. This configuration is not characteristic of structural failure.

This last fact suggested another explanation:

4. The crash was caused by an explosion aboard the plane.

Now if (4) were true, we would expect the crash debris to be widely scattered. We would also expect that evidence of some explosive could be found in the wreckage and that witnesses near the crash site would have heard an explosion. The investigators already knew of the crash configuration. They had also noticed another fact—that the wreckage smelled of gunpowder. Laboratory reports confirmed the presence of an explosive. Witnesses reported hearing or seeing the explosion. With this considerable confirming evidence, the investigators had their answer: an explosion on board caused the crash. This raises another question—the situation is still challenging. How did those explosives get on board? But we cannot develop the details any further. We must get back to the question of what is logical thinking.[2]

What features of logical thinking does this example illustrate? First, notice that each step is relevant to either discovering the appropriate solution to the problem or justifying that solution. We cannot solve a problem unless we recognize it and say what it is. By entertaining various possible explanations, it is hoped that we will include the correct one. By devising tests, we create means for deciding which one is correct. By carrying out these tests, we get the evidence to decide the question properly and to justify our decision. Hence,

I. Logical thinking is *relevant* to the problem being solved or the claim being established.

Notice how the thinking in our other examples is relevant. The scientific evidence presented is presumably relevant to the question of extraterrestrial life. Finding the exits, estimating which is best, proceeding to that exit are all relevant to solving the problem of getting out of the burning movie theater safely.

Second, notice that when the problem was resolved, there was a significant amount of evidence supporting the solution. The widely scattered debris in the crash configuration, the smell of gunpowder, the lab reports, and the eyewitness interviews all converge to constitute a fairly weighty case for the explosion hypothesis. Also, the fact that evidence has ruled out other possible explanations further increases the substantiation. The investigators accepted the explanation only because there was sufficient, adequate evidence to warrant it. Thus,

II. Logical thinking is satisfied with solutions to problems, accepts conclusions, only when *adequate reasons* have been given.

Again, our fire example illustrates this aspect of logical thinking. In locating the exits and estimating which one is safest, I may not be able to get as much evidence as I would like, but I am trying to make do with the most I can get. I want my solution to be based on the most adequate evidence available.

We must highlight a third feature of logical thinking, implicit in our talk of evidence. Notice that our investigators did not just "cook up" data to support their conclusion. Their data were based on the facts. Statements were accepted or rejected because of the way the world is. This is the hallmark of rationality, conforming our thinking to the actual situation. Proverbially, when an ostrich senses danger, it puts its head into the sand. But this is clearly an irrational response to the challenge, precisely because the ostrich has cut itself off from its environment. Being rational presupposes a disposition to be aware of, to be open to, to take account of the situation as it is rather than in any other way. Rationality presupposes a disposition to take into consideration the actual facts of the case, even if they are not what we should like. In short, rationality presupposes being open to reality, and rationality is the third feature of logical thinking.

III. Logical thinking is *rational.*

Logical thinking is relevant, adequate, and rational—that these are the basic features of logical thinking or that logical thinking is concerned with these issues is a theme running through this entire book. But there are other aspects to appreciating the logical thinking enterprise. Our examples illustrate how logical thinking may be expressed, what we can think logically about. The American philosopher of education Robert Ennis has defined logical thinking as "reasonably going about deciding what to believe or do."[3] Explaining the airplane crash illustrates logical thinking about beliefs while safely escaping from the theater involves logical thinking about actions. We want to stress here the great variety of beliefs about which we can think logically. For example, in late December 1984, the news was full of reports that a Soviet missile had invaded Norwegian air space and crashed into a lake in Finland. Can we reasonably decide whether to believe this statement? Of course. That this event was reported by responsible news organizations and that these organizations concurred worldwide constitute strong evidence. Should all else fail to convince, it is in principle possible to dredge the lake and find the missile. That should settle the issue.

News stories that reported this event also contained speculations that the Soviet Union was trying to send the West, the United States in particular, a message. Here we do not have a description of an event but an interpretation— what does it mean? Can we reasonably decide whether to believe the interpretation? Couldn't the testimony of "informed sources" in Moscow, the similarity or lack of similarity of this action to other Russian behavior, and the overall credibility of the act as interpreted give us evidence one way or another?

Again suppose a question arose concerning the rightness of a government policy. Should the United States spend billions to develop high-tech defensive weapons? Certainly, we can predict certain consequences of adopting this policy—consequences that will have an impact on things we value. The high cost of the project may mean cutting funds that would alleviate poverty, necessitating human suffering. On the other hand, if the technology were successful, chances for peace might be greater. Certainly these issues are complex. Certainly coming to a satisfactory assessment of the situation might be difficult. But isn't an appeal to the consequences of the policy and the values it may affect a rational attempt to decide whether to believe it is a good policy or not?

We anticipate here our discussion in Chapter 2, where we distinguish three broad categories of beliefs or assertions: descriptions, interpretations, and evaluations. The point is that we can reasonably go about trying to decide which descriptions, interpretations, and evaluations to believe. Logical thinking occurs in all three areas. We can seek relevant reasons, can assess whether those reasons are adequate, and can seek reasons which are based on the way the world is.

So far, we have been principally concerned with logical responses, with determining when a response to a challenge is an instance of logical thinking. But we may also think logically when we issue challenges. All of us are daily and continually confronted with many messages concerning what we should believe or do. Some may be straightforward and need no challenge. Others are distinctly dubious and should be challenged. Certainly challenging questionable messages is relevant to deciding reasonably what to believe or do. And a logical challenge will demand relevant, adequate, rational reasons. Hence, there are two roles a logical thinker may play: respondent and challenger. To respond to challenges and to issue challenges—these are the activities of the logical thinker.

Clearly being able to recognize and explain why thinking is relevant, adequate, and rational, or why it fails to have these features, is a central skill of the logical thinker as respondent or challenger. This skill enables us to evaluate reasoning logically—our own or others. In both parts of this book, but especially in Part II, we shall examine logical evaluation in detail. The logical thinker as challenger also needs to know when a message should be challenged, when not, and what sort of challenge is appropriate. This presupposes an ability to distinguish various types of messages and to recognize what they are trying to say or do. We focus on these skills in Part I. Together, these two parts should present us with a stock of basic concepts—those central to understanding, appreciating, and evaluating reasoning. These concepts should help us to appreciate just what is logical thinking.

NOTES

[1]The factual details of this example are condensed from W. Edgar Moore, Hugh McCann, and Janet McCann, *Creative and Critical Thinking,* 2nd ed. (Boston: Houghton Mifflin Company, 1985), ch. 4. Used by permission of Houghton Mifflin Company.

[2]For those who want to find out who did it, the complete investigation is discussed in Chapters 4 and 5 of ibid.

[3]"Rational Thinking and Educational Practice," in *Philosophy and Education,* ed. Jonas F. Soltis (Chicago: National Society for the Study of Education, 1981).

PART I   *The Logical Thinker as Challenger*

1

TYPES OF MESSAGES

§1.1 THE THREE BASIC FUNCTIONS OF LANGUAGE

Since different types of messages require different types of challenges, we begin studying the logical thinker's role as challenger by studying the various types of messages that may confront us. What is the difference between these three sentences?

1. Millard Fillmore served as the thirteenth president of the United States.
2. I hate you! I hate you!! Hate!!! DEEP HATRED!!!!
3. Press in the code 109 BR.

There is a very significant difference illustrated here. Sentence 1 gives us information concerning a certain individual, Millard Fillmore. It tells us something about him, claiming to give us a fact. It makes sense to ask: Is this statement true or false? Does (2) give us any information? Is it intended to give us information? Does it express feelings and emotions? Isn't this its primary function? It is taken from an ad where a person is remonstrating with his car for breaking down more times than he could count. Finally, (3) directs behavior. It tells us to perform a specific action. Sentences 1, 2, and 3 illustrate the three basic functions of language. Language may be informative, it may express or arouse emotions or feelings, or it may direct behavior.

6

Let's give precise definitions of these three basic functions of language:

A message serves the *informative function* just in case it claims to say something about the world, just in case we can meaningfully discuss whether it is true or false.

A message serves the *expressive function* if it either purports to express some feeling or emotion or attempts to arouse feelings or emotions.

A message serves the *directive function* if it attempts to guide or direct behavior; it tells us to do something.

We must emphasize an important point about each of these definitions. Note that we have said not that a message is informative just in case it says something about the world but just in case it *claims* to say something about the world. A statement need not be true to be informative. A false statement claims to say something about the world. It is giving misinformation, but its function is still to say something about the world. But notice that if a statement is informative, asking whether it is true or false must make sense. This is the crucial issue. Similarly, we can imagine someone putting on an act—screaming that he is angry, yelling, cursing—when in fact he doesn't feel any of these emotions. We can have all kinds of emotional insincerity. If we had said that a passage is expressive just in case it expresses some feeling or emotion, these cases would be problematic. How could we have expressive language without any emotion to express? But surely this behavior purports to express emotion. The person is creating a strong impression about his or her emotions and using language to foster these impressions is to use language which functions expressively. Last, a message need not actually change behavior to be directive—it's enough that it attempt to. If the person addressed doesn't pay attention or is not disposed to follow the directive, the message still serves the directive function.

How Do We Recognize Whether a Message is Informative, Expressive, or Directive?

We may easily convert our definitions of the three basic functions of language into critical questions to determine which function or functions a message serves:

Can the message be true or false?

What emotions or feelings does the message apparently express or arouse?

What specific action or actions does the message call for?

Let's apply these questions to specific examples.

4. There is a black crow in that tree.
5. All crows are black.

6. Fifty-two percent of the voters favor the Democrats.

7. Detective Most believes more strongly than Sargent Bronson that Alex committed the crime.

8. The results of the New Hampshire primary are a genuine setback for Senator Smith.

In each case, doesn't it make sense to ask whether the statement is true or false? This is enough to show that all these messages are informative. Do any of them clearly express or arouse emotions? Example 8 might dampen the enthusiasm of Senator Smith's supporters or perhaps put Senator Smith's campaign in a bad light, but otherwise these statements are emotionally neutral. Can you cite any particular emotion that the other statements express or arouse? So these messages are not expressive. Do any of them tell us to do anything? Can we cite any particular action we are told to perform? Clearly, the answer is no, and hence, none of these messages serves the directive function.

Now contrast these examples with

9. What a villainous deed!

Example 9 expresses outrage. There is no question of expressive function here. Does it make sense to ask whether (9) is true or false? Some particular deed or type of deed is being called villainous. Since we can specify what it means for a deed to be villainous, we can ask whether the deed satisfies the criterion. The question of truth or falsity is not completely out of place. But is the principal function of (9) to convey information? Again, since most people want to avoid what is villainous, calling an action villainous directs them to avoid similar actions. But is the primary function of (9) to guide behavior? Also, does (9) tell us to do anything about this particular deed? Is any action enjoined on us?

What about the following messages?

10. Please reconsider your plan.
11. You ought to take advanced symbolic logic.
12. It is good to clean house twice a year.
13. It is wrong to lie.

There is no question that these last examples, as did sentence 3, tell us to do something (or refrain from doing something). These messages are obviously directive. Can we meaningfully ask whether (10) is true or false? Does it arouse any emotions? Sentence 10 seems to be purely directive. Sentences 11, 12, and 13 are evaluations. Hence, the issue of their truth or falsity arises. They may also affect our attitudes concerning certain actions. So they are not completely neutral emotionally. But, again, isn't the principal function of these statements to direct behavior?

Our using the term "principal function" several times points to two very important facts about language function. First, some messages may serve several functions. The three functions are not mutually exclusive. A message can be both informative and expressive, or expressive and directive. Some may serve all three functions. Second, although on some occasions saying that a message serves several functions may be technically correct, one function may take precedence over the others. Sentence 9 is principally expressive. Sentences 11 through 13 are principally directive. Here is another example:

14. That gorgeous bouquet contains so many beautiful roses.

Sentence 14 certainly does state a fact about the bouquet: it has many roses. But a number of words in (14) have an emotional charge—"so many," "beautiful," and, most powerfully, "gorgeous." From the presence of these terms, we may judge that (14)'s principal function is not to describe the bouquet but to swoon over it. The principal function of (14) is expressive.

Although sometimes it is appropriate to identify a principal function, at other times we should recognize that we have several language functions going on. We would not be understanding the message fully if we did not recognize this. Let's look at two specific examples applying our questions to see how all the functions of language are served.

Many directives will try to guide behavior by saying something about the consequences of an action, consequences that should affect us emotionally. Ben Franklin's statement after the signing of the Declaration of Independence is a classic example:

15. We must all hang together or assuredly we shall all hang separately.

Is Franklin directing his compatriots to do anything? Surely he is telling them to put aside differences of party, geographic background, and personality and unite behind the cause of a new nation. But he does this by indicating the consequences of disunity. He is making a prediction here. Can't we ask whether Franklin's prediction is true or false? And what about the predicted consequence—hanging separately? Does that fail to arouse emotion? Isn't it necessary to recognize all three functions to appreciate this passage fully? This example is quite instructive, and we shall return to it again in the next section.

What about the following passage?

16. Your moral feelings really torment you for not [repaying that debt], as you well know. You say you have no duty to repay as a feeble effort to quiet your conscience, and free the expression of your crude selfishness.—Charles L. Stevenson, *Ethics and Language.*

What functions does this message serve? First, certain claims are being made about someone's psychology and motivations. Do the moral feelings really torment the person? Is his or her disclaiming any duty to repay an effort to quiet the conscience? Questions of true or false clearly enter here, making the message informative. But that is not all. To assert this message is to attempt to stir up those moral feelings and make the torment more tormenting, to disquiet the conscience, in short to make the person *feel* guilty. The message is expressive. But again, that is not all. Doesn't the speaker want the individual addressed to repay that debt? Isn't the message intended to bring about that behavior? Clearly, then, this passage is informative, expressive, and directive.

Recognizing that a message may be true or false, or that it directs behavior, is relatively straightforward, barring some pitfalls which we shall examine shortly. Recognizing that a message is expressive requires sensitivity to how language expresses and arouses emotion. We can cultivate this sensitivity by becoming aware of various factors which make language expressive.

What Are Some Specific Ways for Language to Express or Arouse Emotion?

The mere description of certain events or situations may be emotion arousing. Consider:

17. Skies were cloudy above the Bal Harbour, Fla., meeting, which was dominated by behind-the-scenes discussion of [the president's] program, [which one labor leader called] "a high risk gamble with the future of America."—From *Time*, March 2, 1981. Copyright 1981 Time Inc. All rights reserved. Reprinted by permission from TIME.

18. The bodies of the U.S. commandos lay in the Iranian desert.—*Newsweek*, May 12, 1980. Copyright 1980, by Newsweek, Inc. All Rights Reserved. Reprinted by permission.

19. The witness was John W. Dean III, who was the White House legal counsel for three years until fired by Mr. Nixon on April 30.—*U.S. News & World Report*, July 9, 1973.

All these statements are informative, but don't they also affect us emotionally, precisely because of what they describe? *Time* conveys a distinct mood of foreboding or apprehension. Saying in particular that skies were cloudy contributes to this overall impression. Clearly, most Americans in May 1980 were not going to react very favorably to the image of U.S. soldiers lying dead *in the desert* of the very country holding American embassy personnel hostage! By presenting this image, the message arouses anger or disgust. Finally, what is the effect of knowing that John Dean was dismissed, fired from his position? Does it put him in a very good light? In all these cases, then, the information the message presents or the image it depicts is emotion arousing. Being sensitive to this helps us to determine that language is functioning expressively here.

We have noted that certain particular words are emotionally charged. Such emotive words are a chief expressive tool of language. What exactly is an emotive word? We approach this by distinguishing literal meaning from emotive meaning. Many words refer to particular persons, objects, or events—President Lincoln, the commander-in-chief, John Lennon, the World Trade Center, the Capitol, the Golden Gate Bridge, the latest presidential inauguration, the first moon landing, the advent of satellite technology—all these expressions refer to something. What they refer to, their *denotations*, are their literal meaning. On the other hand, some words express attributes or relations. Green, house, animal—these are attributes which may be true of things. Parent of, to the right of, between—these relations may hold among things. Given an attribute term, we may talk of the class of objects, the class of green things, the class of houses, the class of animals, of which that term is true. Likewise, we may talk of the class of all those pairs of persons where the first is a parent of the second, or all the pairs of objects where the first is to the right of the second. These classes are the denotations of the attribute or relation terms. The denotation is part, but not all, of the literal meaning of such terms.

Associated with the terms expressing attributes and relations are "rules" or criteria, sometimes not very clearly defined or specifically spelled out, for deciding whether an attribute is true of a certain item or whether a relation holds between or among various things. For example, a skyscraper has to be a tall building, persons are old only when they have attained a certain number of years, a biological human parent is a person who has been involved in the procreation of a human being. These rules or criteria, the dictionary definitions, so to speak, are the connotations of these terms and are also part of their literal meaning. For attribute and relation terms, then, the literal meaning consists of both the denotation and connotation.

Over and above their literal meanings, words may have the capacity to express or arouse feelings. Consider "coolie." In the American West of the late nineteenth century, persons of oriental descent who did hard manual labor, such as building railroads, were called coolies. That definition then spells out the connotation of "coolie." The denotation is the class of all such persons. To-gether, these constitute the literal meaning. But to call someone a coolie was no compliment. Rather, it was a way of casting dispersion, of expressing and arous-ing contempt. Who are the red necks, the red skins? Are these complimentary terms? On the other hand, consider "leatherneck." The connotation is being a member of the U.S. Marines. The denotation then is the class of Marines. But to call someone a leatherneck—this shows real admiration for the macho man. The word expresses and arouses respect. What about "superstar" and "genius"? These words have literal meaning, but they also express and arouse emotions. We may say that the *emotive meaning* of a word is its dimension to express the emotions of the speaker or writer and evoke similar emotions in the hearer or reader. We can similarly speak of the emotive meaning of whole phrases or other expressions which might be parts of sentences. For convenience, we shall call any expressions possessing a distinct emotive meaning emotive words.

In general, there are two types of emotive words. *Laudatory* or *positive words* express or arouse positive or favorable feelings toward what they indicate.

Derogatory or *negative words* express or arouse negative or unfavorable feelings. Words which involve little or no emotion are called *neutral words*.[1] Hence "leatherneck," "superstar," and "genius" are all laudatory words, whereas "coolie," "red neck," and "red skin" are derogatory. We must be careful here because some words will have different emotive meanings depending on context or on who uses them. The word "communist" in the United States has a distinct negative emotive meaning, but just the opposite in the Soviet Union. "Old" is negative at times, but in "old wine," "old castle," "very old antique," it contributes significantly to the positive emotive meaning of the expressions.

The moral of all this is that we cannot be mechanical in judging emotive meaning. We must be sensitive to context—the entire passage in which the word occurs and the circumstances of its use. This touches upon a theme we shall return to again and again. In interpreting passages, we cannot be mechanical; we must be sensitive. Being aware of the issues we discuss in this book should help to develop sensitivity. Thinking specifically about emotive words and emotion-arousing images or descriptions, two specific ways for language to be expressive, should make us sensitive to the expressive power of language. But we must be prepared to exercise sensitivity.

What Are Some Pitfalls We May Encounter in Determining Language Function?

There are three common confusions that may plague our attempts to determine which linguistic functions a passage serves. Consider the following message:

20. Some Puritans felt guilty about being married, since sexual intercourse gave them pleasure.

Is (20) expressive? Although it *talks* about feelings, it does not *express* them. It is not an expression of the Puritans' feelings of guilt or pleasure, but a statement of fact that they had these feelings and that the pleasure caused the guilt. The message is informative—here purely informative. We must distinguish between expressions of feeling and statements about feelings. Only the former serve the expressive function of language.

Another source of confusion comes from our speaking not only of emotions, feelings, wishes, desires, or attitudes being expressed, but also beliefs or opinions. Yet when someone states a belief, he or she need not be using language expressively. After examining a patient, a doctor may render an opinion on the nature of the problem. The doctor is not expressing emotions, but rather is making a statement of fact, using language informatively. In this particular example, we probably would not be tempted to regard the doctor's statement as expressive. The situation becomes more confusing when we have an informative statement, one which can be true or false, which is controversial or based on flimsy evidence, a product perhaps of wishful thinking. For example,

21. The Democrats will win the next presidential election.

Is this statement informative or expressive? Is it, or at least will it be, true or false? It describes the world. Although we cannot say today whether it is true or false, if we wait long enough we shall. Hence the message satisfies the conditions for being informative. Now we can imagine contexts in which the statement might arouse emotions. Democrats might be elated to hear it; Republicans, unhappy. But looking just at the statement, can we say that it was intended to raise the spirits of Democrats or dampen those of Republicans? Are there any emotive words in the statement? By itself, does it express or arouse much emotion? The point is that just because a statement may not be well supported, may be controversial, we cannot say that it is expressive. We must, rather, be able to cite some particular emotion or emotions the message tends to express or arouse.

The word "directive" also may cause confusion. Recall that a message is directive just when it attempts to guide or direct behavior. Hence, when we judge a message to be directive, we must be able to indicate what action or what type of action it impels us to perform. What then about the following message?

22. The Democrats will win the next election because after two terms, Americans will be tired of the Republicans.

We shall have a lot more to say about messages like this in the next section. In a sense, this message may try to direct our thought, to get us to hold a certain belief. But does that make it directive? Does the message try to get us to *do* anything? The answer is clearly no, and therefore this message is *not* directive. To be directive, a message must attempt to get us to choose or perform some action. Without this, we do not have directive function. Keeping these pitfalls in mind should help us to avoid common errors in classifying language function.

Why Is the Informative/Expressive/Directive Distinction Important for the Logical Thinker as Challenger?

There are two significant reasons why distinguishing language function is important for logical thinking. First, how we challenge a message differs, depending on the function of the message. We ask why we should believe an informative message, what evidence or data justify our accepting it as true. If a message is directive, we don't ask whether it is true. Rather, we ask whether the action it commends to us is right. Is it in accord with our moral principles? Does it violate them? What values does it promote? What values are jeopardized? If a message arouses feelings or emotions, we can ask how appropriate are those feelings or emotions. Should I feel this way? In effect, to arouse positive or negative emotions is to make a positive or negative evaluation. Should I accept this evaluation? Why is it correct?

The distinction is important for another reason. Remember our definition. Logical thinking is reasonably going about deciding what to believe or do.

Both informative and directive messages may come heavily laced with emotive words. These may make the beliefs or actions seem attractive. But a logical thinker wants to accept a belief because, on balance, the evidence supports it. He or she wants to perform an action if it is right or justified. Separating the expressive from the directive and informative functions of language can let us distinguish how much hard support we have for a belief or action as opposed to how forcefully someone has tried to sway our attitudes about it. The semanticist Hugh Walpole has said that appreciating the informative/expressive distinction provides "a first-rate umbrella against sales talk and propaganda."[2] Chapters 3 and 4 will show us how apt this is. For now, we have made it plain that to challenge messages critically, we must understand their function, and for that we need the informative/expressive/directive distinction.

Summary

In this section, we have introduced a number of basic concepts concerning language function. A message is *informative* when it claims to say something about the world, when we can properly ask whether it is true or false. It is *expressive* when it either expresses or arouses some feeling or emotion. It is *directive* when it attempts to influence behavior.

We may contrast the literal and emotive meanings of a word. The *literal meaning* of a *referring expression* is the object to which it refers (its *denotation*). The *literal meaning* of an *attribute* or *relation* is the class of objects (pairs of objects, triples of objects) of which the expression is true (its *denotation*) together with some rule for properly applying the expression (its *connotation*). The *emotive meaning* of a word is its capacity to express or arouse emotion. Emotive words can be *laudatory* or *derogatory,* depending on whether they express or arouse positive or negative emotions. *Neutral words* seldom involve much emotion.

Exercise 1-I

What are the functions, or at least the principal functions, of the following?

1. Water is two parts hydrogen, one part oxygen.
2. What an awful mess!
3. Bring me the book on the table.
4. The stock market will continue to rise throughout the coming year.
5. If George comes, give him his wages.
6. $a + b = b + a$.
7. I hope you will come.
8. I know you'll cooperate.
9. All humans are mortal.
10. Wasn't Aristotle the tutor of Alexander the Great?

11. On several consecutive nights, Mary experienced distinct feelings of loneliness.

12. Your children and Dixie cups—they're indispensable.

13. That feather-headed boy had botched things again!—Mark Twain, *A Connecticut Yankee in King Arthur's Court.*

14. Their friends are all of them shamelessly immoral. . . . I know a great number of them . . . , and their immorality gives my judgment no little support.—Charles L. Stevenson, *Ethics and Language.*

15. A heavy wave of perfume came down the jungle on the night.— From *Seduction of the Minotaur* by Anais Nin. Copyright © 1961 by Anais Nin. Copyright © 1985 by The Anais Nin Trust. All rights reserved. Reprinted by permission of the Author's Representative, Gunther Stuhlmann.

Exercise 1-II

In the following passages, identify the emotive words, emotion-arousing images, and statements that excite emotion. Then name the attitudes, feelings, and emotions the writer is trying to convey.

1. Our way of life has been totally destroyed by greedy people and self-serving politicians.—A.T.Z., *Sunday Star-Ledger* (Newark, N.J.), September 19, 1982.

2. All our dignity then consists in thought. We must look to that in order to rise aloft; not to space or time which we can never fill. Strive we then to think aright: that is the first principle of moral life.—Blaise Pascal, *Pensées.*

3. I was heartened to read your editorial . . . commenting on Fidel Castro's claim that he is "nonaligned." If ever there was a case of someone calling "white" "black," this is it. . . . Castro is the lackey of Moscow, its mouthpiece and its recipient of vast amounts of aid to further Moscow's policies in Africa and Latin America and even here in training subversives in Quebec. I only wish more Canadians would realize this and not go on travelling to Cuba for a cheap holiday and put money into the hand that will slap them.—D.J.M., Toronto, Canada.[3]

4. Bureaucratic nitpickers in Washington have pummeled one of the Agriculture Department's most conscientious employees onto the ropes, forcing him into retirement with a series of low blows. The dedicated civil servant is John Coplin. Coplin managed to antagonize his desk-bound superiors . . . , swamping them with memos detailing corrupt practices by meat industry fat cats.—Jack Anderson. Reprinted by permission of United Feature Syndicate, Inc.

5. Poor, handicapped, abused and neglected children have been the primary victims of heartless and relentless Reagan Administration budget cuts, program repeals and regulatory maneuvering.—Children's Defense Fund. Quoted by Carl T. Rowan, April 3, 1983.

6. With a blast comparable to the largest H-bomb ever tested, Mount St. Helens in Washington State blew its top last week—the nation's worst volcanic eruption. At least 18 people died and 88 were missing, and the eastward-spreading cloud of ash dropped a paralyzing blanket of grey soot on cities, farms and highways as far east as Montana.—*Newsweek,* June 2, 1980. Copyright 1980, by Newsweek, Inc. All Rights Reserved. Reprinted by permission.

7. Washington State's Mount St. Helens blows up with 500 times the force of the Hiroshima bomb, killing at least 18, turning lush forest into desolate moonscape and dropping tons of ash on three states.—From *Time,* June 2, 1980. Copyright 1980 Time Inc. All rights reserved. Reprinted by permission from TIME.

8. Fear not torture, for therein lies the crown of martyrdom. The way is short, the struggle brief, the reward everlasting. Yea, I speak now with the voice of the prophet, "Arm thyself, O mighty one!" Take up your arms, valiant sons, and go. Better fall in battle than live to see the sorrow of your people and the desecration of your holy places.—Pope Urban II at Clermont.

9. Americans woke up to a cold splash of reality last Friday. On their TV sets, a tight-lipped Jimmy Carter was explaining that a daring raid to rescue the 53 hostages in Tehran had failed. A series of technical snafus forced the President to abort the mission before commandos got off the ground from a desert staging point 300 miles from Tehran. In the confusion, one of their RH-53D Sea Stallion helicopters . . . collided with a C-130 transport killing eight Americans. The rest fled to safety, leaving the bodies of their comrades behind—and the fate of the hostages more uncertain than ever.—*Newsweek,* May 5, 1980. Copyright 1980, by Newsweek, Inc. All Rights Reserved. Reprinted by permission.

10. Defenceless villages are bombarded from the air, the inhabitants driven out into the countryside, the cattle machine gunned, the huts set on fire with incendiary bullets: this is called *pacification*. Millions of peasants are robbed of their farms and sent trudging along the roads with no more than they can carry: this is called *transfer of population* or *rectification of frontiers*. People are imprisoned for years without trial, or shot in the back of the neck or sent to die of scurvey in Arctic lumber camps: this is called *elimination of unreliable elements*.— George Orwell, "Politics and the English Language."

Exercise 1-III

Each of the following passages involves more than one basic linguistic function. Identify the various functions and be prepared to discuss why you find them. Does the passage involve a claim that can be true or false? Are there emotive words or emotion-arousing images? If so, what emotion, feeling, or mood is the passage trying to arouse? Is some action being recommended, requested, or ordered? If so, what is the action?

1. Late that night, in a small hospital in Elyria, Ohio, a nurse turned away and cried. She knew no one could save the dying boy.

2. It is really a sad culture. And the recent announcement of the operational readiness of the wicked nuclear devices in Europe is so sickening that one dare hardly think of what may so likely take place.—Ben Kimpel, unpublished letter.

3. The white man who had just gotten on the bus . . . stood there. He just stood there. He would not sit down next to the black. Two adult males, living in the most highly industrialized, most technologically advanced nation in the world, . . . faced each other in mutual rage and hostility.—From *Mary* by Mary Mebane. Copyright © 1981 by Mary Mebane. Reprinted by permission of Viking Penguin, Inc.

4. The fireworks were built in the shape of tall trees, and designed to go off in tiers, branch by branch. From the tips of the gold and red branches hung planets, flowers, wheels gyrating and then igniting, all propelled into space bursting, splintering, falling as if the sun and the moon and the stars themselves had been pierced open and had spilled their jewels of lights, particles of delight.—From *Seduction of the Minotaur* by Anais Nin. Copyright © 1961 by Anais Nin. Copyright © 1985 by The Anais Nin Trust. All rights reserved. Reprinted by permission of the Author's Representative, Gunther Stuhlmann.

5. It is only in books that we can deal with those imponderables—our shared knowledge of the powers of love and the forces of memory—that drive us. Daguerre's discovery of photography and the continuation of this in film and television is—as I see it from a highly prejudiced point of view—partly a revelation of the fact that the photographic process cannot equal written language in its intimacy, radiance and fire.—John Cheever, "In Praise of Readers," *Parade,* December 28, 1980.

6. The journey was a swift and pleasant one, and I spent it in making the more intimate acquaintance of my two companions and in playing with Dr. Mortimer's spaniel. In a very few hours the brown earth had become ruddy, the brick had changed to granite, and red cows grazed in well-hedged fields where the lush grasses and more luxuriant vegetation spoke of a richer, if a damper, climate. Young Baskerville stared eagerly out of the window and cried aloud with delight as he recognized the familiar features of the Devon scenery.—Sir Arthur Conan Doyle, *The Hound of the Baskervilles.*

7. The road in front of us grew bleaker and wilder over huge russet and olive slopes, sprinkled with giant boulders. Now and then we passed a moorland cottage, walled and roofed with stone, with no creeper to break its harsh outline. Suddenly we looked down into a cuplike depression, patched with stunted oaks and firs which had been twisted and bent by the fury of years of storm. Two high, narrow towers rose over the trees.—Sir Arthur Conan Doyle, *The Hound of the Baskervilles.*

8. Even as we looked he plucked out from under his covering a short,

round piece of wood, like a school-ruler, and clapped it to his lips. Our pistols rang out together. He whirled round, threw up his arms, and, with a kind of choking cough, fell sideways into the stream. I caught one glimpse of his venomous, menacing eyes amid the white swirl of the waters.—Sir Arthur Conan Doyle, *The Sign of Four.*

9. As we steamed slowly upstream again, we flashed our searchlight in every direction, but there was no sign of the Islander. Somewhere in the dark ooze at the bottom of the Thames lie the bones of that strange visitor to our shores.

"See here," said Holmes, pointing to the wooden hatchway. "We were hardly quick enough with our pistols." There, sure enough, just behind where we had been standing, stuck one of those murderous darts which we knew so well. It must have whizzed between us at the instant we fired. Holmes smiled at it and shrugged his shoulders in his easy fashion, but I confess that it turned me sick to think of the horrible death which had passed so close to us that night.—Sir Arthur Conan Doyle, *The Sign of Four.*

10. "I give you my word on the book that I never raised hand against Mr. Sholto. It was that little hell-hound, Tonga, who shot one of his cursed darts into him. I had no part in it, sir. I was as grieved as if it had been my blood-relation. I welted the little devil with the slack end of the rope for it, but it was done, and I could not undo it again."—Sir Arthur Conan Doyle, *The Sign of Four.*

11. We walk about like a shadow, and in vain we are in turmoil; we heap up riches and cannot tell who will gather them.—Psalm 39:7.

12. The world is too much with us; late and soon;
   Getting and spending, we lay waste our powers:
   Little we see in Nature that is ours;
   We have given our hearts away, a sordid boon!
   —William Wordsworth, "The World Is Too Much With Us; Late and Soon."

13. Tyranny brings ignorance and brutality along with it. It degrades men from their just rank into the class of brutes; it damps their spirits; it suppresses arts; it extinguishes every spark of noble ardor and generosity in the breasts of those who are enslaved by it; it makes naturally strong and great minds feeble and little, and triumphs over the ruins of virtue and humanity. This is true of tyranny in every shape: there can be nothing great and good where its influence reaches. For which reason it becomes every friend to truth and human kind, every lover of God and the Christian religion, to bear a part in opposing this hateful monster.—Rev. Jonathan Mayhew.

14. These are the times that try men's souls. The summer soldier and the sunshine patriot will, in this crisis, shrink from the service of their country, but he that stands it *now* deserves the love and thanks of man and woman. —Thomas Paine, *The American Crisis.*

15. I would say to the House, as I said to those who have joined this Government: "I have nothing to offer but blood, toil, tears and sweat."

We have before us an ordeal of the most grievous kind. We have before us many, many long months of struggle and of suffering. You ask, what is our policy? I can say: It is to wage war, by sea, land and air, with all our might and with all the strength that God can give us; to wage war against a monstrous tyranny, never surpassed in the dark, lamentable catalogue of human crime. That is our policy. You ask, what is our aim? I can answer in one word: It is victory, victory at all costs, victory in spite of all terror, victory, however long and hard the road may be; for without victory, there is no survival. Let that be realized; no survival for the British Empire, no survival for all that the British Empire has stood for, no survival for the urge and impulse of the ages, that mankind will move forward towards its goal.—Winston Churchill, Speech before the House of Commons, May 13, 1940.

§1.2 RECOGNIZING ARGUMENTS

Let's consider once again Ben Franklin's statement:

We must all hang together or assuredly we shall all hang separately.

We saw that this message is directive. But it is different from all the other examples of directives that we examined in Section 1.1. Franklin not only tells his compatriots to do something, he gives them a reason for doing it. Franklin makes a claim about the consequences of not hanging together. If we do not, we shall all hang separately—not an inviting prospect. Hence, this is a reason, and a motivating reason, for hanging together. Many directives operate this way, giving us a reason for doing a recommended action by predicting the consequences of performing or failing to perform that action—consequences which ordinarily we shall want to either possess or avoid. For example,

Ultrabrite gives your mouth sex appeal.

This in effect says, "If you brush with Ultrabrite, your mouth will have sex appeal." Isn't that appealing?

If the Republicans win the White House, can you expect this prosperity to continue?

That is, "If you vote Republican, then you are contributing to ending this prosperity." But who wants to end prosperity? Clearly, these directives give a justification for the actions they enjoin. But to give reasons, to give justification, that is the hallmark of *argument,* the central notion of this book. We must now define this concept specifically and then consider how we may distinguish messages which are arguments from those which are not.

What Is an Argument?

Our discussion so far has already ruled out one popular understanding of this term. By argument, we do not mean the sort of behavior that goes on in barroom brawls or lockerroom fights. Arguments are not the heated exchange of words. Rather when we use the word *argument* in this book, we mean a message which attempts to establish a statement as true or worthy of belief on the basis of other statements. Persons putting forward arguments present certain claims, make certain assertions, which they expect or hope their audience will simply accept. They also put forward some further statement as being supported by these accepted claims. There is, thus, a further claim that because we accept the first statements, we should accept the latter. The former give evidence, justification, support for the latter. There are thus two radically different roles which a statement may play in an argument. A reason for some other statement is a *premise*. A statement defended by some other statement or statements is a *conclusion*. Arguments, then, involve these three factors: premises, conclusions, and a claim that the premises support the conclusions.

Here are some examples of arguments:

1. Anyone who stays out late is a drunken reveler.
   John stays out late.
   Therefore, John is a drunken reveler.
2. On every day in recorded history the sun has risen.
   Therefore, with near certain probability the sun will rise tomorrow.
3. Foreign trade rivals gain an unfair advantage from being subsidized by their governments. Japan's effort to develop its machine-tool industry into a major exporter is in itself an unfair restraint on competition. Therefore, the American government should protect its machine-tool companies from Japanese competition.—Reconstruction of an argument by Houdaille Industries, *The New York Times,* editorial, April 28, 1983. Copyright © 1983 by The New York Times Company. Reprinted by permission.
4. [You should not] throw leaves away! Leaf composting produces rich, black humus that can be used in flower beds, dug into gardens and used as you would use peat moss.

   It is easier to save leaves for mulch or a compost heap than to throw the leaves away. Leaves produce a good soil conditioner inexpensively. Leaf compost can be used to prevent soil erosion, increase soil water retention and improve soil fertility.—P.S., *Sunday Star-Ledger* (Newark, N.J.), October 3, 1982.

Now consider the following argument:

5. The United States does not subsidize its industries.
   Foreign government subsidies make foreign products very competitive in American markets.

> Therefore, foreign trade rivals gain an unfair advantage from being subsidized by their governments.

We have already seen the conclusion before. It is the first premise in argument 3. This highlights a very important point about premises and conclusions. Statements in themselves are not premises and conclusions. They become premises and conclusions when they play these roles in arguments. Hence, one and the same statement may be both a premise and conclusion. It may be a premise in one argument and a conclusion in another. It may even be both a premise and conclusion in the same argument, if it is both supported by some statements and supports some other statement. To say that a statement is a premise or conclusion then is always relative to the argument where it appears and is determined by its role in that argument. What would it look like for a statement to play both roles in the same argument?

Consider:

> 6. There are many problems involved with censorship.
>   Therefore it is not easy actually to carry out censorship.
>   Hence censorship is not an acceptable proposal.

Here the second statement in the argument is supported by the first and, hence, functions as a conclusion. But that second statement in turn supports the third, and so also functions as a premise.

If a message does not present an argument, but merely contains one or more assertions, we call it an *exposition*. This term functions as a catch-all. Whenever a passage presents a number of statements as true, but makes no claim that because one or more of these statements are true, so is some other, we have an exposition. A single statement by itself may be an exposition. For example,

> 7. It was a pleasant-looking old house of two storeys, painted grey, with a red iron roof.—Fyodor Dostoyevsky, *The Brothers Karamazov*.

Again,

> 8. In the fourth century B.C., . . . the unity that the Greek city-states were incapable of achieving by their own efforts was finally imposed by the armed force of Macedon. This was followed by an epoch of empire-building, initiated by Alexander and his generals and continued by Rome, which ended in the unification of the entire Mediterranean world.—Henry Bamford Parkes, *Gods and Men*.

In neither of these passages do we have arguments, but only description. Assertions are made, but there never is a claim that one assertion supports another, that because one assertion is true, so is another.

How Do We Distinguish Arguments from Expositions?

At the outset, we must say that *there is no mechanical procedure for distinguishing arguments from expositions.* We must ultimately use and develop our sensitivity to language. This does *not* mean, however, that we cannot focus our sensitivity on certain elements present or suggested in a passage, to defend our claim that the passage does contain an argument. Nor does this mean that we cannot point to the absence of such elements to claim that no argument is given.

In most examples of arguments just presented, it was straightforward to identify which statements were conclusions, since they were introduced by such words as "therefore" or "hence." Such words are *logical indicators,* more specifically *conclusion indicators.* The presence of logical indicators is a very telling sign that a message presents an argument. Logical indicators are of two types. Besides conclusion indicators, there are also *premise indicators.* Let's be clear about what such elements do. Ordinarily a conclusion indicator signals that the statement immediately following it is a conclusion of the argument. To give a complete list of all the words which may function in English as conclusion indicators is impossible and impracticable. However, it is important to see a sizable list of such indicators:

therefore	we may conclude
hence	let us conclude
thus	allows us to conclude
so	points to the conclusion that
consequently	leads me to believe that
as a consequence	bears out my point that
shows that	the point I am trying to make is that
indicates that	this means that[4]
these facts indicate	
we may infer that	
we can now infer	
let us infer that	
we can justifiably infer that	

Premise indicators are signs that the statement or statements following are premises of the argument. Here is a companion list of premise indicators:

for	in view of the fact that
since	on the correct supposition that
because	may be inferred from the fact that
for the reason that	as shown by
as	as indicated by
inasmuch as	as is substantiated by
whereas	let us take it that
after all	let us begin with
suppose	here are the facts
assume	this is the evidence
assuming, as we may, that	why?[5]

We cannot underestimate the importance of logical indicators in recognizing and analyzing arguments. If there is anything in this book that calls for rote memorization, it is these words. Not only are they major clues in telling us that a passage contains an argument, but they signal the roles—premise or conclusion—that statements play in an argument. Recognizing and correctly identifying these expressions as either conclusion indicators or premise indicators is crucial in analyzing arguments, seeing what supports what. That is crucial for argument evaluation, determining how good a case the argument makes for its conclusion. Thus, these concepts are basic to our discussion in Part II.

What complicates matters is that some logical indicators can on occasion serve other functions. The most notable example is the word "since." Contrast these two messages:

9. The Soviets will break off the arms talks since they are angry over recent U.S. actions.

10. Peter has not left his room since the latest issue of *Popular Mechanics* arrived.

Do we have two arguments here? We see the word "since" in both. The first is an argument. Here "since" functions as a premise indicator, flagging the second statement as a premise. Hence we can readily see that the second statement is claimed to support the first. However, the second message is not an argument. "Since" functions as a temporal indicator rather than a logical indicator in this case. We are saying that one thing happened after another, not that one thing happened because of another or that we should believe one statement because another statement is true. Hence, in judging whether a discourse contains an argument, we do look to see whether logical indicators are present. But if a passage contains a word which may be used as a logical indicator, but which also has some other sense, we must recognize first that the logical indicator sense of the term is being used. There is no mechanical procedure to do this. The sense of the passage must be grasped.

Do the following messages present arguments?

11. If the general economic picture is good, then the stock market will rally.

12. Provided John comes, the party will be a success.

13. You will get an "A" in this course only if you study.

None of these is an argument. Each may look like an argument, but technically all are called *conditional statements*. The particles "If . . . , then," "provided," "only if" are conditional statement indicators. A conditional statement asserts that if one condition holds or one statement is true, then so is another. Hence (11) is a prime example of a conditional statement, since it is of the form "If A, then B."

How do we distinguish conditional statements from arguments? This is to ask: What is the difference between "If A, then B" and "A, therefore B"? In the second, the argument, don't we claim that the premise A and the conclusion B are both true? We assert both A and B, besides claiming that since A is true, so also is B. By contrast, although a conditional statement *as a whole* may be asserted, neither of the component statements is asserted. Consider (11). Does (11) say that the general economic picture is good? Does it assert that the stock market will rally? It asserts that if one, then the other, but it does not assert either one. We are not claiming that a conclusion is true because a premise is true and so there is no argument here. We may repeat this to see that (12) and (13) are not arguments. Conditional statements are frequently confused with arguments, conditional statement indicators with logical indicators. Hence, to identify arguments properly, we must keep these notions distinct.

This does not mean, however, that a conditional statement is a sure sign that we do not have an argument. Consider:

14. If the court does not declare the loyalty oath unconstitutional, then the faculty will strike. Now the court will not declare the loyalty oath unconstitutional. Hence, the faculty will strike.

15. If the current polls are correct, then the Republicans will win the White House. If the Republicans win the White House, then there will be continued attempts to cut entitlement programs. Therefore, if the current polls are correct, then there will be continued attempts to cut entitlement programs.

Both these messages present arguments, although both contain conditional statements. Note that all three component statements of (14) are conditionals. In both cases, several statements are claimed to be true, and one statement is claimed to follow from the others. Therefore, we have an argument each time.

Finally, consider the following message:

16. There is a crafty plan afoot to create an Indian reservation near Cleveland, Ohio.—Jack Anderson, December 30, 1984. Reprinted by permission of United Feature Syndicate, Inc.

This is certainly a controversial statement. It needs defending (and Jack Anderson did give evidence for it in his column). But as the statement stands here, just by itself, do we have an argument? We clearly do not, because no statement is being put forward to support another. Although a message which contains a controversial claim may very well contain statements to support it, an undefended controversial statement by itself is not an argument. We must not let the mere controversiality of a statement mislead us into thinking that we have an argument.

So far we have looked at elements which may be present in a message which may mislead us into thinking the message contains an argument when in fact it does not. On the other hand, a passage may omit certain elements and still be an argument. Often logical indicators may be suppressed. For example, the passage

17. A recession will begin this winter. Inflation is continuing at an accelerated rate, persons are losing their jobs, and our balance of trade is off.

claims that continuing high inflation, job loss, and an unfavorable balance of trade are reasons why there will soon be a recession. The first statement is supported by the others. However, no logical indicator explicitly makes this claim of support. It is implicit in the passage, albeit very clearly suggested.

What about the following?

18. College women—but not their male counterparts—appear almost immune to the government's 15-year-old campaign to curb cigarette smoking. The latest annual national survey by UCLA and the American Council on Education shows that frequent smoking among freshman coeds has gone up "substantially" since the first canvass in 1966. That year, 13.2% of the first-year women considered themselves frequent smokers; the 1978 figure is 17.1%. Male freshmen traced an exactly opposite curve. Among males, the percentage of frequent smokers dropped from 19.4% in 1966 to 10.6% today.—*Forbes*, February 19, 1979.

Here again we have an argument. The first statement is the main conclusion, being supported by subsequent statements, but again, there are no logical indicators.

How are we able to judge these passages to be arguments? This involves sensitivity to three factors. First, in each case subsequent statements support the first. Plain common sense shows us that later statements give evidence for the first. Second, in each case, the first statement is controversial; it needs defending. Although, as we have seen, a controversial statement by itself is not an argument, when defended we *do* have an argument. We might then expect controversial statements to be accompanied by defending statements. Finally, the controversial statements and their defense are closely juxtaposed, set side by side. The defending statements come immediately on the heels of the statements needing defense. This strongly suggests they are there to give support. These three factors, obvious support, a controversial statement needing support, and juxtaposition of supporting and supported statements in a passage are signals that we have an argument present, even when there are no logical indicators.

There is another way in which messages may implicitly suggest arguments. By juxtaposing statements, we may not only suggest that one supports another, we may also suggest some further statement, some implicit conclusion. For example,

19. All philosophers are abstract thinkers and Spinoza is a philosopher.

Doesn't this suggest that Spinoza is an abstract thinker? Don't the two statements made explicitly serve as premises for this conclusion? Here is another example.

20. The AFL-CIO has succinctly torpedoed the myth [that the Western powers are "imperialist"]. . . . In the last three decades, it documents, former colonial powers of the West have granted independence to more than 1.1 billion people. The Soviet Union and Communist China, meanwhile, have brought more than 100 million people under varying degrees of control.[6]—Reprinted by permission of *The Wall Street Journal.* © Dow Jones & Company, Inc., 1972. All Rights Reserved.

Isn't the conclusion left implicit here that it is the communists, not the Western governments, who are imperialists? That claim is clearly suggested and supported by the final two statements in this passage. These messages illustrate that sometimes the actual conclusion of an argument is left unstated, just suggested implicitly. In these cases, we have to supply the conclusion in recognizing that we have an argument.

Our discussion in this section has presented two further ways of classifying messages. Besides distinguishing language function, we may also separate arguments from nonarguments or expositions. In addition, we may classify messages according to whether they are explicitly stated or just suggested. Both these distinctions are important for the logical thinker as challenger. Asking for an argument is one way of challenging a message which is just exposition. We shall study when such challenges should be issued in the next chapter. Recognizing that a message presents an argument brings certain central critical questions into play. We shall examine these questions throughout this book. We cannot challenge a message unless we are aware of it. Realizing that a further message may be suggested by the juxtaposition of what is explicitly stated may heighten our sensitivity to the messages we receive and the power of language to communicate.

Summary

An *argument* is an attempt to establish a statement as true or worthy of belief on the basis of other statements, taken as giving evidence. A defended statement is a *conclusion* of an argument. A statement given as a reason for another is a *premise*. A message not involving an argument is called an *exposition*.

The most important sign that we have an argument is the presence of *logical indicator words*—either *premise indicators* or *conclusion indicators*. However, logical indicator words may have other meanings or be confused with conditional statement indicators. This can mislead us into judging that we have an argument when there is none present, as can the mere controversiality of a statement. On the other hand, arguments may be suggested, without the explicit use of logical indicators. If some statements give evidence for another, if some statement is controversial, and if the evidence statements are juxtaposed with the controversial statement, then we have signals that the message presents an argument. Also, by juxtaposing two or more statements, some further statement may be suggested as conclusion.

Exercise 1-IV

Which of the following passages contain arguments, which do not? If a passage does contain an argument, what is the conclusion and what is the logical indicator?

1. The oil refineries are producing a great amount of gasoline for automobiles this summer. Therefore we can expect shortages of home heating oil next winter.

2. We know that Sherlock Holmes will solve the mystery because he now has all the relevant clues he needs.

3. Mary has been at her desk since the report arrived.

4. The senator refuses to declare herself a candidate for president. We may conclude that she does not want the nomination.

5. The president's economic policies will not help the poor. Why? The president believes in the "trickle-down" theory—by helping the rich, benefits trickle down to the rest of society. But this happens only in a few cases.

6. Congress completed its work around 2:00 A.M. last night. Today many members of the House and Senate were leaving Washington to do some campaigning at home.

7. All Democrats are politicians. All Republicans are politicians. Therefore, all Republicans are Democrats.

8. If the transportation union calls a strike tomorrow, then commerce will be seriously disrupted.

9. If the president vetoes the bill, a two-thirds majority of both houses of Congress is necessary to override the veto.

10. If the challengers are elected, then there will be new economic policies in Washington. The challengers will be elected. Hence there will be new economic policies in Washington.

11. If Alonzo proves the theorem, then Rudolf will publish it. But if Rudolf publishes it, then Bertrand will accept it. From this we may infer that if Alonzo proves the theorem, then Bertrand will accept it.

12. That salesman could not be lying. He gave us facts and figures in rapid-fire succession. Such command would be impossible for someone trying to dupe customers.

13. Since taking the first quiz, Roger has not put in any more effort studying, nor has the material gotten easier.

14. I don't expect Roger to do any better, since he has not put in any

more time studying for the second test than he did for the first, nor is the material any easier.

15. The Westcotts differed from their friends, their classmates, and their neighbors only in an interest they shared in serious music. They went to a great many concerts—although they seldom mentioned this to anyone—and they spent a good deal of time listening to music on the radio. Their radio was an old instrument, sensitive, unpredictable, and beyond repair.—John Cheever, "The Enormous Radio," from *The Stories of John Cheever*. © 1978, Alfred A. Knopf, Inc. Originally published in *The New Yorker*.

Exercise 1-V

Each of the following passages involves an argument. However, in each case the conclusion is implicit, not explicitly stated. In each case, state the intended conclusion.

1. Pride goes before a fall, and several recent U.S. presidents have been proud, arrogant men.

2. She's energetic, intelligent, and ambitious; and energetic, intelligent, ambitious persons quickly get promoted in this company.

3. Coke adds life! Everybody wants a little life!

4. Those who drink and drive are risking a serious accident. Yet Jack persists in driving after drinking.

5. John is wrong in saying that no tests have been done for life on the moon or Mars. But whenever John is wrong, he takes a long time to admit it.

6. Fire-brewed beer tastes best, and Strohs is America's fire-brewed beer.

7. Starbuck and Lieutenant M. had a longstanding grudge. Starbuck had just been ejected from the game. He left threatening to kill M. Furthermore, his gun had been fired exactly once, and the bullet in M.'s body was fired from the gun. Need I say more?

8. According to Shakespeare, if music be the food of love, play on. But music is the food of love.

9. You should convict someone of a capital crime only on very strong evidence, but the prosecutor has not presented strong evidence.

10. The law does not expressly permit suicide, and what it does not expressly permit it forbids.—Aristotle, *Nicomachean Ethics*.

Exercise 1-VI

Indicate which of the following are arguments, which are expositions. If a passage contains an argument, indicate its conclusion (or conclusions). If the conclusion has been suppressed, supply it in your own words. Identify all logical indicators.

1. Every art and every inquiry, and similarly every action and pursuit, is thought to aim at some good, and for this reason the good has rightly been declared to be that at which all things aim.—Aristotle, *Nicomachean Ethics.*

2. All men by nature desire to know. An indication of this is the delight we take in our senses; for even apart from their usefulness they are loved for themselves.—Aristotle, *Metaphysics.*

3. Above all others [i.e., other senses] the sense of sight [is loved]. For not only with a view to action, but even when we are not going to do anything, we prefer seeing (one might say) to everything else. The reason is that this, most of all the senses, makes us know and brings to light many differences between things.—Aristotle, *Metaphysics.*

4. Every state is a community of some kind, and every community is established with a view to some good; for mankind always act in order to obtain that which they think good.—Aristotle, *Politics.*

5. [All communities aim at some good.] But, if all communities aim at some good, the state or political community . . . aims at good in a greater degree than any other, and at the highest good.—Aristotle, *Politics.*

6. Men who are about to make merry should first honor the gods with hymns composed of well-told tales and pure words. After they have poured a libation and have prayed for the power to do what is right—that, indeed, is the first business in hand—then there is nothing wrong in drinking as much as a man can hold without having to be taken home by a servant, unless of course he is very old. The man to be praised is he who, after drinking, can still express thoughts that are noble and well arranged.—Xenophanes.

7. Can we trust the Russians? . . . The simple answer is that "trust" doesn't really matter. The United States can tell whether or not the Soviets are cheating through "verification," using our sophisticated satellites and other detectors to catch any wrongdoing before it gets out of hand.—Union of Concerned Scientists.

8. In the Baltic seaport of Gdansk, sirens wailed to signal the start of a four-hour "warning strike" that interrupted public transport and shut down more than 800 plants. In Warsaw, red-and-white Polish flags fluttered defiantly over idle buses and streetcars as drivers joined workers from some 60 local factories and offices in a related half-day stoppage. . . . Across Poland last week, workers once again served notice that they would bitterly resist any attempt to roll back the rights they had won through a summer of crippling strikes.—From *Time*, February 2, 1981. Copyright 1981 Time Inc. All rights reserved. Reprinted by permission from TIME.

9. It is appalling and disgusting that the housewife is discriminated against.

I do not work according to all current standards. Almost all forms that you must fill in for one purpose or another ask the question: Do you work? You are supposed to reply no if you are "only a housewife."

We get a big $250 to put into an Individual Retirement Account (IRA) whereas the working wife is allowed $2,000.

The working mother can take up to $1,000 off her income tax for child care. Some of the working mothers work because they want to, not because they have to.

A deduction is granted to a family that has both parents working. Of course, we, the housewives, do not work.

When a housewife is injured in an automobile collision, no compensation is available. . . .

Aren't there any housewives . . . who see, as I see it, that the laws are unequal and that we are being discriminated against?

Come on, let's stand up for our rights!—I.M.C., *Sunday Star-Ledger* (Newark, N.J.), November 11, 1984.

10. I have just finished attending "The Hunger Briefing." I was appalled at the fact that 35,000 people each day die from hunger. By the end of the year, 13 to 18 million people will die; 75 percent of these people will be children. How can we let so many people die like this? At the present time we have enough food to feed 7 billion people. There are only 5 billion people on Earth.—D.P., *Sunday Star-Ledger* (Newark, N.J.), November 11, 1984.

11. If in another 34 years from now . . . , the present [world] population doubles, it would be almost 10 billion, and that would be a portentous worldwide disaster. If the rest of the world does not emulate China, the world's largest nation, which has been able to hold down population growth by taking drastic steps of inducing couples to have only one child, then the world will have insurmountable problems and difficulties, not in the United States or Europe, where there is better control of the growth and the resources of food, shelter and other necessities of life are sufficient, but in the Third World, where three-fourths of the people on Earth live in poverty and where the growth is the greatest.—V.V., *Sunday Star-Ledger* (Newark, N.J.), November 11, 1984.

12. We postal workers are both angry and frustrated. For the first time since we were given the right to negotiate our contract, no agreement was reached at the bargaining table. The best offer we got from management was a pay "freeze" that cut our night differential, and eliminated three years' worth of cost of living increases, thereby freezing our present salaries at something in the neighborhood of $1,600 below present levels. We call that a pay cut. This best and final offer also included hiring new employees at a 23 percent reduction in pay and benefits.

Postal workers are tired of losing ground. During the last three years we have had our health benefits gutted—higher premiums out of our pockets and lower benefits given. We have a Medicare tax taken from our pay. In order to "save" Social Security, our pensions have been placed in jeopardy. We have been under constant attack on many fronts and have lost ground in spite of having a contract.—J.S.S., *Sunday Star-Ledger* (Newark, N.J.), August 12, 1984.

13. The podium is set up, the microphone is on, the introduction has

been made, and as the speaker begins his lecture, only one element is missing: the audience.

This is the scenario that has been enacted at the President Club Lecture series speeches far too often. The lectures attract minimal audiences at best, predominately faculty and staff members, and a few students assigned to do classwork on the speech.—Oakland University *Sail,* February 26, 1979.

14. Mankind, he said, judging by their neglect of him, have never, as I think, at all understood the power of Love. For if they had understood him they would surely have built noble temples and altars, and offered solemn sacrifices in his honor; but this is not done.—Plato, *Symposium.*

15. The odds that a dangerous leak in a nuclear power plant would occur are so small as to be almost impossible to calculate. I calculated them about a year ago, but, being realistic, I had the same chance of being seriously injured backing out of my driveway, as I did in living next door to a nuclear power plant for a year. I would feel 100 percent safe living next door to a nuclear power plant.

16. The existence of God is not self-evident to us. . . . Yet from every effect the existence of the cause can be clearly demonstrated, and so we can demonstrate the existence of God from His effects. Hence the existence of God, insofar as it is not self-evident to us, can be demonstrated from those of His effects which are known to us.—St. Thomas Aquinas, *Summa Theologica.*

17. [In killing an animal, do we somehow infringe its rights? Suppose this is the case. Suppose killing an animal does infringe its rights. What follows?] Never may we destroy, for our convenience, some of a litter of puppies—or open a score of oysters when nineteen would have sufficed—or light a candle in a summer evening for mere pleasure, lest some hapless moth should rush to an untimely end! Nay, we must not even take a walk, with the certainty of crushing many an insect in our path, unless for really important business! Surely all this is childish. In the absolute hopelessness of drawing a line anywhere, I conclude . . . that man has an absolute right to inflict death on animals, without assigning any reason, provided that it be a painless death, but that any infliction of pain needs its special justification.—Lewis Carroll, "Some Popular Fallacies About Vivisection."[7]

18. The burglar must have left by the fire escape. No one saw this person leave. But how else could someone leave undetected, since there are guards posted at each entrance to the building?

19. If the way which, as I have shown, leads hither seem very difficult, it can nevertheless be found. It must indeed be difficult since it is so seldom discovered; for if salvation lay ready to hand and could be discovered without great labour, how could it be possible that it should be neglected almost by everybody? But all noble things are as difficult as they are rare.—Spinoza, *Ethic.*

20. Other people were dancing around them, so obedient to the rhythms that they seemed like algae in the water, welded to each other, and

swaying, the colored skirts billowing, the white suits like frames to support the flower arrangements made by the women's dresses, their hair, their jewels, their lacquered nails. The wind sought to carry them away from the orchestra, but they remained in its encirclement of sounds like Japanese kites moved by strings from the instruments.—From *Seduction of the Minotaur* by Anais Nin. Copyright © 1961 by Anais Nin. Copyright © 1985 by The Anais Nin Trust. All rights reserved. Reprinted by permission of the Author's Representative, Gunther Stuhlmann.

§1.3 PERSUADING VERSUS LOGICALLY CONVINCING

Why should we want to give arguments? When we use language informatively, when we claim that something is true, we want not just to communicate our beliefs, we want others to share them also. Should a belief be controversial, should there be some doubt that people will simply accept our claim, we may argue for it to convince them. There are two aspects of arguments which it is crucial for a logical thinker to keep distinct. We must distinguish *persuasive force* from the *logically convincing character*. By persuasive force, we mean an argument's ability to bring people to accept its conclusion. When presenting the argument, how effective will it be in getting people to believe the conclusion is true? The more effective, the greater the persuasive force.

In the Introduction, we characterized logical thinking as having three distinct features: it is relevant, based on adequately strong reasons, and rational. The logically convincing character of an argument concerns exactly these issues. An argument is logically convincing when its premises are relevant to the conclusion, they adequately support it, and they are true or well warranted—based on the facts. A logically convincing argument is a good argument—it gives good reasons for its conclusion. If an argument is logically convincing, any rational person should accept the conclusion or regard the argument as making a worthy case for the conclusion. By contrast, an argument with significant persuasive force is an effective argument; it tends to bring about the desired result of arguing.

Do these two features go together? Need arguments with distinct persuasive force be logically convincing? Need logically convincing arguments always have much persuasive force? The fact that an argument is logically convincing should be one factor in its persuasive force. There should be something compelling about good reasons. An argument which presents good reasons should be persuasive to some extent, precisely because it presents those reasons.

However, as we might already expect, the persuasive force and the logically convincing character are distinct features of arguments. Arguments which are persuasive, at least for some audiences, may not be logically convincing, while some logically convincing arguments might not have much persuasive force. Let's illustrate this point by contrasting two arguments.

While president, Jimmy Carter advocated coal gasification, converting a solid fuel into gas, as a way to deal with the energy crisis. Let's suppose two persons were opposed to this policy. One argues against it by pointing out that coal gasification is not safe, clean, or economical. Suppose he not only makes these claims, but presents detailed, scientific data to substantiate each charge. There is no question that we have three relevant reasons against coal gasification here. Something is not safe, not clean, not economical—these are all relevant reasons to oppose it. And certainly the three reasons together give a rather weighty case against coal gasification. Unless there are some very powerful reasons for this technology, we certainly have strong enough reasons to oppose it. Finally, the scientific data supporting these claims certainly shows they are based on the way the world is—they are rational. Without a doubt, the argument is logically convincing. But what might be the effect of this argument on the audience? Would they be prepared to follow the scientific evidence? Would they find it very interesting? Or would the discussion ultimately bore them and they tune out? Obviously the reaction will be different with different audiences, but bored inattention is certainly possible. So although the argument is logically convincing, it need not be very persuasive.

But remember, two people were going to argue against coal gasification. Suppose the other rises after this presentation and says

> Mr. Smith has just given us a lot of ammunition in our fight against coal gasification and for that we're grateful. I just want to add one further point. Who was it who first used coal gasification? It was the Nazis! So what is the Department of Energy really saying? "Coal gasification will work for us not because it's safe, clean, and economical, but because it's worked before." Auschwitz II—you are just around the corner.[8]

Unless this argument might turn the audience off with emotive overkill, wouldn't it have distinct persuasive force? Wouldn't it bring the audience to its feet cheering, while the first would get just polite applause? Wouldn't it seal opposition to coal gasification? But is the argument logically convincing? Although we abhor the Nazis, and being told that the Nazis used a certain technology may cause us to abhor that also, is it really a good reason to oppose developing that technology? After all, the Nazis drove cars with internal combustion engines, used flush toilets, and breathed. But that is no reason to abandon these activities. It is not relevant, and hence gives no weight to the conclusion. Whether or not the Nazis actually used coal gasification, this argument is not logically convincing.

Our discussion illustrates that persuasive force is intimately connected with the expressive function of language. To say that the Nazis followed a policy is not only informative—we can certainly ask whether this is true or false—but may also be highly expressive. As we shall see in Chapter 3, there are many arguments which are not logically convincing but yet have significant persuasive force because of the emotional appeal they make. All this raises a question. When persuasive force goes beyond the logically convincing character of an argument, when some other factor, in particular some expressive factor, besides the cogency of the reasons contributes to make the argument persuasive, is that bad? Does this mean that the persuasive force is somehow inappropriate or irrational? Is such an argument a bad argument?

We must be very careful in considering this question. If the argument were not logically convincing and yet the persuasive factors made us feel that it was, made us accept the conclusion on poor grounds, that would be bad. But suppose the argument *is* logically convincing. The persuasive factors enhance a good case rather than let a poor one seem good. For example, suppose we wanted to convince people not only that a certain claim was true, but that it was in their vital interests to recognize this fact. In effect, we would have two conclusions: this is true and you ought to be distinctly concerned to know this is true.

Suppose also that we presented logically convincing arguments for *both* conclusions. In arguing for the second assertion, we would be enhancing the persuasive force of our first argument. Would this extra persuasive force detract from the cogency of our argument? The answer is clearly no. Since the argument that we should be vitally interested in this issue is logically convincing, it is quite appropriate that we be concerned. The extra persuasive force leads us to regard a good argument more closely and seriously, to appreciate its point, rather than to overlook the faults or weaknesses of a bad argument.

What is the moral of all this for the logical thinker as challenger? There are two distinct lessons here. First, if an argument seems convincing, we must distinguish its persuasive force from its logically convincing character in assessing how well it establishes its conclusion. We must ask whether it presents a good, logically convincing case, despite how persuaded we may feel. For, as we have seen, these two factors are distinct and one does not necessarily accompany the other. The other moral is that we cannot automatically dismiss the expressive or emotive factors in an argument as irrelevant, if not downright detrimental to presenting a rationally convincing case for the conclusion. To find the discussion memorable, we may need to feel its importance for us. Expressive factors which highlight this importance do not necessarily indicate that the argument fails to be logically convincing.

Distinguishing persuading from logically convincing is central to recognizing properly when to challenge and when not to challenge an argument. In Chapter 3, we shall examine a number of patterns of argument that have persuasive force but fail to be logically convincing. By recognizing these patterns, we can readily challenge such arguments. But arguments are frequently given in response to another challenge—why should we believe a claim? Why should we accept some statement as true? When should this challenge be issued? Understanding that is central to playing the role of logical thinker as challenger effectively. We turn to exploring this question in the next chapter.

FOR FURTHER READING

A classic discussion of the basic uses of language, including a discussion of the performative and ceremonial functions not mentioned here, is contained in Irving M. Copi's *Introduction to Logic*, 6th ed., ch. 2. Monroe C. Beardsley's

Thinking Straight, 4th ed., contains a discussion of the meaning of terms and of a number of expressive devices in Sections 13 and 15. Section 14 considers a number of ways in which language can be suggestive. Both texts contain good discussions on identifying arguments. A number of devices of persuasion are discussed in W. Edgar Moore's *Creative and Critical Thinking* (Boston: Houghton Mifflin Company, 1967), ch. 34. The interrelation of the informative and expressive functions of language in persuasion is discussed in Charles L. Stevenson's *Ethics and Language* (New Haven, Conn., and London: Yale University Press, 1944), ch. 6. Many scholars have sought to investigate persuasion, including how it works and what it should be doing. J. Michael Sproule's *Argument: Language and Its Influence* (New York: McGraw-Hill Book Company, 1980), ch. 7, presents an introduction to this material. Aristotle's *Rhetoric* is a philosophical classic in the field of persuasion.

NOTES

[1]Compare Monroe C. Beardsley, *Thinking Straight: Principles of Reasoning for Readers & Writers,* 4th ed. (Englewood Cliffs, N.J.: Prentice-Hall, Inc., 1975), pp. 180–81.

[2]Hugh R. Walpole, *Semantics: The Nature of Words and Their Meanings* (New York: W. W. Norton & Co., Inc., 1941), p. 40.

[3]Thanks to the *Informal Logic Newsletter,* Vol. II S, June 1980, for this example.

[4]This list of conclusion indicators has been culled from several sources. Most notably, we are indebted to Beardsley, *Thinking Straight,* p. 13. We have also found Irving M. Copi, *Introduction to Logic,* 6th ed. (New York: Macmillan Publishing Company, 1982), pp. 9–10 useful.

[5]Again we acknowledge our debt to Beardsley, *Thinking Straight,* pp. 13–14.

[6]Examples 18 and 20 in this section appear in the *Informal Logic Newsletter,* Vol. I, no. 4, July 1979.

[7]Examples 13 and 15 in this exercise appear in the *Informal Logic Newsletter,* Vol. I, no. 4, July 1979. Example 16 appears in Vol. V, no. 3, and Example 17 in Vol. IV, no. 1.

[8]This argument was actually presented in cartoon form in *Fusion: Magazine of the Fusion Energy Society* (September 1979), p. 2. It appears in the *Informal Logic Newsletter,* Vol. II S, June 1980.

2

EVALUATING ASSERTIONS

In this chapter, we shall be primarily concerned with informative messages which simply state a claim rather than argue for it. When should we accept such messages and when should we challenge them? We saw in the last chapter that distinguishing the various language functions was central to challenging messages properly. So here, the first step in evaluating informative assertions is to classify them.

§2.1 DESCRIPTIONS, INTERPRETATIONS, EVALUATIONS

One principal type of informative assertion is the description. A message is a *description* just in case it is in principle possible to verify or refute it by appealing to the experiences of the five senses, our own or others. For example,

1. There is a knife in the drawer.
2. Hannibal crossed the Alps.
3. Ten percent of all cases of that disease reported in the United States come from a five-block area in New York City.
4. Sixty percent of the voters surveyed said they would vote Democratic.
5. If the election were held today, between 57 and 63 percent of the electorate would vote Democratic.

Clearly seeing how to verify each of these examples by appealing to appropriate experiences should be straightforward. Anyone can look to see whether there is a knife in the drawer. Although we cannot directly observe whether Hannibal crossed the Alps, if the event is historical, other people could and presumably did. We can search for reports of their observations. Clearly we can check health records from across the United States and do some elementary arithmetic to check the statistical statement 3. Examples 4 and 5 are the sorts of statements that polling organizations publish throughout political campaigns, precisely on the basis of their experience with public opinion surveys.

What Types of Descriptions Are There?

Our examples illustrate that there are various types of descriptions. First, there are reports that particular events are happening or have happened, or that particular conditions or states of affairs obtain. Statements 1 and 2 illustrate this. Saying that there is a knife in the drawer, or that there are five red tomatoes on the kitchen windowsill, or that there is a cat on the mat is reporting some particular state of affairs. Saying that John has just driven in the driveway or that Martina has just received her promotion letter reports a particular event. But there is something radically different between these reports and (2). It is quite possible that whoever asserts these reports has directly experienced the conditions or events described. They are reports of his or her own firsthand experience, of what he or she has seen, heard, felt, tasted, smelled. At least, they are claims about such direct experience. We call reports about events, occurrences, conditions directly witnessed *firsthand reports.*

But a report may concern not something which we have directly perceived, but which someone else has. No one may assert (2) today as a firsthand report. Those who were with Hannibal could witness his crossing the Alps, but obviously we cannot. Many reports are like this. A historian generally has not seen the events he is describing. How often have journalists actually witnessed their news stories directly? Whenever a person's report is not based on his or her actual, perceptual witness, but has come through one or more intermediate reporters, we call it a *secondhand report.*

While (1) and (2) concern particular conditions or events, (3) and (4) are more general. In effect, they present summaries of a number of first- or secondhand reports, and for this reason we call them *summary reports.* Statements 3 and 4 are both statistical, and summary reports frequently will be statistical, dealing with numbers or percentages. Hence we count

6. There were 1,257 cases of flu reported in Chicago during January 1983.

7. All (100 percent) of the plants injected with the compound survived.

8. Seventy percent of the animals observed developed tumors when exposed to radiation.

as statistical statements and as summary reports.

But not all statistical statements are summary reports. Consider (5). What is the difference between that statement and (3), (4), and the other statistical summary reports we have seen? Does (5) just report data or does it extrapolate, draw some inference from the data available? We can conduct a poll and report the raw data—so many or such a percentage of voters surveyed said they would vote Democratic; so many said they would vote Republican. But (5) makes a statement not just about the voters surveyed but about all voters. It is a description, since we would properly attempt to verify or refute it by appealing to the polls, which is ultimately appealing to sense experience. But (5) goes beyond just what is observed. Similarly

9. All plants injected with that compound will survive.

10. If you expose animals to that source of radiation, approximately 70 percent will develop tumors.

make claims which go beyond summary reports. Whereas summary reports collate data, in effect collectively making a number of reports, *descriptions involving inferences* go beyond data observed. They may make predictions or general statements about whole populations, not just the individuals or particular events observed.

Descriptions of particular events or conditions may also involve inferences. That is, they may have been arrived at by inference from other beliefs. In one story, Sherlock Holmes told a man, quite to his astonishment, that he had been doing much letter writing of late. This was a true description. How did Holmes know? He observed that the man's right hand appeared shiny. Holmes also knew this appearance was most likely caused by much letter writing and so imposed this interpretation on the situation. But if much letter writing caused this appearance, then the person has been writing a lot of letters. The particular description follows from the interpretation. We may not be able to tell whether a particular description is a first- or secondhand report or whether it involves inference in a given case. We need to know what information was available to the person making the statement. Could he or she have directly observed the event or condition? Could someone else have and told about it? How likely was it derived by inference? If we cannot answer these questions, we cannot make a determination. However, if we *can* answer the questions, then certain critical possibilities open up for challenging the assertion. But more of this in the next section.

Descriptions then may be classed into these two broad types: reports and descriptions involving inferences. Descriptions involving inferences, whether particular or general, go beyond just what has been observed. Reports, insofar as possible, make claims just about what has been observed. Reports may be first- or secondhand, or general presentations of data, summary reports.

What Is an Interpretation?

A message is an *interpretation* just in case verifying or refuting it involves centrally an issue of definition. We can appreciate what this means by contrasting descriptions and interpretations:

DESCRIPTION: The Soviet missile flew over Norway and Finland, crashing into a lake on the Finnish/Soviet border.

INTERPRETATION: The Russians are trying to send the United States a signal by this incident.

DESCRIPTION: In the recent election, most Americans voted for the incumbent, whose policies many poor people dislike.

INTERPRETATION: American voters literally thumbed their noses at the 35.3 million poor people in this land. . . . If the recent elections told us anything it is that most Americans don't want any sharing of wealth with the poor.—Carl T. Rowan, November 18, 1984. © by and permission of News America Syndicate.

DESCRIPTION: The head of Ethiopia's government, Col. Mengistu Haile Mariam, "has diverted supplies to his army" and has spent large sums of money for political rallies "while his people starve."

INTERPRETATION: Col. Mengistu Haile Mariam "has picked the country as clean as the bones of a slaughtered calf."—Jack Anderson, January 6, 1985. Reprinted by permission of United Feature Syndicate, Inc.

If a Soviet missile actually penetrated Norwegian and Finnish air space, crashing into a border lake, it is possible in principle to appeal to experience to verify this, however difficult. If all else fails, we can dredge the lake. On the other hand, to say that the Russians are trying to send a signal by this incident is to interpret it. It is to give it a meaning, significance. What does it mean to send a signal? A question of definition is involved here. We need to spell out what this means to know what evidence counts for the statement. We may very well be able to argue convincingly for or against this interpretation. But can we go out and verify that the Russians are trying to send a signal the way we can go out and verify whether one of their missiles was involved in the incident as described?

Again, whether most Americans voted for the incumbent is a matter of public record. That many poor people dislike the president's policies is a summary report, straightforwardly verifiable by public opinion surveys. But Carl Rowan has given an interpretation to these facts. What does it mean to say that Americans have thumbed their noses at 35.3 million poor? Again a question of definition arises. Proper gathering of intelligence should be able to confirm or deny that Col. Mariam has diverted supplies to his army and spent large sums on political rallies. But to say, with Jack Anderson, that he has picked Ethiopia as clean as the bones of a slaughtered calf involves interpretation. If anything, it involves a graphic comparison. But what exactly does this comparison mean?

What Are the Main Types of Interpretation We May Encounter?

First, interpretations may attribute a significance to an event or condition, as our first two examples do. What does it mean that a woman was nominated for vice-president? What does it mean that the ethnic make up of a neighborhood has shifted? Statements about the internal or mental states of others count as significance interpretations also. We are directly aware of our own pains, feelings, emotions. But can we feel someone else's pain or pleasure, fear or desire? But to say that some other person has pain or feels angry involves interpretation. It involves assigning a significance to certain overt behavior and appearances, seen as signifying these states.

Causal statements, claims that one event or condition has brought about or tends to bring about another or that one event or condition is the effect or result of another,[1] are interpretations. For example,

11. The force of the impact caused the windshield to shatter.

12. Abolishing the death penalty has raised the homicide rate.

13. John's leaving the windows of his house open all winter caused his enormous fuel bill.

All these statements interpret one condition as causing or contributing to another.

Comparisons, like Jack Anderson's, statements that things are like or unlike, similar or dissimilar, are interpretations. Statements assessing the importance of certain facts or conditions are also interpretations. For example,

14. America's critical need for energy and Americans' need for jobs overshadows environmental considerations of offshore oil drilling in the Atlantic.[2]

Finally, a claim that a certain number of alternatives constitute all the alternatives possible in a given situation is an interpretation. For example,

15. We can go either to the mountains or to the seashore for our vacation.

16. Either we develop nuclear power now, aggressively explore for domestic sources of oil and natural gas, or we shall all freeze in the dark.

Each of these statements interprets the world by claiming that a certain small number of alternatives are the only ones possible.

What Is an Evaluation?

An evaluation categorizes something as good or bad, better or worse, in some sense or to some degree. *Evaluations* deal with what is preferable, and this is the principal issue in evaluations. To judge something good is to express a positive attitude toward it. To judge something bad is to express a negative attitude. Conversely, to express a positive or negative attitude toward something, to describe it using laudatory or derogatory words, is to judge it good or bad. Hence evaluations involve the expressive function of language and expressive messages involve evaluations. However, this does not mean that evaluations are mere expressions of feeling or taste. To say that something is good or bad is to make a claim which can be challenged and defended, with stronger or weaker reasons. Here are some examples of evaluations.

17. Of all consumer scandals, nothing is more cruel than shoddy workmanship on pacemakers.—Jack Anderson, November 18, 1984. Reprinted by permission of United Feature Syndicate, Inc.

18. The released draft of the Roman Catholic bishops' pastoral letter on the American economy is "a document of striking intellectual slovenliness."—William Buckley, November 18, 1984.

19. I refer to the astonishing, miraculous and incredible feat our Governor and Legislature have performed in just a few days to bring the seed of an idea to enacted legislation in the matter of a new baseball stadium for our state.—R.B., *Sunday Star-Ledger* (Newark, N.J.), December 30, 1984.

All these messages involve evaluations. To say that a scandal is cruel is not only to say that it shows a delight in hurting people, but to judge it bad. "Striking intellectual slovenliness"—this not only asserts that the document was prepared in a very sloppy, incompetent manner but unequivocally expresses Buckley's very negative appraisal. "Astonishing, miraculous and incredible"—all these say that the feat was very good. Asserting any one of these statements then involves asserting that something is good or bad.

Descriptions, interpretations, evaluations, then, are the three basic classifications of informative assertions. Why these distinctions are important for the logical thinker as challenger will become apparent in the next section, when we discuss challenging these assertions.

Summary

An assertion is a *description* just in case it is in principle possible to verify or refute it by appealing to sense experience, our own or others. In asking whether such statements are true, we appeal straightforwardly and simply to experience, and do not ask what some concept means or what values are involved.

We distinguish reports from descriptions involving inferences. There are three types of reports: *firsthand reports* describe what someone has experienced directly; *secondhand reports* present what someone else has experienced directly; and *summary reports* collect or collate a number of reports. *Descriptions involving inference* go beyond reported data, either asserting some projection or generalization or inferring some particular claim from beliefs going beyond reported data.

A message is an *interpretation* just in case verifying or refuting it involves centrally an issue of definition. In assessing whether an interpretation is true, we appeal not only to sense experience but also to the criteria for determining when some concept applies.

In an *evaluation,* the principal issue is what is right or wrong, good or bad, preferable or not preferable.

Exercise 2-I

For each of the following messages, indicate whether it is a description, interpretation, or evaluation. In some cases different parts of a message may involve different types of assertions. Be prepared to discuss why in each case.

Sample Answer

In Amman, Jordan, Yasir Arafat and the Palestine National Council called for an international conference under United Nations auspices, to negotiate Middle East peace. Clearly the P.L.O. is offering Israel peace.

The first sentence is a description. It simply reports what Yasir Arafat and the Palestine National Council said, which presumably was heard publicly. The second sentence, however, is an interpretation. It makes a claim about P.L.O. intentions and the significance of the call for a U.N. conference reported in the first sentence.

1. The nation's Democratic governors are gathering here in Denver this week.—*Sunday Star-Ledger* (Newark, N.J.), August 3, 1980.

2. The president vetoed the bill to build a dam in that state to punish its residents for voting against him in the last election.

3. That movie was a real thriller.

4. The proliferation of go-go taverns throughout New Jersey is a growing social menace, and strong countermeasures are needed to halt this spreading cancer.—D.V.S., *Sunday Star-Ledger* (Newark, N.J.), January 20, 1985.

5. We have seen and heard enough already to know that the second term of Ronald Reagan is going to be vastly different from the first. . . . I think that what we have seen for years is Ronald Reagan the politician, determined to do and say whatever was necessary to climb politically, saying brilliantly whatever was expedient. . . . I think, though, that having won, Ronald—or Nancy—Reagan has decided that since there are no more re-election campaigns to come, it is time to deal with reality. . . . I think that Nancy Reagan has programmed Ronald Reagan to believe that there is something to be written more indelibly in history than any electoral landslide. I think that Mrs. Reagan, with help from George Shultz and a few others, has convinced the President to shift from his role as Russian-baiter to peacemaker.—Carl T. Rowan, January 20, 1985. © by and permission of News America Syndicate.

6. To reward a crooked cop with a political plum at a yearly salary of $22,000 is a slap in the face to every one of the honest, hard-working Newark police officers who put their lives on the line each day, and to every other law enforcement officer in the state who values the public trust reposed in him or her.—J.H.S., *Sunday Star-Ledger* (Newark, N.J.), December 2, 1984.

7. A day after Army and Navy squared off in Philadelphia for this

year's annual service-academy football classic, a large financial cloud still hovers over last year's game.—Jack Anderson, December 2, 1984. Reprinted by permission of United Feature Syndicate, Inc.

8. United Nations Secretary General Kurt Waldheim arrived here yesterday to try to start a dialogue between the Vietnamese-backed regime in Phnom Penh and Thailand and help resolve the Kampuchean crisis.—Reuters.

9. It is one of their [i.e., those who feel hostility toward nuns because of their "modernized" life-style] insecurities that they cannot accept a show of strength, assertion or individuality in a group of women (would men ever be in this position?) who have been acceptable only in an unquestioning indenture to the patriarchal church.—C.F., *Sunday Star-Ledger* (Newark, N.J.), November 25, 1984.

10. [The National Highway Traffic Safety Administration's] 1980 decision to spare Ford Motor Co. the largest auto recall in history continues to exact a grisly toll of death and injury.—Jack Anderson, November 25, 1984. Reprinted by permission of United Feature Syndicate, Inc.

11. Having already used up most of the $2.6 billion in American aid for the fiscal year that began three months ago, the Israelis now ask for $800 million more in early 1985 *plus* $4.05 billion in the early months of the next fiscal year. All the aid sought and sent is in grants, not loans, half for military equipment and half to be spent at will.—*The New York Times,* editorial, December 24, 1984. Copyright © 1984 by The New York Times Company. Reprinted by permission.

12. Forty percent of the families identified as needing services were not offered or provided any. Thirty-six percent, described as needing multiple services, were provided with only one. Investigations that should be completed in 90 days were drawn out to 145.—*The New York Times,* editorial, December 24, 1984. Copyright © 1984 by The New York Times Company. Reprinted by permission.

13. After a subsequent visit to the White House, perhaps Mrs. Thatcher realized that her schoolgirlish crush on The Russian with the Smile [Mikhail Gorbachev] made her look unstatesmanlike.—William Safire, *The New York Times,* December 24, 1984. Copyright © 1984 by The New York Times Company. Reprinted by permission.

14. Japan's Shinkansen, or bullet trains, are everything they're cracked up to be. Every 20 minutes or so one of the sleek white beauties leaves Tokyo station for the dash west. Superexpresses for Nagoya, Kyoto and Osaka cruise at 125 miles an hour. The trains that serve intermediate stops still manage to average 80. The conductors smile. The cars are spotless. In the buffet car, the white stuff provided with coffee is real heavy cream.—Peter Passell, *The New York Times,* December 24, 1984. Copyright © 1984 by The New York Times Company. Reprinted by permission.

15. We should exploit that fear by linking future deployment of our shield to substantial reductions now and later in offensive missiles and battle-

management radar. We should ultimately dispel that fear by offering to share development of the global shield, reducing the threat to both superpowers from terrorist states.—William Safire, *The New York Times,* December 24, 1984. Copyright © 1984 by The New York Times Company. Reprinted by permission.

Exercise 2-II

We have distinguished four types of descriptions: firsthand reports, secondhand reports, summary reports, descriptions involving inference. For each of the following examples, identify which type of description it most likely is. Be prepared to discuss why in each case.

Sample Answer

The Russians will order all foreign journalists out of Afghanistan shortly.

Since observers stationed in Afghanistan who wait for a short period will be able to tell by direct experience whether the statement is true or not, it is a description. However, since it makes a claim about a future event, it could not be a first- or secondhand report, but must be inferred from certain beliefs about Russian intentions in Afghanistan.

1. There are five birds flying to the right of the ship (said by someone on the ship looking to the right).

2. French police raided two apartments in the student-populated Latin Quarter of Paris at dawn yesterday and arrested two men said to have been involved in the failed attempt on the life of former Iranian Premier Shahpour Bakhtiar.—AP.

3. Twenty-five percent of the students filling out a course evaluation form voted Professor Brown as one of the most outstanding professors.

4. As of today, 68 percent of all Americans approve of the job the president is doing.

5. The Russians have ordered all American reporters out of Afghanistan.—Network newscaster.

6. Independent tests . . . show the contamination in the log pond varies from less than one part per million to 12 parts per million.—Chris Bird, *The Province* (Vancouver, Canada), October 11, 1977.

7. Tuesday night while I was watching the Johnny Carson Show, half-awake and half-asleep, the phone started jumping off the hook, and people were saying, "I got a telegram from Joe Granville—sell me out tomorrow morning at the opening." I said, "You're crazy." They said, "Do it anyhow, it's my money." So, I did it.—Julius Westheimer, "Wall Street Week," January 9, 1981.

8. Almost 900,000 human beings [in Africa] are facing death by starvation this year alone. The drought which has produced widespread famine has

severely affected 13 countries.—M.T.-J., *Sunday Star-Ledger* (Newark, N.J.), December 23, 1984.

9. At least 250,000 Salvadoreans and Guatemalans since 1980 [have arrived] in the United States.—E.I., *Sunday Star-Ledger* (Newark, N.J.), December 23, 1984.

10. Thousands of people who want New Caledonia to remain a French territory defied a government ban and marched through downtown Noumea yesterday as French President Francois Mitterand arrived for a 12-hour visit. —AP.

11. Two hundred thousand [industry] jobs are expected to be lost [to robots] in the next few years.—S.F., *Sunday Star-Ledger* (Newark, N.J.), December 23, 1984.

12. In the late summer of that year we lived in a house in a village that looked across the river and the plain to the mountains. In the bed of the river there were pebbles and boulders, dry and white in the sun, and the water was clear and swiftly moving and blue in the channels. Troops went by the house and down the road and the dust they raised powdered the leaves of the trees. The trunks of the trees too were dusty and the leaves fell early that year and we saw the troops marching along the road and the dust rising and leaves, stirred by the breeze, falling and the soldiers marching and afterward the road bare and white except for the leaves.—Ernest Hemingway, *A Farewell to Arms.*

13. Workers yesterday released about 200 Bolivian and foreign executives held hostage for three days, but kept to their demand for pay raises and threatened to go ahead with a nationwide general strike.—UPI.

14. Even from a stout ally, requests for doubling aid year after year will not be [quickly approved, if at all] in a Congress struggling to make its own severe budget cuts.—*The New York Times,* editorial, December 24, 1984. Copyright © 1984 by The New York Times Company. Reprinted by permission.

15. The maximum energy you can get from the sun is 1 kilowatt per square meter, and you only get that when the sun is shining at right angles to the collectors.—W.P., *Sunday Star-Ledger* (Newark, N.J.), December 23, 1984.

§2.2 CHALLENGING DESCRIPTIONS, INTERPRETATIONS, EVALUATIONS

There are two broad questions involved in challenging an assertion:

1. What does it mean?
2. Why should I believe it?

Since the first question involves problems of meaning, which in turn are connected with questions of argument evaluation and with definition, and properly treating these issues calls for a chapter in itself, we postpone considering the meaning challenge until Chapter 4. We issue the second challenge when we refuse to accept a statement without argument. We are demanding some evidence, justification, support before we accept the claim.

Whenever someone makes an assertion, should we issue this challenge? The answer is clearly no. For in arguing for a claim, we present premises which are themselves asserted. But then, should we *always* demand justification, each of these will have to be supported. But the statements made in their support in turn will have to be supported. But we cannot keep asking why forever. Our argument will never get off the ground. In giving an argument, we assume that our audience already accepts, believes certain statements, and will not demand argument for them. We expect or intend our premises to be among those statements. Without this precondition, we cannot argue with someone. Logical thinkers respect argument. Hence they are not total skeptics demanding justification for absolutely everything. But they do demand justification on occasion. The question is—when should they demand justification for an assertion, and what has this to do with the description/interpretation/evaluation distinction? To answer these questions, we must introduce two very basic concepts in the theory of logical thinking: burden of proof and presumption.

What Do We Mean by Burden of Proof and Presumption?

Suppose that someone were to say

1. The Republicans will win the next national election.

This statement may be true or false. If we wait long enough, we'll find out. But if someone wants us to believe this assertion today, he or she will have to give us reasons. The burden of proof is on him or her. We may define *burden of proof* this way: "To say that the burden of proof rests with a certain side is to say that it is up to that side to bring in the evidence to make its case."[3] One logical thinking skill is recognizing when the burden of proof lies with someone making an assertion. When the evidence is not forthcoming, logical thinkers will challenge the assertion, asking for the reasons to believe it.

Suppose now that evidence is forthcoming for (1). How might someone argue for the contention?

2. The Republicans are currently in office and the economy is strong. Americans surveyed perceive our negotiations with the Soviets as fruitful, and major Republicans as strong leaders.

Given that the Republicans are in office, there are several good reasons here why the American voters would keep them in office. But there is something very interesting about these premises. There was an air of controversiality about (1). Clearly the burden of proof is on someone making that assertion. But is there a similar air of controversiality about the claim that the Republicans are currently in office? That assertion is a straight description which presumably would not be made if false. In saying that Americans perceive our negotiations with the Soviets as fruitful and major Republicans as strong leaders, we have summary reports of public opinion or attitude—something which could be well known. The claim that the economy is strong *is* an interpretation, but if it were not an uncontroversial interpretation, would it be simply offered as a premise? If someone challenges one of these premises, then wouldn't the burden of proof be on the challenger to justify questioning the assertion?

This leads us to the second basic concept in the theory of logical thinking, that of presumption. When there is a *presumption* in favor of a statement, then in the absence of specific counterindications, we may accept it. The burden of proof is on the adversary's side to show it should be challenged.[4]

Clearly, recognizing when there is a presumption in favor of a statement and when the burden of proof lies on the person asserting the statement are two sides of the same coin. This is basic to evaluating assertions. Our distinction among descriptions, interpretations, and evaluations is relevant here. With the exception of descriptions involving inference which make statistical statements about entire classes on the basis of observing a sample, descriptions make statements either based on experience or which can be completely checked by experience. We need not go beyond observation to verify such descriptions. Hence, unless there are reasons to the contrary, why should we question whether persons could have made these observations or were truthfully reporting them? There is a presumption in favor of senses or memory.[5]

There is also a presumption of natural trustfulness, a presumption to accept what is stated as true unless there is cause for distrust.[6] Unless there is evidence of dissembling, why should we demand proof that someone is not? And if someone is just reporting observations, without significant inference, interpretation, or evaluation, or is making a statement which could be checked by simple observation, why should such claims be challenged unless there is evidence to question them?

The situation is different with statistical descriptions involving inferences, with interpretations, and with evaluations. Here, where we are going beyond what is observed, the question of justification naturally arises. Why are we justified in saying that a majority of all the voters will support a candidate? Why are we justified in saying that ingesting certain chemicals causes cancer or that a certain policy is preferable to its alternatives? Such claims, by themselves, call for defense. The burden of proof is ordinarily upon the persons making these assertions. There is, however, one notable exception here. Recall that the interpretation, "The economy is strong," need not be controversial. The following statements need not be either:

3. Americans will generally "vote their pocketbooks" in national elections (i.e., if the economy is going well, Americans will return the party in power to office; if not, they will elect the opposition).

4. Smoking causes lung cancer and other respiratory diseases.

5. Stealing is wrong.

Although all these statements go beyond reports, they are not controversial. Rather, they are part of common knowledge, what is generally agreed to. They are in accord with the normal, usual, customary course of affairs. As such, there is a presumption in their favor.[7] In general, then, there is a presumption in favor of most descriptions, while the burden of proof is on someone asserting interpretations, evaluations, or descriptions involving inference clearly going beyond observation. That is why these distinctions are important for the logical thinker as challenger. Recognizing which class a statement belongs to may be sufficient for recognizing whether there is a presumption in its favor or whether it should be challenged.

However, as we have already suggested, under some circumstances, there may be reason to question a description. The key question here is how could someone know that the description is true? How could he or she have come by this knowledge? This question arises with particular force on certain occasions. Suppose it is obvious that someone's description of a particular event is not based on direct experience or the testimony of others. It is not a first- or secondhand report. Then it was inferred from some interpretation. Here the question immediately arises—how justified is that interpretation and the inference based on it? Unless there is a presumption in favor of the interpretation and inference, recognizing that we have a description involving inference locates the burden of proof on the person making the claim. Our distinguishing firsthand, secondhand, and summary reports is distinctly relevant here. With each type of report, different considerations bring the presumption into question. Knowing what these considerations are is again important for the logical thinker as challenger. Let's look at each type of report in turn.

When Should We Question Firsthand Reports?

Recall that a firsthand report is a description of what a person himself or herself has experienced. Various factors are known to influence perception. Human senses have limitations, and perception can be affected by emotion. Suppose my watch is missing and I claim I have seen it in my neighbor's window across the street. There are a number of critical questions we can ask here.

1. Are your eyes capable of perceiving what you reported? Is human vision, or your vision, accurate enough to discriminate the details that would identify what you saw as *your* watch if viewed from across the street?

Clearly we can ask similar questions about the other sense organs.

2. Would the circumstances allow such an observation? When did you claim to see your watch? If last evening, was there really enough light actually to see it?

3. How carefully did you observe? How much attention did you pay to the observation? Was there concentration over some period or just a quick look?

4. Were you psychologically set to make this observation? Did you "see" what you expected to see?

Our expectations may very well color our sense perceptions.

5. What was your emotional state? How upset were you about losing your watch?[8]

These critical questions can pinpoint when a firsthand report should be challenged, when the burden of proof should be put on the person making the report to give evidence for it or at least to give evidence that undermining conditions do not make the claim questionable. Under these conditions, a challenge would be meaningful and appropriate. If we know that any of these conditions hold, a challenge is called for.

Should We Question Secondhand Reports?

To recognize that a report is secondhand, that it has passed through several sources, is itself to recognize that there is some ground for being skeptical, for challenging the report. Certain crucial questions arise when reports reach us secondhand. The first is just how many intermediate sources did the message pass through? This is distinctly relevant to how much confidence we should put in this description. Even assuming that all the agents in a given chain of communication, one passing a message to the next, intend to tell the truth and not to deceive, it would be hard to guarantee that the whole truth and nothing but the truth characterized the final end product of the chain. Why? Although descriptions principally state facts rather than interpret those facts, almost invariably some interpretation or evaluation of the data is involved in making a report, including a firsthand report. An observer will first judge which observed aspects or details are important enough or relevant enough to be reported. Suppose we have an eyewitness to a crime. Clearly the person will not report *every* detail of the scene. The color of the rug, the style of the furniture, the type of decorations—all these may be deemed insignificant background details irrelevant to the issue of the crime. That the perpetrator had a gun and also wore a mask, that the victim pleaded for mercy—these would be deemed relevant details.

Now we can debate whether the observer's decision was correct or not. Whether some detail should have been included in the description of the scene is not merely a matter of taste. The point is that our witness acts as a filter. Even if he or she intends to be completely truthful, some details will be presented and others left out as judged relevant. A secondhand report will have passed through two or more filters, depending upon how many people have passed the story from one to the next. Each one of these again acts as a filter. It would be surprising if some relevant facts did not get excluded in this process, and the significance of other facts distorted.

Besides judging data relevant, observers may also interpret what they have observed and infer certain descriptions on that basis. Hence at some point in a chain of communication, a reporter may take a message as indicating some further fact, as meaning that some further statement is true, and report that as fact rather than the "original" message. The more persons who have reported a message from one to the next, the more filters our reports have passed through, the more chances such interpretations will have been made at some point in the chain. These interpretations may be mistaken, even assuming goodwill on the part of all our reporters. Hence there is a distinct possibility that these descriptions, these secondhand reports, will involve distortion. And if this may happen, assuming our reporters want to be completely truthful, how much more likely may distortion occur when one or more sources are biased? Recognizing then that a report is secondhand decreases the presumption in its favor. A logical thinker will have these critical considerations at hand when dealing with secondhand reports.

When Should We Question Summary Reports?

Since summary reports involve statistical statements, certain problems with statistics provide grounds for challenging these statements. First is the *problem of the unknowable statistic.* There may be cases where it is quite questionable how someone came to know a given piece of statistical information or even whether anyone could know it. For example, consider the beginning of the following letter:

1. Dear Friend: In the past 5,000 years men have fought in 14,523 wars. One out of four persons living during this time have been war casualties.[9]

Could anyone know the precise number of wars over the past 5,000 years? What is the source of the statistic that 25 percent of the world's population over that time have been war casualties? Is this a credible statistic?

Here is another example:

2. Since the 1973 Supreme Court decision, the number of illegal abortions has decreased by 90 percent.

If this is intended as a statistical report, we may ask how anyone could know that statistic? Since such abortions are *illegal,* they would not be reported to reliable health authorities or agencies. It would seem impossible to get reliable statistics on how many illegal abortions there were before and after the Supreme Court decision. Where did this statistic come from? We should want to challenge statistical reports, and indeed any statistical statement, summary report or inference, when it is questionable whether anyone could know the statistics.

Besides the problem of unknowable statistics, there is the *problem of biased statistics*. Statistics can be biased for various reasons. First, those who gathered them may want to prove a certain point and this can lead to exaggeration or distortion. Only facts favorable to a certain view are summarized in the statistical report. Second, when gathering statistics on public opinion, the way questions are asked, how they are phrased, or to whom they are asked can lead to bias. Consider:

3. Do you support the president's economic recovery plan or do you favor runaway inflation?

There is a false dilemma suggested here—that you must support one or the other of these two alternatives. And who would favor runaway inflation? This question is set to prompt a certain answer. But how reliable would be a statistical report on how this question was answered? Could we properly base any interpretation on it?

In 1976, the Immigration and Naturalization Service surveyed illegal aliens, asking how many "live in a home, their age, how they entered the country, how many children they have, what jobs they have held, how much they earn, what taxes they pay and what use they have made of social welfare services."[10] Although the questions may not be biased, those asked may be very reticent to give wholly accurate answers, even given promises that no action would be taken against them. What would be the value of these statistics? This last example illustrates a distinct problem whenever statistics are gathered by using questionnaires. There is a presumption that those asked will answer these questions truthfully. When people say there are five persons in their household, the data we are gathering are not that they made this verbal response to a particular question but that there are five persons in the household. This, of course, presupposes that those answering told the truth. When this is doubtful, the resulting statistics may be biased.

Biased statistical reports invite mistaken interpretations. In general, statistics may invite interpretations; raw statistical figures are assigned a meaning. Besides the basic statistical data being biased, these interpretations may be questionable. For example, suppose we have statistical reports about the total number of certain types of crimes reported in various cities. Suppose New York City were to head the list. What does this mean? Does it mean that New York is the most crime-ridden city in the United States? Is that a fair interpretation? May we infer that New York is the most dangerous place to live? But wouldn't we expect that the larger a city's population, the more crimes would be committed and reported? A better indication of the crime rate would be number of crimes per 1,000 residents. It is quite possible that a large city could have a greater total number of crimes, but fewer crimes per 1,000 than some smaller cities. Which place has the lower crime rate? This highlights how statistics are subject to interpretation. The raw data can be regarded as giving signs of certain conditions. But these interpretations can be questionable.

Although summary reports are not interpretations, these remarks about questionable statistical interpretations should be kept in mind when evaluating statistical assertions. We must be prepared to challenge statistical statements which may very well be unknowable, which may involve bias, or which may be unwarranted interpretations.

How Else May We Challenge Assertions?

So far, the reason why we ask someone to defend a claim is that there is legitimate doubt the person could know the statement true. If the assertion goes beyond experience, or there is doubt that experience could properly back it up, a challenge may very well be in order. But there is another ground for challenging a claim. If we know the assertion is outright false or have distinct evidence against it, then we should challenge the claim. No one has a right to ask us to believe false statements. We can reject them out of hand. If we have evidence against a claim, then certainly the burden of proof is on the claim's defender to provide opposing evidence supporting it.

But how do we recognize statements as false? When do we see that we have evidence against a claim? In a number of cases, especially descriptions of particular events or occurrences, our general background knowledge may tell us that a certain event did not happen or did not happen as described.

1. Jimmy Carter was inaugurated for the second time in January 1981.
2. Ronald Reagan took the oath of office on the Koran.

Anyone with general knowledge of American politics knows that Jimmy Carter's second inaugural never happened. Ronald Reagan was inaugurated, but he took the oath, as presidents do, on the Bible, not the Koran. Challenging and rejecting such statements when we encounter them is perfectly proper.

The case of generalizations is interesting and deserves special treatment, because here a certain logical concept can pinpoint how evidence may count against or show false such general statements. Let's distinguish first generalizations beginning with "all" or "no"—called categorical generalizations—from those dealing with a certain percentage—statistical generalizations. Hence such statements as

3. All humans are mortal.
4. All men (i.e., human males) are impatient.
5. No college presidents are women.
6. All acts of heroic sacrifice are noble and ennobling.
7. Stealing money is always wrong.

are categorical generalizations. On the other hand,

8. Seventy-five percent of the electorate in that district will vote Democratic.

9. Sixty-six and two-thirds percent of the time that coin is tossed, it comes up heads.

10. Most Republicans are conservatives.

are statistical generalizations proper.

We can find countering evidence to general statements by producing counterexamples. What does this mean? Consider (4) again. If we know of the existence of one patient man, then we know that this statement is false. Pointing out that there is such a man is producing a counterexample. We produce counterexamples to statements of the form

All A are B.

when we exhibit something which is an A but fails to be a B. With (5), if we can cite someone who is *both* a college president and a woman, we show that statement false.

One counterinstance serves to show that a categorical generalization is false, but what about statistical generalizations or less than universal generalizations? One flaming liberal Republican will not show false that most Republicans are conservatives. If several voters in a district say they will vote Republican, this does not show that 75 percent will not vote Democratic. Although one counterexample may not show such generalizations false, several counterexamples, the more the better, may serve as counterevidence. If I can think of ten liberal Republicans offhand, that certainly should give me some rational cause to doubt that most Republicans are conservatives. If, on a number of runs of tossing a coin, it does not come up heads two-thirds of the time, then I have good reason to question the statistical claim that it will do so in the long run. Given such counterevidence, the burden of proof should shift to someone claiming that most Republicans are conservatives or that the coin will come up heads two-thirds of the time.

So far, ability to produce a counterexample has depended on our having certain evidence. We had to know of the counterexample or counterexamples. With certain evaluative statements, normative generalizations such as (6) and (7), on the other hand, it is sufficient to imagine an instance where, contrary to the normative assertion, some action of a certain kind is not right or wrong or permissible, some trait or state of affairs is not good or bad or preferable. For example, suppose someone claimed,

11. It is always wrong to tell a lie.

This is a normative generalization. But consider the following situation. Suppose I were in Germany during the Nazi persecution of the Jews. Suppose I had a

Jewish friend who was fleeing from the Nazis. His only crime is being Jewish. Suppose I know where he is hiding, as do some others. Suppose certain Nazi officers ask me where he is. Apparently I have to say something in reply. If I tell them the truth, then my friend will be caught and an innocent person destroyed. If I say that I do not know, that would be a lie, but at least I would not, in effect, be signing my friend's death warrant. However, since there are other persons who know where he is, and they, let us assume, do not have any desire to protect him, the Nazis could still find out readily where he is. Now suppose I told them that I knew where my friend was and then named a location which would so throw them off his trail that I could get to him, warn him of the danger, and he could escape. This would be a lie also. But would it be wrong under these circumstances? I have saved a life by misinforming the Nazis. How could that be wrong?

This imagined situation is a counterexample to the claim that I should never tell a lie. If it holds weight, then I have conceived of a situation where this moral injunction did not hold. Normative generalizations are intended to apply not just to actual situations but to a wide range of conceivable situations.[11] When we say that lying is always wrong, we mean not just that all actual cases of lying have been wrong, not even that all cases will be, but that any conceivable case of lying is wrong. Imagined counterexamples then count against normative generalizations, showing them strictly false, and not just questionable. Statement 11 must be modified to be adequate. It has told us that in no possible situation is lying permissible, and we have conceived of a situation where it is.

The point of these last considerations is to highlight how we as logical thinkers may have to challenge assertions not just when evidence is necessary before the statement is rationally credible, but when there is counterevidence against the statement, perhaps strong enough to show it false. The point of this whole section is to develop how we as logical thinkers should know when challenging assertions is necessary and what challenges are called for. We must know where the burden of proof lies. Why? Because we do not want to accept statements without proper evidence nor do we want to demand evidence just for the sake of demanding evidence. Recognizing when the burden of proof lies on the person making an assertion distinguishes situations calling for a genuine challenge from those where a challenge would be frivolous. We must also recognize false or unlikely statements. Why? As rational persons, we want to believe what is true. For these reasons, then, knowledge of when to challenge assertions is an indispensable tool of a logical thinker. There is one other reason why logical thinkers must challenge assertions. We turn to that in the next section.

Summary

When the *burden of proof* is on someone making an assertion, it is up to that person to give evidence for the statement. When there is a *presumption* in favor of a statement, the burden is on the challenger to show why it should be questioned.

In general, there is a presumption for those descriptions based on experience or which can be completely checked by experience, while the burden of proof is on someone asserting statements properly going beyond experience. However, in cases of common knowledge, where descriptions involving inference, interpretations, or evaluations are not controversial, are generally accepted, the burden is on the challenger to argue why they should be questioned. However, we should challenge statements based on or verifiable by experience when it is questionable how someone could come to know such a statement.

Specifically, for firsthand reports, we can ask

1. Are human sense organs capable of perceiving what they were reported as perceiving?

2. Could such an observation have been made under the conditions prevailing at the time of observation?

3. How careful was the observer in concentrating on the situation?

4. Did the observer have preconceptions?

5. What was the observer's emotional state?

We may ask whether the report is secondhand and, if so, how many "hands" it has passed through. For summary or statistical reports, we may ask

1. Is the statistic knowable? How could someone gain this information?

2. Are the statistics biased? Were the observers trying to prove a point in gathering the data? Were questions phrased in a leading way? Did those surveyed answer the questions truthfully?

All these critical questions help us identify when it is questionable whether someone knows an assertion is true. We may also challenge a statement when we know it false or have distinct evidence against it. If we know that an event did not happen as described or did not happen at all, we know the description to be false. When challenging generalizations, our evidence may let us construct counterexamples. Citing one A which is not B shows that "All A are B" is false. Citing a number of counterinstances shows a statistical generalization questionable. Imagining a situation where something is not good, right, preferable, or bad, wrong, undesirable shows a normative generalization false.

Exercise 2-III

Produce counterexamples to show that the following generalizations are either false or questionable.

1. All major world political leaders are or have been men.

2. If a person leaves some of his possessions with me for safekeeping, I should return them to him when he asks for them.

3. Human beings always act from selfish motives.

4. If a politician is popular with the voters, he or she is a good public servant.

5. Whatever saves time and money is desirable.

6. Most students find logic easy.

7. All creatures which dwell in the sea are cold-blooded.

8. Killing another human being is always wrong, under any circumstances.

9. Piety is prosecuting any one who is guilty of murder, sacrilege, or of any similar crime—whether he be your father or mother, or whoever he may be—that makes no difference; and not to prosecute them is impiety.—Plato, *Euthyphro.*

10. Two persons are friends just in case each loves the other and wishes the other well for the utility, usefulness the other has for him or for the pleasure the other's company affords him.—Adapted from material in Aristotle's *Nicomachean Ethics.*

Exercise 2-IV

For each of the following assertions, indicate whether the burden of proof would be on someone making the assertion or whether there is a presumption in favor of the assertion. Be prepared to discuss why in each case.

Sample Answer

It is . . . within human capability to overcome the nuclear weapons threat. What is needed is a system of enhanced world order. That system can be built and operating within the next five years, a system providing for powers for a central world authority for planning, resource allocation and development stimuli, as well as for ending nuclear weapons research, production, deployment and the holding of existing stockpiles by nations.—R.H.M., *Sunday Star-Ledger* (Newark, N.J.), December 16, 1984.

We must first ask what "a system of enhanced world order" means. Although saying that such a system would provide a central world authority with certain named powers, what these powers are is left vague. However, even if this were clarified, the claim that it is possible to build such a system within the next five years is a highly questionable interpretation. Certainly nothing in our ordinary experience would suggest such an expectation, that it is in accord with the ordinary state of affairs. Hence, the burden of proof is clearly on R.H.M. to show that such a system is possible.

1. Nancy wore a blue dress to the ceremony.

2. Sixteen ravens were circling to the north of our campsite (said by

someone who just glanced in a northerly direction and was superstitiously afraid of ravens).

3. There's smoke coming from the chimney. That must mean the plant is operating again.

4. It is appalling to see young children dressed in camouflage clothing. This theme condones and encourages a war psychology.—L.R., *Sunday Star-Ledger* (Newark, N.J.), September 23, 1984.

5. The killing of human beings is always tragic and, except in certain exceptional circumstances, is morally wrong.

6. The Central American refugee must be allowed to continue to arrive in the U.S. until conditions of deterioration in Central America cease. And to deport such immigrants, would be like signing a death sentence.—E.I., *Sunday Star-Ledger* (Newark, N.J.), December 23, 1984.

7. The conflicts in Central America have led at least 250,000 Salvadoreans and Guatemalans since 1980 to arrive in the United States.—E.I., *Sunday Star-Ledger* (Newark, N.J.), December 23, 1984.

8. Situations where the cause for washing windshields, collecting contributions or selling merchandise is advanced by banging on car windows or otherwise intimidating drivers . . . is a nuisance and at times blatantly infringes on the rights of drivers.—F.R., *Sunday Star-Ledger* (Newark, N.J.), October 7, 1984.

9. An organization known as the Union of Concerned Scientists is doing its best to give American science a disreputable name. It would be difficult in all the fever swamps of McCarthyism to match the bile of their message, which is, really, to the effect that [the president] is inviting a nuclear war, and presumably doing so because he desires a nuclear war.—William Buckley, February 3, 1985.

10. The absence of any assault on our territory over decades speaks volumes as to the Russians' understanding that any such attempt would be self-defeating; they are too intelligent to try it.—M.S.P., *Sunday Star-Ledger* (Newark, N.J.), February 3, 1985.

11. We can deal successfully with [the Russians] because it is in our mutual interest to do so, and we can verify their cooperation in nuclear arms reduction.—M.S.P., *Sunday Star-Ledger* (Newark, N.J.), February 3, 1985.

12. The auto industry is not developing solar powered cars because of what some call a "concerted, deliberate blockage maneuver" by some interests.

13. It is a blessing, in recognition of which we should someday get around to declaring a national holiday, that the policy that is just is also the policy that is productive. If you were given the choice of poverty or freedom, you might incline to opt for freedom, you might not. But nature has declared that freedom and economic progress go hand in hand.—William Buckley, December 2, 1984.

14. It seems as though our elected officials are pushing this surplus food program [involving a "rancid butter giveaway"] with really no interest for

the health and welfare of our seniors. These same politicians figure a five-pound block of cheese will bring them a vote in November.—J.L., *Sunday Star-Ledger* (Newark, N.J.), January 6, 1985.

15. [By] the Israeli airlift of thousands of impoverished, illiterate Ethiopian Jews into a country beset with enormous financial problems . . . Israel has set an example of courage and integrity for the entire world.—B.C.G., *Sunday Star-Ledger* (Newark, N.J.), January 27, 1985.

16. There are a lot of boys and girls who have the mentality to go to college but can't because of these costs [for higher education in New Jersey]. —A.M., *Sunday Star-Ledger* (Newark, N.J.), August 5, 1984.

17. Nearly 50 percent of the subsidies sent out last year were received by farmers earning over $100,000 per year (12 percent).—William Buckley, February 10, 1985.

18. In addition to creating cultural oases in our urban centers as part of their renaissance, support for the arts creates jobs. That's also good for the state's economy. . . . Funds are important for the academically gifted. They are equally important for the artistically talented. It is not an esoteric issue. It is an economic one.—N.G., *Sunday Star-Ledger* (Newark, N.J.), February 10, 1985.

19. The Ohio Department of Natural Resources said Tuesday the state's first comprehensive roadway and recreational litter survey shows there are 200 million pieces of litter weighing 22 million pounds in Ohio.—U.P.I.

20. To reward a crooked cop [a police officer convicted of bribery and official misconduct] with a political plum at a yearly salary of $22,000 is a slap in the face to every one of the honest, hard-working Newark police officers who put their lives on the line each day, and to every other law enforcement officer in the state who values the public trust reposed in him or her.—J.H.S., *Sunday Star-Ledger* (Newark, N.J.), December 2, 1984.

21. The Mob has moved into a lucrative racket spawned by public concern over the environment: Underworld-connected firms are engaged in the illegal dumping of poisonous and explosive industrial wastes for unethical businessmen who want to get around the new controls.—Jack Anderson, November 16, 1980. Reprinted by permission of United Feature Syndicate, Inc.

22. The proposed resource recovery facility is like the Union Carbide insecticide plant in Bhopal, India, where an accident killed or maimed thousands of people.

23. Uncountable thousands of women carry the scars of rape without their assaulters ever having been brought to justice because, a recent survey shows, half the women raped do not report the crime because they do not want to go through the humiliating ordeal that defense lawyers and judges often impose upon them.—Carl T. Rowan, April 21, 1985. © by and permission of News America Syndicate.

24. The witness, Irish Olympic team coach Padraig Griffin, said the

body was taken away quickly by police, team spokesman John McGouran told reporters.—AP (adapted).

25. Today, the primary needs of our big cities is safety on the streets, both day and night. Crime has built fear and people have lost confidence in the ability of the criminal justice system to control crime. City politicians and the courts have tolerated crime too long and the cities have witnessed an exodus to the suburbs by industry and by families. This is bad.—V.T.R., *Sunday Star-Ledger* (Newark, N.J.), January 27, 1985.

26. The problem is safety first, then economics will work.—V.T.R., *Sunday Star-Ledger* (Newark, N.J.), January 27, 1985.

27. It is apparent that the unnecessary complexity of the tax system comes from concessions granted to special interests.—J.J., *Sunday Star-Ledger* (Newark, N.J.), January 6, 1985.

28. President Harry Truman twice considered threatening the Soviet Union and China with nuclear destruction—"all out war"—in 1952 during the Korean War, handwritten memoranda in his private journal reveal.

Truman considered the threat as a means to end the war, force the Soviet Union to free East European satellites and stop worldwide Communist aggression, Rice University historian Francis L. Lowenheim wrote in a copyright story in the Sunday edition of the Houston *Chronicle.*—UPI.

29. Censorship speaks of insecurity, an obstruction of the free flow of information, and a negation of freedom.

Parents who have a healthy understanding of sexuality and educate their children to their own understanding have nothing to fear from the sale and promotion of pornography within society. It is when parents are insecure about their own understanding of sexuality and about their ability to educate their children concerning sex that censorship and the banning of books and magazines become public issues.—R.K., *Sunday Star-Ledger* (Newark, N.J.), February 10, 1985.

30. As a rule it can be said that censorship is dangerous in all areas of life because it obstructs the free flow of information necessary to finding truth and making decisions vital to the process of living.—R.K., *Sunday Star-Ledger* (Newark, N.J.), February 10, 1985.

31. Promoters of this so-called peace course [a course on the threat of nuclear war] invariably allow no options and probably will tolerate no questions about the wisdom of their proposals.—T.H., *Sunday Star-Ledger* (Newark, N.J.), January 20, 1985.

32. The Comprehensive Employment and Training Act—the federal government's multibillion-dollar program to provide desperately needed jobs and training for low-income citizens—has become the target of an intensive series of FBI investigations focusing on program operations in more than a dozen cities in the state, the *Star-Ledger* has learned.

U.S. authorities revealed they have uncovered evidence of what they portrayed as "rampant" corruption including extortion, kickbacks and fraud involving the "sale" of CETA jobs in return for cash payoffs and political favors.—*Sunday Star-Ledger* (Newark, N.J.), July 27, 1980.

33. UN Secretary General Kurt Waldheim called for the establishment of an independent Palestinian state when speaking at a dinner given by the Arab League Friday night, other guests said yesterday.—Reuters.

34. The streets of New York City are dirtier than at anytime in recent memory. Broadway, Fifth Avenue, Madison Avenue, the wholesale flower market, the theater district, the garment center, Wall Street, Times Square—some of Manhattan's biggest names are dirty.

New York is believed to spend more per capita on sanitation than any major city in the country, but litter clutters nearly every major thoroughfare from the Bronx to Staten Island. The city's own system for measuring street cleanliness shows that the unsightly and sometimes smelly trail of filth is worsening in residential areas from the Upper East Side to Astoria, Queens.—*The New York Times,* August 7, 1980. Copyright © 1980 by The New York Times Company. Reprinted by permission.

35. Our present cars are built for high speeds, and only those who would flee law officers should be made to pay very dearly for their deliberate lawlessness. A fast driver, who is careful, is not a menace on the highway.—J.A., *Sunday Star-Ledger* (Newark, N.J.), January 6, 1985.

36. I have a better way to save lives on the highway [than the 55-mph speed limit]. Since drunken drivers account for most auto wrecks, and more than half of the auto deaths, they should be jailed for life.—J.A., *Sunday Star-Ledger* (Newark, N.J.), January 6, 1985.

37. We are again hearing of widespread famine in Africa. We know, too, that malnutrition on a massive scale there and in other parts of the world is an ongoing reality. . . .

However, . . . there is no reason why humanity should continue to live under these terrible conditions. The world's resources, if properly utilized (and if population growth is curtailed by family planning) are sufficient to both meet needs caused by shortfalls in food under emergency circumstances and to establish sound agricultural practices so that adequate amounts can be grown locally.—R.H.M., *Sunday Star-Ledger* (Newark, N.J.), December 16, 1984.

38. We the people are beginning to expect, as a right, 100 percent protection against everything and that'll never happen in this imperfect world. —D.P.B., *Sunday Star-Ledger* (Newark, N.J.), April 21, 1985.

39. If any citizen thinks he can be exempt from the new warfare the international communist conspiracy is waging against the West in general, and the U.S. in particular, that person lives in a soap bubble. That war is already thrust upon us.

The communist enemy has devised the ingenious ruse of putting its American domestic organizers on our streets disguised as peace marchers.

It is certainly time to investigate the many "peace" groups tied to the international World Peace Council, the granddaddy of most of the peace organizations that tried to sink America during the Vietnam War.—B.B., Ringwood, N.J.

40. I have an idea on how to help relieve two . . . problems—the high federal deficit and high state taxes. Since politicians cannot solve most of the truly pressing problems, I propose the following:

Cut back the U.S. Senate to 50 members instead of 100.

Cut the House of Representatives in half.

. . . we have state senators, freeholders and other elected officials. I'm sure we could cut this number in half. . . .

The savings that these cutbacks would generate would be tremendous. Politicians have large staffs and big expense accounts. But, it's not only money that would be saved. Political institutions would be much more efficient if made smaller. Less in-fighting would take place and politicians should be able to move more swiftly to solve problems. Then perhaps they won't waste their time on trivial matters.

A politician is supposed to serve the people. Unfortunately, many serve themselves and their friends. It's time to end this. I am sure that if you cut back all political institutions by 50 per cent you will see no reduction in service and a high reduction in deficits and taxes. Many private companies are cutting back on employees now and are seeing an increase in profits with no reduction in productivity. It's about time government does the same.—G.S., *Sunday Star-Ledger* (Newark, N.J.), January 27, 1985.

§2.3. THE FALLACY OF FALSE OR QUESTIONABLE PREMISE

We may very straightforwardly relate challenging assertions to the issue of argument evaluation. Not only may people simply assert statements needing evidence or proof without giving that evidence, or simply assert false statements, they may put forward such assertions as premises in arguments. Such arguments will be clearly faulty.

Recall from Chapter 1 what an argument is supposed to do. It is supposed to defend, give evidence for a statement, a conclusion, on the basis of other statements. We asserted in the Introduction that being rational is one feature of logical thinking. But thinking is rational just in case it is based on the facts. In Chapter 1, we pointed out that for arguments, this means that the premises must be true or well warranted. This condition is obviously not satisfied when a premise is false or the burden of proof is on someone asserting a premise which is left undefended—a questionable premise. We may clearly ask whether such arguments are logically convincing.

Just how damaging a false or questionable premise is to an argument depends on various factors. An argument might give several premises to support a conclusion. If only one is problematic, the others may properly logically convince us to accept the conclusion. But this need not always happen. A false or questionable premise may significantly jeopardize an argument's being logically convincing. Certainly having such a premise is a flaw—a flaw important enough to warrant a special name—the *fallacy of false or questionable premise*. Asking whether an argument commits this fallacy is an obvious first question in argument evaluation. The critical questions and considerations developed in the last section are directly relevant here, for they will be precisely what a logical thinker as challenger will ask to identify the fallacy.

We must add two remarks. In the last paragraph we noted that even if a premise is false or questionable, the conclusion of the argument may be defended on other grounds. This point warrants further elaboration. If a premise is false, what does that show about the conclusion? Consider the following simple argument:

> All whales are fish.
> All fish are native to the ocean. Therefore
> All whales are native to the ocean.

Clearly both premises are false. Although whales live in the sea, biologists classify them as mammals, not fish. Also, it's not true that *all* fish are native to the ocean. There are freshwater fish, and many could not survive for long in salt water. But does this mean that the conclusion is false? It clearly does not, because the conclusion is true! This shows that just because we recognize that a premise or all the premises of an argument are false, we are not allowed to infer that the conclusion is false also. The conclusion still could be true. This underscores a very important point. The mere fact that there is a problem with an argument does not mean that we can automatically reject its conclusion. The argument may not have established its conclusion, but that is very different from saying that the conclusion itself is false. We may not be required to accept the conclusion on the basis of the argument, but that does not show that some other argument could not be given to establish the conclusion. Just because an argument is faulty does not mean that its conclusion is not defensible. It is well to emphasize this from the beginning in argument evaluation. We shall develop a number of ways for recognizing that arguments are not logically convincing. This is different from recognizing that their conclusions are false.

For our second remark, recall that a statement's being common knowledge, one generally agreed to, is a presumption in its favor. Now some statements might not be generally agreed to by all persons, but they might well be agreed to by a specific audience. For example,

Republicans tend to be more wealthy and conservative than Democrats.

Not everyone may agree to this, but it is a safe bet that most Americans would. It is the sort of statement we would expect an American audience to accept. It is part of American political common knowledge. This should be recognizable even by non-Americans. If this statement were false or questionable, why should someone address it to an American audience who would easily recognize this? In evaluating an argument for false or questionable premises, then, if we find a premise which we do not know to be either true or false, which is questionable to us, and we know that the argument was intended for a specific audience, we should ask whether that audience would generally recognize the statement as true or false before charging questionable premise.

Exercise 2-V

In each of the following arguments, identify the premises and the conclusions. Remember that a statement may function as either a premise or conclusion. Then in each argument, identify a premise which is either false or questionable. Be prepared to defend why you find the premise false or questionable.

1. Dwight Eisenhower was elected twice to the U.S. presidency in the 1950s. Lyndon Johnson was elected president twice in the 1960s. Richard Nixon was elected in 1968 and reelected in 1972. Hence it looks as if in the third quarter of the twentieth century, Americans were satisfied with their presidents.

2. Harry should not feel ashamed of what he did, for he simply broke a promise when it was inconvenient to keep it, and it is always permissible to break promises when keeping them is not convenient.

3. The Democrats should win the next election. We expect this because voter sentiment has been shifting in their favor. And we know this because American voters never return the current officeholder to power.

4. What struck me as ludicrous were the comments of Kay MacPherson and Marilyn Aarons, who believe that only women can solve the world's problems because they claim women have a "different mind set" and believe in negotiation, whereas men believe in war. These women should be reminded that the toughest, most single-minded rulers in this modern world have been, or are, women—Margaret Thatcher, Golda Meir, Indira Gandhi, to mention but three of many.—A.D.A., Toronto, Canada.

5. In 1978, more than 62,000 Canadian women had their children killed before they could be born. An increase in these numbers takes place every year, so that by the end of 1981, we may nearly have reached the 100,000 level. The percentages are similar in Western Europe. They are greater in the Soviet Union. . . . The present mass fetucide takes place almost always for convenience. The medical professionals tell us that 95% of abortions are now done to kill healthy offspring of healthy women. [Clearly abortion is unacceptable and should be prohibited by law except when necessary to save the mother's life.] —George Grant, "The Case Against Abortion," *Today*, October 3, 1981.

6. The leaders of international communism are the greatest mass murderers in history, and presently hold captive over one quarter of all the humans on the earth. They have stated, without retraction, that they intend to bury the United States, and constitute the single greatest threat to the survival of ourselves and all free nations. They continue aggressively without let-up their drive for total world control. Their bloody invasion of Afghanistan, the brutal crushing of the free labor movement in Poland, massive support for Communist revolutionaries in Central and South America, and the instigation and support of international terrorism, including the recent attempt on Pope John Paul's life, were but their more obvious actions.

Aid and trade with the enemy were once called treason—a word that seems to have disappeared from the American vocabulary—to be replaced by the word profit.

Urge your congressman, senators and the President to stop aid and trade with Communist nations. Stop purchasing at your local stores the Polish hams, Hungarian shoes, Chinese denims, ad nauseam. Wake up, Americans! —J.A.S., *Sunday Star-Ledger* (Newark, N.J.), January 16, 1983.

7. We should legalize possession of marijuana, cocaine, and other hard drugs, for the only victims of these crimes are the users themselves.

8. The military-industrial complex about which President Eisenhower warned us has been raiding the federal Treasury with virtual impunity. Every time someone mentions the Viper antitank rocket, the Trident submarine, the M1 tank, the M2 "Bradley Fighting Vehicle," the C5B cargo transport plane, the Pershing 2 missile or dozens of other weapons systems, you ought to inspect your wallet. You'll find a hole in it reflecting the money taken from you by greedy people who have charged the Pentagon billions upon billions for exotic weaponry that doesn't work, or who have run up the cost of weapons systems in some inexplicable and unconscionable way.—Carl T. Rowan, July 17, 1983.[12] © by and permission of News America Syndicate.

9. Every nation, like every individual, has received a mission that it must fulfill. France exercises over Europe a veritable magistracy that it would be useless to contest and that she has most culpably abused. In particular, she was at the head of the religious system, and not without reason was her king called *most Christian;* Bossuet was never able to say too much on this point. And so, since she has used her influence to contradict her vocation and demoralize Europe, we should not be surprised if she is brought back to her mission by terrible means. —Joseph de Maistre, *Considerations on France.*

10. Some collections of potentially threatened artifacts [remains of California Indians which some present-day Indians wish to rebury] are in museums owned and operated by the tribes. The disputed materials—and the information they hold—are part of the scientific and cultural heritage of all the people of the state of California. As a window on the lives of ancient native Californians, they help us understand the past and therefore ourselves.—Edwin C. Krupp, Direc-

tor, Griffith Observatory, Los Angeles. Letter to *Time,* January 11, 1982. Copyright 1982 Time Inc. All rights reserved. Reprinted by permission from TIME.

11. As the world is, the death penalty can, I believe, be ruled to be morally completely out of the question. The prearranged killing of someone at a stated time is a special outrage against the humane feelings which are an essential part of morality and this is not outweighed by an extra deterrent effect; in fact, the use of the death penalty is likely to increase criminal violence.—J.L. Mackie, *Ethics: Inventing Right and Wrong.*

12. A judge is speaking to a convict upon whom he is about to pass sentence: "You have been convicted of murder in the first degree. Now if you are put to death for this crime, others will think twice before committing murder. Hence there will be fewer murders. Accordingly I sentence you to be put to death in the manner prescribed by law."

13. Our institutions, including the courts, the schools, and the churches have failed us, in not giving positive leadership. Why? Because they have been infiltrated by the "lib-left" and their sympathizers.—D.T., Toronto, Canada.

14. We don't need a government agency to monitor our broadcasters for sex-role stereotyping and tell them when they have offended. If the audience finds the material aired by the broadcasting and advertising industries offensive, those industries will soon know about it, without being told by a government agency that they are doing wrong. The audience itself will always complain about material it finds objectionable.—Adapted from "CRTC: A Dangerous Proposal," *Windsor Star* (Windsor, Canada), November 23, 1982.

15. We must have adequate professional forces to impose our will on the Third World. I am willing to say as a matter of American doctrine, that there are those moments in life when we are going to disagree with other people, and it is my belief that when we fundamentally disagree with somebody we should win.—Senator Newt Gingrich, American Security Council, *Washington Report,* November–December 1980.[13]

FOR FURTHER READING

We are greatly indebted to J. Michael Sproule's *Argument: Language and Its Influence* (New York: McGraw-Hill Book Company, 1980), ch. 3–6, for material in the first two sections of this chapter, in particular for the description/interpretation/evaluation distinction. We recommend these chapters for collateral reading. Burden of proof and presumption are presented in Nicholas Rescher's *Dialectics: A Controversy-Oriented Approach to the Theory of Knowledge* (Albany: State University of New York Press, 1977), ch. 2. The issue of evaluating premises is discussed in Thomas Schwartz's *The Art of Logical Reasoning* (New York: Random House, Inc., 1980), ch. 9. Our discussion of counterexamples is indebted to this treatment. The fallacy of questionable premise is discussed in Ralph H. Johnson and J. Anthony Blair's *Logical Self-Defense* (Toronto, Canada: McGraw-Hill Ryerson, 1977), pp. 22–28, which contains useful supplementary material.

Howard Kahane's *Logic and Contemporary Rhetoric,* 4th ed. (Belmont, Calif.: Wadsworth Publishing Company, 1984), contains much material relevant to this chapter. Sections 4, 5, 9, and 10 of Chapter 4 provide collateral reading on statistical statements. The news media and textbooks, especially in history and civics, are two prime sources of secondhand reports. Chapter 8, "Managing the News," gives a comprehensive analysis of factors in the news media which lead to distortion. Chapter 9, "Textbooks: Managing World Views," analyzes how the desire not just to inform students of our nation's history and the working of our government, but to instill patriotism, affects the presentation of material in history and civics texts.

NOTES

[1] Compare J. Michael Sproule, *Argument: Language and Its Influence* (New York: McGraw-Hill Book Company, 1980), p. 153.

[2] Adapted from a *Newsweek* quote (February 24, 1975), cited in ibid., pp. 151–52.

[3] Nicholas Rescher, *Dialectics: A Controversy-Oriented Approach to the Theory of Knowledge* (Albany: State University of New York Press, 1977), p. 26.

[4] Ibid., p. 30.

[5] Ibid., p. 37.

[6] Ch. Perelman and L. Olbrechts-Tyteca, *The New Rhetoric: A Treatise on Argumentation* (Notre Dame, Ind.: University of Notre Dame Press, 1969), pp. 70–71.

[7] Rescher, *Dialectics,* pp. 36–37.

[8] This is based on a list of "requirements for reliable observation" in W. Ward Fearnside, *About Thinking* (Englewood Cliffs, N.J.: Prentice-Hall, Inc., 1980), p. 318. We are indebted to this list and attendant discussion.

[9] Cited in Howard Kahane, *Logic and Contemporary Rhetoric,* 3rd ed. (Belmont, Calif.: Wadsworth Publishing Company, 1980), p. 100.

[10] *Odessa American,* November 10, 1976, Sec. C, p. 9; quoted in Sproule, *Argument,* p. 113.

[11] Compare Thomas Schwartz, *The Art of Logical Reasoning* (New York: Random House, Inc., 1980), p. 186.

[12] This excerpt involves just the first two paragraphs of Carl Rowan's column for July 17, 1983. The remainder of the article presents evidence to support these assertions. But suppose Mr. Rowan had stopped here. How would we have false or questionable premise? That is what you are being asked to evaluate.

[13] We wish to acknowledge with gratitude our debt to the *Informal Logic Newsletter* and to its contributors for some of the examples in this exercise. Examples 4, 5, 10, and 13 appear in Vol. IV, no. 3, July 1982. Examples 11 and 14 appear in Vol. V, no. 3, July 1983. For example 15, we are indebted to Frank C. Carlon, Karol Dycha, and Leo Raffin, *An Informal Logic Workbook* (Windsor, Canada, 1980).

3
INFORMAL FALLACIES

It is now time to turn our attention specifically to arguments. An argument which fails to give good, that is logically convincing, reasons for its conclusion is *fallacious* or a *fallacy*. We have already identified one type of fallacy in the last chapter—the fallacy of false or questionable premise. Such arguments fail to be logically convincing because the premises are not based on the facts. At least we can question whether they are based on facts. But arguments may be fallacious because the premises fail to be relevant or to give adequate support to the conclusion—the argument fails to satisfy one of the other conditions for being logically convincing.

However, recall from Chapter 1 that we have contrasted the logically convincing character of an argument with its persuasive force—its ability to convince us to accept the conclusion. Although this may be surprising, many fallacious arguments have distinct persuasive force. They do not give good reasons for the conclusion; nonetheless people feel persuaded by them. How can this be—how can fallacies deceive us into being convinced? This can happen for various reasons. First, certain arguments may be of a specific form which resembles a correct pattern of reasoning. If we are not careful, we may easily confuse the fallacious pattern with the correct pattern. These arguments are included in a certain class—the *formal fallacies*—although not all formal fallacies need be persuasive. We may recognize that all such arguments are fallacies by identifying their form. We illustrate formal fallacies as part of our treatment of deduction in Chapter 11.

Second, some arguments are fallacious yet persuasive because they overlook relevant information bearing on the conclusion. Although the premises may appear to give sufficient support, there are factors or conditions that, should they hold, undermine these reasons outright. The argument is fallacious because it has not considered and countered these considerations. Many (although not all) *inductive fallacies* are fallacious precisely for this reason. We shall consider a number of these patterns in Chapter 10, on evaluating specific inductive arguments.

A third way in which fallacious arguments may have deceptive persuasive force is by using ambiguous words or vague language. If we are not critical in asking what is meant, we may not expose the ambiguity or vagueness; we may assent to a conclusion, but may either not know what it means or have very poor grounds for accepting it. These fallacies are discussed in the next chapter, together with problems of meaning and definition.

A fourth way an argument may be persuasive although fallacious is by smuggling in some assumption which itself is doubtful, but which may go unnoticed even though accepted. Recognizing this pattern of fallacy can be a way of bringing these dubious assumptions to light. Finally, and perhaps most important, a fallacy can be persuasive by appeal to some emotion. The persuasive force derives not from good reasons given but from the emotions aroused in the audience.

We have now identified five types of fallacies with persuasive force. It is customary to call all but the first informal fallacies (as opposed to formal fallacies). Since we shall consider formal and inductive fallacies, and those involving vagueness and ambiguity, in later chapters, we confine our attention here to emotional appeals and fallacies of dubious assumption. Since many varieties of emotional appeals, to both positive and negative emotions, abound in everyday life, awareness of these appeals and the major patterns they may take is a central skill of the logical thinker as challenger. Accordingly we turn first to examining a number of these patterns in detail.

§3.1 EMOTIONAL APPEALS

As our emotions are positive or negative, expressions of our desires or fears, so in this section we shall consider first appeals to positive emotions and then appeals to negative emotions. We shall, however, begin with an appeal which can go either way, to either type of emotion. This pattern is a paradigm example of an emotional appeal fallacy.

1. *Grandstand Appeal.* Imagine you are a political candidate about to address a large audience; imagine people assembled before you in a large assembly hall, or better yet, on the grandstands of some major sports arena. You want to persuade the audience to vote for you and your party. How could you appeal persuasively to them? In a group this large some, if not many, may not appreciate good arguments—or may not be in the mood to follow cogent reasoning.

You can't be sure that giving logically convincing arguments will work. But there is one thing you can be sure of. The various members of this audience have gut emotions. If those emotions can be aroused and played upon, you may be able to get those votes or at least to strengthen the audience's tendency to vote for you. How could you do this? Suppose you led your audience to "bask in a warm glow of self-congratulation and smugness."[1] That certainly should make them receptive to your message. Suppose further that you identified yourself with the audience, adopting a "folksy" manner to bring this home. You are just one of these good, decent, down home folks. That would certainly arouse positive feelings toward you. Suppose you also know that your audience thinks of itself as bedrock conservative. You represent your party's policies and platform as being conservative, doctoring it up if necessary. This would raise those positive feelings further.

Suppose in addition you portray the opposing party as scoundrels, deserving to be ignominiously thrown out of office. You arouse anger and hate. Now notice in all this, you may say nothing about your qualifications to hold office or the merit of your programs or party platform. You may not have given much hard information about the shortcomings of the opposition. But you have certainly fostered a very persuasive climate, and you have done it by appealing directly to various gut emotions.

Whenever a person attempts to make a point, get a view accepted, not by presenting cogent reasons, but by arousing the gut emotions of the audience, we have a *grandstand appeal* or the fallacy of *grandstanding*. Although the name "grandstand" derives from this setting of persuading the masses, we shall regard any argument whose persuasive force depends on arousing gut emotions and not on the cogency of its reasons as an instance of the grandstand appeal, whether or not it is addressed to a mass audience, a small group, or even a single person. Here is a classic example of grandstanding which arouses exactly the emotions just mentioned—anger, hatred, and pride:

> If you don't think that the welfare system in this country is a rotten mess that needs complete overhauling, you listen to that great recording by Johnny Cash about the typical families on relief sitting around drinking booze before their color television sets, or driving around in Cadillacs, while you—you, the hard-working, thrifty, honest Middle American—do the work and pay the taxes to make this possible.—In Monroe C. Beardsley, *Thinking Straight: Principles of Reasoning for Readers & Writers*, 4th ed. © 1975, p. 186. Reprinted by permission of Prentice-Hall, Englewood Cliffs, N.J.

"Rotten mess," "typical families on relief sitting around drinking booze before their color television sets, or driving around in Cadillacs"—these words stir up anger and hate. "You, the hard-working, thrifty, honest Middle American"—that certainly arouses the audience's pride, its feeling of self-righteousness. Note how this appeal to pride can heighten feelings of hate in the example. *We*, the honest, hard-working, thrifty Americans *should* not be taken advantage of by these welfare cheats! How dare they take what is rightfully ours,

---

Figure 3.1   GRANDSTAND APPEAL

The fallacy of grandstand appeal occurs when an argument

1. presents essentially no cogent, good reasons for its conclusion, but rather
2. arouses gut emotions to persuade the audience.

The persuasive force in effect rests entirely on arousing passions or gut emotions.

---

especially people so good as we are! Does the argument present any facts for favoring welfare reform? Are these families Johnny Cash portrays typical or "stereotypical"? Paying attention to these factors helps to identify and appreciate grandstanding. Let's summarize this discussion by giving explicit directions for showing why an argument includes the grandstand appeal (see Figure 3.1).

We have emphasized that in grandstanding, we may appeal to a variety of emotions. Arguments appealing to certain particular basic emotions have frequently been treated by logicians as separate fallacies in their own right. We shall follow that procedure here. We might, if we want, view a number of the following fallacies as special cases of the grandstand appeal. However, these fallacies will have additional features which will make them more memorable, and so easier to challenge.

Appeals to Positive Emotions

2. Bandwagon Appeal.   Some students of human behavior believe that humans have a distinct herd instinct—a desire, need, urge to go with the crowd, to do or believe what others are doing or believing. Whether or not this is true, there are arguments which appeal to such an instinct. Wherever there is an attempt to persuade us that a claim is true or an action right because it is popular—because many, most, all people believe it or do it, because the crowd is going in that direction—we have such reasoning. This is the *bandwagon appeal*. Obviously, if there is a crowd instinct, then representing a belief or action as being favored by the crowd is a way of arousing positive feelings, enthusiasm for it. As we shall see in Chapter 5, this fallacious appeal is very popular in advertising. People across the country are switching to a certain product. You should too!

To appreciate the persuasive force of this appeal, ask yourself how you emotionally react to a candidate when you hear that his or her rallies are attended by throngs of happy supporters and the polls project him or her as the clear winner. Surely you feel like getting on the bandwagon. There is a reverse side to this appeal. Suppose we hear that few people have come to see a candidate and that the polls project him or her as a sure loser?[2] Will this person get our vote? The opposite of the bandwagon appeal is the *abandon ship fallacy*. The argument attempts to dissuade us from holding a belief or approving an action just because few or no people accept that belief or support that action. How

---

Figure 3.2 BANDWAGON APPEAL

The fallacy of bandwagon appeal occurs when an argument

1. claims that many, most, or all people accept a certain belief or approve a certain course of action

and

2. therefore claims that belief *must* be true or that action *must* be right.

---

often do we hear "Nobody believes that any more?" If we are being asked to reject a claim solely for this reason, we have the abandon ship fallacy.

Why are bandwagon appeals fallacious? Isn't the fact that everyone agrees on something a mark that it is true or correct? If many people are buying a product, isn't the manufacturer doing something right? Although popularity may constitute some evidence, how much evidence does it give? How strong or weighty is the evidence? An item could be popular for all kinds of reasons, many having little to do with its quality. People might buy the product because it is a status symbol or because it satisfies some subconscious desire. In these cases, the item could be popular but worthless. So popularity is *a* reason, but a weak reason. But how does the bandwagon appeal make us feel about the weight of popularity as evidence? The product *must* be good because it's so popular. Popularity is made a compelling reason. The value of popularity as a reason is inflated beyond all proportion. It is exactly here that the logical error lies. We are duped into thinking that a lightweight reason is a real heavyweight.

How should we argue that an argument involves the bandwagon appeal fallacy? We must establish these two points about the argument (see Figure 3.2).[3]

3. *Fallacious Appeal to Authority or Glamorous Person.* Look at the example of the grandstand appeal again. What is the question at issue? It is whether the welfare system should be dramatically restructured. But who is Johnny Cash? Now this person may rightly be regarded as an authority in country and western music. His comments on the work of aspiring young singers, or on musical instruments (although an expert performer may know next to nothing about the mechanics of his instrument), or on other musical subjects could be very valuable. He is *not* a sociologist. But questions of welfare policy are questions for sociology or social science in general. Yet our argument suggests that because *Johnny Cash* performed this song about welfare recipients and apparently endorsed this view, we should believe what the song says about the welfare system. But this is a *fallacious appeal to authority:* an authority in one field is cited to support some position in an area outside his special field of competence. Here a musician is cited to support a view in social policy.

But even more than being a musician, isn't Johnny Cash a glamour figure? By being a popular singer and recording star, Johnny Cash is surrounded by a special aura. Movie stars, royalty, anyone who is rich or famous shares this aura of glamour. It affects how we feel about them and about what they say. Being an authority is also glamorous. To be told that someone has a doctoral degree, that he or she is a world-famous scientist or a noted scholar calls forth feelings of awe and respect, in short invests that person with a type of glamour. It may not be the same glamour as a movie star or famous athlete, but in some way or other, all these people are glamorous. But this is the point. A fallacious appeal to authority or glamour derives its persuasive force solely from the glamour of someone who endorses some view or action or product, giving us little or no evidence for the correctness of the view.

Now it is perfectly legitimate to appeal to authorities when they are speaking in or dealing with their fields of competence, unless it concerns some issue which is controversial in the field, one over which experts disagree. To look up a word in a dictionary, to follow one's doctor's advice, to accept a professional legal opinion from a trained lawyer admitted to the bar—these are all appropriate. But to buy certain stocks because your physician recommended them or to engage in certain practices because your lawyer claims they are good for the love life—that is fallacious appeal to authority: the glamour of your doctor or lawyer's expertise is convincing you, not sound evidence.

What is wrong with this fallacious appeal? Why is it fallacious? Again we have essentially the same mistake as with the bandwagon appeal. A weak, in some cases, exceedingly weak, reason is regarded as a compelling reason. A movie star may know nothing about the product he or she endorses. On the other hand, a trained scholar, one who has distinguished himself or herself in one field, might bring this same scholarly frame of mind, this inquiring disposition, this rational temper to another field. We have no guarantee that scholars will always do this. Some may have passionate obsessions with various causes, which they will defend and support out of all reason. But if one has carefully investigated some matter outside his or her specialty, and holds a certain view, it is not wrong to consider that as giving some evidence for this view. But in this case, there is much other evidence for the view, and the weight of proof falls on that evidence. What is fallacious is to regard a scholar's endorsing a view as settling the matter, establishing the claim as true beyond question, and silencing all opposition by pointing to the person's greatness, reputation, esteem. When that is done, we have a fallacious appeal to authority (see Figure 3.3).

Figure 3.3 FALLACIOUS APPEAL TO AUTHORITY OR GLAMOROUS PERSON

An argument is an instance of the fallacious appeal to authority or glamorous person when it

1. asserts that some glamour figure or some scholarly authority endorses some view, attitude, course of action, or product, where the authority is speaking outside his field of expertise and

2. therefore concludes that the view, attitude, course of action *must* be correct or the product *must* be good (the best) to buy.

4. *Appeal to Tradition.*   As we may be dazzled by the authority or glamour of some individual, so we may become attached, even passionately attached, to the traditional ways of doing things or traditional beliefs. These attachments may lead us blindly to advocate policies or beliefs when their appropriateness or validity has been challenged. "Why can't we change that?" "Because we've always done things this way." "We can't accept that; this has always been our belief." These are appeals to tradition. Changing circumstances may call for altering policies, changing values, or revising beliefs. At the very least, we may need to rethink the old ways. Under those circumstances, to argue that the old ways should be followed simply because that is the way it always has been done is to commit the fallacy of *appeal to tradition.*

The reaction of some persons to Galileo's discovering the moons of Jupiter is a classic example of this fallacy. Galileo made this discovery by training his telescope on Jupiter. The telescope was a new scientific instrument and Galileo actually constructed the one he used. Yet some persons refused to believe that Jupiter had moons. In fact, they refused even to look through Galileo's telescope. Their traditionally held theories told them that such phenomena were impossible!

The appeal to tradition involves a logical mistake similar to the bandwagon appeal. The popularity of a view is a mark in its favor, but it is a very weak mark. Likewise, that a belief has been held for a considerable period of time is a mark in *its* favor. It is a reason for giving the view serious consideration. There may be significant evidence for it. But long-time acceptance does not *guarantee* that the view is true or even constitute a weighty reason, as opposed to the evidence directly bearing on it. It is in just such an inflation of the value of tradition that the fallacious appeal lies.

Appeals to tradition may actually be counterproductive, focusing our attention on a fallacious argument where a logically convincing or at least logically plausible argument might be possible. Suppose someone argued that abortion is wrong because it has always been regarded as wrong—appeal to tradition. But suppose one argued cogently that reverence for life was a significant value jeopardized by abortion. Here we have a plausible argument against this practice. Appeals to tradition would obscure plausible reasoning here and in many other contexts. Should women be allowed to hold certain jobs? What positions should be open to them in the military? Should women be allowed in combat? If there are any good reasons why not, appeals to tradition (Figure 3.4) would throw us off their trail.

Figure 3.4   APPEAL TO TRADITION

The fallacy of appeal to tradition occurs when an argument

1. concludes that we must hold a certain belief or maintain a certain course of action because
2. we have always believed that or done that, while
3. circumstances have called that traditional belief or practice into question.

5. *Appeal to Pity.* When presenting the grandstand appeal, we said that logicians have frequently treated appeals to certain particular gut emotions as separate fallacies in their own right. One of these special emotions is pity. The appeal to pity is practically self-explanatory. One pulls on the "heartstrings," presents a most pathetic, tear-jerking story to obtain agreement—not because any good reason has been given but because the hearer feels sorry. A classic use of this appeal appears in the following letter to the editor:

> Dear Sir:
>
> As a mother of nine children I would like to speak out on the draft everyone is talking about.
>
> I am one that is very much against it. I lost a husband in Korea and if they draft from age 18 to 26 I stand to lose four sons and one daughter.
>
> As a mother in poor health I don't think I could take that.
>
> Why can't [the president] leave well enough alone and try and find some of our boys still missing or being held some place.—Mrs. L.T.[4]

Regardless of how we feel about war, has Mrs. L.T. given us any relevant reasons for opposing draft registration or any other military measures? Her appeal is persuasive, but it does not offer good reasons.

We should note that the mere arousing of pity does not guarantee that we have a fallacious appeal to pity. Rather, it is the arousing of pity without any reasons why it should be aroused, when we are unable to decide for ourselves whether this emotion is appropriate, or it is using pity to persuade when factual considerations are relevant, that is fallacious. For example, in a trial, the question of whether a defendant is innocent or guilty is a purely factual matter. The person is guilty if he or she actually performed the deed and was mentally competent at the time. Should the defense attorney try to convince the jury of the defendant's innocence by pointing out how he came from a broken home, has never been loved, was forced onto the streets at age twelve, we would have a blatant appeal to pity. Even if true, none of these facts is relevant to the question of guilt or innocence. On the other hand, should the defendant be convicted, they might be relevant to assessing what type of punishment or how severe a punishment should be imposed. Punishment should fit the crime, and to get a proper fit, we may need to look at who the criminal is. In this case, the defense attorney's presenting these facts may be relevant. Again, a graphic description of mass starvation may arouse pity along with other emotions. These may provide the motive force for our giving aid. The persuasive force of the argument to give aid may lie with these emotions. But is this fallacious appeal to pity? When confronted with mass starvation, pity or compassion seems appropriate! But suppose someone tried to arouse pity simply by talking about those poor, helpless, hungry, starving people. Wouldn't this person be trying to manipulate our emotions, rather than to let us properly react to the situation? Could we decide for ourselves to what extent pity was appropriate? If not, we have a fallacious appeal to pity (see Figure 3.5).

Figure 3.5 APPEAL TO PITY

An argument involves the fallacy of appeal to pity when

1. it arouses pity in the course of making its case and
2. that emotion is out of place or questionable because only factual considerations are relevant or we may be unable to decide for ourselves whether the emotion is appropriate to the situation.

Exercise 3-I

All the following arguments involve one of the five fallacies we have discussed so far:

grandstand appeal	appeal to tradition
bandwagon appeal	appeal to pity
fallacious appeal to authority	

In each case, identify the fallacy involved. Then be prepared to argue why that fallacy occurs, citing how the various conditions spelled out for the fallacy are present in the argument. It is possible that a passage may involve two fallacies. It is also possible that a passage may appear to involve two fallacies or that it may sit on the fence between two fallacies. In such cases, ask which of the defining conditions are really satisfied. Remember that although appeal to pity is a special case of grandstanding, where pity is the basic emotion involved, appeal to pity is the correct answer. This may also apply to the other fallacies.

Sample Answer

I shall remember April 16, 1982, for a long time. For me, the 50th milestone had been reached. For a tiny baby in Bloomington, Ind., it meant death after seven days of American humanity.

The passing of Baby Doe for the most part went unnoticed in the hustle and bustle of our mad rushing to get someplace for something. . . .

What made this child's death so remarkably different? We kill 5,000 other babies each day, every day of the year . . . for the most part silently . . . unseen. But this infant was a highly visible newborn babe and, like all other newborns, needed nourishment to sustain his life and water to keep from dehydrating. . . . Without corrective surgery, intake of nourishment was impossible. But nourishment for Baby Doe was not to be, because his parents "chose" neither to operate, nor to feed.

But surely this was not the first case of starving a newborn to death. Why then should I be so upset about one tiny baby dying 600 miles away from my fairly comfortable life? . . . My friends, this killing was done with the blessing of the highest court in the state of Indiana! . . .

That is what is so alarming! We have now reached the next plateau in selective death!—R.J.C., Jr., *Sunday Star-Ledger* (Newark, N.J.), May 9, 1982.

The fallacy here is grandstanding. R.J.C. is surely expressing his anger, bitter outrage at the death of Baby Doe. Talk about killing babies silently and unseen, starving infants to death, a killing being done "with the blessing of the highest court in the state of Indiana," and "selective death" is inflammatory rhetoric. R.J.C. also tries to arouse our guilt by pointing out our apparent indifference to this death and again by referring to killing 5,000 babies. He also arouses pity for Baby Doe by talking about how he was a "newborn babe," needing food and water. (But can we judge for ourselves just how appropriate pity is in this case? So seeing appeal to pity here is not wrong, but there is a lot more going on, many other emotions aroused.) But does R.J.C. give any cogent reasons for regarding Baby Doe's treatment and the decision of his parents as morally wrong, his apparent conclusion? He arouses our gut emotions to feel this way, but has he given any logical defense of his view?

1. If you would take one look at all those long-haired, pot-smoking hippies, you would agree that the only way for this country to return to decency is to round those fellows up, shave all their hair off, and put them in the army.

2. Although in the past President Polk's expansionist policies were quite controversial in America, today we see that he was right. It would be well-nigh impossible today to find a citizen of the United States who would desire to undo President Polk's diplomacy, President Polk's war, and the treaty of Guadeloupe Hidalgo.—Adapted from Samuel Flagg Bemis, *A Diplomatic History of the United States.*[5]
BACKGROUND: President James K. Polk, who served from 1845 through 1849, was known as the expanionist president. During his term, the United States engaged in the Mexican War, bitterly opposed by some Americans, and much new territory, especially what is now the American southwest, came under U.S. jurisdiction.

3. You should buy this peanut butter. Of course it's good peanut butter; Bruce Jenner himself eats this kind.

4. I am not voting for any candidate for senator who does not support volunteer prayers in our schools. For some 200 years, we have honored our Creator (as mentioned in our Declaration of Independence), and all (regardless of their sect or religion) honored Him and respected their neighbors. For many years our children memorized The Lord's Prayer in school.—J.S., *Sunday Star-Ledger* (Newark, N.J.), September 12, 1982.

5. In the 1972 presidential campaign, Senator George McGovern, the Democratic candidate, argued in the following way against the Vietnam policy of President Nixon (and President Johnson): I think it is terrible what we are doing to that poor, little agricultural country.

6. Ethical relativism is clearly the only viable moral theory. Einstein's theory of relativity shows that.

7. Most of the people here seem in favor of building the bridge at Third and Straight Streets, so I'm confident that is a good location.

8. This month I received my first speeding ticket. I am 74 years old.

My father gave me a car on my 17th birthday and I've been driving ever since. I was in World War II and drove jeeps and trucks—five-ton trucks—and feel at this point in time competent to drive a car within the limits of the law.

I was clocked by radar at 40 mph in a 25-mile zone. . . . I'm willing to take my punishment—but I must appeal to the state not to make such harsh punishment. I was fined $60. Isn't that a bit steep?

Livingston must be down on its luck—issuing tickets for speeding to little old ladies who only go to their town to buy cheap bird bread from the Pepperidge Farm outlet. . . .

I live on Social Security only. My car is a 1971, and has been driven 33,000 miles, so you know I don't use it except when I go to get the bread for the birds. . . . I qualify for welfare and food stamps but try in my meager means to provide for myself and not draw upon the state. I have paid the fine with money saved up for the doctor's appointment but I can't see him because I sent the fine in. I have never meaningly broken the law, and I think it's not fair to have such a high minimum penalty.

Can't something be done to give old folks a break?—V.N., *Sunday Star-Ledger* (Newark, N.J.), April 24, 1983.

9. There are some here who say that our organization should discontinue its practice of giving Thanksgiving baskets and begin a year-round distribution of canned and packaged food. They say that many recipients do not have ovens to roast the turkeys in and there is need for food throughout the year. I say they are wrong. This organization has always had a commitment to the poor. We have always shown this by giving Thanksgiving baskets. I for one cannot eat my Thanksgiving dinner in good conscience, knowing that there are others who are going without. I say we must continue to give Thanksgiving baskets!

10. Those guys were cowards who went to Canada or Europe to avoid the war in Vietnam. They grew up in America, but when it was time for them to serve their country, they were afraid to die. Why should we let them back in?

11. Workers up and down the country are tired of parties which can do nothing but promise more and more doles when they know full well that the money is not in the till. What we want is a Government which will honestly try to bring back work in the mines, the mills, and the workshops.—Stanley Baldwin.[6]

12. Many people have criticized me for driving a Japanese car. At times they made me feel guilty for buying a Honda. But now I know I made the right choice. I want to tell all my critics that Doug Boast [a writer for a major Canadian newspaper] test-drove a Honda and he said that it is fun to drive and almost sporty. Furthermore, he said the car "drives like all other cars should." I just want to add that Mr. Boast has been test-driving cars for years; he's an expert, my critics aren't.—F.C.

13. The death of Mrs. Indira Gandhi was mourned by people throughout India and in fact throughout the world. This means that she was an unusually able political leader.

14. Of course the political patronage system is corrupt, but that's the

way things have always been done around here. Just look at the situation at City Hall. Just about everyone there has gotten his job through patronage. Can you expect such a system to change?

15. I hope that the good citizens of this state will rouse themselves and begin to respectfully demand that our Legislature . . . pass an acceptable initiative and referendum bill post haste.

The small businessman, homemaker, office worker, and countless other hard working citizens of this state are [its] governors and it's about time we stand up and demand that our right to petition our government be made law.

A strong, united voice of common sense will cut through the Legislature's excuses and pat answers as to why they balk at passing an I&R bill; then the truth will be known, and the bad apples will be kicked out of the barrel.—D.D., *Sunday Star-Ledger* (Newark, N.J.), August 19, 1984.

16. In 1974, contrary to what was then canon law, a group of Episcopal bishops ordained several women to the priesthood in Philadelphia. At the beginning of the ceremony, a group of clergymen opposed to women's ordination addressed the bishops with words like these: "Most reverend sirs! God is to be called Father and so are his priests."

17. The Reagan administration may have a legal point in dropping an 11-year-old government policy of denying tax-exempt status to private educational institutions that practice racial discrimination. But it is on shaky ground from a moral standpoint.

In justifying the reversal of an Internal Revenue Service policy dating back to the Nixon administration, the Justice and Treasury departments argue that IRS has no clear basis in law for denying tax-exempt status to private schools and colleges that discriminate. . . .

That legal technicality, if indeed it is one, didn't seem to bother the Nixon, Ford and Carter administrations. They denied tax-exempt status to 100 private institutions on the ground that taxpayers should not have to subsidize practices that run contrary to the nation's firm policy against racial discrimination. . . .

[This means that the legal point the Reagan administration is raising, even if valid, is clearly outweighed by the moral considerations here.] We think the Reagan administration made a mistake.—*Citizen-Journal* (Columbus, Ohio), editorial, January 14, 1982.[7]

18. On behalf of our police departments, let us not forget our men and women who gave their lives while fighting crime.

Let's protect our protectors.

Reinstate capital punishment; change the laws of jurisprudence that protect and enrich the guilty. It's about time that the citizens fight back on this important issue.—J.K., *Sunday Star-Ledger* (Newark, N.J.), August 1, 1982.

19. Thomas I. Kidd, a labor union officer, has been charged with criminal conspiracy. Clarence Darrow speaks these words in his defense:

I appeal to you not for Thomas Kidd, but I appeal to you for the long line—the long, long line reaching back through the ages and forward to the years to come—the long line of despoiled and downtrodden people of the earth. I appeal to you for those men who rise in the morning before daylight comes and who go home at night when the light has faded from the sky and give their life, their strength, their toil to make others rich and great. I appeal to you in the name of those women who are offering up their lives to this modern god of gold, and I appeal to you in the name of those little children, the living and the unborn.—Irving Stone, *Clarence Darrow for the Defense*. Copyright 1941 by Irving Stone. Reprinted by permission of Doubleday & Company, Inc.

20. For fifty years this family has been going to the shore for its vacation. That's an awfully long time! So how can you possibly propose that we go to the mountains this summer?

21. I would like to express my support for [the president] and his proposed budget.

Our country has become like a spoiled child. We have become complacent and have taken many things for granted. We have allowed ourselves to get fat on our pleasures and immoralities to the point where we are not able to raise ourselves from our "chair of selfishness." To quote from Abraham Lincoln:

"We have forgotten God.

"We have forgotten the gracious hand which preserved us in peace, and multiplied and enriched and strengthened us; and we have vainly imagined in the deceitfulness of our hearts, that all these blessings were produced by some superior wisdom and virtue of our own."

We think that the more we have the better (or richer) we are. We should be ashamed of ourselves.—D.D., *Sunday Star-Ledger* (Newark, N.J.), March 28, 1982.

22. It is pretty obvious that the music played on Detroit's rock stations is better than punk rock. The Sex Pistols [a punk band] have sold very few albums in North America. The Ramones [also a punk band] have had only one hit after five years of trying. A.C.-D.C. probably outsells all those punk bands put together. Punks always seem to forget this fact.—F.C., Windsor, Canada.[8]

23. Dr. Sol Blumenthal, director of biostatistics for the New York City Health Department, gives rather straightforward explanations, even if they are only partial explanations, for what is happening [illegitimacy rising with increased spending on poverty]. There are two reasons for the growth of illegitimacy, he says. "People who were in that class were once held to ridicule and abuse." When the scarlet letter was implanted on the mother bearing an illegitimate child, there were fewer illegitimate children. And the second reason: "Society has cushioned the blows of having children outside marriage by providing welfare payments and day-care programs."—William Buckley, November 18, 1984.

24. The famous American lawyer Clarence Darrow is giving a summation in his own defense against charges of attempting to bribe a jury:

"Gentlemen of the jury . . .

"I am a stranger in a strange land, two thousand miles away from home and friends. I think I can say that no one in my native town would have made to any jury any such statement as was made of me by the District Attorney in opening this case.... But here I am, in his hands. Think of it! In a position where he can call me a coward—and in all my life I never saw or heard so cowardly, sneaky, and brutal an act as Ford committed in this courtroom before this jury.

"In examining you before you were accepted as jurors, the District Attorney asked you whether, if I should address you, you would be likely to be carried away by sympathy. You won't be if you wait for me to ask for sympathy. I have never asked sympathy of anybody, and I am not going to ask it of you twelve. I would rather go to the penitentiary than ask for sympathy....

"Gentlemen, don't ever think that your own life or liberty is safe; that your own family is secure; don't ever think any human being is safe when, under evidence like this, I, with some influence and some respect, am brought here and placed in the shadow of the penitentiary.

"I know my life. I know what I have done. My life has not been perfect; it has been human, too human. I have tried to help in the world. I have not had malice in my heart. I have done the best I could. I ask you to save my liberty, and my name."—Excerpt from *Clarence Darrow: A One-Man Play* by David W. Rintels. Copyright © 1975 by Dome Productions (USA). Reprinted by permission of Doubleday & Company, Inc.

25. I believe articles ... which tell of the death of the independent family farms in our country should appear more often on the front page of newspapers throughout this land.

The small, independent family farm was the backbone of our country. If we lose these small farmers we are headed for serious trouble.

As it is with other small businesses, the operating costs for farmers are too high and the market prices are too low. But the small farmer provides more than just an average service for the people; he provides food. The large corporate farmers don't have their whole lives involved in the land as does the family farmer. Large corporations, to a great extent, do not care anything about providing food to their fellow man, they just care about making a profit.

I'm not a farmer, but I know it takes a special strength to work the earth and provide for one's family and for one's neighbors. Most large corporations rely on their "bottom line" for their strength, and not their heart.

Major factors in the foundation and strength of our country were the individual's faith in God and the independence of men such as the family farmer. Without these, our nation cannot and will not stand.—D.D., *Sunday Star-Ledger* (Newark, N.J.), February 20, 1983.

Appeals to Negative Emotions

6. *The Ad Hominem Appeal.* The Latin expression *ad hominem* literally means "to the man." Suppose a person has just made a statement or presented an argument for some position we do not accept. Suppose we want to convince others that this view is incorrect or unwarranted. If we want to convince them logically, we shall present evidence that the claim or conclusion is false or that at key points in the argument, there has been unclear meaning or equivocation, false or questionable premises, errors in the reasoning. In all this, we shall be speaking directly to the issue at hand—the correctness or incorrectness of the claim being discussed. If our argument is cogent, it should convince our audience.

However, there is another way, a very persuasive way, of trying to convince people that our opponent is wrong—and that is to attack *him* or *her* as opposed to his position, to say something derogatory, demeaning, damaging about him as a person as opposed to saying what is wrong with his position. For example,

> "Only in the United States would quite such a vulgar spectacle be mounted." A quote published in the *Star-Ledger* and attributed to Andrew Alexander, a reporter for the *London Daily Mail*. Mr. Alexander is referring to a program produced by the U.S. government entitled "Let Poland Be Poland." . . . I suspect the theme of the program hits close to home. After all, all one has to do is switch two words in the title, "Ireland" and "Irish," and it becomes apparent that British and Soviet governments parallel each other in their policies towards people who would be autonomous in their national affairs.—R.A.Q., *Sunday Star-Ledger* (Newark, N.J.), February 21, 1982.

This is a classic example of an *ad hominem* argument. If R.A.Q. wanted to rationally convince us that Andrew Alexander's claim was false, his best strategy would be to argue that the program "Let Poland Be Poland" was not a "vulgar spectacle" but simply an attempt to give moral support to the Polish people at a difficult time in their history. As such, morally sensitive individuals everywhere could find merit in the program. If Mr. Alexander had defended his assertion with argument, R.A.Q. could have included a critical examination of this reasoning. All this could be good argument. But R.A.Q. does nothing of the kind. Rather, he suggests that Andrew Alexander endorses or condones repression—specifically by accepting British policy in Northern Ireland, and so is sensitive to any criticism of repression anywhere. This blackens not only Mr. Alexander's character, but that of his whole nation as well. Attention has been completely diverted from the question at issue—the merits of Mr. Alexander's statement—to Mr. Alexander himself. R.A.Q. has made very derogatory allegations about the man's character in an attempt to undermine his claim. This is the pattern in *ad hominem* appeals. Attention is diverted from some statement to the person who made the statement. This is done attempting to undermine what he or she says by saying something derogatory about who or what he or she is.[9]

Another classic example of the *ad hominem* appeal comes in this anecdote about Abraham Lincoln:

> In a case where Judge [Stephen T.] Logan—always earnest and grave—opposed him, Lincoln created no little merriment by his reference to Logan's style of dress. He carried the surprise in store for the latter, till he reached his turn before the jury. Addressing them, he said: "Gentlemen, you must be careful and

not permit yourselves to be overcome by the eloquence of counsel for the defense. Judge Logan, I know, is an effective lawyer. I have met him too often to doubt that; but shrewd and careful though he be, still he is sometimes wrong. Since this trial has begun I have discovered that, with all his caution and fastidiousness, he hasn't knowledge enough to put his shirt on right." Logan turned red as crimson, but sure enough, Lincoln was correct, for the former had donned a new shirt, and by mistake had drawn it over his head with the pleated bosom behind. The general laugh which followed destroyed the effect of Logan's eloquence over the jury—the very point at which Lincoln aimed.[10]

Did Lincoln say anything here about the case he was arguing with Logan? His remarks are totally irrelevant to that issue. Yet they were very effective in neutralizing Logan's argument.

There are several varieties of the *ad hominem* appeal. The two preceding examples illustrate the *abusive* form of this fallacy. Here the derogatory comment is aimed directly at the person's character, background, associates, or competence. The strategy is to undermine a person's credibility by blackening his reputation, putting him under a cloud.

Another way of attacking a person's view by attacking the person is attempting to explain away the view by explaining how the person came to hold it in the first place. This is called the *genetic fallacy*. We claim or suggest that someone holds a view not because he or she has arrived at it rationally or logically, but because it solves some personal conflict, is the product of some mental condition, or has just been inherited from the person's social or cultural background, accepted uncritically. Now although in some cases this charge will not be a vicious personal attack, as the abusive *ad hominem* tends to be, it will be at least a put down. For example,

> Much of Aristotle's ethical and political theory can be set aside as having only historical interest. For Aristotle was just expressing the preferences of the wealthy, educated Greek society of his time.

This certainly does not attack Aristotle's character or even his overall intellectual competence. Still it does allege that in one aspect of his thinking, Aristotle uncritically accepted the views of his age.

By contrast, consider:

> We must take Schopenhauer's famous essay denouncing women with a grain of salt. Any psychiatrist would at once explain this essay by reference to the strained relationship between Schopenhauer and his mother.—Example in S. Morris Engel, *With Good Reason.*

Clearly we are not to accept Schopenhauer's views on the nature of women, nor are we to have a particularly high opinion of Schopenhauer, at least of his psychosexual development. But are we given any evidence showing that Schopenhauer's opinions were false or his reasoning faulty? Rather, Schopenhauer's view is explained away with reference to a personal problem.

Don't believe what Schopenhauer said about women. It all comes from his neurosis!

Psychological and sociological material can especially tempt persons to commit the genetic fallacy. If we say that a person holds a view because of some psychological problem, some unresolved conflict or complex, and we feel that therefore we have discredited the view, that it may be dismissed without further considerations, then we have committed the genetic fallacy. If we claim that a person's class background is responsible for his or her view, thereby suggesting that it need not be seriously considered, we have again committed the genetic fallacy. Although fallacious, we can see the great persuasiveness of such an argument. For we may frequently want to dismiss someone's views. To explain how some features of his background led him to arrive at them may suggest that these views are based on nonrational factors, that they are prejudices or mere opinions—not defensible or not to be taken seriously. But to explain why someone holds a view, even if an explanation incorporates impressive psychological or sociological theory, is not to have established that the view is false.

Now consider the following argument:

> Senator Smith believes that the proposed dam project for his state will bring significant long-term economic and energy benefits to the whole region. But we need not consider his reasons. We would certainly expect him to support the project. It will create thousands of jobs in his state right away, and next year, Senator Smith is up for reelection.

What is going on here? Senator Smith has asserted a claim—the proposed dam project will bring long-term benefits to the region. The arguer clearly rejects the senator's claim. But instead of giving counterevidence, or showing that the senator's reasoning is faulty, the arguer attacks the senator, specifically by alleging the senator is making his claim because he has a vested interest in people's accepting it. Ultimately what is alleged here is that the senator holds his view and wants others to accept it because it will bring him votes—and certainly a politician has a vested interest in getting votes! This charge of vested interest is called the *circumstantial ad hominem.* The attacker does not say anything to disprove the claim at issue, but rather attacks the person who made the claim, saying that he or she was motivated by self-interest in proposing it. This allegation—that the person has made his or her claim not out of a sincere belief but because he or she has a vested interest in the claim—is offered as compelling evidence that the claim is false.

Jack Anderson has reported a classic example of this fallacy. In the following, the first two paragraphs give the background of the case. The third presents certain claims. The fallacy occurs in the last paragraph.

> The Federal Trade Commission is just wrapping up an investigation of Dr. Kenneth P. Berg, a retired minister. He has been one of the nation's biggest entrepreneurs in providing so-called "life care" for older Americans. . . .
> According to a still-unpublished FTC staff report, Berg's life-care system

guaranteed a senior citizen a home for life—whether an apartment, a duplex or a detached house. . . . The resident of a retirement "village" or apartment complex got a lifetime lease, utilities and maintenance, one to three meals a day and lifetime nursing care (exclusive of hospitalization) as needed. . . .

In interviews with industry representatives, the FTC staff reported, "Berg and Christian Services International were almost invariably mentioned by home operators in unfavorable contrast to their own policies." Berg and Christian Services International "are well known to other managers and home operators in the industry, and are considered notorious in terms of their practices and the problems which they have caused," the report adds.

When this was read to Berg, he attributed the criticism to "cutthroat competition."—July 10, 1983. Reprinted by permission of United Feature Syndicate, Inc.

Now, clearly, Rev. Berg wants to persuade us that his critics are wrong, that their claims about the overall conduct of his Christian Services International are false. But he does this by saying that his critics were motivated by "cutthroat competition."

In effect, Rev. Berg is saying that those criticizing his business practices were doing so primarily to improve their own business prospects. By knocking out Berg, they will have more of the business themselves. It is in their self-interest to make these claims and that is why they are doing it, not because they know Dr. Berg is an incompetent or dishonest businessman. Note that Rev. Berg presents no evidence that he has run his business in a competent and responsible manner. He attacks his critics not by giving evidence that their allegations are false but by charging that it is in *their* self-interest to make these allegations.

We must mention one further version of the *ad hominem* fallacy. Charging someone with not believing or not practicing what he or she preaches seriously diminishes that individual's credibility. But does it show, does it give much evidence that what the person preaches is false? Clearly not. Here again, we attempt to undermine what someone says by discrediting the person rather than the person's views. This particular attempt is the *you-too* version of the *ad hominem* appeal. "Do as I say, not as I do," is met with "Why should I do as you say, since *you don't* do as you say?" For example,

[I don't for one minute accept the position of the Audubon Society and other environmentalists that America should not develop the energy and mineral resources on its public lands.] Could someone explain why it is O.K. for the Audubon Society to permit three oil companies to pump oil and gas on their Rainey Wildlife Sanctuary in Louisiana, but it denies similar use of "our" mineral-rich government lands to be used for multiple purposes.—K.S., *Sunday Star-Ledger* (Newark, N.J.), August 8, 1982.

Has K.S. given us *evidence* that the environmentalists are wrong in saying we should not develop the energy and mineral resources on our public lands? (In her original letter to the editor, K.S. did point out that such development would allow America to be energy and mineral independent, a cogent consideration. But she is still arguing fallaciously here.) Rather, she has tried to discredit the

Audubon Society by alleging they are allowing on their own lands what they would prohibit on public lands. If you don't believe these resources should be developed, you-too shouldn't allow their development on your lands. But even if the Audubon Society does this, does that show their environmentalist position false?

What exactly is wrong with *ad hominem* reasoning? Why is it fallacious? Let's look at each variety in turn. Blatant, abusive *ad hominems* may frequently involve outright irrelevant premises. An *ad hominem* argument attempts to show that some particular statement is false by attacking the person making the statement. But is the fact that persons have "bad" characters, backgrounds, associates in general relevant to establishing that their claims are false? "Jones has been seen in a seedy neighborhood." Is that relevant to "Jones's statements are false?" Persons committing the genetic fallacy may simply assume the view that they are attacking is false and then seek to explain why someone could still hold this falsehood. If so, they are assuming what has to be proven, reasoning from a very questionable assumption or premise. But if they intend their explanation that someone's view is the product of personal conflict or individual upbringing as evidence that the view is false, how good is that evidence? Now if someone has accepted a statement at issue not because it is rationally justified but for some other reason, that is a mark against the statement. But by itself, it is a very weak mark.

Similarly, with circumstantial *ad hominem*, the fact that someone who advances a view has a vested interest in people's believing it is a mark against the view. It may be put forward not because it is true, but because it is expedient for the person advocating it. We have some reason to suspect the view is false. But *by itself* is this information sufficient to show it false? Again, if people do not follow their own advice, practice what they preach, perhaps there is something wrong with the advice. But is this by itself much reason for rejecting the advice?

So the genetic, circumstantial, and you-too varieties all involve that inflation of the weight of the premises which we have seen in other fallacies. If anything, the premises of these arguments give rational grounds for being skeptical of the claims being attacked. But there is a very great difference between being cautious, wary, skeptical, demanding further corroboration or confirmation, and rejecting what is said out of hand, regarding it as false.

In *Fallacy: The Counterfeit of Argument,* W. Ward Fearnside and William B. Holther point out that

> The idea of "not accepting" is not equivalent to "rejecting." . . . Personal considerations are certainly relevant for judging the reliability of a man, his willingness to tell the truth. If judgment of a man holds him unreliable, then his statements are rightly suspect. But there is a difference between "suspect" and "false." And there is a difference between taking into account the reliability of a witness and blindly assuming that personalities dispose of issues.[11]

Let's summarize this entire section on the *ad hominem* appeal by giving explicit instructions for arguing that we have an *ad hominem* fallacy (see Figure 3.6).

Figure 3.6 *AD HOMINEM* APPEAL

The *ad hominem* fallacy occurs when someone

1. argues that the claim, conclusion, opinion, or view of some individual is false, should be rejected but

2. supports this not with evidence relevant or adequate to show that view false but, rather, with a personal attack on the individual holding the view. The derogatory attacking statement is intended to undermine what the person says by undermining credibility, confidence in the person. The personal attack may concern

    a. the person's character, background, associates, or competence (abusive),

    b. the genesis or origin of the person's view (genetic fallacy),

    c. the person's vested interest in having people accept his or her position (circumstantial), or

    d. the fact that the person does not practice what he or she preaches (you—too).

---

7. *Appeal to Ignorance.* The *ad hominem* appeal aroused negative feelings toward someone who made a claim. But we can have feelings about claims themselves in addition to feelings about the persons asserting them. In particular, how do we *feel* when we are told that some assumption or assertion is unproven? Doesn't that make us feel the statement is somehow silly or believing it is somehow silly? But if so, shouldn't we then reject the claim, dismiss it, and believe the opposite? Although this trend of thought may be emotively or persuasively attractive, although it may depict how we actually reason on occasion, it involves a fallacy. For how are we reasoning? Aren't we saying that a statement is false, just because it has not been proven? But just because we don't have proof that a statement is true, does that mean the statement is false? When a detective investigating some crime gets some clues as to who the culprit is, when the detective considers the statement "so-and-so perpetrated this crime," there may be far too little evidence at hand to prove in court that the suspect actually committed the crime. More data may be necessary. But this does not show that the statement is false. Rather, it shows that the detective has more work to do. More evidence may indeed show it true that so-and-so committed the crime. Concluding that it is false would be fallacious, but it is just such a conclusion that we may be persuaded to make, when someone calls the statement unproven. If an argument claims that some statement is false, just because it is not known to be true or has not been proven, or it claims that a statement is true just because it is not known to be false or because it has not been refuted or disproven, then that argument commits the *fallacy of appeal to ignorance*.

Clearly there may be times when there is not enough evidence to decide a question one way or the other. Is it in principle possible to build safe nuclear power plants to generate electricity? On the basis of current technology, we may not be able to guarantee the safety of such plants. But do we know whether or not technology can be improved to guarantee safety? The evidence may not be conclusive either way. Notice that in a case like this, if the appeal to ignorance argument were genuine and not fallacious, we could justify an outright contradiction! For we could argue

It has not been shown that a potentially devastating nuclear accident will occur. Hence it's safe to build nuclear power plants and to further develop nuclear power

and

No safe way of constructing nuclear power plants or disposing of nuclear waste has been discovered. Hence nuclear power plants are inherently unsafe.

But it cannot be both safe and unsafe to build nuclear power plants.

Can lack of supporting evidence ever support saying that a statement is false or lack of refuting evidence support saying that it is true? This can happen, provided one crucial condition is satisfied. Suppose someone alleges that there was a nuclear explosion at a certain point in Kansas in 1955. If that were true, we would expect a number of other things to be true even today about that place— Geiger counter readings should indicate an unusual amount of radioactivity, there may very well be signs of destruction, medical records should show a greater incidence of various forms of cancer, to say nothing of the news stories we would expect such an explosion to generate. Suppose competent researchers could discover no such evidence or any other evidence of a nuclear blast, employing all the equipment and knowledge available to them. Then if someone argued

> Even after detailed competent scientific investigation, there is no evidence of a nuclear explosion at the alleged point in Kansas. Hence we may conclude that no such explosion occurred.

we would not have an appeal to ignorance. In this situation, the lack of such evidence in the face of the scientific procedures employed constitutes very good warrant for saying no such explosion occurred.

This highlights what is wrong with the appeal to ignorance fallacy. That we have no evidence to support a statement is relevant to saying that the statement is false only when competent appropriate procedures for gathering data have been used and have failed to produce any evidence. Likewise, that we have no evidence to refute a statement is not relevant, by itself, to show the statement true or support our believing it. We must also know that there has been a genuine search for such evidence. Without this additional statement, the premise is not relevant to the conclusion. But it is precisely this second premise which fails in the appeal to ignorance fallacy (see Figure 3.7).

8. *Straw Man.* Saying that an assumption or assertion is unproven is not the only way to generate negative feelings about statements. Some claims are

> **Figure 3.7 APPEAL TO IGNORANCE**
>
> An argument involves the fallacy of appeal to ignorance when it argues either that
>
> 1. because a statement is not known to be true or has not been proven, therefore
> 2. it is false
>
> or
>
> 1'. because a statement is not known to be false or has not been disproven, therefore
> 2'. it is true,
>
> where there is no reason to believe that competent, adequate procedures have been undertaken to gather the appropriate supporting or refuting evidence.

just downright implausible, false, or even silly in their own right. They are not worthy of belief, and recognizing this casts them and anyone who allegedly accepts them in a negative light. But this leads directly to another fallacy. Consider the following exchange:

> CONCERNED CITIZEN: It would be a good idea to ban advertising beer and wine on radio and television. These ads encourage teenagers to drink, often with disastrous consequences.
> ALCOHOL INDUSTRY REPRESENTATIVE: You cannot get people to give up drinking; they've been doing it for thousands of years.[12]

Has the concerned citizen maintained that it would be a good idea if teenagers or people in general gave up drinking? Is abstinence the conclusion this person is arguing for? If beer and wine ads were banned on radio and TV, would alcoholic beverage consumption cease? The answer to all these questions is clearly no. But doesn't the alcohol industry representative want to make us believe the concerned citizen advocates total abstinence? Isn't that how he represents the concerned citizen's position or doesn't he suggest that this is implied in that position? Now ask yourself which of the following two statements is easier to refute, show false? Which is less plausible?

> A: It would be a good idea to ban advertising beer and wine on radio and television (the concerned citizen's original conclusion)
> B: It would be a good idea to get people to stop drinking (the alcohol industry representative's portrayal of that conclusion)

Isn't B far easier to argue against? Isn't it much easier to cast doubt on B rather than on A? Is B plausible?

What does this mean? In attacking the concerned citizen's position, the alcohol industry representative has not only misrepresented that position, but has misrepresented it in a way making it easy to refute, making it look almost silly. The alcohol industry representative does not, then, attack the concerned citizen's actual view but, rather, this misrepresentation which is designed to be easily attacked. What we have here is a classic example of the *straw man fallacy*. This fallacy arises in adversary contexts. An opponent allegedly attacks a statement made by an adversary, be it a conclusion or a supporting premise. But the statement attacked is not the adversary's actual claim, but a misrepresentation which is easy to refute, perhaps even obviously false or silly. The opponent does not attack the real "man" (woman) or "his" (or her) position, but a straw man—and straw men are not noted for their effectiveness in fighting back.

What is wrong with this procedure? Why is it a fallacy? Since not the adversary's original statement but a straw man is attacked, the reasons for rejecting the straw man may not be relevant at all to refuting or casting doubt on the original position, which is what the argument is allegedly trying to do. Straw man is a fallacy of relevance. The reasons which allegedly refute an opponent's position are really not relevant to showing it false. Rather, they show false a straw man misrepresentation. Why is the straw man argument persuasive? Since the substitute is easily refutable, it looks bad. And since it is substituted for the original position, it makes that look bad also. If an opponent's view can be so easily knocked down, both the opponent and the view must be rather stupid. But that is not a very favorable evaluation of either the opponent or the view, and neither are the emotions this judgment evokes.

Sometimes in adversary contexts, no reasons may be presented to refute the straw man. The opponent may trust that the misrepresented position is really so fantastic as not to need refutation. For example,

> One advocate of the public school system, R. Freeman Butts, defends it because it imposes uniform values—"common commitments"—on students. Its whole purpose, he says, has always been to make them "self-governing citizens rather than . . . private persons loyal primarily to their families, their kinfolk, their churches." . . .
>
> There we have it. The mission of the American school is to homogenize American children. Not for their sake, but for the State's. The best way to make them "self-governing citizens" is apparently to take them from the plural influence of their parents and to submit them to a monolithic state program.
>
> If this is the defense, the prosecution rests.—J.S., Sacramento, Calif.[13]

Does Mr. Butts really advocate the eradication of children's diverse ethnic heritages by forcing them to undergo a "monolithic" educational program which will in effect "brainwash" them into being good servants of the "State"? That clearly is a very extreme view. Isn't he really arguing that public education broadens the horizon of children so that they can live in a pluralistic society with others of diverse background? That is a different view entirely. Education does not destroy ethnic background, but it helps one to work with others of different backgrounds through common commitment to one society. Can J.S. refute that?

Obviously, the straw man fallacy is popular in politics. To make one's adversary look bad by refuting his position could cost him votes. The ease with which straw men can be knocked over is a strong temptation for politicians to use this trick.

Did Jimmy Carter make such a move in his debate with Ronald Reagan in the 1980 presidential campaign?

> CARTER: In the past the relationship between Social Security and Medicare has been very important to provide some modicum of aid for senior citizens and the retention of health benefits. Governor Reagan, as a matter of fact, began his political career campaigning around this nation against Medicare.

Here is Ronald Reagan's reply:

> REAGAN: There you go again. When I opposed Medicare, there was another piece of legislation meeting the same problem before the Congress. I happened to favor the other piece of legislation and thought that it would be better for the senior citizens and provide better care than the one that was finally passed. I was not opposing the principle of providing care for them. I was opposing one piece of legislation as versus another.

If what Mr. Reagan says is true, does Mr. Carter's statement involve straw man?

Figure 3.8 gives explicit instructions for identifying the straw man fallacy.

Figure 3.8 STRAW MAN

The straw man fallacy occurs in an adversary context when

1. an opponent attacks an adversary's position by attributing to the adversary a statement S, as constituting or being implied by the adversary's position.
2. The opponent may present reasons showing S false or may take it for granted that S is obviously false. However
3. S is not the adversary's position but, rather,
4. S is a misrepresentation which is easy to refute.

---

9. *Appeal to Fear.* We began this discussion of emotional appeals with the fallacy of grandstanding, appealing to strong gut emotions and presenting little or no evidence to convince anyone logically. As we singled out the appeal to one positive emotion, pity, as a special fallacy in its own right, so we also single out one negative emotion, fear. This fallacy is practically self-explanatory. The *appeal to fear* attempts to frighten someone into accepting a conclusion by threat or by arousing fear where that is not relevant to the conclusion being argued. Here is a classic example:

> MILL OWNER: I have a good reason why the mill workers should not go on strike. If they strike again, I shall close the mill and go back to England, where workers do not strike.

Now given the mill owner's threat, it may be imprudent to strike. But is the threat really relevant to showing it wrong or unjustified for the workers to strike? Relevant reasons here would concern adequacy of pay and benefits, and the impact of a strike on the employer. The threat covers none of these.

Here is another example, where irrelevant fear is aroused, although not by a threat:

It is wrong to believe there will be a slump in business next year. Such propheses are self-fulfilling.

What is this argument saying? If the conclusion is that the statement—there will be an economic slump next year—is false, then we have appeal to fear. For the argument gives no clear reason to justify this claim. Rather it tries to frighten us into accepting the conclusion by alleging that believing there will be a slump will actually cause the slump.

We should note that the mere arousing of fear is not enough to show we have a fallacious appeal to fear.

You should not drink what's in that bottle. It's poison.

There is no fallacy here. Although the premise may arouse fear of the consequences of drinking the bottle's contents, considering those consequences is certainly relevant to deciding whether or not it's a good idea to drink what is in the bottle (see Figure 3.9).

Figure 3.9   APPEAL TO FEAR

An argument involves the appeal to fear when

1. it attempts to discourage some action or belief by arousing fear

and

2. that fear is not relevant to evaluating properly whether to perform the action or accept the belief.

---

10. *Slippery Slope Fallacy.*   There is one special version of the appeal to fear which merits consideration in its own right as a separate fallacy. It occurs quite frequently. President Reagan and his administration often used this argument to justify American efforts against communist activities in Central America, particularly Nicaragua and El Salvador:

If we let the Communists take over Nicaragua or El Salvador, pretty soon they will be in other countries like Guatemala and Honduras. The upshot will be that all Central America will be Communist. But then the Communists will take over Mexico, and we'll be looking at Russian troops and missiles from El Paso.

This is not the first time Americans have heard such arguments. They were prevalent during the Vietnam era. If America lets South Vietnam fall to the communists, then Laos and Cambodia will follow shortly. And after that the rest of Southeast Asia, and then. . . .

What is wrong with these arguments? We can challenge the Reagan administration quite effectively by asking why the fall of El Salvador or Nicaragua would lead to the fall of other countries in Central America and why the fall of these would cause the fall of Mexico. We could ask analogous questions about the fall of South Vietnam. Such causal assertions that the fall of one country would cause the fall of others are at least suggested in these arguments. But why should we accept these causal claims? Are they true?

Not every slippery slope argument involves causal assertions or causal suggestions. These arguments may rather claim that performing a certain action or permitting an action establishes a precedent—a very dangerous precedent. Once established, we have to permit all sorts of other undesirable actions. Here is a classic example:

> Although I of course sympathize with the students picketing the Admissions Office in protest against what they call a "discriminatory" policy of admissions, I cannot condone their disruptive action. They claim that their demands are moderate, and negotiable; but the point is that they *are* demands, and we would be negotiating under compulsion. We must not give the students what they ask for, when they ask for it; that would set a dangerous precedent. Once we gave in on the Admissions policy, they would propose changes in the curriculum and the course schedules, and we would have to negotiate and compromise on that. They might then ask for students to serve on faculty committees and on the Board of Trustees, and we could not consistently deny them this, since we would have in effect conceded their right to make demands. What if they then came to dominate the University, and determine what is taught and who is hired? The ultimate consequence is too horrible to contemplate; the only logical policy is to stop at the beginning, and refuse all demands.—Example in Monroe C. Beardsley, *Thinking Straight: Principles of Reasoning for Readers & Writers*, 4th ed. © 1975, p. 149. Reprinted by permission of Prentice-Hall, Englewood Cliffs, N.J.

What's wrong with this argument? Is it really true that if the university administration negotiates on moderate student demands concerning admissions policy, this would set a precedent requiring concessions on *all* student demands? We may practically use the words of the argument to refute it. The current student demands are moderate and negotiable. But not all student demands will be moderate, nor will students always be open to negotiation. But these are very relevant differences in making demands. Negotiating with students in the present case may establish a precedent that when students press moderate, negotiable demands, the administration should hear them in a responsive, open manner. But this precedent certainly does not necessitate the administration's negotiating on every student demand, especially those which are radical.

What is going on in slippery slope arguments? How may we analyze them? Whether a slippery slope argument proceeds from causes or from precedents, it alleges that there is some end stage of a process, some final state which is highly undesirable—something to be avoided, abhorred, in short feared—communists invading California, Russian missiles on the Texas/Mexico border, students in control of the university. Fear of this end stage or state gives these arguments their persuasive force. A slippery slope argument also alleges that this end stage will definitely be reached, once a certain step is taken. The claim is that taking this step will either set a causal process in motion which will inevitably lead to the end stage, or it will establish a precedent mandating the end state come about. Some slippery slope arguments may actually spell out some intermediate stages of this process. Others will just allege that once we take the first step, we will have to take the last. In either case, the conclusion is that we should not take the first step. If we do, we shall end up at the bottom of the slippery slope.

However, the assertion that the first step will lead to the last is highly questionable. One or more of the alleged causal links may be very dubious. It may not be obvious at all that one particular step causes the next in the causal chain. A step may establish some sort of precedent. But this need not cover cases on the next step. There may be relevant differences between them. Slippery slope arguments are fallacious precisely because they involve this questionable or false assertion that the first step will unavoidably lead to the last. Hence the disastrousness of the last step is really not relevant to deciding whether or not to take the first step and the fear aroused by contemplating the last step is inappropriate, irrelevant here.

We must add, however, that there can be legitimate appeals to precedent. Not every appeal to precedent involves slippery slope. Suppose I come up to the cash register in a store 15 seconds after closing time. The clerk is sorry, but cannot take my purchase. Otherwise anyone who comes up to the register late (at least not too late) would have to be helped and that could keep the clerk there long overtime. This is not slippery slope. By helping me, the clerk has established a precedent, and if five other people come up to the register within a minute or so, would there be a relevant difference between their cases and mine? This is not clear. Suppose, however, that I have been standing on line for a half hour and get to the clerk 5 seconds after closing. The clerk refuses to help me with my purchase, saying otherwise anyone could be helped. Here we do have slippery slope. There is a distinct, relevant difference between my case, where I have been waiting for some time and have gotten on line before closing time, and someone else who walks up to the cash register right after closing. Helping me

---

Figure 3.10 SLIPPERY SLOPE

An argument involves the slippery slope fallacy when

1. it concludes that a certain action or situation should not be permitted because
2. if permitted, it would lead to a further situation, and so on down to an end stage where
3. the end stage is obviously disastrous. However,
4. the claim that once begun the process will inevitably lead to the last stage is false or highly questionable.

does not establish a precedent requiring the clerk to help them. The two arguments may look similar, but only the second is slippery slope, because in the second the alleged precedent does not hold (see Figure 3.10).

Exercise 3-II

All the fallacies that are listed are instances of the appeals to negative emotions we have just discussed:

ad hominem appeal	appeal to fear
appeal to ignorance	slippery slope
straw man	

In each case, identify the fallacy involved. Also, if the fallacy is an *ad hominem* appeal, state which variety

abusive	circumstantial
genetic fallacy	you—too

is involved. Then be prepared to defend why the fallacy occurs, as in Exercise 3-I, citing how the various conditions spelled out for the fallacy appear in the argument. Again, an argument may be an instance of more than one fallacy or more than one variety of the *ad hominem* appeal.

Sample Answer.

> The struggle to preserve St. Bartholomew's Church has become a struggle to preserve the landmarks law itself. For, if the church can successfully claim exemption from the law on the pretext of religious freedom and transfer that claim to a private developer, then the landmarks preservation law is not long for this world. . . .
>   If the claim prevails, it won't be long before every landmark is donated to a church and—after obtaining a religious exemption—leased back to its former owner for private development.
>   To preserve the landmarks law, therefore, the public must fight to preserve St. Bart's.—Edward C. Wallace, *The New York Times*, August 21, 1982. Copyright © 1982 by The New York Times Company. Reprinted by permission.

BACKGROUND: St. Bartholomew's Church in New York City proposes to allow a developer to demolish its parish house, not the church itself, and build a fifty-nine story office tower on the site. In return the church would receive $9.5 million a year for ten years, and proposes to use the money both to put the church on a better financial footing and to aid the poor. But to do this, the church must get an exemption from the New York City Landmarks Preservation Committee, since it has been designated an historic landmark.

This is clearly an example of the slippery slope fallacy. The conclusion is that St. Bartholomew's Church should not be permitted to demolish its parish house. It is alleged that if permitted, the city landmarks law itself would be rendered ineffective and all historic buildings in New York City destroyed or modified. However, it is very questionable whether this would happen as a result. Certainly permitting St. Bartholomew's plan would not establish a precedent for destroying *every* historic landmark. If anything, the church did not acquire its parish house with the purpose of allowing a developer to demolish and rebuild. Also, it is the church itself, not an associated office building, which is of historic interest. Yet St. Bart's wants to demolish only the office building. These are relevant differences.

1. Jones says he had an interview with extraterrestrial, intelligent life forms. But we all know that Jones has been in and out of mental institutions and that he is a heavy drinker.

2. In his February 20, 1950, speech in the Senate, Joe McCarthy announced that he had penetrated "Truman's iron curtain of secrecy" and that he proposed forthwith to present 81 "cases in which it is clear there is a definite Communist connection . . . persons whom I consider to be Communists in the State Department". . . . Of Case 40, he said, "I do not have much information on this except the general statement of the agency unidentified that there is nothing in the files to disprove his Communist connections."—Richard H. Rovere, *Senator Joe McCarthy* (Harcourt Brace Jovanovich, Inc.).

3. Modern psychological and anthropological research has shown how religion originates as a response to man's feeling helpless in the face of his environment. Man believes in gods because he needs protection. Hence as technology increases and man comes to control more and more of the world, he will replace belief in God and the rest of religious superstition with a scientific picture of the world.

4. You have said that a great many women just ask their husbands whom to vote for and then vote the way they are told. In fact, you say specifically "Seventy per cent of the women vote for the person their husband tells them to." That you would assert such a ridiculous statement seems unbelievable. But to set the record straight, let me say that women need rely on no one in making their decisions as to which way to vote. Contrary to the beliefs of many, women have the power to think and reason out problems without having to rely on the so-called "stronger sex" for answers. In the future, I suggest that you think more carefully before making such statements as you have.[14]

5. The FDA has responded swiftly and vigorously to charges by an anonymous whistleblower against a pacemaker manufacturer. The target of the FDA investigation is the Cordis Corp. of Miami, one of the five biggest pacemaker producers. Harold Hershenson, the company's executive vice president, told my associate Tony Capaccio that the FDA sent a "very zealous group of inspectors" to pore over the company's books for nine months.

An FDA compliance officer said that "in general" the investigation supported the whistleblower's charges. The results of the investigation were summarized in a private letter Sept. 7 to the company from John C. Villforth of the FDA. . . . Villforth's concluding paragraph was particularly blunt: "I must say that the problems referred to in this letter appear to reflect a corporate practice and a pattern of serious disregard for the requirements of the Federal Food, Drug and Cosmetics Act."

Hershenson commented, "We took issue with the last paragraph. They did it to get our attention."—Jack Anderson, November 18, 1984. Reprinted by permission of United Feature Syndicate, Inc.

6. Of course, Green is guilty. I'll beat your brains out if you say anything different!

7. My opponent maintains that members of my staff have been engaged in some unscrupulous financial activities. But you should look at him to see that he has no grounds for these charges. The only reason he and his allies haven't been involved in financial irregularities is because they haven't been close enough to the till to take any money.

8. We must recognize that once the practice of exaggeration is begun, there is no logical stopping-place. The reporter can justify to himself ever greater and greater exaggeration, till he finally arrives at the position held by the man who justified an utterly false report, the product simply of his own vivid imagination, in the words, "But I had to have a story! I must make a living!"—Edwin Leavitt Clarke, *The Art of Straight Thinking*.

9. [The Australian postal workers' offer of support to the striking Canadian postal workers (during their 1978 strike) does not show the Canadians have a worthy cause.] After all, didn't Australia used to be a penal colony?—J.L., Toronto, Canada.

10. PRESIDENT CARTER: The air pollution standard laws that were passd in California were passed over the objections of Governor Reagan, and this is a very well-known fact. Also, recently, when someone suggested that the Occupational Safety and Health Act should be abolished, Governor Reagan responded, "amen."

GOVERNOR REAGAN: If it is a well-known fact that I opposed air pollution laws in California, the only thing I can possibly think of is that the President must be suggesting the law that the Federal Government tried to impose on the state of California—not a law, regulations that would have made it impossible to drive an automobile within the city limits of any California city, or have a place to put it if you did drive it against their regulations.

It would destroy the economy of California. And I must say, we had the support of Congress when we pointed out how ridiculous this attempt was by the Environmental Protection Agency. We still have the strictest air control, or air pollution, laws in the country.

11. PRESIDENT CARTER: As long as there's a Democratic President in the White House we will have a strong and viable Social Security system, free of the threat of bankruptcy.

Although Governor Reagan has changed his position lately, on four different occasions he has advocated making Social Security a voluntary system which would in effect very quickly bankrupt it.

GOVERNOR REAGAN: This statement that somehow I wanted to destroy it, and I just changed my tune, that I was for voluntary Social Security, which would mean the ruin of it—Mr. President, the voluntary thing that I suggested many years ago was that a young man, orphaned and raised by an aunt who died, his aunt was ineligible for Social Security insurance because she was not his mother.

And I suggested that if this is an insurance program, certainly the person who's paying in should be able to name his own beneficiaries, and that's the closest I've ever come to anything voluntary with Social Security. I, too, am pledged to a Social Security program that will reassure these senior citizens of ours that they're going to continue to get their money.

12. So you doubt the accuracy of the standard geneological history of the Japanese imperial family. Would you like to end up the victim of an assassination?[15]

13. Jones believes in the importance of hard work, and he practices what he preaches. He is in the office a half-hour before everyone else and doesn't leave until a half-hour later. But, poor man, this all comes from the Protestant work ethic of his family environment. He grew up with that, and it is as ingrained in him as the English language.

14. I am truly saddened by the unnecessary deaths and injuries sustained by paratroopers in the southern California desert in a so-called "rapid deployment" maneuver. . . .

They were ordered by Army Lt. Gen. Robert Kingston to do the necessary parachuting despite very windy conditions.

The general now insists that the wind prevailing at the time of the jumps was within safe limits although it is rather strange to contemplate that one of the parachutists upon hitting ground was carried away by the wind and killed. . . .

I was wondering whether this general also parachuted with the men.
—L.H.R., *Sunday Star-Ledger* (Newark, N.J.), April 11, 1982.

15. The professional whiners of the National Union of Students (NUS) [lobbying against university tuition increases] tax one's patience.

Tuition fees today probably represent a smaller percentage of the total cost of education than 20 years ago. . . .

Contrary to NUS statements, university budgets are not declining nor is funding by government. The rate of increase might not meet the unrealistic expectations of some students—notably those in liberal arts.

The shaggy, shouting, banner waving yahoos who seem dedicated to making confrontation a way of life whether with university administration or government would have minimal representation from faculties like commerce, engineering, medicine, law or agriculture.

The student should feel some moral obligation to contribute a small percentage of the total required for his or her education. The middle class taxpayer becomes a bit weary of carrying them on his back with their hands in both his pockets.—Letter to the Regina, Canada, *Leader-Post,* October 1979.

16. This is directed at the politicians and/or persons responsible for the reconstruction of the congressional districts in the state of New Jersey. . . . I was shocked to see the "jigsaw" effect on the New Jersey map in connection with the redistricting.

It is clearly evident what motivates people responsible for this fiasco. I ask what difference is there between these people and the basketball players who shaved points as in the recent Boston College scandal? Also, what difference is there in drugging horses for a race? They are all "fixed."—N.M.B., *Sunday Star-Ledger* (Newark, N.J.), March 7, 1982.

17. No mathematician has been able to prove Goldbach's theorem. Hence it must be false.

18. No mathematician has been able to give a counterexample to Goldbach's theorem. Hence it must be true.

19. The German philosopher Arthur Schopenhauer held a pessimistic view of the world—life is doomed to destruction. In fact, reality is self-destructive, he maintained. He saw confirmation of this in the reaction of an Australian bulldog ant when it is cut in two pieces. "If it is cut in two, a battle begins between the head and the tail. The head seizes the tail with its teeth, and the tail defends itself bravely by stinging the head; the battle may last for half an hour, until they die or are dragged away by other ants."

Thank heavens that Freud has shown us how properly to appreciate such a view! For by applying psychoanalytic techniques, we can show how such a pessimism arises from a neurotic character structure. And we have plenty of independent evidence that Schopenhauer was neurotic. Apparently the only creatures he ever loved were his dogs, and he positively hated women. He had to pay damages to his maid for the rest of her life after he broke her arm. What's more, he was not on very good terms with his mother. The relation ended completely when he yelled at her that the name of Schopenhauer would be remembered not for her novels but for his philosophy.

20. BACKGROUND: Entrapment means that although a person committed acts which ordinarily would be illegal, the individual is not guilty because government agents actually led him to commit these acts which he otherwise would not have done. In returning a verdict of innocent because of entrapment, a jury is applying the law that entrapment is improper and cannot lead to conviction. In the summer of 1984, in a widely publicized trial, John DeLorean was acquitted of drug dealing charges precisely on this ground.

I read with disgust the verdict of the jury in the DeLorean drug plot case—innocent of all charges. The jury believed the defense that the government entrapped an innocent victim by pretending to be criminals. . . . However, thousands of citizens are in state and federal prisons at this very moment convicted of crimes that involved phony scams and required the testimony of under-cover agents. . . . [Not only is this DeLorean verdict unfair to these persons, it says something loud and clear—the government can't use scams to catch criminals.]

Let the debate begin.

Must we assume that these men are innocent because the government had no business acting like criminals in order to obtain evidence?

Must we do away with undercover agents whose sole purpose is to gain access to criminal activity that might otherwise go unnoticed?

Must we do away with phony police "fencing" operations that ensnare hundreds of criminals who bring in stolen watches, television sets, automobiles, etc.?—G.H., *Sunday Star-Ledger* (Newark, N.J.), August 26, 1984.

21. We think that Mayor Ed Koch should take another look at his pro-posal to have New York City's radio station, WNYC, broadcast the "John Hour." The Mayor believes that by publicly exposing the patrons of this city's "ladies of the night," he will discourage prostitution. But what does this proposal entail? If we are to decrease prostitution by shaming those who participate in it, then why shouldn't we broadcast the names of those who have gotten tickets for speeding or other moving violations? But then it would seem we should broadcast the names of those whose cars have been towed away for alternate side of the street parking violations. The real clinker comes when we see that proceeding accord-ing to this logic, we must broadcast the names of those who violate the city's "pooper-scooper law." But clearly this is ridiculous. Mr. Mayor, yes, we must decrease prostitution, but the "John Hour" is not the way to do it.—Freely adapted from a Channel 2 (CBS, New York City) editorial.

22. Now gentlemen I would like to hear your responses to my proposal. But before you respond, let me remind you that current company policies are under review, and a number of positions have to be cut.

23. Thank heavens that the judge in Arkansas had the courage to stop those creationists in their tracks and prohibit teaching creationism as a scientific alternative in the public schools. For if once that were allowed, other religious groups would demand the teaching of their views on the origin of the world as science. Then would come all the cults. And who is to say what is science and what lies outside science? Pretty soon, the schools would have to teach just about any religious view on anything.

24. When Mrs. Macaulay argued boldly for the equality of mankind—in the presence of her servants—Dr. Johnson replied by asking her to allow a footman to sit down beside her.—James Boswell, *The Life of Dr. Johnson.*[16]

25. Officials of the county assessor's office confirmed today that the assessed valuation of the Seattle First National Bank Building has increased only about 2 percent since 1971. The building's assessment was questioned last night by a former employee of the assessor's office at a candidate's forum on Mercer Island. The former employee, Bob Clymer, accused Assessor Harley Hoppe of giving the Sea-First Building and other major businesses special consideration

while residential-property values have risen as much as 50 percent in King County. However, Loran Clark, Hoppe's chief deputy who represented him at the meeting, said Clymer was a "disgruntled former employee" [and so would want to press such a charge of favoritism] and that the valuation was proper. —*The Seattle Times,* October 17, 1975.

26. One can see a tendency to pass from withdrawing life support from the moribund to facilitating the death of the suffering, and from there to the neglect or even abandonment of the profoundly defective, and from there to the degradation or liquidation of any whom society might consider undesirable. The undisciplined making of life-and-death decisions tends to corrupt the individual who makes them, and corrupted individuals tend to corrupt society.[17]—Mortimer Ostrow, M.D., *The New York Times,* June 1, 1977. Copyright © 1977 by The New York Times Company. Reprinted by permission.

27. Dr. Arthur Avella, medical director at the Essex County psychiatric hospital, suggested a need for psychiatric nursing homes. I would like to point out that there is danger in again advocating separate facilities for the mentally ill. As past history has taught us, this leads to continued misunderstanding of the illness along with prejudice and stigmatization of the patient. . . . No longer should mental illness be considered out of the mainstream of the health profession. . . . Let's not again return to the dismal days of separation and create new mini warehousing and institutionalization under another disguise.—A.J.M., *Sunday Star-Ledger* (Newark, N.J.), December 30, 1984.

28. Imagine what would happen if our police went on strike. Criminals would perpetrate crimes with impunity. We would be safe neither on the streets nor in our homes at any hour. Not even in a bomb shelter could we find protection. People would be forced to take the law into their own hands and justice would be dispensed vigilante style. The very fabric our our society would be torn. A firefighters strike is equally horrible to contemplate. Buildings would be simply left to burn! Our cities would be enveloped by huge confligrations. Before long, our country would look like one vast bombed-out war zone. Our society depends on certain necessary social services. Under no circumstances should we give the right to strike to these workers.

29. Governments can only take from some and give to others—which is a form of robbery under another name. Under no circumstances should we compel help through taxation for any group no matter how small or disadvantaged. For once we begin to help some, we shall inevitably be forced to help more and more individuals. This help leads invariably to the welfare state, and that leads to the proliferation of wasteful bureaucracies, and finally to Stalin's collectivization of the farms for the people's "own good," no matter how many had to be killed to do it.

30. We representatives of the packaged-food industry do not, of course, object in principle to what is called "truth-in-packaging." But for Congress to pass a new bill under this title is to suggest that all packaging in the past has lied to the consumer or deceived him or misrepresented the amount of food the

package contains. Sure, I know that a steady stream of housewives trooped before Senator Hart's committee telling about alleged malpractices in packaging baby foods, cereals, cookies, candy, detergents, cake mixes, etc. No doubt it taxed their brains to do the calculations necessary to realize that sometimes a pound package is bound to contain only $14\frac{1}{2}$ ounces, and that the bigger package does not always contain the most, and that rice that costs 29¢ for 14 ounces is more expensive than one that costs 12¢ for 5 ounces. The point is that the industry is being hurt by all this bad publicity; as our trade paper *Packaging* has said, "If we don't smother all this talk about how the consumer is being deceived and cheated, our whole economy will emerge sell-shocked."—Example in Monroe C. Beardsley, *Thinking Straight: Principles of Reasoning for Readers & Writers,* 4th ed. © 1975, p. 198. Reprinted by permission of Prentice-Hall, Englewood Cliffs, N.J.

§3.2 FALLACIES INVOLVING DUBIOUS ASSUMPTIONS

We have already seen, both in the last section of Chapter 2 and with slippery slope fallacies, that when an argument rests on a false or questionable premise, it is faulty. This is one problem with arguments. Why would someone put forward such an argument? One possibility is that he or she simply assumed the false or questionable premise to be true, uncritically accepting it without supporting evidence or proof. In such cases, it is appropriate to say the argument involves a dubious assumption. Our discussion so far, however, illustrates only one way dubious assumptions may enter into arguments. For in our examples, the dubious premise is manifestly, explicitly stated. We can identify one or more of the given premises as dubious. But what about the following argument:

Jones has used cocaine on occasion at parties. So I would not put much confidence in his research on electromagnetism.

This is a clear abusive *ad hominem.* For all we know, the premise is not false but simply irrelevant to the conclusion. But, we may ask, why might someone think the premise supported the conclusion, and so was relevant to it, in the first place? Hasn't the person assumed that

Those who use cocaine (on occasion at parties) in general make unreliable statements (at least on scientific subjects).

Doesn't this statement enter into the reasoning, although it is not explicitly stated? Hasn't it been simply assumed, although it is itself highly questionable? So here we have a second way in which dubious assumptions may enter into arguments. We shall discuss nonexplicit or suppressed premises in detail in Chapter 9, and so leave this type of dubious assumption for now.

The third way that arguments may involve dubious assumptions concerns false or questionable presuppositions. What do we mean by presupposition? Consider the following statements:

Jean Paul is no longer a member of the Communist Party.

Jones has ceased frequenting the Times Square area.

Alice (of *Alice in Wonderland* fame) would like some more tea.

The present king of the United States is a constitutional monarch.

Look at the first statement. Suppose Jean Paul never was a member of the Communist Party. Would that statement make sense? Can it make sense to say that he no longer is a member if he never belonged in the first place? Similarly, can the second statement make any sense if Jones never was in the Times Square area? What about the third statement. Can Alice have some *more* tea, if she hasn't had any to begin with? If Alice hasn't had any tea, how can she want some more? Finally, does the fourth statement make any sense? There is no present king of the United States. No such person exists. So what sense does it make to say he is a constitutional monarch? Would it make sense to deny it? The point is that all four of these statements involve presuppositions. For each of these statements to make sense, some other statement must be true. If the presupposed statement is false, the presupposing statement hardly seems meaningful. If arguments involve false or questionable presuppositions, we again have the problem of dubious assumption.

There are three frequently studied fallacies involving dubious assumptions. Two involve problematic presuppositions. The third involves either an explicit questionable premise or an explicit premise with a questionable presupposition. Let's examine each in turn.

1. Complex Question.   Not only may declarative statements have presuppositions, so may questions.

Consider the following:

Have you given up drinking?

Have you stopped abusing your mother-in-law?

When did you leave the scene of the crime?

Why did you rob the Andrews?

Will agriculture benefit by the increased prices which will follow the increase of taxes on imported food?—Robert H. Thouless.

Each of these questions presupposes that some other statement is true. You cannot give up drinking if you have not been a drinker. You cannot tell when you left the scene of a crime unless you both were there and at some time left the scene. We cannot tell whether agriculture will benefit from the increased prices unless those prices actually will increase. Each of these questions is complex. To be meaningful, each presupposes another statement is true, that another question has been answered affirmatively.

Now consider the following two exchanges:

ADELE: Have you stopped beating your wife?
BERTRAND: Yes.
ADELE: You admit, then, that you have beaten your wife!

ADELE: Have you stopped beating your wife?
BERTRAND: No.
ADELE: I see, then, you still are beating your wife!

Poor Bertrand. No matter how he answers Adele's question, it seems he has to admit having been a wife beater. We might even congratulate Adele on tricking such a confession out of him. And asking a complex question might in fact be a way to trick someone into making a confession. But unless that person actually admits that he or she has been engaging in some behavior, the complex question may not so much trick the person into making a confession but us into committing a fallacy. For to infer that the presupposed statement suggested by the complex question is true simply because that question has been asked and perhaps answered "yes" or "no" is to commit the *fallacy of complex question*. Committing this fallacy could easily have serious and significant consequences. If a prosecutor asks a witness whether he still attempts to perjure himself, the witness's testimony could very easily be discredited. But unless the prosecutor, independently of asking the question, has established that the witness had attempted perjury in the past, this discrediting involves the fallacy of complex question. The jurors will be led to believe that the witness had lied because of the question asked, not because evidence has been presented that the witness actually has lied. This in turn might result in the jury's rendering a faulty verdict.

It bears emphasizing that we are using the expression "complex question" in two senses. Any question which involves a presupposition, which presupposes that some statement is true, is a complex question. On the other hand, the *fallacy* of complex question occurs when someone infers just because such a question has been asked, or has been asked and answered "yes" or "no," that the presupposition is true. We have a fallacy because the mere fact that a statement is presupposed by a question is not good evidence that the statement is true. To assume that it is true just on these grounds is to make a dubious assumption.

Complex question is a tool of persuasion in other adversary contexts, not just the courtroom. "Why are the Republicans going to drag us into the Third World War?" "Why are the Democrats in favor of inflation?" "Why does the nuclear industry put profits over safety?" When confronted with a question involving a presupposition, a complex question, the proper response is to recognize this presupposition and to refrain from assuming it, to refuse to accept it as true, unless we have evidence for it. Being aware of the presupposition and being able to formulate it precisely can go a long way in preventing us from committing this fallacy (see Figure 3.11).

Figure 3.11 **COMPLEX QUESTION**

The fallacy of complex question occurs when someone assumes that a statement presupposed by a complex question is true simply because that question has been asked or has been given a "yes" or "no" answer.

---

2. *False Dilemma.* Suppose I say to a child, "You can have apple pie or ice cream for dessert." Suppose my young friend responded, "I'll have cake." Is that socially acceptable? It's clearly not, because there was a presupposition in my offer: you have a choice between apple pie and ice cream, just those two, and no other. Here are some further expressions involving alternatives:

> Do you believe in restoring the death penalty or letting innocent people get murdered?
>
> With assaults, abductions, rapes and even murders growing more of an everyday occurrence, why not legalize such materials as Mace for the everyday citizen to carry on his/her person? Or haven't we the right to protect ourselves against crime?—B.G., *Sunday Star-Ledger* (Newark, N.J.), March 20, 1983.
>
> Either we take some drastic steps to prevent the influx of illegal immigrants from continuing forever or we abandon protecting the American worker and his right to have a job without competition from those who have entered the country illegally.—S.H. (adapted), *Sunday Star-Ledger* (Newark, N.J.), February 9, 1984.

The first question suggests that there are really just two possibilities: there is no other way to control potentially murderous violence in society than by imposing the death penalty. The second again suggests just two possibilities: either we legalize certain chemical means of self-defense or we must concede the right to self-defense. According to the third statement, it seems we either take drastic measures or abandon the American worker. Notice that in each of these examples, the last alternative is distinctly unpleasant or undesirable. Hence these expressions could be quite persuasive in leading people to adopt the other alternative or alternatives.

But in each of these cases, we can ask whether this presupposition that the stated alternatives are the only possible alternatives is correct and in each case, this seems quite doubtful. Is the death penalty the only deterrent to murder? Is our choice just between allowing chemical self-defense weapons or denying the right to self-defense? Must we either adopt *drastic* measures to curb the flow of illegal immigrants or say to American workers that they don't have a right to a job without unfair competition? Clearly, in all these cases, the suggestion that the presented possibilities exhaust the open alternatives is either false or questionable. Assuming that they are the only alternatives available is making a dubious assumption. It is, in fact, to commit the *fallacy of false dilemma.* More specifically, the fallacy of false dilemma occurs when we simply, but falsely or questionably, assume that the stated alternatives are the only possible alternatives, even though this is suggested or presupposed. It is precisely because of this dubious assumption that the reasoning becomes fallacious.

Sometimes false dilemma occurs when the various stated alternatives are compound.

Are you for the Democrats and inflation or the Republicans and unemployment?

Are you for the current administration and its economic policy or not— yes or no!

Are these my only choices? Do the Democrats necessarily bring inflation and the Republicans unemployment? Do I have to approve both the current administration and its economic recovery program or neither? Can't I be in favor of one without the other? As with complex question, recognizing the presupposition and refusing to accept it without evidence, is the key to handling false dilemmas. Recognizing some other genuine alternative exposes the false dilemma (see Figure 3.12).

Figure 3.12   FALSE DILEMMA

The fallacy of false dilemma occurs when

1. certain alternatives are presented,

 2. there is a suggestion or presupposition that these are the only possible alternatives available in the situation,

3. this suggestion or presupposition is false or highly questionable,
yet

4. it is assumed true.

---

3. *Begging the Question.*   Consider the following argument:

The death penalty offends moral sentiments or feelings, because the prearranged killing of someone at a stated time is a special outrage against the humane feelings which are an essential part of morality.—Adapted from an argument in J. L. Mackie, *Ethics.*[18]

Look at the conclusion of this argument and then at the premise. Do you see something funny? What is "the prearranged killing of someone at a stated time" if not carrying out the death penalty? What is "a special outrage against the humane feelings which are an essential part of morality"? Isn't that offending moral sentiments or feelings? What does the premise do? It simply restates the conclusion, using more elaborate language. But what are we trying to do in giving arguments? We are trying to give reasons to support a conclusion. Hence, our conclusion may very well be questionable, at least to some people. But if our premise says the same thing, it too is questionable. So what was the point of the argument? It should leave our audience no more logically convinced than they were before. If they feel persuaded, it is because they have not noticed that the premise and conclusion say the same thing. Restating the conclusion in other words may give the argument some persuasive force, but it fails to make it logically convincing.

Notice that in this particular example, the question of presupposition does not arise. The premise does not presuppose the conclusion, it just *is* the conclusion, in other words. But if I introduced a premise which presupposed the conclusion, would that be legitimate? If for my premise to be meaningful my conclusion has to be true, then the questionability of the conclusion casts doubt on the meaningfulness of the premise.

Any argument which introduces the conclusion as a premise, in the same or other words, or introduces a premise which presupposes the conclusion commits the *fallacy of begging the question* (see Figure 3.13). This is a fallacy because the truth or meaningfulness of the premise is questionable—at least as questionable as the conclusion one is trying to prove. Question begging frequently occurs when in the course of an argument a second question (or perhaps a third or fourth question) arises and the original conclusion is put forward to settle one of these later questions. It is easy to see why question begging could more easily arise unnoticed in such a situation. To state or restate the conclusion as one of the premises from which that conclusion is to be derived may be rather blatant. But to restate it when attention has been diverted to establishing some other proposition, to deciding some other question, allows its introduction to go more unnoticed. Perhaps the very familiarity of the statement which is the question begged may make the argument more persuasive. A classic illustration of such question begging occurs in a motion picture starring the French comedian Sacha Guitry:

> Some thieves are arguing over division of seven pearls worth a king's ransom. One of them hands two to the man on his right, then two to the man on his left. "I," he says, "will keep three." The man on his right says, "How come you keep three?" "Because I am the leader." "Oh. But how come you are the leader?" "Because I have more pearls."—Example in Irving M. Copi, *Introduction to Logic*.

Figure 3.13 BEGGING THE QUESTION

An argument begs the question when the conclusion, in the same or different words, or a statement presupposing the conclusion is introduced as a premise. The case for the conclusion ultimately depends on accepting the conclusion itself.

Exercise 3-III

The following arguments are all instances of the three fallacies discussed in this section:

complex question   false dilemma   begging the question

In each case, identify the fallacy involved. Then be prepared to defend why that fallacy occurs.

Sample Answer

If you think education is expensive, try ignorance.—Derek Bok, president, Harvard University.

President Bok presents two alternatives: expensive education (as expensive as Harvard's?) and ignorance. His statement suggests or may be taken as suggesting that these are the only two alternatives. But is there no third? Can the costs of education be contained; can there be lower-cost public institutions? If we overlook this possibility and assume these two alternatives are the only two, we have false dilemma.

1. A: Are you still a member of the Communist Party?
   B: No.
   A: Aha! I see. You admit then that you were a member of the Communist Party!

2. When Junior presented his report card to his father, it contained mostly D's and F's. "We'll, Dad, what is it," he said, "heredity or environment?"

3. The Rainbow Room is clearly a superior restaurant to Harvey's Clam Bar. How do you know? People with taste consistently prefer the Rainbow Room. But how do you decide who has taste? Someone has taste just in case he prefers the Rainbow Room to Harvey's Clam Bar.

4. At a breakfast a few weeks before the election, where [pollster Peter D.] Hart incidentally forecast the results almost perfectly, he cautioned reporters not to accept the White House view that the voters had to choose between continuing on the course Ronald Reagan had set, or rejecting it and going back to traditional Democratic programs.—David S. Broder, November 7, 1982.

5. a. Are minority groups any less in trouble with the law than they used to be?
   Yes. It's obvious, exposure to civilization improves the lesser races.
   b. Are minority groups any less in trouble with the law than they used to be?
   No. It all goes to show that you can't reform people.

6. According to Helmuth Von Moltke, "Without war the world would sink into materialism." How may we defend this statement? Consider that without armed conflict between nations, the human race would drift decadently into a preoccupation with amassing pleasures and possessions.

7. I am afraid that there can be no such thing as a politics of happiness for America. For either we'll have a Democrat as president and he will get us into war, or we'll have a Republican and he'll get us into a recession—or worse!

8. Sextus Empiricus has an argument for the existence of the gods. He points out that "you do not serve the centaurs because the centaurs are non-existent." But you do serve the gods. So the gods certainly exist, or else "you could not serve them."[19]

9. Why did you kill your husband with that meat ax? Was it because he threatened to leave you for another woman or because you stood to gain $1 million from his insurance policy?

10. Why do educators place a stumbling block in front of learning?

Why do they insist that kids master the basics, that is—learn to read—before they can learn art, music, science and even math? Why do they waste hours, months and even years of many children's lives in remedial reading and comp ed classes before they allow them to use a microscope, watch *Gone with the Wind,* use a calculator, build and fly a kite (measuring its height in "arms lengths" when the string is back on the ground), or watch other students act out Shakespeare, or listen to other students or the teacher read to them?

Why are most "special education" and comp ed classes insults to the students' intelligence—presenting materials on such a babyish level that most of the students are turned off? Why aren't they fascinating places full of stimulating materials and activities so that the children will be anxious to learn?

Why do we say to a majority of our public school children, "You are in a below average reading group," or "You are a poor reader," or "You will fail history because you cannot read" or "You have a 'learning disability' "—when teachers, and most students, know that only a select few are supposed to succeed in school, that only a few will be allowed to learn?

Why? Because it is partly a natural desire on the part of "successful" parents (who happen to be those with money and influence) to see their children succeed. We see it on a state and a local level. The only factor that correlates with reading test score results is the socioeconomic factor. The financial status of the parents is an accurate predictor of the reading success of the child.

Why? Because that's the way society—influential, controlling, successful members of society (the ones who elect or appoint school board members)—wants it.

How can society control what is happening in the schools when so often we are told that schools are "out of control" and unresponsive to the community? Why is community involvement a reality in some communities and not others? Because it is a reality in communities made up of people who agree with the goals of their schools which allow upper income students to be at the top—or lower economic level communities that have been convinced that roller skating and good dental health rather than job or college related skills are the proper goals of their schools. Where middle or lower income level parents want more than this for their children, they are not welcome in the schools.—S.M., *The Sunday Star-Ledger* (Newark, N.J.), May 2, 1982.

FOR FURTHER READING

Logicians have distinguished a great number of fallacies over the centuries since Aristotle first drew up his list of thirteen. Indeed, some books distinguish so many that it would be practically impossible to remember all of them. One very useful handbook of the fallacies, with succinct definitions of over ninety faulty patterns of reasoning, is Alex Michalos's *Improving Your Reasoning* (Englewood Cliffs, N.J.: Prentice-Hall, Inc., 1970). W. Ward Fearnside and William B. Holther's *Fallacy: The Counterfeit of Argument* (Englewood Cliffs, N.J.: Prentice-Hall, Inc., 1959) features "fifty-one fallacies named, explained, and illustrated." David Hackett Fischer's *Historians' Fallacies* (New York: Harper & Row, Publishers, 1970) distinguishes a vast number of flaws in reasoning, illustrating how they may arise in the scholarly work of historians.

Concentrating on recognizing fallacies is one approach to teaching basic critical thinking. We have found two texts which emphasize this approach especially helpful here: Ralph H. Johnson and J. Anthony Blair's *Logical Self-Defense,* 2nd ed. (Toronto, Canada: McGraw-Hill Ryerson, 1983), and Howard Kahane's *Logic and Contemporary Rhetoric,* 4th ed. (Belmont, Calif.: Wadsworth Publishing Company, 1984). Both texts discuss a number of fallacies we do not mention here. We recommend them as collateral reading. In particular, Johnson and Blair present a good technique for identifying straw man. We must mention two other texts we have also found helpful. Irving M. Copi's *Introduction to Logic,* 6th ed. (New York: Macmillan Publishing Company, 1982), ch. 3, and Monroe C. Beardsley's *Thinking Straight: Principles of Reasoning for Readers & Writers,* 4th ed. (Englewood Cliffs, N.J.: Prentice-Hall, Inc., 1975), pp. 185–88. All this material may be read with profit to supplement our discussion in this chapter.

NOTES

[1]Monroe C. Beardsley, *Thinking Straight: Principles of Reasoning for Readers & Writers,* 4th ed. (Englewood Cliffs, N.J.: Prentice-Hall, Inc., 1975), p. 187.

[2]For a discussion of how public opinion polls create a bandwagon effect and may actually significantly influence the outcome of elections, see Michael Wheeler, *Lies, Damn Lies, and Statistics: The Manipulation of Public Opinion in America* (New York: Liveright, 1976), ch. 6.

[3]The grandstand and bandwagon appeals are sometimes presented as two varieties of one fallacy, the *appeal to the people.* That label may also be applied just to grandstanding. We feel there is enough difference between these two patterns of fallacious reasoning to warrant two different labels.

[4]Example courtesy of the *Informal Logic Newsletter,* Vol. II, Supplement, June 1980.

[5]Cited in David Hackett Fischer, *Historians' Fallacies* (New York: Harper & Row, Publishers, 1970), p. 302.

[6]From a speech during the 1931 British Parliamentary elections. Quoted in L. Susan Stebbing, *Thinking to Some Purpose* (Harmondsworth, England: Penguin Books, 1939), p. 98.

[7]Example courtesy of the *Informal Logic Newsletter,* Vol. IV, no. 3, July 1982. We also wish to thank Charles Kielkopf for granting the *Informal Logic Newsletter* permission to reproduce a portion of his study guide from which this example is taken.

[8]We are indebted to Frank C. Carlone, Karol Dycha, and Leo Raffin, *An Informal Logic Workbook* (Windsor, Canada: 1981) both for this example and Example 12.

[9]Compare Beardsley, *Thinking Straight,* p. 187.

[10]Paul M. Angle, ed., *Herndon's Life of Lincoln* (New York: Da Capo Press, 1983), p. 291. Quoted in Fischer, *Historians' Fallacies,* p. 291.

[11]W. Ward Fearnside and William B. Holther, *Fallacy: The Counterfeit of Argument* (Englewood Cliffs, N.J.: Prentice-Hall, Inc., 1959), pp. 100, 99.

[12]Paraphrase of an actual exchange aired on CBS News with Dan Rather, December 24, 1984.

[13]Example courtesy of the *Informal Logic Newsletter,* Vol. II, Supplement, June 1980.

[14]Adapted from a letter to the editor of the Windsor (Canada) *Star,* which appears in Ralph H. Johnson and J. Anthony Blair, *Logical Self-Defense* (Toronto, Canada: McGraw-Hill Ryerson, 1977), pp. 35–36.

[15]See David Hackett Fischer, *Historians' Fallacies,* p. 294.

[16]Example cited in David Hackett Fischer, *Historians' Fallacies.*

[17]We again want to thank the *Informal Logic Newsletter* and its contributors for several of the examples in this exercise. Examples 9 and 26 are from Vol. I, no. 4, July 1979. Example 15 is from Vol. II, Supplement, June 1980.

[18]Example courtesy of the *Informal Logic Newsletter,* Vol. V, no. 3, July 1983.

[19]Example in Fearnside and Holther, p. 166.

4

VAGUENESS, AMBIGUITY, DEFINITION

It is now time to specifically address an issue we left hanging in Chapter 2, right at the beginning of discussing challenging assertions. We noted that there were two broad questions we could ask of an assertion:

1. What does it mean?
2. Why should I believe it?

It is now time to specifically address the issue of unclear meaning. Why should someone pose this challenge? When is it appropriate? How can problems with meaning lead to mistakes in reasoning, to fallacies? What is involved in giving definitions to clarify meaning? What problems may plague definitions? These are the issues connected with this challenge which we shall examine in this chapter.

§4.1 PROBLEMS WITH MEANING—VAGUENESS AND AMBIGUITY

Why should we ask what a statement means? One good reason is because the assertion involves a totally unfamiliar word, one whose meaning we do not know. We want information on how that word is used, on how it should be applied. This should be the easiest type of challenge involving meaning to meet. There can be two reasons why a word is unfamiliar. Either it has an established usage which someone has not yet learned, or it may be a new word or expression coined for some special purpose. In the first case, someone need only repeat the established meaning to answer the challenge. If someone cannot clearly phrase what the unfamiliar word means, explain its meaning in more familiar terms, dictionaries are ready at hand to supply this information. On the other hand, those who coin words should be able to explain what they mean, if they have been thinking carefully.

But there are other reasons, besides unfamiliarity, why the meaning of a word should be unclear. Suppose our neighbor told us that she had just rented her second floor apartment to a young married couple. Imagine our surprise on finding that both our new neighbors are males! Can there be homosexual marriages? Our neighbor was perhaps right in saying she had rented her apartment to a couple, but was she right in saying they were a *married* couple, even if these gentlemen had entered into some formal contract which, should they have been man and woman, would have clearly been a marriage contract? Suppose our new neighbors are both a man and a woman, but, upon getting acquainted with them, we find they have contracted to live with each other for only 5 years? They have an option to renew after that. The are a couple, but are they *married?* Or suppose we recognized the couple moving in and knew they had been living together for 20 years, but had never formally entered into a marriage contract; they had never formally exchanged vows before an officer of the peace or a clergyperson. Their relationship is a "common law marriage," but are they truly married?

Your response may be that this all depends precisely on what we mean by a marriage. But that reaction just highlights an important feature of this and certain other terms. If a man and a woman have entered into a legal contract binding them to live together in exclusive monogamy for the rest of their lives, and creating various rights and duties for each partner, we have no hesitation in saying they are married. On the other hand, if two persons have never entered into any contract, agreement, or arrangement resembling this, they are not married. However, there is a range of indefiniteness, a gray area, where we are not sure whether the term applies. Such terms are *vague.* Prime examples of vague terms are adjectives which admit of more or less. One object may be more heavy than another, but how heavy is heavy? That is, how much must an object weigh to be correctly described as heavy? Must it be 10 pounds, 50 pounds, 100 pounds, 1 ton? How much must an article cost to be properly called expensive?

Notice that many times when something is said to be heavy, expensive, tall, we mean that it is heavy, expensive, tall for or relative to some class to which the item belongs. A 100-pound elephant may not be heavy for an elephant, although a baby weighing 10 pounds at birth is certainly heavy for a baby. Specifying the class may clarify meaning, but need not remove vagueness altogether. For can't we ask how heavy an elephant must be to be a heavy elephant? How heavy must a newborn be to be a heavy baby? Vagueness then is one problem with meaning. Although we understand the meaning of a word, and may be able to identify a number of correct or incorrect applications, there are a number of cases, a range of indefiniteness, where whether or not the term applies is unclear.

There is another problem with meaning however. A number of words have *multiple meaning;* they may express a number of distinctly different senses depending on the context. Consider "block." This means something quite different depending on whether we are talking about a city block, a building block or chopping block, or a block of seats. The deck of a ship is a very different thing from a deck of cards. Ordinarily, the context in which a word appears clues us to which of the various meanings is intended. "There is a new family on the block"—we wouldn't for one minute interpret this as asserting that a family had recently gotten on top of a piece of wood or stone. "In a storm, everything must be lashed to the deck"—this doesn't tell us to tie everything to a deck of cards when we see a storm coming.

However, there may be contexts which fail to eliminate all but one of the various meanings of a term. We expect there should be just one meaning in the context, but it is not clear which one is intended. Suppose we heard someone say "Remove the joint." What was intended? Was a plumber telling his assistant to remove a certain piece of connecting pipe? Was this an anxious directive to get rid of a marijuana cigarette so there would be no evidence of illicit drugs? Is a gangland figure telling someone to destroy some building—perhaps we should have heard "Torch the joint." Or is a very proper gentleman telling his butler to remove the piece of meat he has been serving his guests for dinner? The context has said too little; we have not heard enough to decide which of these meanings is intended. We say then that the word "joint" is *ambiguous* in this context. Notice that ambiguity is context relative. We do not say simply that a word with multiple meaning is ambiguous, but rather that it may be ambiguous in certain contexts.

Vagueness and ambiguity, then, are two significant problems with meaning. We challenge an assertion, asking what it means, when we recognize that it contains vague or ambiguous expressions. When challenged, we may attempt to eliminate ambiguity by defining the particular sense intended for the ambiguous term, or by proposing a definition to reduce vagueness. This involves giving definitions. But what is it to give a definition? We shall take up that question specifically in Section 4.3. First, however, we want to see how inattention to vagueness and ambiguity can lead to fallacies. We turn to that in the next section. For now, we want to emphasize how we have two distinct problems with meaning here. When dealing with vague terms, we may have no question as to the general sense of the term, but for a certain class of cases it is unclear whether or not the term applies. There is no general agreement as to where to draw the line in this range of indefiniteness. With ambiguous terms, we cannot, given the context, tell which sense is intended. The context does not select one particular meaning from among the various multiple meanings available. Should the specific sense be identified, the term may not be vague at all. We may be able to determine precisely what does and what does not fall under this term. However, it is possible that an expression be both vague and ambiguous. The specific senses of a word with multiple meaning may themselves be vague. Some terms then can be both vague and ambiguous, although vague terms need not be ambiguous nor ambiguous terms vague.

Exercise 4-I

In the following statements, identify any words or expressions which are vague or ambiguous. Are there any examples where words with multiple meaning occur more than once and display two radically different meanings? For those words which are ambiguous or which shift their meaning, restate the various meanings involved.

1. John is an extremely tall person.
2. Mary had a little lamb.
3. The mayor's antics are to come before Judge Grieg.
4. All motor vehicles must be licensed.
5. That tree is certainly diseased. But to find the root we must dig beneath the surface.
6. Suicide, whether direct or indirect, should be strongly condemned.[1]
7. All men are created equal.—Declaration of Independence.
8. Revolting police take over Bolivia.—Example in Monroe C. Beardsley, *Thinking Straight: Principles of Reasoning for Readers & Writers,* 4th ed. © 1975, p. 135. Reprinted by permission of Prentice-Hall, Englewood Cliffs, N.J.
9. Countersuit threatens movie actress's appeal.
10. General Brown's inspection will check their battle readiness.
11. Although LMK was a championship bridge player, he couldn't build a bridge over the stream on his property to save himself.
12. Ace Construction Company did a very poor job paving the new parking lot. They left a lot to be desired.
13. I don't know why they put that overlook where they did. It seems that what we saw we could easily overlook.
14. My opponents claim that because of low salaries, teachers will not come to this city. Yet if you look at where some teachers actually live, you can see they do come here from quite some distance.
15. Without Him, nothing is strong. And nothing can be very strong indeed!—Adapted from C. S. Lewis, *The Screwtape Letters.*

§4.2 FALLACIES OF VAGUENESS AND AMBIGUITY

How can inattention to vagueness and ambiguity lead to fallacious arguments? There are two basic problems here. First, the presence of a vague or ambiguous expression in either the premises or conclusion may make the entire assertion unclear. This is a distinct fault in an argument. How can we rationally accept a conclusion if we do not know what it means in the first place? How can we rationally regard a premise as giving relevant evidence unless we know what that premise says to begin with? How can we assess how much evidence a statement gives unless again we know what it means? In Chapter 2, we saw that if an argument contained a false or questionable premise, it was distinctly faulty. But how can we tell whether the premises are false or questionable until we know what they say? Hence, lack of clarity, besides being a fault in itself, blocks critically evaluating arguments on other grounds.

The second basic problem caused by vagueness or ambiguity arises when an unclear expression occurs several times in an argument. An ambiguous expression has several meanings. It may shift from one to the other in the course of the argument. The result may be an argument which only appears correct but which is actually fallacious. Similarly, as we have suggested in the last section, we may give definitions to reduce vagueness. But if a vague term appears twice, there may be a temptation to reduce the vagueness in two different ways, compromising the cogency of the argument. Let's now look at these two problems in detail.

1. *Fallacy of Unclear Assertion.*   If either a premise or a conclusion of an argument contains a vague or ambiguous expression, so that, upon reflection, we cannot be certain what is being asserted or how the conclusion is being supported, the argument involves the *fallacy of unclear assertion*. How could such a fallacy have persuasive force? Although expressions may be vague or ambiguous, we may not recognize this problem. Their vagueness or ambiguity may slip by unnoticed, leading us to think we understand the statement when we really do not, or to supply our own interpretation or clarification, when that may not be what the arguer intended. For example,

> [The courts are] providing a handsome income for all those involved. Each crime brought before the court is prolonged, processed, and milked for months—and even years. . . . The bureaucratic conglomeration of judges, prosecutors, lawyers, policemen, social workers, court staff, sheriffs, criminals, and still more lawyers all get paid.—S.S. (adapted), Vancouver, Canada.[2]

What is a "handsome income"? If any expression is vague, that one is, and until it is clarified, we cannot assess how much evidence the premises give for the conclusion.

Wonder Bread is the bread for you. It's baked for America.

What does "baked for" mean? The very familiarity of the expression masks its ambiguity until we start to think about it. Does "baked for America" mean "baked for sale in the United States"? If so, then what's so special about Wonder Bread? How many American baking companies prepare regular table bread for export? Perhaps "baked for America" means "baked with American tastes or preferences in mind." But if that's what it means, then the statement is questionable. Are there American preferences in table bread? Until that is established, the premise is not credible. Even if this is established, is Wonder Bread different from other companies in baking for America? Maybe "baked for America" means that all the bakers go about their tasks feeling particular pride and satisfaction that their bread will be eaten by Americans. The workplace is suffused with patriotic symbols, and each worker imbibes this spirit. But if that's what it means, what does that have to do with quality bread? All this might be fine for heightening the grandstand appeal, which certainly is involved in this argument, but is irrelevant to giving us a reason for buying Wonder Bread. In both these examples, then, the vagueness or ambiguity of a component expression makes it impossible to properly evaluate the argument.

There is one question we must address here. Is vagueness always a fault in an argument? Does the presence of a vague term automatically signal the fallacy of unclear assertion? Suppose a premise asserts that something is expensive or a conclusion that a couple is married. Does the vagueness of these expressions mean there is a problem with the argument? The answer is not necessarily. The question is—does the vagueness hurt the argument.[3] Consider:

You should not buy that baseball glove, for it is expensive and a cheaper glove would do just as well.

Do we need to know how expensive is the baseball glove or how expensive is expensive to determine that the premise is relevant to the conclusion? In

John and Patty have been going by the name Mr. and Mrs. Thompson for as long as I have known them. I assume that they are married.

do we need to specify a sense of marriage to see that the premise supports the conclusion? It is not vagueness in itself which leads to the fallacy of unclear assertion, but vagueness which renders it impossible to assess what a statement says or whether it properly supports or is supported by other statements. As in the last chapter, let's sum up this discussion by giving explicit directions for identifying this fallacy (see Figure 4.1).

Figure 4.1 FALLACY OF UNCLEAR ASSERTION

An argument involves the fallacy of unclear assertion when

1. some component assertion contains a vague or ambiguous expression
and
2. because of this, we cannot be certain of what is said or how the conclusion is supported.

---

2. Fallacy of Equivocation. Perhaps the most frequently mentioned fallacy connected with ambiguous words or expressions concerns how such words may shift their meaning in argument. This results in reasoning which may appear cogent, but is actually fallacious. If we are not careful, we may well judge the argument logically convincing. Alternatively, we may feel there is something wrong with the argument, the conclusion may appear outlandish, while the premises seem plausible, but without recognizing the shift in meaning, we may be unable to say what is wrong. Consider this instance:

> The end of a thing is its perfection.
> Death is the end of life. Therefore
> Death is the perfection of life.

Is the conclusion credible? Can we possibly agree that the termination, dissolution of life is its highest state, its perfection? But are the premises implausible? Certainly from the first premise we may infer

> The end of life is the perfection of life.

Taking this statement as our first premise we have

> The end of life is the perfection of life.
> Death is the end of life. Therefore
> Death is the perfection of life.

Although this may look like a good argument, let's ask ourselves: Are both premises true? We might accept the first premise, if we understood it as saying that achieving the goal of life, realizing that state which life is striving for, is to reach the perfection of life. We certainly will agree with the second premise, if we understand it as saying that death is the final stage or final event in life. But wait! We have used "the end of life" in two different senses here. Certainly, achieving the goal need not mean arriving at the final event. "The end of life" then is ambiguous in this context. Does the meaning shift affect the cogency of the argument? Let's rewrite it, substituting the different senses of "end of life" for their occurrences in the original.

> The goal of life is the perfection of life.
> Death is the final event in life. Therefore
> Death is the perfection of life.

Is this argument cogent? "The end of life" served to connect the two premises in the original. But here there is no connecting term. Are the original premises relevant to the conclusion? If they are, "the end of life" must have the same meaning in both. However, for the first premise to be true, "the end of life" must mean "the goal of life." But then the second premise will be

> Death is the goal of life.

—a highly questionable assertion. For the second premise to be true, "the end of life" must mean "the final event of life." But isn't

The final event of life is the perfection of life.

again a highly questionable assertion? So either the premises of this argument are not relevant to the conclusion or at least one premise is false or questionable. In either case, we fail to have a logically convincing argument.

An argument in which an expression shifts its meaning in a way affecting the cogency of the reasoning commits the *fallacy of equivocation* (see Figure 4.2). This problem can arise not only with ambiguous words but with vague expressions. If the statements containing those expressions are to be true, we must reduce the vagueness in different ways. But then the premises may no longer be relevant to the conclusion. Here is an example:

No one can safely predict that a new drug will not have adverse side affects for at least some of its users.

If you cannot safely predict that a drug is free of adverse side effects, you should not administer it. Therefore

No one should administer new drugs.

The expression "safely predict" is vague. If the first premise is to be true, "safely predict" must be given a strict interpretation, "predict with a very high degree of certainty." But under this interpretation, the second premise turns out false. If we are reasonably sure, although not totally or near totally certain, that a drug will not have adverse side affects, are we being irresponsible in using it? To make the second premise true, "safely predict" must mean "predict with reasonably high certainty." But then is the first premise true under that interpretation? At best, it seems highly questionable. But if "safely predict" shifts its meaning from the first to the second premise, what about the cogency of the argument?

Figure 4.2   FALLACY OF EQUIVOCATION

An argument involves the fallacy of equivocation when

1. a vague or ambiguous expression occurs several times in the argument;
2. if the premises and conclusion are to be plausible, this expression must be interpreted as shifting its meaning from one occurrence to another; but
3. for the argument to be logically cogent, it must have only one meaning throughout.

Exercise 4-II

For each of the following arguments, identify whether it is an instance of the fallacy of unclear assertion or the fallacy of equivocation. Be prepared to discuss why in each case.

Sample Answer

Only man is rational. No woman is a man. Therefore no woman is rational.[4]

This is an obvious example of fallacy of equivocation. "Man" is used with two distinct meanings. In the first premise, it means "member of the human race" as opposed to any other living thing. In the second, it means "male" as opposed to female. Once we recognize this shift, we see that the premises are irrelevant to the conclusion.

1. Those who feel free to criticize our president and his policies, either foreign or domestic, should leave the country at once. These people are clearly bad citizens for they are unpatriotic.

2. To enact responsible drug laws, we need the testimony of authorities. Hence we should hear from Detective Smith, the head of the narcotics division, since he is the chief drug authority here.

3. We may be confident that there are more people who want to adopt children than there are children up for adoption. People are on waiting lists for years applying for the adoption of a child. This means that, in our country at least, there is no such thing as an unwanted child. Hence banning abortions except when necessary to save the life of the mother will not result in unwanted children.—Adapted from a speech by Canadian Justice Minister Otto Lang.[5]

4. Lewis is sometimes late for work. So he's a bit unreliable. Unreliable people should be fired. So Lewis should be fired.

5. It doesn't make any difference whether you win or lose a war. War, as I look at it, is a game which everyone loses.[6]

6. What I find so exasperating and unsatisfying about contemporary visual art is that it is simply not sincere: The painters seem to paint less from what they feel in their hearts and need to express than from a desperate desire to startle and shock, to gain notoriety by starting some new and short-lived movement.—Example in Monroe C. Beardsley, *Thinking Straight: Principles of Reasoning for Readers & Writers,* 4th ed. © 1975, p. 140. Reprinted by permission of Prentice-Hall, Inc., Englewood Cliffs, N.J.

7. Present-day painters, more than any of their predecessors, paint what they want to paint, and are free to follow their own inclinations and wishes. What could be more sincere than that?—In Monroe C. Beardsley, *Thinking Straight: Principles of Reasoning for Readers & Writers,* 4th ed. © 1975, p. 140. Reprinted by permission of Prentice-Hall, Inc., Englewood Cliffs, N.J.

8. The historian Herbert Aptheker claims that "there were many revolts in the history of American [black] slavery." He defines a revolt "as something involving 'a minimum of ten slaves' with 'freedom as its object.'" To substantiate this claim, Aptheker cites revolts "involving fewer than ten people, risings not directed toward freedom, revolts in French and Spanish colonies, conspiracies, and alleged conspiracies."—David Hackett Fischer, *Historians' Fallacies.*

9. Beware of Mr. Justice Brandeis, Judge Mark, and Felix Frankfurter. They are gentlemen whose activities since Armistice Day would make a very interesting story.[7]

10. There has been something said lately which I cannot quite fully understand about the right of this Parliament to impose a permanent tariff. Parliament cannot impose anything that has a permanence. Every Parliament has a perfect right, if it thinks fit, to rip up the work of its predecessor. No Parliament could pass a law saying that this or that shall be permanent.—Stanley Baldwin.[8]

11. Power corrupts, and luxury when available is a powerful temptation. Therefore when luxury becomes available to rulers, they become powerfully corrupt.—Adapted from Byron Farwell, *Prisoners of the Mahdi*.[9]

12. Joe has been spending his time rather frivolously this year. He's been involved with the games.

13. If we cannot fund all programs at requested levels, there's not enough money to go around. But if there is not enough money to go around, some programs will have to be cut (i.e., discontinued). Now we cannot fund all programs at requested levels. So some programs will have to be cut.

14. Although the senator has perpetrated a few campaign dirty tricks, sought to launder PAC contributions in excess of the legal limit, and is perhaps beholden to certain special interest groups and lobbies, he is still an honest politician. But someone who is honest is virtuous, and a virtuous person is a good role model for our youth. So I do not hesitate to hold up our senator as someone for our young people to emulate.

15. Antipornography laws destroy liberty and therefore promote slavery, for whatever destroys liberty promotes slavery.—Thomas Schwartz, *The Art of Logical Reasoning*.

§4.3 TYPES OF DEFINITIONS: REPORTS AND PROPOSALS

We said in Section 4.1 that when a statement is challenged because it contains a vague or ambiguous term, we may respond to that challenge by providing a definition. In the last section we used definitions to expose the fallacy of equivocation. For one statement to be true, an ambiguous term must have one meaning. For another statement to be true, it must have a different meaning. We express the meanings by giving definitions. Similarly with vague expressions, we expose the equivocation by presenting definitions, making the term more precise in various ways. But what is a definition? It is important to ask this question, because definitions themselves may be challenged. There are various types of definitions, and the type determines what challenges are appropriate. We shall distinguish two basic types in this section, and then consider various challenges and where they apply in the next.

Definitions given to eliminate ambiguity and definitions to reduce vagueness illustrate nicely these two basic types of definition. When I attempt to eliminate ambiguity by defining the particular sense of the word I am using on a given occasion, I am reporting one of the meanings the word has in general usage. This is the hallmark of a *definition report,* which claims that some group of people regard a certain word or expression in some contexts as having the same meaning as some other word or expression. But when I attempt to reduce the vagueness of a term by proposing some rule, criterion, or principle which will decide borderline cases, my procedure is in part arbitrary. For example,

"Being intelligent" means "having an IQ of at least 120."

The specific IQ of 120 is not part of the generally accepted meaning of being intelligent, although it does not run counter to it. Drawing the line at 120, as opposed to 115 or 125, is arbitrary, although it is not arbitrary as opposed to 90 or 180. I am proposing a specific borderline for the term "intelligent" where one does not exist in ordinary usage.

This leads to the other basic type of definition. As we noted in Section 4.1, we can coin new terms and present definitions to explain how we shall use them, what they shall mean in our discussion. Here it seems I am free to propose whatever meaning I want for my new term. (However, as we shall see in the next section, there are certain rules we must not violate.) A *definition proposal* announces that a new term is to be regarded as synonymous with another expression. When we offer a definition proposal, we indicate that we are using a term in a certain way and would like others to follow our use at least for the duration of the discussion. Definitions reducing vagueness, then, are in part definition proposals. They propose drawing the line somewhere through the range of indefiniteness.

Why is it important for the logical thinker as challenger to distinguish definition reports from definition proposals? In presenting a definition report, we are using language informatively. We are making a claim about how a word is used in ordinary discourse. Definition reports, then, can be true or false, depending on whether the definition correctly informs us of how the term is used. Definition proposals, on the other hand, state how a particular person intends to use a term and invites others to adopt that usage. These definitions, then, have a significantly directive language function. They aim to have persons apply a term in a certain way, not to inform someone of how a term is used. Hence they are *not* true or false. We may then challenge definition reports on the grounds of not being true. We cannot do that for definition proposals.

Notice that saying all definitions are arbitrary, as is sometimes thought, is not accurate. Although definition proposals may be arbitrary, there is no intrinsic reason why the term being coined is assigned its particular meaning, definition reports, since they are true or false, are in a distinct sense not arbitrary. Consider:

"Horse" means "hoofed four-footed animal of the genus *equus.*"

It is true that there is no intrinsic connection between the ordered sequence of letters constituting the word "horse" and actual horses which explains why this term came to be applied to those animals. But this definition is *not* arbitrary, for it reports how one sense of "horse" is actually used in English and so makes a statement which could be true or false.

There is one feature common to both definition reports and definition proposals which we should make explicit. It has been implicit in our discussion so far. Both display a certain structure, involving three basic components: the *term being defined,* the *defining expression,* and a signal (usually the word "means" or "is") that one is taken as synonymous with the other. Where the term being defined has multiple meaning, varying from context to context, the definition may also include a scope indicator identifying the context where this particular definition applies. The general form of these definitions then follows this pattern:

term being defined (scope indicator) means *defining term*[10]

The two examples just presented follow this pattern. To illustrate the pattern with scope indicators, here are definition reports for four senses of "set":

"Set" (in mathematics) means "a collection of objects."

"Set" (in psychology) means "the direction an individual employs in approaching a problem."[11]

"Set" (in tennis) means "a series of games."

"Set" (in dancing) means "the number of persons necessary to perform some sort of square dance."

These structural features will be very important in framing challenges to definitions. But how can definitions be challenged?

§4.4 PROBLEMS WITH DEFINITIONS

In the last section, we stressed the difference between definition reports and definition proposals. The importance of this distinction emerges here where we present three challenges to definitions. The first, being too broad or too narrow, applies exclusively to definition reports. The second, being obscure, applies primarily to reports. The third, involving incompatibility, applies to both reports and proposals.

When Are Definition Reports Too Broad or Too Narrow?

Recall that definition reports can be true or false. They are claims that the term being defined means the same as the defining expression, at least as used by a certain group of people in certain contexts. How could we show such a claim false? Consider that if the claim is true, the term being defined and the defining expression will both express the same concept or property, since they have the same meaning. Hence the term being defined and the defining expression will be true of, will apply to, exactly the same things, be they persons, places, physical objects, events. For example, the definition

1. "Quadrilateral" means "closed plane figure having four sides."

is a true definition report. Notice that any object which is a quadrilateral is a closed plane figure having four sides, and any closed plane figure having four sides is a quadrilateral. Similarly, since it is true that

2. "Doe" means "female deer."

exactly the same animals which are does are female deer.

We can illustrate this correct definition report very clearly by a diagram. Let Figure 4.3 represent the class of does and Figure 4.4 the class of female deer. Since these two classes coincide, we may represent their relationship by Figure 4.5. Whenever a definition report is correct, such a diagram will display the relation between the things indicated by the term being defined and the defining expression, since both designate exactly the same things.

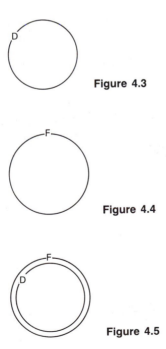

Figure 4.3

Figure 4.4

Figure 4.5

The converse is not true: two terms could be true of exactly the same objects, yet they would not *mean* the same thing. For example, exactly the same triangles that are equilateral are equiangular. Hence the triangles whose sides are equal are exactly the same as the triangles whose angles are equal. Yet it would be wrong to propose the following as an adequate definition of "equilateral triangle":

    3. "Equilateral triangle" means "triangle all of whose angles are equal."

It would be wrong because the term being defined simply does not mean what the defining expression claims it does.

However, the fact that two terms must be true of the same objects if the definition is to be correct provides a test for definitions. If the term being defined and the defining expression do not refer to the same objects, if they do not pick out the same class, then the definition will not be correct. Two problems can arise here, either separately or together. The class indicated by the defining expression may include objects which are not members of the class indicated by the term being defined. In this case, the definition is *too broad*. For example, the definition

    4. "Brother" means "sibling."

is too broad. A sibling can be either male or female, a brother or a sister. All persons who are sisters are included in the class indicated by "sibling," but not, of course, in the class indicated by "brother." We can represent this situation diagrammatically also (see Figure 4.6).

Here the brother circle is completely within the sibling circle, but clearly, as the x's indicate, there are siblings which are not brothers. The defining expression applies to objects which the term being defined is not true of. On the other hand, the term being defined may be true of objects which the defining expression is not true of. In that case, the definition is *too narrow*. For example,

    5. "Kitten" means "young female cat."

is too narrow. There are male kittens just as well as female kittens. But the males are excluded from the class of young female cats, making the definition unacceptable. Figure 4.7 is a diagram of this situation. The young female cat circle is completely within the kitten circle and the x's indicate there are kittens not young female cats.

What about the following definition?

    6. "Conservative" means "a person who advocates reducing and then freezing property taxes."

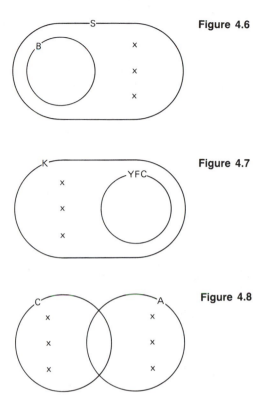

Figure 4.6

Figure 4.7

Figure 4.8

Now someone could want his or her property taxes reduced and then kept down, but yet not be properly a conservative, not accepting other conservative policies. On these grounds, the definition is too broad. On the other hand, someone who generally favors conservative policies, who supports conservative candidates, and who should be considered a conservative might not support this policy, regarding it as unwise or unsound. On these grounds, then, the definition is too narrow. This shows that definitions can be too broad and too narrow simultaneously. We may diagram the situation as done in Figure 4.8.

As the x's indicate, there are conservatives who do not advocate this property tax reform, and there are advocates of the property tax reform who are not conservative. Asking whether a definition report is too broad or too narrow is one way to test whether it is true or false. If it fails, we know there is something wrong with the definition.

We must add one further note about this test. To show that a definition is too broad, it is not necessary to exhibit an actual object which the defining expression is true of but not the term being defined. It is enough just to show such an object is imaginable or conceivable. Similarly, to show the definition too narrow, it is enough to show that an object which the term being defined but not the defining expression is true of is conceivable or imaginable. At present, by law all U.S. presidents are commanders-in-chief of the U.S. armed forces. But isn't it conceivable that the law could be changed? Then there could be presidents who were not commanders-in-chief and commanders-in-chief who were not presidents, making the definition too broad and too narrow. Why are these conceivable examples sufficient to show a definition too broad or too narrow? If a definition report is true, the terms equated are synonymous, do mean the same thing. Hence, in any conceivable circumstance, they should be true of exactly the same things. Showing this false is sufficient to show the definition false.

When Are Definitions Obscure or Circular?

A definition is supposed to explain meaning. Hence, if the defining expression is obscure, if it is as hard or harder to understand than the term being defined, if the defining expression contains a term as unclear as the term being defined, then the definition defeats its purpose. That a definition must not be expressed in vague, ambiguous, obscure, or figurative language is a traditional rule for giving definitions. Does Khalil Gibran's statement

7. Beauty is eternity gazing at itself in a mirror.[12]

really advance our understanding of beauty? Does it clarify its meaning? Pointing out, then, that the defining expression is obscure, figurative, or contains a term itself needing definition is a second way of challenging definition reports. It may also be a way of challenging definition proposals. It is certainly conceivable that a proposal to define a term in a certain way could leave us mystified as to what it really means.

There is one special way this problem may arise. Surely if the term being defined were to itself appear in the defining expression, the definition would not go very far in advancing our understanding. We shall be no better off than when we started. For example,

8. "Father" means "a person who is a father."

is obviously circular. If we do not know what "father" means, (8) will not help us. For a definition to be *circular*, the *entire* term being defined must appear in the defining expression. This is exactly what happens in (8). Notice, however, that

9. "Three-piece suit" means "suit consisting of a jacket, vest, and trousers."

is *not* a circular definition. Although the word "suit" appears in both the term being defined and the defining expression, the entire expression "three-piece suit" does not appear in the defining expression, and so (9) is not circular. What about the following?

10. "Economics" means "the science which treats of the phenomena arising out of the economic activities of men in society."[13]

Sentence 10 certainly looks circular, but according to our definition, it is not. "Economics" and "economic" are different words, actually serving different parts of speech. So the term being defined does not appear in the defining term, and, technically speaking, the definition is not circular. However, for those who do not understand the term "economics," it is doubtful that they will understand the expression "economic activities." If, in turn, we propose this definition for "economic activities":

11. "Economic activities" means "the activities studied by the science of economics."

then circularity will have entered. Sentences 10 and 11 together comprise a *circular definition set,* "a set of definitions in which at least one term is ultimately defined in terms of itself."[14] In (10), "economics" is defined in terms of "economic activities," while in (11), "economic activities" is defined in terms of "economics."

It is easy to see how circularity can creep into definition sets much more easily than into single definitions. The circularity of (8) is blatant. The circularity of {(10), (11)} is less so. Clearly a sizable definition set might be circular without that fact being readily noticed. However, the circularity may be exposed in the following way: start with one definition in the set. Where the defining expression contains a term itself defined in the set, replace that term in the defining expression by the expression defining it. Continue this process, until all terms defined in the set have been replaced by their respective defining expressions. If the resulting definition is explicitly circular, then the definition set was circular. To make this plain, let's consider this example.

12. "Obedience" means "the disposition to obey a law, principle, or directive."

13. "Law" means "a rule mandating certain specified behavior."

14. "To mandate" means "to command."

15. "To command" means "to demand obedience in performing."

Sentences 12–15 tell us first that

16. "Obedience" means "the disposition to obey a rule mandating certain specified behavior, or to obey a principle or directive."

Or, shortening this as we clearly may, we have

16'. "Obedience" means "the disposition to obey a rule mandating certain specified behavior."

Next,

17. "Obedience" means "the disposition to obey a rule commanding certain specified behavior."

And, finally,

18. "Obedience" means "the disposition to obey a rule demanding obedience in performing certain specified behavior."

Sentence 18 is manifestly circular, and so {(12), (13), (14), (15)} is a circular definition set.

When Is a Definition Incompatible or Inconsistent?

There is one final problem which may plague definitions and definition sets. For a definition report to explain meaning or a definition proposal to give meaning, the defining expression must make sense. But no defining expression makes sense if its component terms are incompatible with each other. For example, nothing can be square and circular simultaneously. Hence

19. "Quirkle" means "square circle."

just does not make sense. Neither does

20. "Gred" means "being green all over and red all over simultaneously."

These examples illustrate the most striking incompatibility we may have—the defining expressions are *inconsistent*. It is plainly impossible that anything should fall under the defining expression. It is true of nothing. But if the defining expression cannot be true of anything, what sense does it make?

We may also have definitions where, strictly speaking, the defining expressions are consistent, but given what we know, it is highly unlikely that they are true of anything. Suppose someone offered the following:

21. "To be a good teacher" means "to be popular with all your students and to be a strict disciplinarian."

Now although it is imaginable that someone could both be popular with all of his or her students and be a strict disciplinarian, don't these qualities go against each other? A strict disciplinarian will make hard and comprehensive tests, require work on time, and tolerate no nonsense. Are such teachers likely to be popular with *all* their students? Given what we know of human nature, can there be any good teachers under this definition? Again, suppose someone says

22. A law is just if and only if it guarantees to all persons their due and equalizes the distribution of wealth.

Thinking logically, we should ask: What does this definition mean? More precisely, what does it mean to guarantee persons their due? If one recognizes property rights, rights to own things privately, then guaranteeing persons their due involves respecting these property rights. On the other hand, don't rights to private property foster unequal distribution of wealth? Some people own more than others. So how can a law be just on this definition? Note that incompatibility or inconsistency can be a problem for definition proposals as well as definition reports, since here terms are being put together to construct a defining expression for the term being defined. It is quite possible to put incompatible terms together.

As with circularity, inconsistency can much more easily creep into a definition set than appear manifestly and blatantly in one definition. We may define an inconsistent definition set as one in which one term is ultimately defined by means of an inconsistent defining expression. As with circular definition sets, we can expose the inconsistency by making appropriate substitutions. For example,

23. "Centaur" means "gryphon with the head of a man."

24. "Gryphon" means "beast with the head of a bird and the body of a lion."

If we substitute the definition of "gryphon" for its occurrence in (23), we get

25. "Centaur" means "beast with the head of a bird and the body of a lion, with the head of a man."

Now presupposing that our beast has only one head, (25) is a manifestly inconsistent definition. As with circularity, it should be clear that the larger the set, the greater the chance for inconsistency to occur.

Being too broad or too narrow, being obscure, in particular being circular, being incompatible, especially being inconsistent, are problems that can beset definitions or definition sets. Any acceptable definition must avoid these problems. When they occur, they show that the definition or definition set is defective. Recognizing these problems with definitions is a skill of the logical thinker as challenger. Part of the task of being a logical thinker is challenging problematic definitions when recognizing them.

Summary

A definition is *too broad* when the defining expression is true of certain items which the term being defined is not true of. A definition is *too narrow* when the term being defined is true of items the defining expression is not true of. A definition report may be both too broad and too narrow. A definition is *circular* when the entire term being defined appears in the defining expression. Circular definitions are obscure, and obscurity is a problem for definitions. A definition is *incompatible* when it is problematic whether the defining expression applies to anything. Given what we know, it seems unlikely that the component concepts of the defining expression can be jointly true of anything. In particular, a definition is *inconsistent,* when it is impossible for the defining expression to apply to anything. Besides single definitions, sets of definitions may be circular or inconsistent.

Exercise 4-III

Are the following definitions or definition sets too broad, too narrow, both, neither? Are any obscure or circular? Are any incompatible or inconsistent? Are any of them unproblematic? Be prepared to discuss why in each case.

Sample Answer

An antique is an old piece of furniture.

First, this definition is too broad. An old, beat-up sofa qualifies as an old piece of furniture, but it is certainly not an antique. The definition is also too narrow. Antique cars, antique books, and other such items qualify as antiques, but they are not pieces of furniture, old or otherwise.

1. "Professor" means "a person who works in some educational institution."
2. "Musician" means "a member of a symphony orchestra."
3. And what, then, is belief? It is the demicadence which closes a musical phrase in the symphony of intellectual life.—Charles Sanders Peirce, "How to Make Our Ideas Clear."
4. A genuine scientific contribution means a discovery which is quickly accepted by the scientific community at large and which calls for a major revision in scientific modes of thought.
5. A vigilante is one who usurps the duly constituted law enforcement functions of arrest, trial, and conviction.—J.H., *Sunday Star-Ledger* (Newark, N.J.), February 10, 1985.
6. A colt is a young horse.
7. A kitchen is a place where one cooks food.
8. An urn is a receptacle for human remains.
9. Penicillin is a type of medicine used in the treatment of flu.
10. A garage is a place where people park their Cadillacs.
11. A journal is a diary recording the daily events in someone's life.

12. A student is a person attending high school.

13. A murderer is a person who kills people.

14. A murderer is a person who kills people, but not in war.

15. A murderer is a person who kills people, but neither in war nor in prison, but in their homes.

16. A parallelogram is a four-sided closed plane figure whose opposite sides are parallel.

17. A home is a building which serves as a home.

18. A spatular is a married bachelor.

19. "Grog" means "green smog," and "brog" means "blue grog."

20. A beastie is any animal and an animal is a dumb brute. Now a dumb brute is a wee beastie.

21. The camel is the ship of the desert.—Example in Howard Kahane, *Logic and Philosophy.*

22. Economic stability means economic growth for society in general without any upward economic mobility.

23. An entertainer is someone who appears on television.

24. A cynic is a man who knows the price of everything and the value of nothing.—Oscar Wilde, *Lady Windermere's Fan.*

25. A fanatic is a man who does what he thinks the Lord would do if He knew the facts of the case.—Finley Peter Dunne.

26. A quatragon is a square pentagon.

27. A reel is the opposite of a real slow drag, and a real slow drag is the opposite of a reel.

28. A steeple is a tower on top of a church, and a tower is a narrow, tall building standing separately from other buildings.

29. That a work of art is beautiful means it is appreciated by the general public and displays technical abilities which only experts appreciate.

30. What, then, is the government? An intermediate body established between the subjects and the sovereign for their mutual correspondence, charged with the execution of the laws and with the maintenance of liberty both civil and political.—Jean Jacques Rousseau, *The Social Contract.*

Propaganda is frequently considered an enemy of logical thinking. But getting a precise definition of "propaganda" can be tricky. What problems can you find with the following definitions?

31. Speaking generally, propaganda is the art of making up the other man's mind for him. It is the art of gaining adherents to principles, of gaining support for an opinion or a course of action.—Raymond Dodge, *The Psychology of Propaganda.*

32. Propaganda is the deliberate effort to affect the minds and emotions, chiefly the latter, of a group in a given way for a given purpose.—M. K. Thomson, *The Springs of Human Action*.

33. [Propaganda] is the presentation of a case in such a way that others may be influenced.—Sir Campbell Stuart, *Secrets of Crewe House*.

34. [Dishonest propaganda is] the creation of public opinion by the spread of misinformation which is known to be such by those who spread it. —Edwin Leavitt Clarke, *The Art of Straight Thinking*.[15]

35. Propaganda is "the dissemination of conclusions"—just this, nothing more, nothing less.—Frederick E. Lumley, "The Nature of Propaganda."[16]

FOR FURTHER READING

Chapter 4 of Monroe C. Beardsley's *Thinking Straight: Principles of Reasoning for Readers & Writers*, 4th ed. (Englewood Cliffs, N.J.: Prentice-Hall, Inc., 1975) contains an excellent discussion, with many illustrative examples, of vagueness and ambiguity. We have relied on this discussion in developing our account here. We have also found Chapter 6 helpful, where Beardsley presents a full discussion of types of definitions and how definitions may be problematic. Jerry Cederblom and David W. Paulsen's *Critical Reasoning* (Belmont, Calif.: Wadsworth Publishing Company, 1982), pp. 56–65, contains a very clear discussion of vagueness, ambiguity, the fallacy of equivocation, and the significance of definitions. Pages 182–86 contain a good discussion of problems with definitions. Michael Scriven discusses a number of issues connected with definition and meaning in *Reasoning* (New York: McGraw-Hill Book Company, 1976), ch. 5. Irving M. Copi's *Introduction to Logic*, 6th ed. (New York: Macmillan Publishing Company, 1982), ch. 4, examines many issues connected with definition.

NOTES

[1]Example in Jerry Cederblom and David W. Paulsen, *Critical Reasoning* (Belmont, Calif.: Wadsworth Publishing Company, 1982), p. 63.

[2]Example courtesy of Frank C. Carlone, Karol Dycha, and Leo Raffin, *An Informal Logic Workbook* (Windsor, Canada: 1981), p. 36.

[3]Compare Michael Scriven, *Reasoning* (New York: McGraw-Hill Book Company, 1976), p. 106.

[4]Example in Stephen N. Thomas, *Practical Reasoning in Natural Language*, 2nd ed. (Englewood Cliffs, N.J.: Prentice-Hall, Inc., 1981), p. 261.

[5]An excerpt from this speech is presented in Ralph H. Johnson and J. Anthony Blair's *Logical Self-Defense* (Toronto, Canada: McGraw-Hill Ryerson, 1977), p. 110.

[6]Example in W. Ward Fearnside and William B. Holther, *Fallacy: The Counterfeit of Argument* (Englewood Cliffs, N.J.: Prentice-Hall, Inc., 1959), p. 161.

[7]Adapted from a quote taken from *The International Jew, the World's Foremost Problem*, Vol. I (Dearborn, Mich.: The Dearborn Publishing Company, 1921), p. 75. Quote appears in Edwin Leavitt Clarke, *The Art of Straight Thinking* (New York: D. Appleton-Century Co., 1929), p. 347.

[8]From a speech during the 1931 British Parliamentary elections. Quoted in L. Susan Stebbing, *Thinking to Some Purpose* (Harmondsworth, England: Penguin Books, 1939), pp. 99–100.

[9]Cited in David Hackett Fischer, *Historians' Fallacies* (New York: Harper & Row, Publishers, 1970), p. 274.

[10]Compare Monroe C. Beardsley, *Thinking Straight: Principles of Reasoning for Readers & Writers,* 4th ed. (Englewood Cliffs, N.J.: Prentice-Hall, Inc., 1975), pp. 208, 212.

[11]See Fillmore H. Sanford, *Psychology: A Scientific Study of Man,* 2nd ed. (Belmont, Calif.: Wadsworth Publishing Company, 1965), p. 417.

[12]From *The Prophet,* quoted in Patrick Suppes, *Introduction to Logic* (Princeton, N.J.: D. Van Nostrand Company, Inc., 1957), p. 151.

[13]J. N. Keynes, *Scope and Methods of Political Economy,* quoted in Irving M. Copi, *Introduction to Logic,* 6th ed. (New York: Macmillan Publishing Company, 1982), p. 171.

[14]Beardsley, *Thinking Straight,* p. 222.

[15]Examples 31–34 are all quoted in Frederick E. Lumley's *The Propaganda Menace* (New York: The Century Co., 1933), ch. 2, to which we are indebted for them.

[16]Quoted in Terence H. Qualter's *Propaganda and Psychological Warfare* (New York: Random House, Inc., 1962), p. 24.

5

SOME FURTHER CONSIDERATIONS ON PERSUASION

So far, we have been concerned with persuasive force primarily in connection with the fallacies. Why are some arguments that fail to be logically convincing still persuasive? But someone can be persuasive without specifically arguing for a position, fallaciously or otherwise. In Chapter 1 we discussed emotive words and expressive language. Surely by being expressive, a statement may be persuasive. Hence we can inquire about the persuasive force of a passage, whether or not it specifically presents an argument. Furthermore, to assess this persuasiveness properly, we may need to look not just at various specific factors in a passage, the marks of a fallacy, the emotive words or emotion-arousing images, but at the passage as a whole. We may have to assess the cumulative expressive force of what is said (and of what is left unsaid). This is to determine the slant of the passage. In the case of the media, we can speak not only of an article or story being slanted, but of the entire coverage of some topic. In an election, a paper could be slanted for one candidate and against the opponent. Or a paper could be slanted toward one party in general, or against a certain racial minority.

As we might expect, emotive words are a principal ingredient of slanted messages. In addition, there are two specific slanting techniques we must introduce here, along with developing how to assess the overall slant of a passage. This shall occupy us in the first section. In the second, we turn our attention to advertising—perhaps the most prevalent persuasive medium today. The persuasive techniques we are studying, including slanting, have specific advertising applications. As we shall see, being aware of these applications constitutes some of the skills of the logical thinker as challenger. In fact, this whole chapter deals with further honing our skills on when to challenge a message and what sort of challenge should be made.

§5.1 SLANTING

What do we mean by the *slant* of a passage? What does it mean to say that a newspaper story or the newspaper itself, a book, or a television program is *slanted?* Webster's *New World Dictionary* defines "slant" as "point of view, opinion, attitude, bias" and bias as involving prejudice. This definition highlights an important fact: to be slanted, a passage must express an attitude toward what it is describing or interpreting. There must be some claim that something is good or bad, there must be some expression of preference for or against. But we would not ordinarily count a straightforward evaluative assertion, especially one defended by cogent argument, as slanted or making a passage slanted. By mentioning bias and prejudice, our definition highlights another feature of slanting. It seeks to convey and mold attitudes ordinarily without being concerned for their rational justification. With slanting, the purpose is to express an attitude and get others to share it, not to make and defend evaluative claims. How then may we correctly assess what attitude is being expressed? How do we determine the slant of a passage so we can see what evaluative claim is being made and challenge it, if necessary?

There are three slanting techniques. We have already met one—emotive words. Laudatory and derogatory emotive words convey attitudes. Consider the following two passages:

> President Reagan is launching the nation on a dramatic and unexplored course that reverses decades-old policies in Washington.
>
> If Congress goes along with his revolutionary program of huge tax and spending cuts, business will improve—at least for the short run. . . .
>
> With the plan in place, most economists believe, the economy should start to shake off its doldrums this summer and shoot up next year. Consumers, with a big cut in taxes, will spend billions more. Firms will pour cash into new buildings and equipment. Defense contractors will enjoy a boom in orders. The military will get more of the taxpayers' dollars.—Reprinted from *U.S. News & World Report,* March 2, 1981. Copyright 1981, U.S. News & World Report, Inc.

> . . . The President is taking a whole series of high-risk gambles. He is betting first that Congress can be persuaded to pass at least the key elements in his program in recognizable shape. That is at least questionable: . . . [Reagan] is asking Congressmen to vote for spending cuts that will hurt their own constituents—and there is something in his plan to offend just about every lobby in Washington.
>
> The President is also taking a long chance that the deep tax cuts he wants will prompt savings, investment and hard work, and thus healthy economic growth. They could instead deepen deficits, lead to a consumer buying spree, or both; either would make inflation worse.
>
> That prospect troubles many economists and businessmen who applaud what Reagan is trying to do. Says Otto Eckstein, a member of TIME's Board of Economists: "With only a little additional bad luck, the Government could expe-

rience a deficit of $100 billion." Adds DuPont Chairman Irving Shapiro: "I have a lot of trouble with this new economic religion. No businessman would run his business on the basis of an untested thesis."—From *Time*, March 2, 1981. Copyright 1981 Time Inc. All rights reserved. Reprinted by permission from TIME.

Both these passages are discussing the same thing—President Ronald Reagan's nationally televised speech on February 18, 1981, to a joint session of Congress outlining his economic recovery program. Both excerpts are from much longer articles. But just from what is given here, we can detect a distinct and different slant in each. "Launching," "dramatic," "unexplored"—this whets our appetite for adventure. "Shake off its doldrums," "shoot up," "spend billions more," "pour cash into new buildings and equipment"—all this, emotively, is very up-beat. Taking all these factors into account, we can predict that *U.S. News*'s attitude to President Reagan's economic recovery program is favorable. But now compare *Time*. "High risk gambles," "questionable," "long chance," "deepen deficits," "consumer buying spree," "make inflation worse," "a deficit of $100 billion," "new economic religion," "untested thesis,"—these expressions are not emotively neutral. They convey a distinctly downbeat feeling. *Time* seems to be highly skeptical of the president's program.

In Chapter 1, we noted that not only the emotive words used but what is described can contribute to the expressive character of a passage. Pointing out that someone is guilty of various crimes arouses negative emotions, while reports of heroic deeds are positive. We must also take these factors into account when assessing the slant of a passage. But this leads us directly to the other two slanting techniques, slanting by selection and slanting by association.

Slanting by Selection

If we wanted to form a rational attitude toward certain persons or their actions, policies, events, what should we want to know? Shouldn't we want to know all the facts relevant to assessing these actions, policies, events? Ideally, we should like to base our attitude on all the available relevant information. But suppose someone presented only that information which supported his or her attitude toward the subject at hand and omitted other relevant facts? The message expresses an attitude, but it is biased and prejudicial. In short, it is slanted. This technique is *slanting by selection*, displaying or giving undue prominence to information supporting an attitude and downplaying, suppressing, or omitting other factors relevant to forming a proper attitude. Notice that contrary information does not have to be completely omitted in slanting by selection. Suppose someone actually presented all or most of the relevant facts, but highlighted what supported his or her attitude and downplayed conflicting considerations. Wouldn't that have a similar effect in conveying a prejudicial attitude? Here is a classic example of slanting by selection:

Pointing to great progress in his community and the nation, a politician boasted in a National Book Week speech that 220 libraries have been built in the U.S. in the past fifteen years. He did *not* mention that during the same period some 10,000 pizza parlors, 15,000 frozen-custard stands, 9,180 bowling alleys, and 3,500 drive-in theaters went up.—Samm Sinclair Baker, *The Permissible Lie*.

Looking just at what the politician said, we may develop a positive attitude. But looking at the whole picture could change that attitude dramatically.

Newspaper reporting, not only in individual articles but in the overall treatment of certain topics, can provide good examples of slanting by selection. The physical layout of a newspaper fosters this. What is the most prominent part of a newspaper? Certainly, it is the front page. If a story occurs there, it is far more likely to be read by more people than if it is "buried," that is, placed on some inside page. Similarly, what is the most prominent part of a news story? It is the headline. Next to that come the opening paragraphs in the story. Not only will more people read these paragraphs, they can set the whole tone in which the rest of the article may be read. The farther down some statement appears, the less its prominence. How may we exploit these features to slant by selection? The Chicago Commission on Race Relations once accused the *Chicago Tribune* of presenting a prejudicial picture of blacks. In one year, the *Tribune* published

> 145 articles which, because of their emphasis on crimes, clashes, political corrup-
> tion, and efforts to "invade white neighborhoods" definitely placed [blacks] in an
> unfavorable light. . . . It also published eighty-four articles dealing with [black]
> soldiers, sports, industry, and personalities, which . . . did not place [blacks] in an
> unfavorable light. The unfavorable 145 articles contained 487 inches of printed
> matter, while the less colorful items contained 223 inches.
>
> Front page space amounting to eleven inches was given to favorable articles,
> and 158 to unfavorable.[1]

The *Chicago Tribune*'s picture seems lopsidedly against blacks. Not only were more articles and more space given to unfavorable material, but this imbalance was increased by where the information occurred—front-page coverage was heavily against blacks. Can we really believe that the newsworthiness of these unfavorable stories justified such an imbalance of negative over positive information?

This last question highlights a problem in assessing whether slanting by selection is taking place. We cannot know for sure that we have slanting by selection unless we know that certain relevant facts have been left out or downplayed while other information is unduly featured. But it might seem that we cannot know this unless we have witnessed what is being discussed. Only then can we tell whether a report has left out relevant factors to create a biased impression. But for most messages that we receive, this is not possible. The next best thing, in detecting slanting by selection, is to consider two or more reports side by side. How facts are given contrasting emphases in these reports, how prominently they are featured, can indicate whether or not either or both involve slanting by selection. Let's illustrate how this comparison can reveal slanting by contrasting two series of headlines. The first appeared on successive days in September 1952 in the front-page area of the New York *Post*: "SECRET

NIXON FUND"; "SECRET RICH MEN'S TRUST FUND KEEPS NIXON IN STYLE FAR BEYOND HIS SALARY"; "DICK'S OWN WELFARE STATE"; "IKE BACKS NIXON BUT—I'M TRYING TO PHONE HIM"; "NIXON PUT IKE ON SPOT"; "CH 4 9:30—NIXON; SUBJECT $18,000, COST $75,000"; "TAX MEN PROBING NIXON"; "STEVENSON SHIFTS TO ATTACK"; "STEVENSON SUPPORTER TELLS OF $1,000 DONATION." (The last two headlines appeared on the same page, but the first was in larger print.) Over the same few days, the *Chicago Daily Tribune* ran these headlines: "NIXON DEFENDS $16,000 FUND DONATED FOR HIS USE"; "POLITICAL POT SET TO BOILING BY NIXON FUND. Ike Voices Faith in Running Mate"; "LIST DONORS TO NIXON FUND; NEVER TRIED TO CONCEAL FUND: NIXON"; "NEW FUND BARED; IT'S ADLAI'S"; "[STEVENSON] ADMITS TAKING PRIVATE AID FOR STATE OFFICIALS"; "SEN. NIXON TELLS LIFE STORY; CHALLENGES STEVENSON TO REVEAL FUND RECORDS"; "GIVES VIGOROUS SUPPORT TO NIXON AFTER SPEECH."[2]

These headlines concern two similar and potentially explosive events in the 1952 presidential campaign: the revelations that Richard Nixon, the Republican vice-presidential nominee, and Adlai Stevenson, the Democratic presidential nominee, both had "secret" funds. Mr. Nixon's fund, allegedly for his "financial comfort," amounted to $18,235, contributed by seventy-six donors. Contributions were continuing while he was a U.S. senator. Then Governor Adlai Stevenson's fund amounted to $18,150. It consisted of surplus campaign contributions to Stevenson's successful run for governor of Illinois, made by 1,000 donors. Stevenson was using it to supplement the salaries of eight persons appointed to state office.[3] Whatever should be the relevance and importance of this information in assessing the fitness of the Republican or Democratic tickets to be elected, comparing the headlines brings into strong relief the differing attitudes of the *Post* and the *Chicago Daily Tribune*. By emphasizing that Nixon's fund was secret, that it was established by rich men to keep him in luxury, that Nixon had embarrassed Eisenhower, his presidential running mate, and that Mr. Nixon might have tax troubles, the *Post* coverage puts Nixon in a bad light. The *Chicago Daily Tribune,* by contrast, seeks to minimize the damage of this story by emphasizing that Nixon will defend the fund, that his party still supports him, and that it really wasn't secret after all. In addition, the *Chicago Daily Tribune* goes on the offensive, suggesting Stevenson has something to hide with *his* fund. By contrast, the *Post* tries to put Stevenson in a strong position. By looking at these headlines side by side, we can readily recognize their different attitudes and question whether either is justified. Certainly slanting is going on somewhere.

Slanting by Association

Slanting by selection basically concerns relevant information—giving some undue prominence while downplaying or suppressing other necessary data. It takes relevant information out. By contrast, slanting by association puts irrelevant information in. To illustrate, let's look at another excerpt from *Time*'s coverage of President Reagan's speech unveiling his economic recovery program:

> The President prepared the address in what is now becoming the usual way. White House Speechwriter Ken Khachigian put together a rough draft, which Reagan reworked sporadically during a Camp David weekend. Crammed as it was with fiscal details, the speech could not display Reagan at his rhetorical best. For once, the master of the TV homily and the after-dinner pep talk appeared not only ill at ease but even a bit defensive, as he spent some of the opening minutes talking earnestly about programs he would not cut, most notably, veterans' and basic Social Security retirement benefits.
>
> The President originally had wanted to speak for 20 or 25 minutes, but found after practicing and timing himself that his talk was longer than that—it took 34 minutes to deliver—and he decided there was nothing he wanted to cut. As a result, his rushed delivery caused him, uncharacteristically, to misjudge some of his applause lines. Late in the speech, he drew a loud and long ovation by asking the assembled Congressmen and Senators to make his program not just the Administration's idea but "our plan." Reagan flashed his widest grin and remarked, "I should have arranged to quit right there"—then went on speaking for another 4½ minutes.—From *Time*, March 2, 1981. Copyright 1981 Time Inc. All rights reserved. Reprinted by permission from TIME.

Remember that judging from the emotive words used in a previous excerpt, we considered the slant of *Time*'s article to be skeptical of Mr. Reagan's economic policy. Doesn't the information in this passage reinforce that slant? Not only do we have a real putdown, describing Mr. Reagan as "the master of the TV homily and the after-dinner pep talk"—the implication being that the president is a real intellectual lightweight—but telling us that Mr. Reagan reworked the rough draft "sporadically," that the speech "could not display [him] at his rhetorical best," that Mr. Reagan appeared defensive, that he misjudged some of his applause lines, is all uncomplimentary. It certainly does not put Mr. Reagan in a favorable light or foster confidence in him. But obviously there is a close association between the president and his policies. Arousing negative feelings about one can easily lead to negative feelings about the other. By including this unfavorable information in a report on the speech and the new economic program, *Time* is using this connection, the association between the president and his economic policy, to express and reinforce its overall skeptical attitude toward that policy.

But since the issue concerns the merits of Mr. Reagan's program, how relevant are these facts about how the speech was prepared and delivered to assessing that program? As logical thinkers, we want to know what the president said and how we could evaluate it. That might involve expert testimony on the policy's consequences and their economic and social impact. We do not care particularly about how the president presented the speech. These facts then serve to reinforce the attitude *Time* is trying to convey, to further mold our attitude, but are not relevant to the main issue. By including them, *Time* is arousing skeptical feelings about Mr. Reagan's performance and then transferring those feelings by association to the economic recovery program itself. This is slanting by association.

There is a special form of slanting by association that we must identify—
innuendo. We may define it as presenting facts in a manner to suggest relationships, connections, conclusions which are either highly questionable or do
not hold outright.[4] These suggestions, of course, will be prejudicial to what is
being discussed. For example, suppose we hear that there are communists in a
certain neighborhood and that Senator Smith has been seen in that neighborhood.[5] Both these statements may be true. But what may we suggest by
juxtaposing them? That Senator Smith is a communist and perhaps was in the
area to attend a communist meeting? Juxtaposing these statements may make
such suggestions, but do we have logical grounds for accepting these suggestions? Do the juxtaposed statements give us good reasons for believing what
they suggest? However, how do these suggestions make us *feel* about Senator
Smith? Do they foster such prejudice, such a negative attitude that we will not
think to challenge them?

In the first example, there was an obvious association between President
Reagan and his policies. That enabled *Time* to reinforce its skeptical attitude
toward the president's policy by presenting negative information about Mr.
Reagan. In this example, we set up an association between Senator Smith and
communists, sure that the negative emotional reaction communism elicits will
transfer to Senator Smith. *Slanting by association,* then, involves either introducing irrelevant but prejudicial facts into a story or juxtaposing, arranging certain
material to suggest descriptions, interpretations, or evaluations which are prejudicial and which also may very well be untrue.

Determining the Slant

We have already stressed how comparing and contrasting different accounts of the same subject may reveal that one or both are slanted. Determining
the political affiliations and editorial biases of the media can also put us on guard
against slanting. We would expect newspapers to slant their stories in favor of
what they endorse and against what they oppose. We should also ask about the
opinions and biases of the intended audiences. There are white-collar papers
and blue-collar papers. These groups may have different attitudes on various
issues, and papers will slant their stories to conform to, reflect, and reinforce
these attitudes. We must further ask who the major advertisers are, for these
sources can manipulate the news media. Newspapers, radio, and television get
much of their income from advertising. Hence they may be extremely reluctant
to publish stories which adversely affect big advertisers, and may be willing to
publicize a manufacturer who advertises with them. Profits from advertising
open a channel of controlling influence for advertisers, an influence which
results in news being slanted in their favor.

Asking these questions about opinions, biases, points of view is important not only for guarding ourselves against slanted accounts. Seeking contrasting points of view can be a way of critically assessing the merits of some issue or
critically developing and refining our attitudes. In effect we may use various

slanted accounts to become aware of the different positions concerning an issue. This can help us get at the truth by making us aware of the factors involved in properly assessing what to believe or do. What should be our attitude toward our government's policies and actions in Central America, the Mideast, in relations with the Soviet Union? What about its policies on domestic social issues? American newspapers have longstanding political affiliations. We might expect Republican and Democratic papers to differ on these issues. By consulting papers on both sides, we may become aware of factors bearing on the issue which hearing just one side could not make us aware of. However, major American papers might not differ so much that they question significant middle-of-the-road American values. How do foreign papers view American policy on these issues? What about the "underground press," small papers put out by dissenting groups? By contrasting these sources with major American news media, we may not only point out how major news organizations slant the news, but we may become aware of facts, values, insights which we should take into account in properly developing our own beliefs and attitudes about government policy.

We should make one additional point in connection with slanting. In determining the slant of a passage, we are interpreting it. We are trying to determine the author's underlying attitude. It is worth emphasizing that it is the *author's* attitude, feelings, point of view that we are concerned with. In determining how a passage is slanted, we are not asking how we react to the passage, whether the author's treatment is congenial or uncongenial to us, nor are we asking about our emotional reaction to what is described. We are trying to assess the author's reaction to the material. Hence, we should be on guard against reading into a passage what we might like to see there or what the author might have said but did not. When we read something into a passage, we misinterpret it.

However, there is a distinct but subtle difference between reading something into a passage and reading between the lines. Appreciating innuendo, in general appreciating what is suggested by juxtaposing several statements, involves ability to read between the lines. How is this different from reading into a passage? When we read between the lines we discern something the author intended but only suggested, said implicitly rather than explicitly. When we read something into a passage, we claim to see something which isn't there. An example may help make this distinction clear. If someone says, "The wheat crop has not been good this year. The corn crop will not be good either," we have just two assertions. The passage does not communicate the message that because the wheat crop was poor, so will be the corn crop, that one caused the other. To claim that is to read something into the passage. But to say, "Our opponents took office four years ago. Since then inflation has run wild, unemployment has gone through the roof, and apparently our government policy is dictated abroad," *is* to suggest that the opposition is responsible for these disasters. That is not *explicitly* stated, but it is certainly there between the lines.

As we noted when beginning to discuss slanting, the slant of a passage is a matter of the passage as a whole, of the entire passage. Proper interpretation involves looking at what is said on the whole, rather than concentrating just on particular points. Consider the following statement from *Time:*

> On his ninth international junket, Pope John Paul II tours the Philippines with stagecraft, statecraft and devotion, making a stirring declaration against the world's unequal distribution of wealth.—From *Time,* March 2, 1981. Copyright 1981 Time Inc. All rights reserved. Reprinted by permission from TIME.

What is *Time*'s overall attitude toward Pope John Paul II and his trip? Is it positive or negative? Doesn't the writer describe the Pope as having skill, affection, and social conscience? Doesn't saying this about a person foster a positive attitude? Isn't this the main thrust of the statement? But what is the emotive meaning of "junket"? Is it laudatory or derogatory? When we say a congressional representative has gone on a junket, we suggest that the official is not tending to business but is having a good time at government expense. That doesn't put the individual in a very good light. However, if someone said that *Time* feels that the Pope's trip is silly and unnecessary because "junket" appears in this message, that person has focused in on one point in the passage and failed to look at the whole. We call this pointed thinking, and we must avoid pointed thinking to interpret passages properly, to assess the slant adequately.

Of course, individual emotive words or emotion-arousing expressions can be quite revealing. The position of a word in a passage is important. The beginning of a passage is crucial, for that sets the tone. The conclusion is also important for that is how the writer leaves the reader. Laudatory or derogatory emotive words in these positions can be especially important for revealing the overall slant. The point is that if we say the overall attitude of a passage is favorable or unfavorable, that assessment must be borne out when we look at the passage as a whole. Judging the whole just from one point is pointed thinking.

Why is it important to be aware of the slant of a passage? Why should we pay attention to the emotive words, the emotive impact of the information presented, the suggestions and innuendo? Why should we compare different accounts of the same story? Through slanting, the author is expressing an attitude, and at least implicitly asserting an evaluation. We can ask whether this attitude is appropriate, whether the evaluation is correct. When made explicit, should the evaluation be challenged? Recognizing the slant of a passage helps us to think logically about what is said, rather than be carried along by its persuasive force.

Summary

A passage is *slanted* when (1) it expresses a distinct attitude toward something it discusses and (2) it does not attempt to justify that attitude rationally, but to sway the audience to accept it through various persuasive devices. We identify three slanting techniques: emotive words, slanting by selection, and slanting by association. In *slanting by selection,* some relevant information is downplayed or omitted altogether, while other relevant information may be highlighted or given undue prominence. *Slanting by association* involves either putting in prejudicial irrelevant information or arranging information, juxtaposing information to create a biased impression by suggesting dubious relationships or connections.

Exercise 5-I

Discuss how emotive words, slanting by selection, and slanting by association may slant the following messages. Think about what a message says explicitly and what it suggests. In some cases, background information is given. You are to evaluate the message against that background information.

Sample Answer

BACKGROUND: Ace Steel Company employs 5,000 workers at its Elmtown plant. For the past eighteen months, there have been labor troubles at the plant, which have been increasing.

MESSAGE: MID AMERICA CIRCUS COMES TO ELMTOWN.

> Ace Steel President Bertrum Hogenthorp announced today that his company is bringing the Mid America Circus to Elmtown. It will give three performances for the whole community and all Ace Steel employees get free tickets for themselves and their families. "We want to show our workers our appreciation for the fine job they have been doing and show our concern for their well-being," Hogenthorp said.

We have grounds for charging slanting by selection here. The message portrays Ace Steel as really caring about its workers, as being benevolent. This makes the company look good. But should we suppose the labor troubles of the past eighteen months are all the workers' fault? Is Ace Steel really as nice as it is portrayed to be? Does the passage lead us to formulate a correct evaluation of Ace Steel?

1. BACKGROUND: In 1919, Massachusetts Governor Calvin Coolidge waffled in the extreme before the Boston Police strike. On the day it occurred, the mayor of Boston had to settle it himself; Coolidge was no where to be found.[6]
MESSAGE: When the Boston Police struck in 1919, Governor Calvin Coolidge, that strong, silent man of destiny, telegraphed these words to the president of the American Federation of Labor: "There is no right to strike against the public service by anybody, anywhere, any time."

2. In 1926, the first report ever in Minneapolis of a black man's attempting to abduct a white woman was recorded. Seizing on this fact, one propagandist declared, "Never before have such crimes been as frequent in Minneapolis as they are now."[7]

3. Congress will shortly take up the issue of child labor when it votes on the Child Labor Amendment. There will be many watching this debate who

have other interests to heart than child welfare. The socialists have generally been for abolishing child labor. Russia prohibits children from working in its factories so they can be free to attend compulsory propaganda classes. Never mind that the parents want the children to work and need the money! Parents rights are superseded by the State's rights. Why we need this measure now is a mystery, since responsible employers have clearly reformed their child labor policies. Isn't it good for a kid to work a couple of hours a day after school?

4. The saloon is the storm center of crime; the devil's headquarters on earth; the schoolmaster of a broken decalogue; the defiler of youth; the enemy of the home; the foe of peace; the deceiver of nations; the beast of sensuality; the past master of intrigue; the vagabond of poverty; the social vulture; the rendezvous of demagogues; the enlisting office of sin; the serpent of Eden; a ponderous second edition of hell, revised, enlarged and illuminated.[8]

5. MESSAGE: If you are a slum dweller you can get an apartment with eleven-foot ceilings, a twenty-foot balcony, a swimming pool and gymnasium, laundry room and playroom, and the rent begins at a hundred and thirteen dollars and twenty cents and that includes utilities.—Ronald Reagan referring to Taino Towers, a subsidized housing project in New York City, during the 1976 campaign.
BACKGROUND: Only 92 of 656 units had high ceilings, and these were in six-bedroom units for large families that paid from $300 to $450 a month, depending on income. Also, the pool, gym, and other facilities were public, shared with the surrounding community of 200,000 Puerto Ricans and blacks.—From *Marathon, The Pursuit of the Presidency* by Jules Witcover. Copyright © 1977 by Jules Witcover. Reprinted by permission of Viking Penguin, Inc.

6. The Republican candidate for Governor [of New Jersey], Thomas H. Kean, . . . reminded his hosts [at a federally financed lunch program for the elderly] that he had co-sponsored many pieces of legislation benefiting the elderly while in the state General Assembly, and that his father, the late Representative Robert W. Kean, was known in Washington as "Mr. Social Security." —*Star-Ledger* (Newark, N.J.), dateline September 24, 1981.

7. In Mexico, unemployment is about 50 per cent, and the peso is worth about a penny, down from eight cents a while back. Mexico is run by a self-denominated socialist. To the north, Canada has unemployment of almost 11 per cent, inflation higher than that, corporate profits down 50 percent, a stock index down 40 per cent, and just about everybody in a towering rage over Canada's leader, a nonself-denominated socialist.—William F. Buckley, Jr., Copyright 1982 Universal Press Syndicate. Reprinted with permission. All rights reserved.

8. In a memo to the President, [then Interior Secretary James] Watt recommended establishing new guidelines for determining how much of a water project's cost should be borne by the federal government. Agricultural water projects—for the Administration's Republican strongholds in the West—would get up to 65 per cent of the costs paid by Uncle Sam; but municipal water projects—in the largely Democratic cities of the Northeast—would get zilch.

—Jack Anderson, March 6, 1983. Reprinted by permission of United Feature Syndicate, Inc.

9. The President, for obvious reasons, chose to overlook the implications of the history of his Administration's two phases. In 1981, when his tax and budget cuts were swept through Congress with alacrity, the reaction on Wall Street, the financial markets and the economy was one of doom and gloom.

In 1982, when Congress rejected his budget, rewrote it on its own, and forced him to accept a tax increase he had opposed, Wall Street boomed, interest rates cracked and at least some sectors of the economy showed signs of revival.—David Broder, October 17, 1982.

10. Clarence Darrow is speaking: This is an historic case which will count much for liberty or against liberty. Conspiracy, from the days of tyranny in England down to the day the railroads use it as a club, has been the favorite weapon of every tyrant. It is an effort to punish the crime of thought. *If there are still any citizens interested in protecting human liberty, let them study the conspiracy laws of the United States* which have grown until today no one's liberty is safe.—Excerpt from *Clarence Darrow: A One-Man Play* by David W. Rintels. Copyright © 1975 by Dome Productions (USA). Reprinted by permission of Doubleday & Company, Inc.

Exercise 5-II

We have pointed out that a good way to expose slanting is by juxtaposing passages from different sources discussing the same material. Discuss the contrasting slants in the following pairs of passages.

1. Imagine that the following are reports in two news mgazines of a campaign debate between the incumbent president and his opponent, the challenger:

a. A highlight of the debate came when the challenger outlined his comprehensive program of welfare reform. After delivering a trenchant criticism of the current administration's policies, he indicated in some detail how he would handle the problems of food stamps, housing, unemployment, and medical care. The audience knew what the challenger would do, and could join him when he later repeated and shrewdly thrust the question, "But what are you going to do about this?" when the president discussed these issues. The president apparently had no more to say than that he was aware of the problems.

b. The challenger continued to serve up the same warmed-over liberal fare which has dominated the Democratic party since the time of Franklin Roosevelt. He went on and on about his welfare proposals, and perhaps he may even have convinced some people. He appeared to know something about dealing with welfare problems. But his whole harangue was really an unscrupulous electioneering manifesto. His attacks on the current administration's welfare policies were really a vulgar campaign of personal abuse. The challenger continued this abuse even while the president was speaking with his unmannerly interruptions of "But what are you going to do about that?" The president had to endure this behavior while he was trying to show his sensitivity to the plight of America's underprivileged.

2. a. The flood control measures taken here by the Federal Government, following the disastrous flood in 1936, received their crucial test last night when Callahan Dam broke, spilling 2,000,000 gallons of water into the Joralemon River. Although the flood crest in the downtown section reached within two feet of the all-time high recorded in 1936, little damage was reported. The flood waters were carried safely between the concrete walls built by WPA labor in 1936–38.

b. The city received its worst flood scare since the disaster of 1936 last night when Callahan Dam broke without warning, spilling 2,000,000 gallons of water into the Joralemon River. Although all local emergency relief units were mobilized, their services were not needed. At the height of the flood the waters reached to within two feet of the peak recorded during the 1936 disaster, and engineers for a time expressed anxiety whether the retaining walls, built in 1936–38, could resist the unprecedented pressure. However, the waters receded by 4 A.M. and little damage was reported.[9]

3. a. If one is determined to find a supernatural explanation for the strange goings-on in the old, grand, snowbound hotel in the Rockies, it is just barely possible to do so. But Stanley Kubrick really does not care. His adaptation of *The Shining*, Stephen King's pulpy haunted-house novel, keeps forcing reasonable—or non-occult—interpretations on the behavior, variously bonkers and bloody, that his camera records with its customary elegance. Whether his stylistic mastery and rigorous intelligence will carry this film to commercial success with the bedrock audience for horror—a young crowd that likes its metaphysics murky and its menaces crude—is problematical.—From *Time*, June 2, 1980. Copyright 1980 Time Inc. All rights reserved. Reprinted by permission from TIME.

b. Stanley Kubrick hungers for the ultimate. In *The Shining* he has gone after the ultimate horror movie, something that will make *The Exorcist* look like *Abbott and Costello Meet Beelzebub*. The result is the first epic horror film, a movie that is to other horror movies what his *2001: A Space Odyssey* was to other space movies. In *2001*, Kubrick understood that the point was not all the ravishing technology but its interaction with human beings. In *The Shining*, he understands that the point is not all the supernatural machinery but its effect on human beings. For all its brilliant effects, the strangest and scariest element in *The Shining* is the face of Jack Nicholson undergoing a metamorphosis from affectionate father to murderous demon.—*Newsweek*, May 26, 1980. Copyright 1980, by Newsweek, Inc. All Rights Reserved. Reprinted by permission.

4. a. A very sound moral argument can be made that America is honorbound to assist those patriotic Nicaraguans who are attempting to hold the Sandinistas to the promises they made in 1979 to the O.A.S.: free elections, respect for human rights, political pluralism and a mixed economy—promises cynically flouted in Managua.

But U.S. policy is more than altruistic. Our own national interests are at stake. For the past five years, Nicaragua has undertaken the most massive military buildup in the history of Central America, exceeding even that of Cuba in 1962.

The number of men under arms has grown from 6,000 in 1979 to over 119,000 today. In 1979, Nicaragua had three tanks. Today, it has 100 Soviet medium tanks, over 20 light amphibious tanks and 120 other armored vehicles. And that is just a sampling. The Sandinistas are armed by the Soviets, trained by the Cubans, Libyans and Bulgarians, and animated by the fervor to export their revolution throughout the rest of this hemisphere.

Tomas Borge, the Sandinista Minister of the Interior and chief of the secret police, was asked to respond to President Reagan's expressed concern that after the revolution triumphed in Nicaragua it would be exported to "El Salvador, then Honduras and then Mexico." "That," said Mr. Borge, "is one historical prophecy of Ronald Reagan's that is absolutely true."

As the mother of a draft-age son, I am especially grateful that this Administration favors prophylactic measures, which, if endorsed by the Congress, would make U.S. military engagement in Central America completely unnecessary.—Faith Ryan Whittlesey, *The New York Times*, December 24, 1984. Copyright © 1984 by The New York Times Company. Reprinted by permission.

b. Karen Brudney is a 33-year-old American doctor who has worked for the past year in Nicaragua. Back here on a holiday visit, she talked with me about work and life in Managua. Her experience, described in homely detail, brought the large political abstractions of the debate about U.S. policy into human focus. . . .

"Life is dominated by the war," Dr. Brudney said. "There's not a day goes by that I don't have a patient telling me her son has been mobilized, or a son who's been wounded or killed. It's a constant theme in daily life, you never forget it.

"The contras aim to disrupt, and they do. They go into the villages, and the first thing they do is go for all the things the revolution has built. They go for the clinic, the day-care center, the schools, the grain-storage areas. And the numbers are pretty staggering."

"What numbers?"

"Of dead people. I don't know what the official figures are, but I think 80 or 90 a week are being killed, civilians and soldiers: in a country of 3 million. That means 4,000 to 5,000 a year, in population terms equal to 200,000 to 300,000 in the United States—which is unthinkable.

"It's a war. I don't think Americans know that. For reasons I don't understand our press is not really covering the war in Nicaragua. . . .

"In any case," she said, "the way our Government has chosen to act, through the contras' war, is unforgivable. I am a doctor. I don't have to come up with political solutions. But I know the war has to be stopped."—Anthony Lewis, *The New York Times*, December 24, 1984. Copyright © 1984 by The New York Times Company. Reprinted by permission.

5. a. After hours of skirmishes with police, tensions ran high outside the high school in the "colored" (mixed race) Cape Town suburb of Elsie's River. Bands of youths pelted passing cars with rocks. Then someone threw an unlit gasoline bomb at a truck driven by two white plainclothes policemen. Two other officers in camouflage riot gear suddenly sprang from the rear. Without warning they fired directly into the crowd, wounding six and killing two 15-year-old colored students.—From *Time,* June 9, 1980. Copyright 1980 Time Inc. All rights reserved. Reprinted by permission from TIME.

b. Bernard Fortuin, a 15-year-old of mixed race, was on his way to buy groceries for his mother in Elsies River, a suburb of Cape Town, South Africa, when he saw other colored teen-agers throwing stones at white motorists. Suddenly, one of the cars stopped. Four white policemen jumped out and opened fire with shotguns. Two youths died on the spot, including Bernard Fortuin. When his mother heard the news, she ran to the scene and, hysterical, tried to approach the body of her son. A policeman in camouflaged riot fatigues beat her back with a truncheon, shouting in Afrikaans: *"Luat die donder vrek"* ("Let the bastard die").—*Newsweek,* June 9, 1980. Copyright 1980, by Newsweek, Inc. All Rights Reserved. Reprinted by permission.

§5.2 ADVERTISING AND ITS PLOYS

I think most will agree that a main source, if not *the* main source, of persuasive messages in our lives today is advertising. We are continually being bombarded by claims that we should not only believe but especially do certain things. Now there is nothing wrong *in itself* with attempting to persuade people to buy certain products. Providing information about a product available on the market, telling what is offered, what it does, where to buy it, what the price is, presenting accurate, understandable, and reasonably comprehensive information would be rational advertising. A logical thinker ordinarily should not need to challenge such advertising messages. They would give us reasons, good, plausible, logically convincing reasons why we should buy the product.

But how many of the ads we encounter *should* be challenged? How many ads rationally persuade us to spend our money? Did Will Rogers get it right when he said, "Advertising persuades people to buy things they don't need with money they ain't got"? Don't people generally feel that ads con them into buying products rather than giving them good reasons? If they do, this shows that at least on the level of reason and argument, people aren't fooled by these ads.

But ads do have distinct persuasive force. They *do* persuade people to buy things. Indeed advertisers spend huge sums of money to make their ads persuasive. They employ psychologists to do motivation research to find out just what the audience desires and how to appeal to those desires. There are certain distinct advertising techniques, advertising ploys, which facilitate appealing to those desires. They let the advertiser tell what Samm Sinclair Baker calls "the permissible lie,"[10] the half-truth, of which it has been said: "A half-truth is generally the worst half."[11] Recognizing these techniques should be part of the skills of the logical thinker as challenger. They help us separate the persuasive force of an ad from its informative content. If by doing this, we see that the ad's appeal is quite questionable, we can challenge it. What better way to avoid being conned or duped than to be aware of the techniques for conning and duping? What are these ploys? We shall distinguish seven.

1. Emotional Transfer by Association.

This technique might very well be called the "fundamental principle of advertising." The idea is illustrated in this quote from Dr. Ernest Dichter, an authority on motivation research: "To women, don't sell shoes—sell lovely feet!"[12] Similarly, a Milwaukee advertising executive points out that "The cosmetic manufacturers are not selling lanolin, they are selling hope. . . . We no longer buy oranges, we buy vitality. We do not buy just an auto, we buy prestige."[13] How do ads get us to do this? Many ads sell their products by setting up an association between the product and some situation or person or setting which is very desirable or appealing. Practically the whole persuasive force of the ad lies in transferring these feelings to the product. At one time Maxwell House ran an ad featuring an around-the-world solo sailor. We saw him on his boat, in the midst of a gale, adjusting the rigging, and then going below for—Maxwell House coffee. Topside on the boat we have romance and high drama! When we go below we bring all this to the coffee. Maxwell House is the coffee of bravery, daring do, romantic adventure. The excitement of the adventure, our admiration for the man's bravery, strength, and masculinity all get transferred, by this association, to the coffee. We are asked to feel that by drinking it we too will share in all these wonderful things. Notice that the ad does not—and cannot—say this outright. It would be silly! But the suggestion is there and gives the ad its persuasive force. Do we have any information about the coffee here?

This is only one example. A few moments reflection on the ads we have seen should convince us of the pervasiveness of this technique. What are advertisers doing when they get attractive young females to model jeans, sometimes babbling nonsense in the process? The moment when smoldering old love bursts again into flame—that's the Gallo Chablis moment! How often do we see athletes endorsing all sorts of products? By using those products, we too will share in their strength, youth, glamour. We are to become winners the way they are. This is how the advertisers want us to feel.

Notice that by setting up these associations and making these emotional transfers, ads may make a very persuasive appeal without saying anything about the product or what may make the product better than any competitor. Indeed, there may be no difference between the product and its competitors. Don't most brands of coffee taste the same? What distinguishes one brand of beer from another? Why is one brand of gasoline superior to others? There may be little difference between products. Yet if advertisers can associate some appealing image with one of these competing brands, can construct a "personality" for it, can tie it especially to something which touches deep urges, and do this in a way to make the product "distinctive," they may get sales. They will at least have made the product distinguishable from its competitors, even though the distinction has nothing to do with the product itself. At one time, advertisers for three different brands of gasoline created three different images for these brands. One had an image for bigness, authority. The second was friendly and folksy. The last was pictured as a playboy. As these images appealed to different people, they consistently bought these different brands. Being aware of this technique then may allow us to separate the feelings aroused by an ad from the central question at issue—why should I buy that product? If we do not see why, we should challenge the ad.

     2. Bogus Information. If emotional transfer by association is the fundamental principle of advertising, giving bogus information comes in a close second. But what is this? An ad gives *bogus information* when it appears to be giving significant information and, yet, has practically no information value. It gives us the feeling of being well informed without saying anything. Our feeling well informed is just that—a feeling. For example, we are a scientifically minded society. "Science" has a laudatory emotive meaning, and the procedures of science are viewed with favor. So many ads claim that their products have been tested, scientifically tested, and proven effective. How many ads for patent medicines claim that their products are doctor tested, hospital tested, clinically tested? This is the brand doctors recommend. Patent medicines are not the only thing tested or endorsed by "experts." "Wine connoisseurs" are lined up to testify that this brand is superior. Tests have shown that brand X of low-tar cigarettes has better taste than any other competitors.

     All this sounds impressive, but does it tell us anything? What are those tests which have generated such valuable consumer information? Who are these doctors who have tested the products? How often are they identified? Are they impartial investigators, especially qualified to carry out the tests? And what about the tests themselves? How extensive were they? Would they be regarded as scientifically respectable by competent judges? Who are these wine experts? Are they recognized in the field of wine tasting, or did they become experts when they signed on to do these advertisements for the wine company? Why should we buy a certain brand of wine? Because the experts recommend it. But who are the experts? Those who recommend that wine? That's circular, question begging, fallacious reasoning. A really flagrant example of bogus information is the ad for Trident sugarless gum. "Four out of five dentists surveyed recommend Trident gum for their patients who chew gum." That *sounds* impressive. The statement itself may very well be true. But the more we think about it, the more we look at its details, the less can we be sure that it says anything. A survey, of course, sounds scientific. But how many dentists were surveyed? Maybe there were only five, and the one who didn't recommend Trident was the only one not employed by the company. Do these dentists really recommend Trident, do they think it is a good thing, or do they only grudgingly recommend it as the least of possible gum chewing evils? If you have to chew gum, this is the least harmful. In this light, how much information does the ad give? It is our desire to be scientific which is being manipulated here. These ads would have little power if we did not desire to have expert justification for our actions. "The advertiser reckons upon your not pausing to ask for any evidence that 'they all' swear by the goods offered, nor for evidence of the credentials of 'the expert' who hides so modestly behind the description. The purpose of the whole lay-out of the advertisement is to persuade you that you have been offered reliable evidence, although, in fact, you have not."[14]

Although these advertising claims in the end tell us little, and so are bogus, we can still understand them. Another form of bogus information involves presenting *meaningless* claims, meaningless at least for the average member of the audience. They are meaningless because they contain technical or technical sounding terms. The claim might be informative for someone with special training, but not for the general audience—who is being impressed by this technical-sounding jargon. Why should I eat a certain breakfast cereal, even if it has riboflavin in it? Or what about a product containing activated chlorophyll? What are the virtues of activated chlorophyll over chlorophyll which has been left alone, unactivated? Or is all chlorophyll activated? What is hydrocortizone and how does it aid in making a preparation effective? Who can explain what rack-and-pinion steering is? How big (or small) is a 1.5-liter engine? What is an independent suspension system—and why should it make a new car more desirable? All these words give the impression of expertise and erudition. But using them in advertisements gives people the impression that they have sound scientific reasons for buying the product even when they have no comprehension of those reasons at all.

One particular way in which ads use meaningless terms is by inventing a special name for one of the ingredients in the product, copyrighting the name, and then claiming that its product is unique, because it is the only one with that name. It sounds like it is the only product with that ingredient. In truth, it is the only product whose manufacturers can legally use that name to refer to the ingredient. For example, Colgate claimed that it was the only toothpaste with MFP. Yet MFP was just their special trademark designation for a fluoride ingredient, and many other toothpastes have fluoride.[15] What, of course, MFP is, or what ABC, 47-11, AC-6, or any other such cryptic names mean, the consumer does not know. Their informational value is entirely bogus.

Advertisements with various types of bogus information may have a serious tone, but they do not give us relevant information that we can assimilate to decide properly whether a product is worth buying. Instead of giving us a logically convincing argument, they pander to our image of ourselves as rational, scientific persons. The arguments may leave us with a strong impression or feeling for the superiority of a product, but this is basically just an emotional response. We have been persuaded even to feel that we are rationally persuaded, but we have not been rationally convinced. We have the impression that we have good reasons for buying something, when in fact we have not thought critically about the issue at all.

3. Fallacies.   We could count fallacies as another type of bogus information. However, since we have devoted a whole chapter to the fallacies, we give this type of bogus information a separate heading. Three fallacies especially may occur in advertising: fallacious appeal to authority or glamorous person, bandwagon appeal, and appeal to fear. Ads which feature a famous athlete, movie star, or performer endorsing some product are trying to transfer this person's glamour to the product, and by doing so they are creating a fallacious appeal to authority or glamorous person. These persons rarely will be experts on the products they endorse. They will be making comments completely outside their field. The bandwagon appeal is also very popular. Everyone is doing it, so you should too. People are drinking lighter these days, so stock your home with Cold Springs mineral water. All across the nation, people are switching to the uncola! Last year, 10 million models were sold. All this can be persuasive, especially since it appeals to our desire to conform to general behavior, to our herd instinct. But, as we noted in Chapter 3, in itself this gives us no good reason to prefer these products.

Ads appeal to fear by threatening people with social ostracism, failure in the love life, or embarrassment if they do not use certain soaps, deodorants, mouthwashes, detergents. This is all a way of scaring people into buying certain products. What housewife would not find it embarrassing to have some one proclaiming loudly, "Ring around the collar! Ring around the collar!" when seeing shirts she has just laundered? Who wouldn't be anxious that people might be gossiping behind his back if he didn't use Right Guard or Ban? A particularly flagrant example here occurs in ads for home computers, suggesting that children may fail in school unless they have a personal computer at home. The question is whether these fears are legitimate and whether the products advertised will do anything to help the consumer avoid these anxiety-laden situations. Studying the informal fallacies is an excellent way of being innoculated against advertising and propaganda in general. The fallacies are easily recognizable persuasive techniques. "Once we know that a speaker or a writer is using one of these propaganda devices in an attempt to convince us of an idea, we can separate the device from the idea and see what the idea amounts to on its own merits."[16]

4. Slanting by Selection.   Recall from Section 5.1 that in slanting by selection, certain facts are prominently featured, while others are downplayed or omitted. How does this provide an advertising ploy? We can all remember ads which tell us good things about their products (or at least appear to). But how many tell us about the product's faults? We sometimes see ads for luxurious resorts. Do we hear about the rates? They may be as stunning as the resort! Or what about auto ads which feature in banner headlines how powerful or sexy the car is yet bury the price in small print? An ad may truly state that a certain product was safest when compared with three leading brands. It doesn't say that five other leading brands were safer. Nor does it say the three leading brands were only insignificantly behind in safety but were distinctly ahead in being efficient and economical. "The advertiser accents the one hazy positive, bypassing completely the significant negatives."[17] In a way, this is what we should expect. Advertisers are interested parties. They want to make a sale. Consequently, they do not want to say anything in an ad which would dissuade the consumer from buying.

What about ads for state lotteries? They may picture many happy people who have won all sorts of money. But do they tell us the odds of winning a million dollars? Do they tell us the odds of winning anything? Where can we find out this information? Do the ads create the impression that the chances of winning are good?[18] What about those ads which present testimonials from average, ordinary product users who allegedly have used the product and been satisfied with it? Even assuming that what they say is true, are they representative of all the people who have used the product? Or if 3 testify, were they the only 3 who liked it, the fact that the other 9,997 found it worthless being omitted?

Slanting by selection may also create a misleading impression of a product's uniqueness. For example, some feature in the composition or manufacturing process may be prominently mentioned, say, a certain wine is aged in special wooden casks. Now this may be perfectly true. But then again, many other wines may be aged in similar wooden casks and that information is suppressed. The suggestion that the feature is unique to the brand is false. And our feeling, brought about by this slanting by selection, that the wine is uniquely satisfying, is totally groundless.

Notice that telling us just the good features of a product and not the bad may say nothing false explicitly. But suppressing the bad may certainly create a misleading impression. And this misleading impression may lead us to *feel* that the product is especially desirable when in fact it is not. And, of course, this feeling can be very persuasive.

5. Emotive Words.   We do not have to spend very much time to find many advertisements bestrewn with words arousing admiration, interest, excitement, desire. Here is a list taken from just three ads in one weekly news magazine: "state of the art," "incredible," "blazing," "total automation," "rugged," "spectacular," "ultimate," "exact," "authentic," "flawless," "mirror-smooth."

Frequently, it is hard to see what literal meaning these emotive words have, and so to assess what information claim the ad is making. What does it mean to say that our product is "superior"? Superior to what? "Our product is the ultimate"—what is that supposed to mean? "New," "improved,"—we hear these two words practically all the time. They arouse feelings of admiration and approval, but what do they mean? The literal meaning of "different" is also very unclear. Advertisers want you to confuse it with "better." But clearly a product can be different from its competitors without being any better.[19] Clearly these words are being used not for their literal meaning, but for their emotive impact. They make us feel that the product is great without giving us any reasons.

6. Slogans.   Sometimes ads may include short phrases or statements, which may be repeated again and again in various settings, always claiming to tell us something about the product. These are slogans.

Extra value is what you get, when you buy Coronet.

Chock-Full-of-Nuts is that heavenly coffee—heavenlier coffee a millionaire's money can't buy.

It's a Sealy Posturepedic morning!

You can be sure, if it's Westinghouse.

Prudential has the strength of Gibraltar.

Although slogans may appear to make informative claims, they give little information. And if they do make informative claims, they do not lead us to investigate the data on which those claims were based, but rather to just accept them. Their primary purpose is to sway us emotionally, and not to convince us logically. They tend to cut off logical thinking rather than stimulate it. The advantage of slogans is that they involve an easily repeated, catchy, and so easily remembered phrase. And if the phrase can be easily remembered, so can the product. By repeating slogans *ad nauseam,* advertisers hammer the product into the audience's consciousness.

7. Exaggeration or Outright Falsehood.   Ordinarily advertising does not tell outright lies. All the techniques discussed so far illustrate how advertising can be highly persuasive without being explicitly false. Indeed, how can we accuse an ad of being false when, informatively, it says practically nothing? Yet, on occasion ads may exaggerate or present outright falsehoods, and this should lead us to be critical, if not downright skeptical, about advertising claims. For example, one electric razor company once advertised that its shaver was so gentle that it could shave a peach. When the FCC tested this, investigators found the shaver tore the peach skin to shreds. Listerine for years claimed that its mouthwash prevented colds by killing germs. Yet there was no solid evidence to support this.

At least in the United States, if an ad makes claims which are outright false, the FCC can demand a retraction, and this is publicly embarrassing. If you gain a reputation for spreading falsehoods, you ruin your credibility. To create a misleading impression is different from saying something out-and-out false, and is a far subtler and safer way to proceed. It's far better to remain in the realm of the "permissible lie." We should not, then, be overly hasty in charging an ad with exaggeration or outright falsehood. For when we do, the burden of proof is on us to say why the ad is exaggerated or false. It is incumbent on us to present evidence supporting why the ad overstates its case or makes false claims. If we cannot produce this evidence, if we do not have it ready at hand, we should be hesitant about saying that the ad is exaggerated or false.

Studying these seven advertising techniques should not only give us insight into how advertising works, but also show how we can cultivate a critical, skeptical attitude toward advertisements. As we said before, recognizing these techniques helps us to separate the persuasive force of an advertising message from any informative content. Doing so, we may find that the ad just claims we should buy something without giving us any credible justification. Here the claim is open to challenge. Recognizing these advertising ploys, then, is a useful skill in playing the role of logical thinker as challenger.

Exercise 5-III

Here is a list of the seven advertising techniques discussed in this section:

emotional transfer by association   emotive words
bogus information   slogans
fallacies   exaggeration or outright falsehood
slanting by selection

For each of the following ads, identify as many of these techniques being used as you can, and be prepared to discuss why.

1. CURB THAT APPETITE WITH SWEETS
Recent clinical studies have shown that when you eat a small amount of sugar, your appetite is suppressed. Eating candy can actually be a way to control weight! Star Confections makes its candy in scientifically sized pieces so that one nibble gives you just the right amount of sugar to control your craving. Try Star Candies for the SCIENTIFIC NIBBLE.

2. CALIFORNIA BATHROOMS—THE ULTIMATE
Ultimate in style. Our bathroom fixtures define the standard of elegance in the trade. Expert designers have crafted unique combinations of color and contour co-ordinations to satisfy the most discriminating buyer.
Ultimate in luxury. What does a bathing experience in one of our tubs promise? Our exclusive water reconditioners guarantee that you are surrounded by a tingling smooth medium. Our energizers deliver 156 HPZ for uplifting sensations. Our solarizer surrounds your body in undulating pulsations of light.
Ultimate in every way.

3. STOPS FALLING HAIR
My hair came out in patches and I was totally bald in spots. I used two bottles of Essence of Youth Oil. You can see my hair now! It not only stopped my hair from falling out but grew new hair in the bald areas.
ESSENCE OF YOUTH OIL—Used by Thousands.[20]

4. PINE WOOD KNOLLS

At Pine Wood Knolls, you can forget about outside chores. Summer or winter, it's all taken care of for you. So you can enjoy the pool, tennis courts, golf course, jogging trails, and our own private clubhouse.

Our houses are full of outstanding features—cathedral ceilinged living rooms, fireplaces, designer kitchens, complete laundry, state of the art appliances, spacious bedrooms, skylights, the most modern bathrooms.

Pine Wood Knolls offers you the life you want.

5. COME ON OVER TO LAWRENCEBURG, INDIANA, and BUY AT TRI-STATE DISCOUNT LIQUORS

Our prices are 25 percent lower than those offered in Ohio and Kentucky.

FACT: According to Hamilton County, Ohio, Judge Robert Blackmore, it is illegal to carry purchased liquors across state lines.[21]

6. VANGUARD LAUNDRY DETERGENT—FOR THE CLEANEST WASH EVER

Vanguard really gets your clothes clean. That's because Vanguard has an exclusive combination of cleaning agents. First our heavy duty chemical agent DIRTBUSTER with hexachlorinol attacks heavy dirt and stains. Then our general cleaning agent with pentapure dissolves anything making dirt adhere to your clothes. Finally our finishing agent with tridure rinses everything away and leaves your clothes looking fresh and soft.

7. MEGAPOWER BATTERIES—CHARGED UP FOR ENERGY

8. No Medical Evidence
or Scientific Endorsement
Has Proved Any Other Cigarette
To Be Superior to KENT

9. THE LEADER IN SEDAN MPG

With 52 MPG, it's no wonder that all across America people are buying Dorval.

And with such features as a 1.5 litre engine, rack and pinion steering, and a scientifically designed, computer-crafted body construction, Dorval is truly a high tech car.

10.   LASERCAR RATED
BEST
IN GAS MILEAGE

(*In a company sponsored test. Actual mileage will vary with speed and driving conditions.)

11. At DayStar Oil, we believe we can develop new energy sources and respect the environment, too. We did not begin to build our offshore oil wells in the Gulf of Mexico until marine biologists had certified that our construction would preserve and even enhance the ecology of marine life. It's true that our coal-shale mines in Colorado will be productive for at most fourty years. But we shall not leave the land wasted and scarred when mining is no longer profitable.

Our plan is already in place to restore the contour of the land and reforest it. We've even taken care to preserve the remains of the region's prehistoric cave dwellers.

DayStar Oil—committed to environmental integrity.

12. *Illya Darling* rests on the premise that Melina Mercouri is irresistible. Even if one accepts this unlikely premise, this is a tasteless, heavy-handed show beyond anyone's capacity to bring to life.—Edwin Newman, Critic for NBC.

Edwin Newman says "Melina is irresistible."—Advertisement for *Illya Darling*.[22]

13. LOSE ANY ITEM FROM OUR FABULOUS 56-PIECE SET AND GET A REPLACEMENT FREE

Just send $1.00 to cover postage and handling to P.O. Box XYZ, New York, New York.

FACT: The price of the entire set is $19.95. Are you being led down the garden path?

14. The old homestead—a white farmhouse on a country road—the swing on the front lawn—the smell of grandma's apple pie in the kitchen— GRANDMA HARRIS'S APPLE PIE

15. SOUTHERN ISLES—The Vacation of a Lifetime

16. Revlon Ultima II non-makeup makeup . . . transparesscent . . . souf-fléd texture . . . spins out a complexion like a sweep of silk . . . sweeps across your cheeks like an unexpected compliment . . . as though this were not makeup at all but something fed to you on a silver spoon.[23]

17. Doctor tested Hypermedrol Cough Syrup—the cough medicine with two special ingredients to stop your cough fast and keep your cough away. A laryngotolator goes directly to your throat and chest to smooth irritated tissues. A cerebellator relaxes the cough center in your brain. One teaspoon in the morning and you can forget your cough for the rest of the day. One teaspoon at bedtime for a sound night's rest.

18. Prunes help bring color to your blood and glow to your face. When you feel good, good things happen to you. So start eating prunes today till you have energy to spare.[24]

19. SILENTIUM with dextromethorphan is the cough medicine most doctors recommend.

20. Mr. Clayton's direction [referred to earlier as "photographic fidgets"] is somewhat mechanical, too, tumbling his drama in a confusion of jump cuts and fleeting images. The cutting style is distracting, but some striking effects are achieved."—Bosley Crowther, *The New York Times*.

"STRIKING EFFECTS! . . . . . Bosley Crowther, *N.Y. Times*."—Advertisement in *The New York Times*.[25]

21. "TransAfrica Airlines offered me the best meal I have ever had on an airline."—P.D.

"The attendants were friendly and helpful; the food was really great;

and the movie was outstanding. TransAfrica Airlines did a great job on this flight."—Q.B.

"I've flown many times before; finding seats this wide and roomy in coach was a real surprise."—H.J.

You've heard our passengers.

Fly TransAfrica for a great trip!

22.   SO EXCLUSIVE . . . IT MUST BE PAOLETTI
The opulence . . . the unparalleled
workmanship . . . a combination only
Paoletti can achieve.
   Upholstery so superb, each piece is a
veritable work of art. Fabrics so beautiful,
you simply will not find their equal anywhere.
Workmanship unsurpassed, accomplished by
master craftsmen in Paoletti's own workrooms.
The result: upholstered furniture uniquely
yours, and exclusively Paoletti.
PAOLETTI—DISTINCTIVE FURNITURE

23.   Kids and Winter—Snow, sleds, skates, skis, snowball fights. What fun they're having! What a treasury of memories they're building! You remember your childhood, and the appetite you built up on those cold days. There's nothing like a good, hot bowl of Mrs. MacGregor's Soup—steaming with all the flavors you used to know—for when the kids come in. Beef Barley, Tomato Vegetable, Chicken Noodle. Give them the soup you used to know. What could be finer?

24.   JOHNNY'S FAILING!

What parent wants to hear that? Your youngster seemed to be doing fine in school—right up there with the best. But then he seemed to be falling behind, not able to keep up. He seemed discouraged, left out. His friends seemed to know something he didn't. And now Johnny's teacher has called you in for the real shocker.

What's the problem? Could it be that you don't have a personal computer in your home while other parents do? Educational experts agree a PC can be a big help in educational achievement and DeltaSys makes the PC educators prefer most. Don't let Johnny fall behind. Give him the edge he needs to compete.

A MESSAGE FROM DELTASYS.

25.   APEX MEANS TOTAL ENTERTAINMENT

With an APEX 10-11 Omega Home Entertainment Center you've got it all!

First there's a truly sophisticated, 26″ digital, stereo ready, color TV monitor. With such high-tech features as our gamma filter system, computer-controlled equalizer, and a fully programmable scanner, this truly state of the art unit is cable ready for 200 channels.

Next, there's a complete stereo rack system. The AM/FM stereo receiver has a built-in synthesizer. Delivering 50 watts per channel, distortion is at −.075 MST, fully correctable for varying recording curves. Add our Maxima S−1000 speaker systems, a PC−780 digital tracking turntable, and an AST−87 analog convertible Cassette Deck.

Last but not least, there's the fully programmable LS−10,000VCR, with HT−noise reduction filter, advanced tape drive, and internal memory.

With such high-powered, high-tech, high performance features, the APEX 10−11 Omega system is simply unmatched.

FOR FURTHER READING

Monroe C. Beardsley's *Thinking Straight: Principles of Reasoning for Readers & Writers,* 4th ed. (Englewood Cliffs, N.J.: Prentice-Hall, Inc., 1975), Sects. 13 and 14, presents a sensitive discussion of certain expressive and persuasive resources of language, relating them to slanting. Howard Kahane's discussion of statistics in *Logic and Contemporary Rhetoric,* 3rd ed. (Belmont, Calif.: Wadsworth Publishing Company, 1980), ch. 5 illustrates how slanting by selection and association may be used to present misleading statistical statements. In ch. 9, Kahane turns specifically to the news media, discussing how bias and slanting occur there. In *The Art of Straight Thinking* (New York: D. Appleton-Century Co., 1929), pp. 283 ff., Edwin Leavitt Clarke presents a number of factors leading to newspaper bias, misrepresentation, and slanting. The section, "On Reading Newspapers," in Richard D. Altick, *Preface to Critical Reading* (New York: Henry Holt and Company, 1946), also discusses these issues, considering especially factors which may cause slanting.

Ralph H. Johnson and J. Anthony Blair's *Logical Self-Defense* (Toronto, Canada: McGraw-Hill Ryerson, 1977) contains a very useful, informative, and entertaining chapter on advertising (ch. 10, "Advertising: Games You Can Play"). Included are a number of suggestions for viewing ads critically and formulating critical questions about what ads claim. Kahane's *Logic and Contemporary Rhetoric* also contains a chapter specifically on advertising. Samm Sinclair Baker's *The Permissible Lie: The Inside Truth About Advertising* (New York: The World Publishing Company, 1968) presents a hard-hitting and frequently very humorous exposé of advertising deception. How propaganda and advertising seek to manipulate through appealing to deep needs, anxieties, fears, and emotions is discussed in Vance Packard's *The Hidden Persuaders* (New York: David McKay Company, Inc., 1957).

NOTES

[1]Chicago Commission on Race Relations, *The Negro* [sic] *in Chicago* (Chicago: The University of Chicago Press, 1922), pp. 531–32. Quoted in Edwin Leavitt Clarke, *The Art of Straight Thinking* (New York: D. Appleton-Century Co., 1929), pp. 283–84.

[2]These headlines, along with much additional material documenting how the New York *Post* and *Chicago Daily Tribune* handled the Nixon and Stevenson fund stories, appear in Arthur Edward Rowse, *Slanted News: A Case Study of the Nixon and Stevenson Fund Stories* (Westport, Conn.: Greenwood Press, Publishers, 1957), pp. 45–47 and pp. 71–73. In this book, Mr. Rowse compares and contrasts accounts in thirty-one newspapers across the United States to assess slanting.

[3]Rowse, *Slanted News,* p. 8.

[4]Monroe C. Beardsley calls this slanting by distortion. See *Thinking Straight: Principles of Reasoning for Readers & Writers,* 4th ed. (Englewood Cliffs, N.J.: Prentice-Hall, Inc., 1975), p. 175.

[5]This example is adapted from material in Thomas Merton's *Conjectures of a Guilty Bystander* (Garden City, N.Y.: Image Books, 1968), p. 236.

[6]Clarke, *The Art of Straight Thinking,* pp. 319–20.

[7]Ibid., p. 323.

[8]Quoted in Leonard Broom and Philip Selznick, *Sociology: A Text with Adapted Readings,* 3rd ed. (New York: Harper & Row, Publishers, 1963), pp. 292–94, "from the Kentucky Edition of *American Issue,* April 1912, the national organ of the Anti-Saloon League."

[9]These contrasting examples appear in Richard D. Altick, *Preface to Critical Reading* (New York: Henry Holt and Company, 1946), p. 292.

[10]Samm Sinclair Baker, *The Permissible Lie: The Inside Truth About Advertising* (New York: The World Publishing Company, 1968), p. 5.

[11]Ibid., p. 14.

[12]Quoted in Vance Packard, *The Hidden Persuaders* (New York: David McKay Company, Inc., 1957), p. 32.

[13]Quoted in ibid., p. 8.

[14]L. Susan Stebbing, *Thinking to Some Purpose* (Harmondsworth, England: Penguin Books, 1939), pp. 82–83.

[15]Compare Ralph H. Johnson and J. Anthony Blair, *Logical Self-Defense* (Toronto, Canada: McGraw-Hill Ryerson, 1977), p. 224.

[16]Broom and Selznick, *Sociology,* p. 287, commenting on propaganda techniques in general.

[17]Baker, *The Permissible Lie,* p. 127. Both the quote and the example discussed occur here.

[18]For details of how Lotto Canada could be charged with deceptive advertising on these grounds, see Alex C. Michalos, "Advertising: Its Logic, Ethics and Economics," in J. Anthony Blair and Ralph H. Johnson, eds., *Informal Logic: The First International Symposium* (Inverness, Calif.: Edgepress, 1980), pp. 95–100.

[19]Compare Johnson and Blair, *Logical Self-Defense,* p. 223.

[20]Adapted from Frederick E. Lumley's *The Propaganda Menace* (New York: The Century Co., 1933), p. 142.

[21]Adapted from J. Michael Sproule, *Argument: Language and Its Influence* (New York: McGraw-Hill Book Company, 1980), p. 279.

[22]A statement to this effect appeared in a full page ad in *The New York Times.* See Baker, *The Permissible Lie,* p. 39.

[23]Ibid., p. 50.

[24]Adapted from Packard, *The Hidden Persuaders,* p. 139.

[25]Baker, *The Permissible Lie,* p. 40.

PART II Argument: Analysis and Evaluation

6

ARGUMENT STRUCTURE

In Part I, our central concern has been with the logical thinker as challenger. It is now time to give the challenger specific tools to use in the most logically important activity of challenging arguments. One central question sums up our inquiry: How can we tell whether an argument is logically convincing? In Chapter 1, we spelled out the three conditions an argument must satisfy to be logically convincing: the premises must be true or well warranted—based on the facts; they must be relevant to the conclusion; and they must give it adequate support. In Chapter 2 we discussed examining arguments for false or questionable premises. In Chapter 8, we turn our attention to argument strength and in Chapter 9 to the question of relevance. These three chapters, then, spell out a basic method of argument evaluation, one we can apply in assessing the merits of any argument.

Although our central concern is now with argument evaluation, we do not lose sight of the challenger role. We in effect will be playing this role when we probe arguments for weaknesses. We shall be using this role even more. Before we evaluate an argument for strength or relevance, we should ask: How does the argument hang together? This introduces the concept of argument structure, which we develop in this chapter and the next. How can the challenger role help us to appreciate argument structure? Consider, there is something very concrete in imagining two persons discussing some issue, one challenging the other. I expect we all have participated in such dialogues. Argument structure is somewhat abstract. Hence, if we can motivate it by relating it to this basic concrete exchange, the whole subject will be more comprehensible.

How can we do this? Let's imagine two people discussing some issue. One wants to defend a certain position. The other is concerned not with defending an opposing view, or with knocking down the first person's claim, but with drawing out the argument for it, helping the first person develop the best argument he or she can. The challenges then will be positive challenges, intended to maintain discussion, continue the dialogue, rather than to cut it off. They are intended to help the respondent think logically. Just by asking "Why should I believe it," our challenger has called for argument. Suppose the respondent has given a reason. The challenger could ask all sorts of questions at this point. But four are especially revealing for argument structure:

     (I) Can you give me another reason?
    (II) How do you know that reason is true?
   (III) Why is that reason relevant to supporting your claim?
   (IV) Given your reason, how confident should I be of your claim?

We call these the four *basic dialectical questions*. Each question generates a different argument structure.

    Given an argument with a certain structure, we can imagine the respondent offering its premises when the challenger has asked certain of these questions. This should make the whole subject of argument structure more concrete. Notice that (I) and (II) are really special versions of the challenge—Why should I believe that? Accordingly, we study them together in Section 6.1. We turn to (III) and (IV) in Sections 6.2 and 6.3, respectively. In Section 6.4 we see how these various structures may occur together in a single argument. But what do we mean by the way an argument hangs together, by argument structure? Let's proceed directly to Section 6.1.

§6.1 THREE TYPES OF ARGUMENT STRUCTURE: CONVERGENT, SERIAL, DIVERGENT

Notice that if our respondent were content just to assert his claim and our challenger never asked for a reason, never asked why she should believe it, we would have no argument. But should the respondent accept the challenge and give one single reason, we would have an argument—and the structurally simplest type of argument possible: one premise, one conclusion. Any argument must have at least these two elements.

    Let's begin our analysis of argument structure with such simple arguments. This will enable us to introduce the basic features of structural analysis without worrying about complications at this point. Even at this basic level, there can be differences in argument structure.

    Consider the following two arguments:

I. (1) Mary did not leave the porch light on when she went out last night. Therefore
   (2) It was very dark when she returned.

II. (1) Art will give up eating peanut butter, because
   (2) He has just discovered that he is allergic to peanuts.

Can you see the structural difference here? Argument I states the premise first, then the conclusion. Argument II gives the conclusion first and then the premise. This illustrates the two possible different structures arguments with just two statements may have. We represent the structures as shown in Figure 6.1. We call these representations *tree diagrams* or *circle and arrow diagrams*. The information they give should be clear. In I, statement (1) is shown to support statement (2). In II, statement (2) supports statement (1). These two diagrams already illustrate some important features of the tree method. First, component statements of arguments are always represented by encircled numbers, the numbers reflecting the order in which the statements appear in the argument. Logical support is represented by downward-directed arrows, and arrows are always written in a downward direction. Since the premise supports the conclusion, we use the direction of the arrow to picture the direction of logical support. At the conclusion of this section, we shall see why we also need to write our arrows pointing downward.

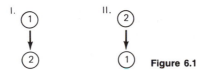

Figure 6.1

Diagrams I and II exhaust all the possibilities for arguments containing exactly two component statements. The situation becomes much more interesting when an argument involves three or more statements. Our respondent's presenting one premise to support his conclusion may leave our challenger unsatisfied. The reason may be all right as far as it goes, but it is not sufficient to convince her. She wants more justification, more support before she will accept the claim. That's why she asks the first basic dialectical question: Can you give me another reason? Let's look at some concrete exchanges where this might arise. Here R stands for respondent, C for challenger:

R: Jones is certainly the best person to run for president next year.
C: Why?
R: She has consistently shown herself very competent in administrative positions.

But should this be enough for C? Asked for another reason, R might respond

R: Jones has more experience than any of her competitors.

Here is another example:

R: We should not develop star wars–type technology to defend ourselves against Soviet missiles.
C: Why shouldn't we?
R: It is only a matter of time before the Russians develop further weapons to knock out our laser beams, particle beams, and other defenses.
C: All right, but can you give me another reason?
R: Such technological development will divert funds needed for social programs.

In both these cases, R has given an additional, different, independent reason for his original claim. Of course, we can imagine that C might still not be satisfied. Two reasons might not be enough. Perhaps in some cases, C will demand a certain number of independent reasons right off. Give me three good reasons why I should vote for Jones!

   Before proceeding further, we should make perfectly plain what we mean by two reasons for a conclusion being independent of each other. Consider the two reasons R has given C for supporting Jones: consistent competence and most experience. Notice that each of these reasons, by itself, gives some justification for R's original claim that Jones is the best person to run for president. They may not by themselves be totally convincing, taken together they may make a stronger case for R's claim than if taken separately, but each by itself is obviously relevant and obviously gives *some* justification for R's claim. Even before R tells us that Jones has the most experience or even if that should prove false, we can see that R has given some justification for his claim. And the situation would be parallel, if R had said first that Jones had the most experience of all the competitors and *then* told C of her consistent competence. When several premises present distinct, separately relevant evidence, we say they are *independent*.

   How should we diagram R's argument here? Since two different independent reasons are given for one conclusion, we represent the structure as shown in Figure 6.2. Since our premises in a sense converge to support one and the same conclusion, we say that this argument has *convergent* argument structure. As we mentioned, someone presenting a claim could be asked to give three good reasons for it. Clearly he could be asked for more or might give more. As long as they were all independent reasons supporting one conclusion, we would

Figure 6.2

have an argument with convergent structure. Convergent arguments can have any number of premises. Now consider the following argument:

(1) Our 40,000 GIs stationed in South Korea support a corrupt regime.

(2) The savings in dollars which would result from their coming home could make a sizable dent in the projected federal deficit. Furthermore

(3) The Korean conflict ended 30 years ago. Hence

(4) It is time we brought our troops home.—E.B. (adapted), *Sunday Star-Ledger* (Newark, N.J.), March 13, 1983.

Here again, we have convergent argument structure, but the conclusion is stated last. The diagram looks like that in Figure 6.3.

Figure 6.3

Theoretically, the conclusion of a convergent argument, indeed of any argument, may come at any place in the passage, although the beginning and the end are preferred positions. We need to keep these points in mind, so as not to fall into a habit of thinking that the first statement of an argument is its conclusion or that a convergent argument has only two premises, from looking at examples with these features. We correctly recognize the structure of a convergent argument when we identify the premises and the conclusion, and see that the premises give independent support to the conclusion. Our diagram then represents the actual support structure in the argument. Notice how the logical indicators, "furthermore" and "hence," in this argument, help us identify premises and conclusion, along with the fact that (1), (2), and (3) do intuitively present evidence for (4). We cannot stress enough the importance of recognizing logical indicators, premise indicators, and conclusion indicators, in properly analyzing the structure of arguments. These, together with our intuitive sense of what supports what, are the keys to disclosing logical structure.

Let's go back to the star wars discussion. When R responds to C's initial challenge by saying that American weapons technology would soon be matched by the Russians, C could be dissatisfied with that answer. Is it obviously true? She could again challenge R, demanding justification for this premise. Here she is asking the second basic dialectical question: How do you know that reason is true? Notice that here C is not asking for another independent reason for R's original claim. Rather, she is questioning R's response, demanding that he justify this response in turn. R must respond, then, not with an additional reason for his first claim, but with a reason for his second statement. How might he respond?

R: All the star wars technology is as readily available to the Russians as it is to us.

This, surely, should give some justification for why the Russians would soon develop weapons to knock out our superdefenses.

Numbering R's assertions (1), (2), (3) in the order he has presented them under C's prompting, we may display the structure of his argument in Figu. 6.4. Notice that when diagrammed, the component statements in this argument line up in a series. This motivates saying that the argument has a *serial* argument structure. Also notice that statement (2) is both a premise and a conclusion. The diagram brings this out clearly. Statement (2) supports (1) and is thus a premise, but in turn is supported by (3) and so is a conclusion. Statement (1) is the final conclusion or the point of the whole argument. Only (3) is purely a premise.

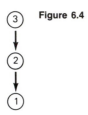

Figure 6.4

In the foregoing argument, the main conclusion was stated first and each statement was supported by the following statement. Many serial arguments will have exactly the opposite order.

(1) Mr. Nearthewind's closest friend is Mr. Closerstill. Hence

(2) Nearthewind knows all the current public opinion. Therefore

(3) He is the best man to answer that question.—Charles L. Stevenson, *Ethics and Language* (adapted).

Here the conclusion indicators readily let us see the structure (see Figure 6.5).

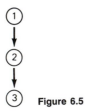

Figure 6.5

Although all serial arguments must have at least three statements, we can certainly have serial arguments with more than three or even four components. Any finite number is possible. What is necessary is that all the statements line up in a row or series. Each premise in the argument up above the one directly supporting the final conclusion could be an answer to the second dialectical question.

Both of the examples so far are well ordered, "logically ordered," we could say, since the order in which the component statements are presented mirrors the order of logical support. But this need not always happen. The component statements may also be scrambled, although this may not be good rhetorically.

(1) Alice's psychoanalyst could not help with her problem, because
(2) She dislikes talking about such things and so
(3) She did not tell him about it.

The diagram is given in Figure 6.6.

Figure 6.6

Again, we see that the structure is serial. But we must pay special attention to the logical indicators to determine what supports what. The order in which the statements were presented does not straightforwardly reflect the order of logical support. Clearly there are many more ways that the component statements of a serial argument may be scrambled.

One question may be nagging you here (or may begin to nag and confuse you as you work on the exercises). Consider the second example again. Does statement (1) also support statement (3)? If so, should the diagram be amended to look like Figure 6.7?

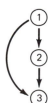

Figure 6.7

Such a change is unnecessary. To use a technical term, logical support is *transitive*. If (1) supports (2) and (2) supports (3), then (1) supports (3). When we represent the support (1) gives to (2) and (2) gives to (3), we have already, automatically represented the fact that (1) supports (3) and no further arrow is necessary. So in each of these examples, all the reasons given support the final conclusion, and our diagrams are sufficient to show this. The *notion* of transitivity, although perhaps not the term, should already be familiar. The relation of identity is transitive. If a = b and b = c, then a = c. To say that a = b and b = c implies that a = c.

To introduce the third type of argument structure, consider the following exchange:

R: The motel business will be very bad this summer.
C: Why do you say that?
R: With the current recession, people cannot afford expensive vacations.
C: OK.
R: We may also expect sales of camping equipment to rise this spring and summer.
C: Why is that?
R: For the same reason: with the current recession people cannot afford expensive vacations.

What is going on here? R is justifying two *different* claims on the basis of one premise about the current economic situation. Numbering R's statements (1), (2), (3) again in order, (2) is given as a reason for both (1) and (3), although (1) is not a reason for (3), nor is (3) a reason for (1). The structure of the argument is represented in Figure 6.8.

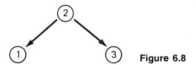

Figure 6.8

Since two distinct conclusions are drawn from one premise, we may say that the premise or the argument diverges to those two conclusions. Hence we call this type of structure *divergent* argument structure. Again, as with convergent and serial structures, a divergent argument may have more than three component statements. As long as one premise is used to support several conclusions, none of which support each other, we have divergent argument structure. Also, the premise may be stated first, last, or, as here, between two of the conclusions it is used to support.

Unlike convergent and serial argument structures, divergent structure is not motivated by a basic dialectical question. However, it is motivated by a dialectical exchange. We can think of the challenger asking, for each conclusion, why she should believe it, and the respondent answering each time by giving the same premise. Since, as we pointed out, the first two basic dialectical questions are really special versions of the challenge—Why should I believe that?—it is appropriate to consider all three structures together in this section.

I. convergent

II. divergent

Figure 6.9

We can now explain why we require the arrows in an argument diagram to be always pointing downward. Contrast the diagrams in Figure 6.9 for convergent and divergent arguments.

Here not only the direction of the arrows, but the total configuration of each diagram serves to display the difference in logical support between these two argument structures. We can see in the first that two premises converge on one conclusion, while in the other one premise diverges to two conclusions. But suppose we made no restrictions on the direction of arrows. Then we might write II as shown in Figure 6.10.

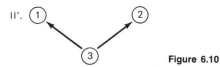

Figure 6.10

Although the heads of the arrows show that (3) supports (1) and (2), II′ looks confusingly like I. Why couldn't we say here that two conclusions converge on one premise? Similarly, if we wrote I as shown in Figure 6.11, then we would have a diagram looking confusingly like II. By requiring that the arrows be written in a downward direction, we avoid these problems and are able clearly to distinguish convergent from divergent arguments.

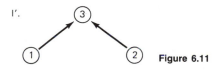

Figure 6.11

Summary

In this section we have introduced three types of argument structure, convergent, serial, and divergent. For convenience, we illustrate these structures again (see Figure 6.12).

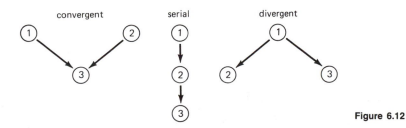

Figure 6.12

In a *convergent argument,* two (or more) premises independently support a conclusion. By saying that two premises give independent evidence or independent support for a conclusion, we mean that we may recognize separately that each is intended to support the conclusion, without having to take the other into account. In a *serial argument,* one statement supports another, that a third, and so on until we reach the final conclusion in the argument. The statements form one series. In a *divergent argument,* at least two different conclusions are drawn from the same premise.

Exercise 6-I

Show the structure of each of the following arguments by means of a tree diagram. Label the diagram as being either convergent, serial, or divergent.[1]

Sample Answer

(1) The reason the Navy is finding it tough to hang onto its pilots is strictly economic:

(2) An experienced pilot can earn up to four times his military pay by becoming a commercial airline pilot. As a result,

(3) The Navy's pilots are peeling off at an alarming rate to pursue the more lucrative careers offered by commercial aviation.—Jack Anderson, March 22, 1981. Reprinted by permission of United Feature Syndicate, Inc. (See Figure 6.13.)

This is not a straightforward example. "As a result" is a conclusion indicator, showing here that (2) supports (3). The colon after "economic" suggests that a reason for (1) is coming. Certainly (3) (and (2)) presents evidence for (1). Hence (2) supports (3) and (3) supports (1).

Figure 6.13

I. (1) The one-third of U.S. passengers who smoke on airplanes are subjecting two-thirds of us to discomfort—sometimes acute—and

(2) They are putting our lives at risk. Therefore

(3) It is time federal regulators put a stop to this outrage.—Carl T. Rowan, June 12, 1983. © by and permission of News America Syndicate.

II. (1) The president was elected largely by voters who are fed up with high taxes and federal interference in their lives. Therefore

       (2) They can be expected to bring pressure on Congress to help him keep his campaign promise to "get the government off our backs." From this we may conclude that

       (3) Few modern presidents should be in a more advantageous position to attack governmental waste, fraud and mismanagement.—Jack Anderson, January 11, 1981. Reprinted by permission of United Feature Syndicate, Inc.

III. (1) Most of the registered voters in this district do vote in the general election. From this it follows that

       (2) It is very important that you make a good impression on them and

       (3) You remind them of your running mates on the ticket.

IV. (1) Smoking should be banned not just on long flights but on short flights too, because

       (2) It only takes minutes for smoke to cause great misery to persons acutely sensitive to it, and furthermore

       (3) CAB policy ought to be based on the point that it is a lot easier for a passenger to endure an hour without smoking than it is for a person with serious allergies to endure an hour of breathing someone else's acrid puffs.—Carl T. Rowan, June 12, 1983. © by and permission of News America Syndicate.

V. (1) Since Croesus attacked Cyrus,

       (2) A mighty kingdom was lost. From this it follows that

       (3) Croesus was very angry with the Oracle of Delphi.

VI. (1) Croesus was very angry with the Oracle of Delphi. Why?

       (2) A mighty kingdom was lost because

       (3) Croesus attacked Cyrus.

VII. (1) Two weeks ago, Ronald Reagan was a hero.

       (2) He had won wide support for his spending cuts,

       (3) [He had] stirred a rebellion among Southern Democrats and

       (4) [He had] driven his budget to victory even in the Democratic House.—*The New York Times,* editorial, May 24, 1981. Copyright © 1981 by The New York Times Company. Reprinted by permission.

VIII. (1) The withholding law on interest and dividends will force those who would otherwise under-report (or not report) income from these sources to declare such income and pay taxes on it. Consequently

       (2) The government will reap an additional $8 billion in revenue, and

       (3) The "little guy" will be happy.—T.M., *Sunday Star-Ledger* (Newark, N.J.), March 20, 1983.

IX. (1) Since if this measure is enacted, investors will lose the interest on these monies,

       (2) The ultimate consequence will be a decrease in total savings as funds are diverted into other assets. Therefore

       (3) The bill will reduce capital available for economic growth.—T.M., *Sunday Star-Ledger* (Newark, N.J.), March 20, 1983.

X. (1) Senate Bill 597 specifically says, "It shall be the duty of both spouses to support the family and both shall be liable for 1) responsible and necessary medical and dental services rendered to either spouse or their minor children; 2) the cost of any dwelling unit . . . and 3) any article purchased by either spouse for the reasonable and necessary support of the family." Hence

(2) This bill imposes on the mother and homemaker the financial obligation to pay for that home and all the expenses. It follows that

(3) The bill will undermine her independence and will force her to go into the job market to meet her obligations. Therefore

(4) The bill will obliterate the traditional family that has made this and other nations strong. We may conclude that

(5) Senate Bill 597 will have serious social consequences and should not be treated lightly.—R.M., *Sunday Star-Ledger* (Newark, N.J.), March 20, 1983.

XI. (1) Since a holocaust is a wholly prospective rather than a present calamity,

(2) The act of thinking about it is voluntary, and

(3) The choice of not thinking about it is always available.—Jonathan Schell, *The Fate of the Earth.* © 1982. Published by Alfred A. Knopf, Inc.

XII. (1) The airlines won't hire a pilot who's over 30, so

(2) The service pilots [i.e., those in the armed forces] can't afford to stay on much past 28. Result:

(3) One hitch and they're gone, leaving the taxpayers stuck with their training bill and the recruiters trying to hire replacements—who will presumably start the whole cycle over again.—Jack Anderson, March 22, 1981. Reprinted by permission of United Feature Syndicate, Inc.

XIII. (1) Our moral solidarity [with Poland] is so important now. [Therefore]

(2) We must let the Polish people know that we will respect their decision [on how to respond to the imposition of martial law], whether it be sullen patience or outright defiance;

(3) that we will give their quislings no unrestricted aid; and

(4) that if events reach the stage where Marshall Kulikov and his invaders take personal control, our reaction will be to launch an all-out economic and political crusade to make continued oppression in Poland too great a burden for the Communist world.—William Safire, *The New York Times,* December 20, 1981. Copyright © 1981 by The New York Times Company. Reprinted by permission.

XIV. (1) The [presidential] commission was set up in the emotional aftermath of the hostages' return to decide whether the Government should pay financial compensation to them, or make such payments to possible future hostages. It finds that benefits they receive under existing laws are more than generous.

(2) Those laws, including one passed last year specifically to benefit the

hostages, made sure they were paid their full salaries while in captivity—and exempt from income tax.

(3) The Government will pay their Iran-related medical expenses and college expenses incurred by their families while they were in captivity.

(4) Former hostages may also claim up to $40,000 for property losses in Iran.—*The New York Times,* editorial, September 25, 1981. Copyright © 1981 by The New York Times Company. Reprinted by permission.

XV. (1) The president's reelection is assured. We may infer this from the fact that

(2) He is the incumbent,

(3) His foreign policy has been successful, and

(4) In a crisis, Americans do not change leadership.

XVI. (1) We are all, in one way or another, . . . customers [of the sex industry].

(2) Sex sells more jeans than "marital aids."

(3) [It sells] more slick magazines than porno comics.

(4) [Sex sells] more TV shows than X-rated movies.

(5) The pursuit of better sex even has a Federal benediction: sex counseling can be a medical tax deduction.—*The New York Times,* editorial, February 15, 1981. Copyright © 1981 by The New York Times Company. Reprinted by permission.

XVII. (1) Many authorities warn of worldwide fuel shortages.

(2) The U.S. government has been urging fuel conservation.

(3) Even oil exporting countries are begging that consumers conserve fuel. Hence

(4) It looks like the days of plentiful oil and gas are over.

XVIII. (1) Not only all artificial satellites currently orbiting the earth but

(2) All interplanetary space vehicles launched from this planet will eventually crash back to its surface, since

(3) All that goes up must come down.

XIX. (1) No one afraid that the sky will fall on him is rational. From this it follows that

(2) All those afraid that the sky will fall on them are irrational. Hence

(3) Some irrational people are afraid that the sky will fall on them. We may conclude that

(4) Some people afraid that the sky will fall on them are not rational.

XX. (1) Because ultraviolet radiation breaks down DNA, which regulates reproduction, and because

(2) It also represses photosynthesis, which is the chief metabolic process of plants,

(3) The direct effect of increased ultraviolet radiation on plant life is likely to be widespread and serious.—Jonathan Schell, *The Fate of the Earth.* © 1982. Published by Alfred A. Knopf, Inc.

§6.2 A FOURTH TYPE OF ARGUMENT STRUCTURE—LINKED

R: Sam should get rid of that old jalopy he is driving.
C: Why do you say that?
R: It uses too much gas.
C: How do you know it uses too much gas?
R: It is a 1968 model car.

C could find this argument unconvincing. To see why R's claim that Sam's car is a 1968 model is relevant to his claim that it uses too much gas, we have to know that cars built during that period were not fuel efficient, or comparatively, were less fuel efficient than were cars built later. Without that information, R's second reason would seem irrelevant to his claim about gas use and so would seem quite puzzling and inappropriate. Hence, we can imagine C challenging R again, here with the *third* dialectical question:

Why is that relevant?—What does being a 1968 car have to do with gas use?

R might respond:

Cars made around 1968 are far less fuel efficient than later models.

How does this premise function? It functions to explain why being a 1968 model car is relevant to using too much gas. It does not so much provide new evidence for the conclusion as explain why certain evidence already given is relevant to that conclusion. We call such premises *warrants*. That is, a premise is a warrant or functions as a warrant just when it serves to explain why some other premise is relevant to the conclusion it is claimed to support.

Notice here that the data and warrant, that Sam's car is a 1968 model and such models are not fuel efficient are *not* independent reasons. It is not true that either one, by itself, gives some justification for the claim of excessive gas use. If all we knew was that Sam had a 1968 car, and nothing about the connection of that feature with excessive gas use, we would not see why that fact supported the claim. Likewise, if we knew that 1968 cars were not fuel efficient, but we did *not* know that Sam had a 1968 car, we would similarly be puzzled about the relevance of that response to the claim of excessive gas use. But put these two responses together, and we see that R has given us a good, or at least a plausible, reason for his claim.

What does all this have to do with argument diagramming? Since the evidence-premise and the warrant-premise are not independent reasons, both have to be taken together. The two in effect jointly constitute one reason for the claim. In other words, they must be linked to support the claim. Arguments involving such premises have *linked* argument structure. Let's restate R's argument this way:

(1) Sam's car uses too much gas since

(2) It is a 1968 model car and

(3) Such cars are far less fuel efficient than later models.

We represent its structure by the diagram in Figure 6.14.

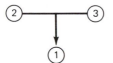

Figure 6.14

This diagram represents the logical situation that statements (2) and (3) must be taken together to constitute a reason for (1). Here is another example:

(1) If the economy continues to recover, then the current administration will be reelected. Now

(2) The economy will continue to recover. Hence

(3) The current administration will be reelected.

Notice that here the conclusion is stated last, rather than first. Statement (2) presents data to justify (3), while premise (1) constitutes a warrant, explaining why (2) is relevant to (3). Again in this argument, neither (1) nor (2) by itself justifies (3). Rather, together they constitute a joint reason for (3) (see Figure 6.15).

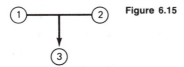

Figure 6.15

We should emphasize specifically what these diagrams say and do not say. Notice that there is no arrowhead at either end of the horizontal line connecting the linked premises. Logical support, the premise/conclusion relationship is represented in our diagrams by arrows from premise to conclusion. Since the horizontal line is in no way an arrow, it in no way says that either of the linked statements supports the other. Any sense that the diagram says or suggests this should be resisted. In the last example, premise (1) does not support premise (2) nor does premise (2) support premise (1). (Ask yourself: Does either give evidence for the other?) The lack of any arrow going from (1) to (2) or from (2) to (1) shows that neither supports the other. The horizontal line connecting (1) and (2) shows that both are taken together to get a proper reason for the conclusion (3).

Would an argument presenting just (2) to support (3) have some plausibility? It would if we were aware of some connection between the economy's continuing to recover and the current administration's being reelected, that is, if we were aware of (1). This raises an important point in argument analysis. Frequently arguments may be presented with warrants left unstated. Some warrant may be assumed in the reasoning, may actually enter into the argument, but especially if it seems obvious, may not be stated manifestly. The arguer may be confident that the relevance of the evidence to the conclusion is understood and need not be made explicit. If we recognize that a warrant is suppressed, how should we diagram the argument?

Here we must introduce another important distinction, that between the *manifest* and the *developed structure* of an argument. We display the manifest structure when we produce a tree diagram showing how just those elements actually presented in the argument hang together. Hence the diagram in Figure 6.16 adequately represents the *manifest* structure of the argument from just (2) to (3). The point is that even when we sense that some other unstated information is used as a premise, when to see why a premise is relevant to a conclusion, some other information is needed, when diagramming just the manifest structure, we are justified in drawing an arrow from one statement to another if the first is intended as a premise for the second.

Figure 6.16

When we make implicit premises explicit, we develop the argument. The tree diagram then pictures the developed structure. We may do this to get a clearer understanding of the reasoning or to target a problem in the argument. Is the implicit premise a dubious assumption? To answer that question properly, we must make the warrant explicit and display where it fits into the reasoning. This opens up the thorny problem of supplying suppressed premises, intimately connected with evaluating arguments for relevance. Hence, we postpone further discussion of these issues until Chapter 9. For now, when we ask for argument structure, we ask just for the manifest structure.

Sometimes when we link two premises, it may seem that they mutually explain why each other is relevant to the conclusion. Consider the following argument, familiar perhaps for thousands of years to beginning students of logic:

(1) All Greeks are humans.
(2) All humans are mortal. Therefore
(3) All Greeks are mortal.

The structure is shown clearly in Figure 6.15.

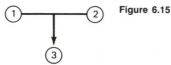

Figure 6.15

Here instead of one premise giving some data and the other explaining why it is relevant to the conclusion, doesn't each premise explain the relevance of the other? Imagine that someone had no idea of the connection between being human and being mortal. Then asserting that all Greeks are humans would seem to give little reason for why they are all mortal. We need (2) to establish the relevance of (1) to (3). Similarly, if someone had no idea of the connection between being Greek and being human, saying that all humans are mortal would be a mystifying justification for (3). Statement (1) then explains the relevance of (2) to (3). So we must be prepared for the possibility of two warrant-type premises in arguments.

Are there times when we need to link together premises just giving data, where no premise apparently functions as a warrant? This is also possible.

(1) John smoked two packs of cigarettes a day since he was fifteen. He ate a diet rich in fatty foods and never exercised.

(2) Sam, John's brother, does exactly the same things.

(3) John died at age fifty-two of a heart attack. Hence we may expect that

(4) Sam will die prematurely of a heart attack also.

To see why the data in each premise are relevant to establishing this conclusion that Sam will die prematurely of a heart attack, we have to consult the information in the other premises. We must take all these data together, to understand their relevance to the conclusion. If all we knew was that John smoked two packs of cigarettes a day since he was fifteen, why should we conclude that *Sam* will die prematurely? Even if we had the other information about Sam's life-style, we could ask why this was relevant to the conclusion. We must link together the information about the similarities between John and Sam and the fact that John died at age fifty-two, to see *why* we have a reason for our claim about Sam's mortality.

Not only does our argument show that just data may be linked together to establish a conclusion, it also shows that linked arguments may have more than two premises. To link together three premises, we diagram the argument as in Figure 6.17.

Figure 6.17

Linked structure can be frequently confused with convergent or serial structure. We should, then, review the differences between arguments which have these structures, and how we can determine which structure an argument has. If an argument has convergent structure, the premises independently give support to the conclusion. To see why a premise is relevant to the conclusion, we do not look to the other manifestly stated premises. They do not provide an explanation as to why the premise is relevant. If the manifest structure of an argument is linked, the reason why a certain premise is relevant to the conclusion is offered in another explicitly stated premise or premises. In determining whether two premises should be linked or whether they converge on a conclusion, the following question should be helpful.

> If we knew that just one of the premises were true, and had no knowledge of the other, would we see why that premise was relevant to the conclusion?
> If we blocked the other premise completely out of our mind, would we see why the first still gave a reason for the conclusion?

If the answer is yes, then the premises are convergent. If no, then they are linked.

There is also frequent confusion as to whether an argument has linked or serial structure. In a way, this is very understandable. If one statement supports another, they are in a sense linked. But the sense is not that represented in linked argument structure. To see how we can distinguish these two structures, contrast the following serial argument with the Greeks/human/mortal argument on page 176:

(1) Sawatski is the front runner. Therefore

(2) We may expect her to win the nomination next year. Hence we may expect that

(3) She has a very good chance of becoming our next president.

The structure of this argument can be seen in Figure 6.5.

Figure 6.5

Now our diagram clearly shows that both (1) and (2) support (3). But they are not linked. How do we determine that the argument has this structure? Clearly the conclusion indicator "therefore" between (1) and (2) gives a clear signal that (1) is a reason for (2). Statements (1) and (2) are not two separate, unjustified statements linked to support (3). If one statement logically supports another, gives a reason for another, we should not link them together in our diagram, but draw an arrow from the support statement down to the supported statement.

The case is quite different for the argument on page 176. Here there is no logical indicator between (1) and (2). Nor, intuitively, is there any logical support either way. Does "All Greeks are humans" give a reason for saying that "All humans are mortal," or vice versa? The answer is clearly no, and so serial structure is inappropriate. The first statement does not logically support the second, nor does the second statement logically support the first, although the two together guarantee that "All Greeks are mortal" is true. Notice that even though there may be a natural flow from the first premise to the second in this argument, that the first may lead into the second quite naturally, or that it seems "logical" to follow the first premise by the second, this does not indicate logical *support*. Logical support occurs when one statement gives a reason or is claimed to give a reason for another statement. Don't be misled by these other functions.

Hence serial structure may be distinguished from linked structure in the following way:

> If one statement gives a reason for another, even if the latter statement gives a reason for a third or the two support a third, the first logically supports the second, we should draw a downward-directed arrow from the first to the second, and the structure is serial, not linked. If, however, one statement does not give a reason for the second, nor the second for the first, but the two together support a third, then we have linked argument structure.

Notice that in the system of diagrams we have developed, horizontal lines are introduced to link *premises only*. They are *never* introduced between conclusions. Such a diagram is here meaningless. Premises are linked to support conclusions. If we ever have reason to link a conclusion with another statement, it is because the two of them are used as premises to support some further statement. We emphasize this point, because there is a temptation, in diagramming divergent arguments, to draw a horizontal line between the two conclusions supported by some one premise. There is a feeling that some further connection between the conclusions must be shown. But all the connection necessary to show has already been shown. The same premise supports several conclusions and the diagram displays that fact. A further connecting line is unnecessary, given our methods of diagramming divergent arguments, and confusing.

Summary

In a linked argument, a conclusion is drawn from two (or more) premises taken together. By saying that several premises are taken together to support a conclusion, we mean that each one, strictly by itself, seems irrelevant to the conclusion. However, when the premises are taken together, we have a relevant and significant reason for the conclusion. Typically, when two premises are linked together, the structure of the argument is represented in Figure 6.15.

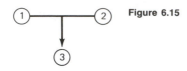

Figure 6.15

Exercise 6-II

Show the structure of each of the following arguments by means of a tree diagram. Label the argument as being either linked, convergent, serial, or divergent.

Sample Answer

(1) Voluntary decisions about death presuppose freedom of choice.

(2) Freedom of choice presupposes the absence of freedom—limiting constraints.

(3) Such constraints almost always are present in cases of the terminally ill. Therefore

(4) Terminally ill patients cannot make a voluntary decision about death. (Refer to Figure 6.17, adding the label "LINKED.")

Figure 6.17

  I. (1) All houses are costly.
     (2) All costly things are protected by insurance. From this it follows that
     (3) All houses are protected by insurance.
 II. (1) The son of Supreme Court Justice William J. Brennan, Jr. has been and continues to represent Great Adventure.
     (2) Our newest U.S. Supreme Court appointee, Sandra Day O'Connor, was told that she could not hear any cases involving her husband's law firm. Therefore
     (3) Justice Brennan should not be allowed to decide a case involving Great Adventure.—B.H., *Sunday Star-Ledger* (Newark, N.J.), November 1, 1981.
III. (1) Some animals are brown, since
     (2) All cows are animals and
     (3) Some cows are brown.
 IV. (1) Harold has just enrolled at the state university. So
     (2) Helen should enroll there shortly, since
     (3) If Harold does one thing, Helen is soon to follow.

V. (1) If the current crisis is not resolved soon, then the Soviet Union will intervene.
   (2) If the Soviet Union intervenes, then the United States will suspend all trade relations with the Soviet Union. But
   (3) If the United States suspends all trade relations with the Soviet Union, then American business will be hurt. Therefore
   (4) If the current crisis is not resolved soon, American business will be hurt.

VI. (1) This Administration's foreign policy involves CIA plans for a covert assault on an African country. This suggests that
   (2) The United States is heading for more and deeper troubles in Africa, because
   (3) This policy is based on dangerously insensitive assumptions.—Carl T. Rowan, August 2, 1981. © by and permission of News America Syndicate.

VII. (1) The Planning Commission scheduled the hearing on the Fox Hill apartment complex for 2:00 P.M. Wednesday.
   (2) Most residents of Fox Hill work from nine to five, Mondays through Fridays. It looks like
   (3) The Planning Commission does not want the residents of Fox Hill at the hearing.

VIII. (1) All logicians are mental cases. From this it follows that
   (2) Bertrand Russell is a mental case and
   (3) So also is Gottlob Frege.

IX. (1) After being convicted of six brutal slayings, DB was sentenced to life in prison.
   (2) Upon conviction of killing his girlfriend, RT was put to death. This should show that
   (3) The punishment RT received was unfair.

X. (1) Three hundred and fifty years ago the Catholic hierarchy condemned Galileo for his claim that the earth revolves around the sun.
   (2) We are confronted today with statements by the American Catholic hierarchy indicating that military service and/or massive retaliation is immoral or at least morally questionable.
   (3) The Catholic hierarchy in the Vatican has recently belatedly admitted that its judgment in the Galileo case was wrong. Hence
   (4) If the judgment of the American Catholic hierarchy on military involvement is wrong, they may take a long time to admit it.—C.M.H., *Sunday Star-Ledger* (Newark, N.J.), May 22, 1983.

XI. (1) In regular private construction work, there never are such ridiculous cost overruns of 50 per cent of the contract bid price, as there have been on this Justice Office building complex. But
   (2) Private construction and public construction are still basically the same thing—construction work. Therefore

(3) It should not be up to the taxpayer to pay for the 50 per cent cost overrun.—W.S., *Sunday Star-Ledger* (Newark, N.J.), May 22, 1983.

XII. (1) When I went to the nearest Unemployment Compensation office in Harrison, located about three miles from my home in North Arlington, the clerk informed me that because I resided in Bergen County, she could not take my claim; rather I would have to file in either Bloomfield or Passaic.

(2) I called the Bloomfield office. I was told that they did not process claims from North Arlington; Hackensack (Bergen County) would be the appropriate place.

(3) Four days after I filled out the required forms at the Hackensack office, I received a phone call from them that I had filed at the wrong office, and that I should apply at the Passaic Office.

(4) In Passaic I went through the same routine. A week later, I received a telephone call from the Passaic UC office. "Mr. J.," the caller said sternly, "you have already opened up a claim in Hackensack. Are you trying to collect twice? Besides, we don't handle North Arlington claims. You are supposed to file in Newark." Based on these experiences,

(5) I do not think that the personnel in these offices are well informed. —H.J., *Sunday Star-Ledger* (Newark, N.J.), January 3, 1982.

XIII. (1) Ten soldiers were sick with a fever.

(2) On the same day, the doctor prescribed the same medicine for all ten soldiers.

(3) Nine of the soldiers took their medicine.

(4) Jackson did not.

(5) On the following day, all nine soldiers who took their medicine had died.

(6) Jackson was still alive. Hence it looks like

(7) The doctor's medicine did in the nine soldiers.

XIV. (1) La Petite Coloumb has the best chef in town.

(2) The live entertainment there is outstanding.

(3) The menu is also quite varied. Thus

(4) We should go there for dinner.

XV. (1) "Detention benefits" . . . were established in 1948 for World War II veterans who had been locked up in enemy prison camps. In 1948, the benefit was $2.50 for each day in prison.

(2) Vietnam P.O.W.'s, too, received these benefits at an inflation-adjusted rate of $5 per day.

(3) For the hostages in Iran the commission adjusted the figure again, to $12.50. . . . So

(4) The $12.50 figure is not capricious or stingy.—*The New York Times*, editorial, September 25, 1981. Copyright © 1981 by The New York Times Company. Reprinted by permission.

§6.3 MODALITIES

Our discussion so far may have left you with a question or misgiving. Let's look again at our argument about Jones being the best candidate to run for president.

(1) Jones is certainly the best person to run for president next year, because

(2) She has consistently shown herself competent in administrative positions and

(3) She has more experience than any of her competitors.

We diagrammed this argument in Figure 6.2.

Figure 6.2

But the conclusion claims that Jones is *certainly* the best candidate. Does either reason (2) or (3) separately, by itself, establish that? Don't we have to take (2) and (3) together (and perhaps add in further information) to see why Jones is *certainly* the best candidate? That is, to represent the structure of this argument adequately, shouldn't the premises be linked?

There is something right about this objection, which we need to incorporate into our account of argument structure, but not by linking the premises.

Suppose the word "certainly" were left out of the conclusion (1). Suppose we were just arguing that

(1') Jones is the best person to run for president next year.

Then the temptation to link (2) and (3) would certainly be lessened. If we replaced "best" by "good" in (1'), arguing that

(1″) Jones is a good person to run for president next year.

our desire to link (2) and (3) should be completely gone. But what does this show? It shows that we can appreciate why (2) and (3) are independently relevant to establishing (1). Taking each by itself we can understand why it contributes something to establishing the conclusion. But linked structure was introduced to represent argument situations where two or more premises were *not* independently relevant to establishing the conclusion, but had to be taken together to see why we had a relevant reason.

Seeing that (2) and (3) are independently relevant to establishing (1) should convince us that the linkage we may feel is necessary is not required on relevance grounds. The problem is not that we cannot see how (2) and (3) independently support (1), but we doubt that each by itself has the power or weight to establish that Jones is certainly the best candidate. The problem is with the word "certainly"—what does that word do? It indicates how confident the arguer is of the conclusion, given the premises. In short, it answers the fourth basic dialectical question: Given your reasons, how confident should I be of your claim? It serves to itself make a claim about how strongly the premises support the conclusion.

Our respondent R could have been more modest in this claim. He might have said that

(1)   Jones is *most likely* the best person to run   or

(1′)   It is *likely* that Jones is the best person to run   or

(1″)   Jones is *probably* the best person to run   or

(1‴)   Jones is *presumably* the best person to run.

The words "presumably," "probably," "likely," "most likely," and such expressions as "necessarily," "a sure thing," "cinch," "evidently," all serve as "certainly" to express a level of confidence in the conclusion, given the evidence for it. We call these expressions *modalities.*

As we have just seen, the amount of confidence expressed can vary. To anticipate for a moment our discussion in Section 8.1 of Chapter 8, modalities such as "necessarily" and "must" make the strongest claim possible, if intended literally. "Cambridge is north of London, so it must be that London is south of Cambridge." Here "must" claims that since the premise is true, the conclusion has to be true also. There is no hedging here. This is the deductive claim, as we shall develop in Chapter 8, and we may call these modalities deductive modalities. Similarly, "certainly," "consequently," "surely," "implies," "entails," "proves," if not always making such a strong claim, can be used to make it. They are very strong modalities. They indicate a high degree of confidence. "Presumably," "probably," "likely," "suggests," and "supports" claim that we should accept the conclusion, given the evidence, but the degree of confidence is not so high. We are not claiming that the premises guarantee the truth of the conclusion, but only that they give significant evidence for it. These modalities, and indeed any which make a weaker than deductive claim, are called inductive modalities. Again, we shall develop the significance of this in Chapter 8. For now, where our main focus is on argument diagramming, the important point to remember is that a modality makes a claim about how strongly the premises support the conclusion, about how weighty is their evidence for it.

Since a modality indicates how confident we may be of a statement, given the evidence, or how strongly the premises support the conclusion, the modality is not properly part of the conclusion. So in our argument about Jones, the conclusion is really not (1), that Jones is certainly the best person to run next year, but (1′) that Jones is the best person to run. "Certainly" is the modality. Just as conclusion indicators are not parts of the conclusion but serve to introduce conclusions, to indicate that statements are conclusions, and premise indicators are not part of the premises, but serve to introduce premises, signaling that certain statements function as premises, so modalities are not part of the conclusions, but serve to indicate the amount of support the argument claims its premises give the conclusion.

Grammatically, modalities frequently are adverbs or adverbial phrases. Hence our linguistic habits tend to place them within the conclusion of an argument, modifying the verb. Therefore we have to resist the force of natural English to count the modality as part of the conclusion itself. Rather, as we have done, we need to paraphrase our conclusion to get the modality "out," where it belongs, where it more obviously describes how strongly the premises support the conclusion. Consider another example:

(1) The only tracks leading away from the house were a man's.
(2) Joanne and Franklin were the only two people at the house. Hence
(3) The tracks must have been Franklin's.

Doesn't "must" here describe how strongly (1) and (2) support (3)? To make its role plainer, we should paraphrase the last sentence to read

Hence it must be that (3) the tracks were Franklin's.

One other caution is necessary with modalities. Just because they may frequently be expressed by adverbs does not mean that every adverb expresses a modality. "Happily," "freely," "quickly," and "pleasantly" are all adverbs. But could we use them to make a claim about how strongly the premises support the conclusion?

(1) John heard the dinner bell ring. So
(2) He ran quickly to the dining hall.

In this argument, does "quickly" serve to indicate how strongly (1) supports (2)? Clearly not. We have to think about what modalities mean to judge properly whether an expression is a modality.

How can identifying modalities help us in structurally analyzing arguments? Since a modality makes a claim about how strongly the premises together support the conclusion, about the force of their combined weight, when we may have several independently relevant premises converging on a conclusion, explicitly including the modality in the argument diagram would allow representing that cumulatively such premises support the conclusion to a certain degree. Representing the modality allows us to represent modal "linkage" in addition to and in contrast with relevance linkage. What we need then is a way of structurally representing modalities and then connecting the modality with the premises and conclusion.

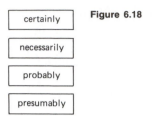

Figure 6.18

In our diagrams, we shall represent a modality by writing it out and enclosing it in a box. Thus, the entries in Figure 6.18 all represent modalities. Since a modality claims that the premises support the conclusion to a certain degree, in the diagram the modality will be placed between the premises and the conclusion. The downward-directed arrows from the premises will be "interrupted" by the box. That is, there will be a solid line from each of the reasons to the modality box, and there will be a downward-directed arrow from the box to the conclusion. Hence we represent our argument about Jones by the diagram in Figure 6.19.

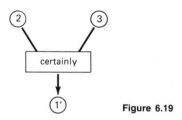

Figure 6.19

Here is another example:

(1) In the winter of 1979, the government of Cambodia, one of the most repressive regimes in the world, collapsed.

(2) In February 1979, the Shah of Iran's regime, which he had maintained with torture and repression, ended.

(3) Idi Amin's dictatorship was in a desperate position by the spring of 1979.

(4) Clearly, government by oppression will not work.

The structure is shown in Figure 6.20. Here (4) is the statement, "Government by oppression will not work." We do not regard "clearly" as part of (4).

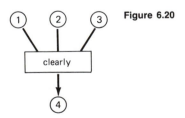

Figure 6.20

We cannot stress how central is the concept of modality in logically appraising arguments. To be logically convincing, the premises of an argument must support the conclusion with adequate weight. That means we must be justified in using a modality at least as strong as "presumably." All things being equal, the stronger the argument, the more weight the premises give in supporting the conclusion, the better the argument. This means that the stronger the modality we are justified in using, the more logically convincing the argument. When given an argument, we as challengers can ask two questions:

(1) How strong a modality is justified to describe the weight of evidence the premises give for the conclusion?

(2) If the arguer himself or herself has supplied a modality, is that modality justified?

Answering these questions is at the core of logically evaluating arguments. We begin developing what this means in Chapter 8. We make these remarks here to stress the importance of the concept. We introduce modalities at this point to highlight that they are a separate element in arguments and to contrast relevance linkage with modal "linkage" for proper argument diagramming.

Summary

Modalities indicate the strength of support which arguments claim their premises give to their conclusions. Modalities claim that given the premises, we may repose our confidence in the conclusion to a certain degree. In argument diagrams, modalities are represented by modal words enclosed in a box, interposed between the arrows connecting a premise or premises and the conclusion they support.

Exercise 6-III

Construct tree diagrams to represent the structure of each of the following arguments, explicitly displaying the modality in each by the box method described in this section.

Sample Answer

(1) Congress is very angry with the president over his sponsoring covert operations in Third World countries.

(2) Many moral leaders have criticized this action.

(3) Many Americans see these activities as reckless adventurism. Hence it is quite likely that

(4) The president's popularity will decline (see Figure 6.21).

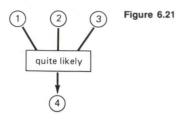

Figure 6.21

I. (1) In twenty-five years of marriage, John and Patty have never exchanged an unkind word. Presumably,
   (2) They have a stable and happy marriage.

II. (1) Jim is Andy's uncle. So necessarily
   (2) Andy is Jim's nephew.

III. (1) Last night, Harry came home yelling and cursing.
   (2) He was red in the face.
   (3) He even smashed his fist through the window. Hence we can be pretty sure that
   (4) Harry was mad about something.

IV. (1) The witness remained calm and cool under cross-examination. Evidently,
   (2) He was telling the truth.

V. (1) La Petite Coloumb has the best chef in town.
   (2) The live entertainment there is outstanding.
   (3) The menu is also quite varied. Certainly
   (4) That would be a good place to go for dinner.

VI. (1) Congress may, in fact, object [to dismantling the Department of Energy and assigning its tasks to other departments, mainly Commerce].
   (2) Senate conservatives are unhappy about assigning nuclear weapons production to Commerce.
   (3) House Democrats see dismemberment as a partisan slap.—*The New York Times,* editorial, December 21, 1981. Copyright © 1981 by The New York Times Company. Reprinted by permission.

VII. (1) Some change [in offshore development policy] is clearly desirable.
   (2) The cumbersome regulatory process has resulted in needless delay and duplication of environmental studies.—*The New York Times,* editorial, July 25, 1981. Copyright © 1981 by the New York Times Company. Reprinted by permission.

VIII. (1) Con Ed failed to identify and correct the root cause of numerous leaks which eventually led to the flooding at the Indian Point nuclear plant last October.
   (2) It coped poorly with the flooding once it occurred, and
   (3) It failed to report the accident promptly to regulatory authorities. Clearly
   (4) The blame for the accident lies primarily on Con Ed's management. —Nuclear Regulatory Commission investigation as presented in a

New York Times editorial, December 14, 1980. Copyright © 1980 by The New York Times Company. Reprinted by permission.

IX. (1) A substantial majority of the nation's gun victims are felled by relatives or friends, not by criminals, often in the heat of anger or passion, using readily available handguns.

   (2) If a gun were not so handy, it is possible a less deadly weapon would suffice to release the momentary surge of aggression.—*Sunday Star-Ledger* (Newark, N.J.), editorial, April 5, 1981.

X. Presumably
   (1) It is well not to seek to have as many friends as possible, but as many as are enough for the purpose of living together; for
   (2) It would seem actually impossible to be a great friend to many people.—Aristotle, *Nicomachean Ethics.*

§6.4 ARGUMENTS WITH MIXED STRUCTURE

We have at this point studied convergent, serial, divergent, and linked argument structure and have considered how modalities could indicate how strongly one or several premises support a conclusion. These are basic concepts of argument analysis. But now a very important question arises: Does every argument have just one of these basic structures? Could an argument display both linked and divergent structure, for example, or convergent and serial? Could we have a number of premises linked together and a modality claiming how strongly that one reason, or that together with the weight of several other reasons, support the conclusion? You may already have asked such questions. The answer in all cases is yes. We can have arguments with mixed structure, and we must recognize this to diagram the structure of arguments correctly. To try to see exactly one of the four basic structures as *the* unique structure of any argument we might encounter is a distinct mistake. How do we diagram arguments with mixed structure? That is the issue in this section.

   To motivate the notion of mixing the basic types of argument structure, recall that at the very beginning of Section 6.1, we examined arguments with the very simplest possible structure. There was exactly one premise, exactly one conclusion, and the structure is given in Figure 6.22.

Figure 6.22

   Now notice that each of the three argument structures discussed in Section 6.1 can be generated from this basic structure given certain conditions. The two arguments shown in Figure 6.23 both display this basic structure. But

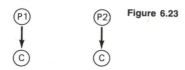

Figure 6.23

the conclusions are the same statement. Hence we can think of pushing these two arguments together over their shared component (see Figure 6.24).

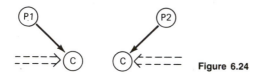

Figure 6.24

The result when we are finished, when the two representations of (C) coincide, is a combination of the diagrams that displays convergent argument structure (see Figure 6.25).

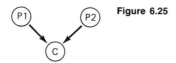

Figure 6.25

We can similarly generate serial or divergent argument structures. Consider two arguments with simple structure where the conclusion of one is the premise of the other. Combine these two diagrams, letting the common statement coincide. We have serial structure. Again consider two simple arguments where the premise is the same in each. Combining their diagrams, we get divergent argument structure.

Clearly, if arguments with more complex structure share some statement, we should be able to combine them, producing a yet more complex argument with more complex structure. Here is a concrete example:

(1) Since you cannot learn logic unless you make a significant effort and
(2) Alfred never makes much of an effort, it follows that
(3) Alfred will not do well in logic. This means both that
(4) His overall grade point average will suffer and
(5) He will be disgruntled with the professor.

The structure of this argument is given in Figure 6.26.

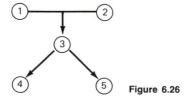

Figure 6.26

Now the configuration (Figure 6.27) displays linked structure, while Figure 6.28 displays divergent structure. The conclusion of I, statement (3), is the premise of II. As the diagram displays, this argument has a mixed structure, combining both the linked and divergent structures. We could say that the structure is linked/divergent. We might even say we have serial/linked/divergent structure here, for (1) and (2) are combined to provide one reason for (3) and (3) in turn supports (4)—here we have a series—and (3) again supports (5), producing another series. Each series differs from plain serial structure since the first reason consists of two statements linked rather than one individual statement.

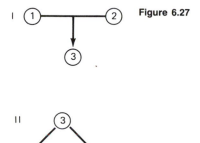

Figure 6.27

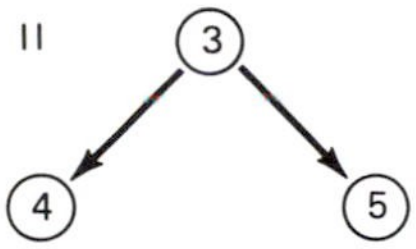

Figure 6.28

Since all these ways of looking at this structure are justified, we need not prefer one way above the others in describing this combination. In general, although it is important that we be able to distinguish convergent, serial, divergent, and linked arguments displaying exactly one of these structures, labeling combinations of these structures is relatively unimportant.

Obviously we can imagine how a number of premises can converge on a conclusion, which in turn serves as a premise for one or more further conclusions (see Figure 6.29). Or we can imagine a straight serial argument diverging at some point to several conclusions (see Figure 6.30). Or an intermediate conclusion in a serial argument may be supported by several independent premises (see Figure 6.31).

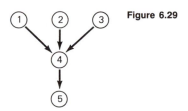

Figure 6.29

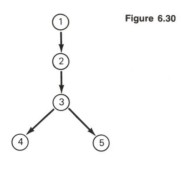

Figure 6.30

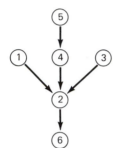

Figure 6.31

But our mixture of structures can go far beyond this. For example, a conclusion of one argument might be linked together with some further statement (or statements) to yield some further conclusion. Or a conclusion supported by two or more premises linked together might be supported by some further premise or premises, either convergently or linked. Here are some examples of these further structures:

(1) If Israel and the United States sign the agreement, then Israel will share the lessons of the Lebanon war. But

(2) The Defense Secretary has refused to sign the agreement which would make this vital information available. Hence

(3) The United States is not going to avail itself of the lessons of the Lebanon war. However,

(4) If the United States were to put the lessons of the Lebanon war to use in Europe, then the Warsaw Pact's enormous numerical superiority over NATO forces could be nullified practically overnight. Hence

(5) We are losing a splendid advantage in our contest with the Soviets.
—Adapted from Jack Anderson, February 27, 1983. Reprinted by permission of United Feature Syndicate, Inc.

What is the structure here? Clearly (1) and (2) are linked to support (3). But (3) in turn is linked with (4) to support the conclusion (5). (See Figure 6.32.)

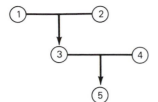

Figure 6.32

Now consider the following argument:

(1) The administration's economic program is unwise, because

(2) Any program which hurts the poor is ultimately unwise, and

(3) The administration's program takes significant benefits away from the poor. Furthermore,

(4) It is very questionable whether Congress will pass the program in its current form.

Here (2) and (3) together are put forward as a reason for (1), while (4) is given as an additional reason. Hence we represent the structure in Figure 6.33.

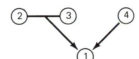

Figure 6.33

By now, the reader should already suspect that this combining process can go on and on. This point is so crucial that it bears repeating:

> CRUCIAL POINT: Given any argument, no matter how complex, we can always in principle build on further. The structure of the resultant argument is a mixture of the structures of the component arguments composing it. Given any diagram representing argument structure, we can represent an argument with more complex structure.

We have now seen how the four basic argument structures can be combined to produce arguments with mixed structure. Arguments with such mixed structures may also involve modalities. Whenever a claim is made that one or more statements support another, this claim may be specifically modified by some modality. For example, a modality may "interrupt" any of the arrows in an argument with serial structure. Some modality can describe how strongly a reason of two or more premises linked together support a conclusion. Divergent structure is especially interesting. We may claim that one premise supports two or more conclusions with the same weight (see Figure 6.34). Or the premise may support each separate conclusion with a different weight. Here each arrow must be interrupted by a different modality (see Figure 6.35). Clearly all these things can happen when we have mixed structure.

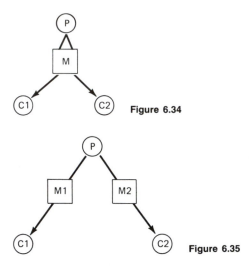

Figure 6.34

Figure 6.35

The second possibility for divergent arguments raises a more general point: we may have "mixed" modalities. When an argument has several conclusions, either where some are intermediate or where there are several final conclusions, each may be introduced by some modality, and not necessarily the same modality in each case. For example,

(1) John's fingerprints were all over the gun. Hence it must be that

(2) He committed the murder. But from this we may suspect that

(3) His motive was revenge. Now

(4) Frequently those who commit murder for revenge are remorseful over their deeds. So possibly

(5) John will express remorse over the murder.

The structure appears in Figure 6.36, where three different modalities are used to introduce the three different conclusions of this argument, and so each must be represented in the diagram.

Clearly arguments with mixed structure will frequently contain a fair number of statements. But when confronted by an argument with six, ten, or even more component statements, how do we begin to analyze it? How do we diagram the structure of such complex arguments? We want to offer several suggestions here. The idea is to break down a big problem into smaller, more manageable units. Take care of those and you are well on your way to diagram-

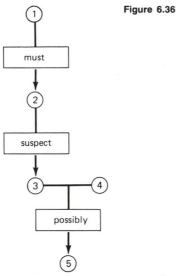

Figure 6.36

ming the whole argument. Upon examining the argument, does one statement appear as the main conclusion? If so, what reasons immediately support it—that is, what premises are just an arrow away from that conclusion? Diagram the subargument from these reasons to the conclusion. Are any of these premises supported? Diagram these subarguments. Does the main conclusion support any other statement? Diagram those subarguments.

Instead of seeing one statement as main conclusion, when examining an argument, a certain subargument may readily emerge. Diagram that. Then ask yourself how the rest of the argument "fits on" to this subargument. Or perhaps several subarguments appear. Diagram those. How do these subarguments fit together? Perhaps no subarguments readily appear. Then we should go looking for them. Start with the beginning of the passage. When you come to the point where you have an argument, a subargument of the whole, stop there and diagram it. Proceed, fitting on the rest to your growing diagram. If we follow these rules of thumb, we should find diagramming arguments with mixed structure less daunting than it first might appear.

We cannot stress enough how crucial is careful attention to the logical indicators. Logical indicators, in a sense, are the joints of an argument. They show what is connected to what, and in which way. Failure to pay attention to logical indicators or to distinguish premise from conclusion indicators correctly can only lead to confusion in determining the structure of an argument. By paying attention to them, we may more readily recognize the subarguments in a passage. Reviewing the lists of premise and conclusion indicators in Chapter 1 could be very helpful before attacking the exercises in this section. Beyond this, we must be sensitive to what the component statements of an argument are saying. If one assertion gives evidence for another claim, and in particular the two are juxtaposed, then it would seem that the first is a reason and is being put forward as a reason for the second. Working through the exercises should be helpful in developing these sensitivities. Indeed, getting practice through exercises is the only way to gain confidence in argument diagramming.

Exercise 6-IV

Show the structure of each of the following arguments by means of tree diagrams. Remember that modalities are as much a part of tree diagrams as circles and arrows.

Sample Answer

(1) It is very characteristic of friendship that friends live together. Now

(2) That one cannot live with many people and divide oneself up among them is plain. Further

(3) A person's friends must be friends of one another, if they are all to spend their days together; and

(4) It is a hard business for this to be fulfilled with a large number.

(5) It is found difficult, too, to rejoice and to grieve in an intimate way with many people, for

(6) It may happen that one has at once to be happy with one friend and mourn with another. Hence, apparently,

(7) It is impossible to be a great friend to many people. Presumably, then,

(8) It is well not to seek to have as many friends as possible, but as many as are enough for the purpose of living together.—Aristotle, *Nicomachean Ethics*.[2] (See Figure 6.37.)

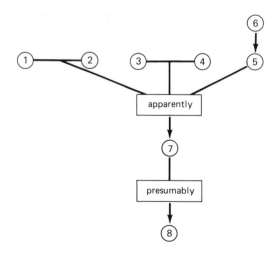

Figure 6.37

"Hence" flags (7) as a conclusion in the argument. How is (7) defended? We should already sense that reasons have been given. Sentences (1) and (2) together tell us that we cannot have a great number of friends. "Further" suggests a different reason may be coming, so functioning as a premise indicator. Sentences (3) and (4) together give us a different reason for (7). Sentence (5) also gives us a reason for (7). "For" signals that (6) is a reason for (5). Finally, the modality "presumably" followed by "then" indicates that (8) is drawn as a conclusion from (7)

I. (1) All Republicans are either moderates or conservatives, and
   (2) Senator Malcolm is not a moderate. It follows that
   (3) She is a conservative. But from this we may expect that
   (4) She supports most legislation favoring big business.

II. (1) Most Democrats are liberals and
    (2) Senator Cherry is a Democrat. Hence probably
    (3) He is a liberal. Therefore we may expect both that
    (4) He is opposed to a further nuclear arms buildup and
    (5) He will favor legislation creating jobs for the unemployed.

III. (1) The Secretary of State is beginning his Mideast peace mission in Egypt. But from this we may expect that
     (2) He wants to enlist Egypt's aid in getting foreign troops out of the region. But this leads us to believe both that
     (3) The Secretary of State feels that his peace mission to the Mideast is difficult, and
     (4) Egypt has some influence with other countries in the Mideast.

IV. (1) The president wants to keep his campaign promises. Hence
    (2) He will not raise taxes. But
    (3) If taxes are not raised, then we shall not have a balanced budget. Thus evidently
    (4) We shall not have a balanced budget.

V. (1) John got sick after eating at the Dog'N'Suds.
   (2) Jim got sick after eating there also. Hence quite possibly
   (3) The food at the Dog'N'Suds is not sanitary. But from this we may infer that
   (4) The Dog'N'Suds is not run conscientiously and therefore
   (5) John and Jim will sue the Dog'N'Suds.

VI. (1) John was satisfied with his VW.
    (2) So was Jill.
    (3) Harry, too, was satisfied, and
    (4) Tom was very happy. Therefore, most probably,
    (5) Dick will be happy with his VW. From this it follows that
    (6) He will buy two of them.

VII. (1) Organic chemistry is a difficult subject.
(2) Differential equations is difficult also. Hence
(3) Anyone who takes either subject will have a hard semester. From this it follows that
(4) Art will not take either organic chemistry or differential equations, and
(5) Jim will not take both.

VIII. (1) If Art and Stan both come to the party, then they will get into an argument.
(2) But if they get into an argument, then there will be a fight.
(3) But if there is a fight, then the party will be ruined. Hence,
(4) If Art and Stan both come, the party will be ruined. Now
(5) The party is not going to be ruined. From this we can be sure that
(6) Either Art or Stan won't come to the party.

IX. (1) If we cannot safely dispose of waste products from nuclear power plants, then we should not allow them to operate.
(2) At present, there is no way to safely dispose of such nuclear wastes. Hence,
(3) We should not allow nuclear power plants to operate. But from this it follows that
(4) Current nuclear plants should be shut down and
(5) New ones should not be allowed to start operating.

X. (1) Senator Wheelpower's arguments against higher auto emission standards are all bad. We say this because
(2) Anyone who is part of the automobile industry is too emotionally involved to see the issues clearly, and
(3) The Senator's main campaign contributors are all auto industry executives. Hence
(4) They are too involved to see the issues clearly. But
(5) These contributors have made up the arguments the Senator is using.

XI. (1) The chances of obtaining money from each source are 50-50, and
(2) We have four sources available to fund this project. So necessarily
(3) The chances of no source coming through with some money is one in sixteen. Hence, it is quite likely that
(4) We shall get some money for the project. From this it follows that
(5) We can start reviewing specific bids.

XII. (1) The majority of males who desert their wives and children cannot fulfill their natural role as protector and provider for their families because
(2) They cannot secure work, due to the fact that
(3) They lack training and
(4) Employers use discriminatory hiring practices.—H.A.M., *Sunday Star-Ledger* (Newark, N.J.), January 3, 1982.

XIII. (1) In twelve years, the EPA has taken action to protect public health against only four of the at least forty airborne chemicals known or suspected of causing cancer or other serious diseases.

     (2) For the past five years EPA has been reviewing thirty-seven suspect pollutants but has controlled none. Hence

     (3) Under current law, the EPA has been dragging its feet on public health issues.

     (4) Under the proposed law the EPA will no longer be able to ignore regulatory function as has been done in the past with unnecessarily lengthy data collection programs. Therefore

     (5) This proposed legislation is an improvement over the current Clean Air Act. But

     (6) That act was still a good piece of legislation. Hence

     (7) The new clean air law deserves support.—J.A.C., *Sunday Star-Ledger* (Newark, N.J.), October 3, 1982.

XIV. (1) The Iraqis were indeed in the business of creating an A-bomb. How may we support this? Consider first that

     (2) The Iraqis need nuclear energy to produce electrical power as Eskimos need icemakers. Why?

     (3) If you stumble in Iraq, you strike oil. Secondly,

     (4) The configuration of the nuclear plant ordered by the Iraqis from France was such as to permit it to go into the business of plutonium production, because

     (5) Any plutonium the Iraqi plant produced could more conveniently have been "withdrawn" than from a conventional power reactor. Thirdly,

     (6) On Oct. 4, 1980, Al Thawra, an official Baghdad newspaper, said "The Iranian people should not fear the Iraqi nuclear reactor, which is not intended to be used against Iran, but against the Zionist enemy." Finally,

     (7) The state of Iraq and the state of Israel are technically "in a state of belligerency" with each other.—William Buckley, June 14, 1981.

XV. (1) I was disappointed with the performance of a team of Division of Motor Vehicles examiners conducting a roadside check, which I observed recently.

     (2) They did not start to check cars until after 9 A.M.

     (3) When I passed the area again at about 3:15 P.M., they were gone.

     (4) The actual test procedures left much to be desired. Why?

     (5) It did not appear that they were checking brakes or steering.

     (6) Most of what was going on could have been done by the police without the help of the DMV examiners. Apparently

     (7) The site is repeatedly used for the roadside check.

     (8) My neighbor, a senior citizen with a new car, was stopped there twice.—B.W., *Sunday Star-Ledger* (Newark, N.J.), March 20, 1983.

XVI. (1) The postal service is starting new rates for bulk third-class mail on May 22, largely reductions in the current third-class or "junk mail" rates. Hence we may expect that

(2) The junk mail will get a bit junkier, with an extra 227 million pieces being mailed each year under the new rates. Therefore, perhaps,

(3) More pieces of first-class mail would be sent if they reduced first-class rates as well. But

(4) If more pieces of mail were sent, the postal service might have an even larger surplus than the one it recently achieved for the first time in many years. So it is possible that

(5) If the first-class rates were reduced, the postal service would have an even larger surplus.—S.K., *Sunday Star-Ledger* (Newark, N.J.), May 22, 1983.

XVII. (1) To some extent, the West should blame itself [that television projections of Ronald Reagan's victory in the presidential election cut the Democratic turnout and caused some regional Democrats to lose their elections]. We say this because

(2) Those early network projections wouldn't be so conclusive if there were real doubts about how the West would vote. In fact, however,

(3) Nothing is as certain in Presidential politics as that the West is now solidly Republican, so much so that Democratic candidates . . . mostly waste their time campaigning out there in the wide open spaces. To see this, consider that

(4) California, with the exception of the Johnson landslide in 1964, has not gone Democratic since 1948.

(5) In the same span and with the same exception, only Hawaii, Texas, Nevada, New Mexico and Washington have voted Democratic even once.

(6) In all the region, only Texas appears to be a real "swing" state, where either party has a chance to win, and

(7) Only Hawaii usually goes Democratic.—Tom Wicker, *The New York Times,* November 9, 1980. Copyright © 1980 by The New York Times Company. Reprinted by permission.

XVIII. (1) We should not build nuclear power plants to generate electricity because

(2) Alternative and better means to generate sufficient electricity are readily available. This is substantiated by considering that

(3) During the Carter administration, an Army Corps of Engineers survey showed that even without building additional dams, there are now 48,000 water dams, just sitting there, across the United States.

(4) These dams can all be adapted to hydroelectric generation—cheaper than building equivalent nuclear or even fossil fuel generating stations—and with far less impact on people and the environment! Further

(5) These water dams can provide so much electricity that we do not need nuclear generating plants. For

(6) The report showed that they could produce a staggering 30 million kilowatts, and

(7) In 1975, nuclear energy provided only 20 million kilowatts per hour average, by comparison.—M.P.G., Williamstown, N.J.

XIX. (1) Since man's body is doomed to die, evidently

(2) His task on earth must be of a more spiritual nature. Therefore,

(3) It cannot be unrestrained enjoyment of everyday life. In addition,

(4) It cannot be the search for the best ways to obtain material goods and then cheerfully get the most out of them. But rather,

(5) It has to be the fulfillment of permanent, earnest duty so that one may leave life a better human being than one started it.—Alexander Solzhenitsyn.[3]

XX. (1) Demographic and sociological data contradict the proposition that family-planning programs have significantly figured in the decline of premarital chastity. This is indicated by the fact that

(2) The "sexual revolution" (to use that phrase to refer to the breakdown of prohibitions against premarital intercourse) was well under way before the 1970's, when family-planning programs first provided their services to teenagers. In addition,

(3) Before the 70's, it was virtually impossible for unmarried adolescents to obtain birth-control aid from publicly and privately funded family-planning programs. Yet,

(4) It is hardly the case that teenagers resisted premarital sex, because

(5) In the 50's and 60's, more than half of all teenage women entering marriage were pregnant, and

(6) Many others who became pregnant escaped notice by obtaining illegal abortions.—Frank F. Furstenberg, Jr., *The New York Times,* February 15, 1981. Copyright © 1981 by The New York Times Company. Reprinted by permission.

XXI. (1) In less than three years that alleged cure-all, deregulation, has produced a semi-disaster in the airline industry. Consider first

(2) Since deregulation some 40 per cent of U.S. airports have lost service in terms of weekly departures, because

(3) Airlines have abandoned marginal routes to join the scramble on transcontinental and other lucrative routes. Secondly,

(4) Deregulation has produced a "competition" madness in which airlines are experiencing the worst financial period in their history.—Carl T. Rowan, April 26, 1981. © by and permission of News America Syndicate.

XXII. (1) Extinction is, in truth, even less tangibly present than death, because

(2) Death continually strikes down those around us. Therefore

(3) It at least reminds us of what death is and that we, too, must die. On the other hand,

(4) Extinction can, by definition, strike only once. Therefore

(5) It is entirely hidden from our direct view. Thus

(6) No one has ever seen extinction and no one ever will.—Jonathan Schell, *The Fate of the Earth.* © 1982. Published by Alfred A. Knopf, Inc.

FOR FURTHER READING

The circle and arrow method is gaining wide popularity in argument analysis. To our knowledge, it first appeared in Monroe Beardsley's *Practical Logic* (Englewood Cliffs, N.J.: Prentice-Hall, Inc., 1950), ch. 1, and was presented again in the first chapter of his *Thinking Straight: Principles of Reasoning for Readers & Writers,* 4th ed. (Englewood Cliffs, N.J.: Prentice-Hall, Inc. 1975). Stephen N. Thomas, in *Practical Reasoning in Natural Language,* 2nd ed. (Englewood Cliffs, N.J.: Prentice-Hall, Inc., 1981), modifies Beardsley's presentation. The labels, "serial," "divergent," "convergent," and "linked," are due to Thomas. Our discussion of the circle and arrow method is especially indebted to the latter two presentations.

Stephen Toulmin's *The Uses of Argument* (Cambridge: Cambridge University Press, 1958), especially the first two sections of Chapter 3, has also greatly stimulated our thinking about argument structure and its motivation. Our four basic dialectical questions are motivated by Toulmin's distinction of data, warrants, qualifiers, rebuttals, and claims contained in his account of "the layout of arguments." Our explicitly including modalities in argument diagrams is due to Toulmin. Toulmin's views are also developed in the text, *An Introduction to Reasoning,* which he co-authored with Richard Rieke and Allan Janik (New York: Macmillan Publishing Company, 1979). We have found Chapter 6, "Modalities and Rebuttals," especially useful both here and in Chapter 8.

NOTES

[1] In the Part I exercises, we were careful to keep our examples taken from newspapers, news magazines, or other sources as close to the original as possible. In Part II, we are being more liberal. Some examples that are credited to various writers have been edited and adapted for our purposes here. In some cases, material has been added. However, we have endeavored to preserve the spirit of the original in each case.

[2] Compare Example X, Exercise 6-III.

[3] We have adapted Examples XVIII and XIX from material in the *Informal Logic Newsletter,* Vol. I, no. 4, July 1979, for which we express our thanks.

7

ANALYZING ARGUMENTS

The examples in the last chapter were all somewhat artificial. In natural language, arguments do not have each separate premise and conclusion written on a different line and numbered. This is all too neat. In ordinary contexts, arguments are presented within paragraphs, one sentence following the next, and with no numbering. Unless our tree method can be applied to arguments presented this way, it may have points of intrinsic interest, but will not be a serious method for argument analysis or ultimately for argument evaluation. In this chapter, we show how to apply the tree diagramming technique to everyday arguments. This is our principal business. We conclude by relating diagramming to evaluating arguments. Why is constructing tree diagrams helpful, why is recognizing the information they give crucial, in determining whether an argument is logically convincing?

We should make one point clear from the start. Argument analysis is not a mechanical procedure. We cannot give a cookbook approach to displaying the structure of arguments in natural language, something which can just be followed step-by-step to get an acceptable result. We must be sensitive to what the author of a passage intends. By carrying out our diagramming procedure, we hope to develop our sensitivity further. However, we must be prepared from the start to think about what an arguer is specifically defending and to try to formulate exactly what that is. Let's now see how these considerations enter into the practical procedure of argument analysis.

§7.1 DIAGRAMMING ARGUMENTS IN NATURAL LANGUAGE

Consider this passage:

> That American parents are under an increasing strain in bringing up children is shown by the rapid and horrible rise in the incidence of child abuse. Obviously the government must provide substantial help to the family, which means there should be a broad system of day-care centers for children of working parents. The number of working mothers is constantly increasing, so certainly small children will be even more neglected unless there are day-care centers. Moreover, we now know how important it is for children to be stimulated and given the chance to learn at the earliest ages, and this need can best be filled by such centers.—Adapted from Monroe C. Beardsley, *Thinking Straight: Principles of Reasoning for Readers & Writers,* 4th ed. © 1975, p. 31. Reprinted by permission of Prentice-Hall, Englewood Cliffs, N.J.

The Five-Step Procedure

How may we construct a tree diagram for this argument? We need to work up this material—at the very least to get numbers assigned to statements—before we can begin to diagram. How may we do this? We offer a five-step procedure—the last being actually constructing the tree diagram itself. This constitutes a method of argument analysis. To begin, recall that at the end of the last chapter, we said that logical indicators were the joints of an argument. Identifying them and recognizing whether they are premise or conclusion indicators may give us a preliminary indication of how the argument hangs together. So our first step in argument analysis is not surprising:

STEP I. Circle all logical indicators in the passage to be analyzed.

Looking at our passage, we can readily identify two logical indicators: "so" occurring in the third sentence and "moreover" introducing the fourth. But there are two further indicators here. In the first sentence, "is shown by" indicates that the rise in child abuse is being given to support the claim that parents are under greater strain. It functions as a logical indicator, and should be circled. Similarly, the second sentence puts forward the assertion, "The government must provide substantial help to the family" to support the claim that "There should be a broad system of day-care centers for children of working parents." This is signaled by the expression "which means," which should also be circled as a logical indicator.

Logical indicators are not part of either the premises or the conclusions of an argument. In effect, they are connecting material. So also are modalities, as we emphasized in the last chapter. Our next step should be to identify them, but in a way marking them off from logical indicators:

STEP II. Enclose all modalities in rectangles.

Turning to our passage again, we see that there are two modalities: "obviously" introducing the second sentence and "certainly" which immediately follows the logical indicator "so."

If logical indicators are the joints of an argument, then the statements constituting the premises and conclusions are the bones. Having isolated logical connectives and modalities, we are now ready to identify these components.

STEP III. Enclose the separate statements constituting the passage in square brackets ([ ]) and number them with encircled numerals in the order in which they appear in the passage.

Here is how our argument looks after completing these three steps:

That   ①   [American parents are under increasing strain in bringing

up children]   (is shown by)   ②   [there is a rapid and horrible rise
                                              [the rapid and horrible rise

in the incidence of child abuse.]
in the incidence of child abuse.]

     Obviously   ③   [the government must provide substantial help

to the family,]   (which means)   ④   [there should be a broad system

of day-care centers for children of working parents.]   ⑤   [The number

of working mothers is constantly increasing,]   (so)   certainly   ⑥

[small children will be even more neglected unless there are day-care

centers.]   (Moreover,)   ⑦   [we now know how important it is for

children to be stimulated and given the chance to learn at the earliest ages,]

and   ⑧   [this need can best be filled by such centers.]

The point, of course, in rephrasing (2) is to recognize it as a separate component statement in the discourse, should there be any question of this. Note that the modality "obviously" is not included in statement (3), nor is "certainly" included in (6). As we have stressed, modalities and logical indicators are connecting matter, not parts of the argument's component statements. In the last sentence, notice that the coordinating conjunction "and" is not included within any square brackets. This is because it links two statements together, but is not properly a part of either of them.

Just because a statement appears within an argument does not guarantee that it is part of the argument. It could merely give background information, helping to make the discussion more intelligible, increasing our interest in the issue or our sense of its importance, but not being either argued for or used to establish other statements. Such statements should not appear in the final tree diagram. If we can recognize them at this point, we can simplify our final task.

STEP IV. Decide which, if any, of the numbered statements are clearly background material, and so do not constitute part of the argument proper.

This step is not mechanical. Answering this question may require a close and sympathetic reading of the text and a feeling for what are the author's intentions. In other words, it may require that we have a good feeling for what the argument is about or what is the conclusion. Not every argument need have statements which just serve as background material. Every statement in the argument we are currently analyzing pulls its weight as an actual part of the argument. Also, just because a statement does not appear clearly as background material at this point does not guarantee that it is part of the argument. We may find during constructing the tree diagram that there is no obvious place to fit it in. Its status as background material may only appear after construction has actually begun. However, it is useful that we have this step at this point. By eliminating those statements which are clearly background, we can focus just on the material to go into the tree diagram.

What have we reached at this point? We now have the argument worked up for diagramming. We have the information in front of us which the artificial presentation of arguments in the last chapter gave us. It only remains to take the last step and complete the whole process.

STEP V. Construct a tree diagram representing the structure of the argument.

Remember the hints we gave in the last chapter for diagramming arguments with mixed structure. Does a main conclusion stand out, or a subargument? Starting from the beginning, when do we recognize a subargument? How does the rest fit on? These hints are still helpful.

Let's carry out this final step, starting with the beginning of our argument. The first sentence itself contains a subargument. The logical indicator makes plain that (2) is being put forward as a reason for (1) (see Figure 7.1). The modality "obviously" suggests that (3) is a conclusion. Modalities frequently in effect do double duty as conclusion indicators also. What supports (3)? Doesn't

Figure 7.1

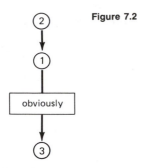

Figure 7.2

the author intend that the increasing strain in bringing up children is the reason why the government should provide substantial help to the family? Sentence (1) supports (3). Building on our diagram, we have Figure 7.2. The conclusion indicator "which means" shows that (3) in turn supports (4). Hence our diagram at this point looks like that in Figure 7.3.

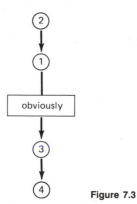

Figure 7.3

Turning to the third sentence, the conclusion indicator "so" shows that (5) is a reason for (6). The modality "certainly" indicates that strong support is claimed here (see Figure 7.4).

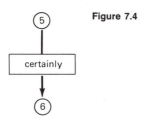

Figure 7.4

How do these two subarguments fit together? Clearly neglecting small children is undesirable. Surely our author agrees to this. But (6) says that if we don't have day-care centers, this will result. Isn't that a reason for having adequate day-care centers, that is, (4)? So (6) supports (4). To represent all the information we have up to this point, our diagram should look like that in Figure 7.5.

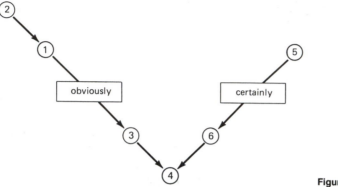

Figure 7.5

Turning to the last sentence, we see that it is introduced by the premise indicator "moreover," in effect "here is another reason." Another reason for what? So far we have two distinct lines of reasoning for statement (4). We should expect another such reason here. Looking at the last sentence confirms this. Saying that young children need stimulation and learning opportunities and that these things can be provided by day-care centers certainly gives us a reason for having day-care centers, that is, for (4). Notice also that (7) and (8) have to be linked together to get a reason for (4). Hence this part of the argument should be represented as shown in Figure 7.6. Incorporating this information into our diagram, we complete the representation of this argument's manifest structure (see Figure 7.7).

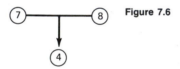

Figure 7.6

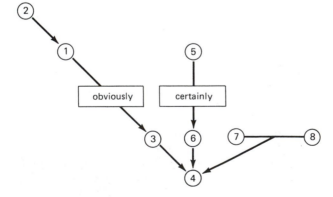

Figure 7.7

We should note that this five-step procedure will not always produce a unique diagram of an argument. There are various factors which could lead different readers to interpret a passage differently. Does a sentence contain one statement or two? In some cases, we might even ask which way the logical support was directed. The point of constructing diagrams for arguments in natural language is not to produce the one true picture of an argument's structure, but to provide a defensible account of how the argument hangs together. We want to get a defensible picture of the logical links, the connections between premises and conclusions, in an argument. Once we see what supports what, or have a reasonable picture of what supports what, we can proceed cogently to evaluate whether the premises really do support their conclusions, and if so, how strong is this support.

The one step our example did not illustrate was determining which statements were just background. All the statements entered into the argument. Let's analyze one further passage which definitely includes background material.

> Autumn comes, and the ubiquitous green of summer briefly explodes into autumn's warm golds and russets. Autumn comes, and while the harvest of the summer fields is gathered, another crop—a repulsive one—is revealed by the receding roadside vegetation. Covered by the summer's green, but now exposed to the recoiling senses, are countless littered beer bottles and soft drink cans.
>
> There is a solution to this disgrace: A so-called "bottle bill"—a bill requiring beer and soft drinks to be sold only in returnable bottles and requiring a refundable deposit on each bottle. If you give people a monetary incentive to return the bottles, then they will. But if people return the bottles, then they will not be discarded as litter. But a monetary incentive is precisely what the bottle bill provides. Hence the bottle bill would remove a major source of litter. Thus, I repeat, a bottle bill would remove this disgraceful blight on our landscape.
> —N.K., *Sunday Star-Ledger* (Newark, N.J.), November 28, 1982.

Turning to Step I, we see two logical indicators in this passage: "hence" introducing the next to the last sentence and "thus" introducing the final sentence. Accordingly, we circle both these words. There are no modalities, so we move at once to Step III. The first sentence contains two assertions joined by "and." Mrs. N.K. is saying two different but related things here. Hence we bracket each assertion, assigning (1) to "Autumn comes" and (2) to the material after "and." The second sentence again contains two assertions. The first is (1) again. This raises an interesting question: Should we assign that statement (3) in its second occurrence or (1) again? When we repeat an assertion, ordinarily we do not mean to say something different but to emphasize our point, or make clear what we are arguing for, or to increase the emotive force of our statement. Hence, when an arguer in effect says the same thing twice, we should assign the same number to both occurrences. So in the second sentence, we assign (1) again to "Autumn comes" and (3) to the material following "and." The next sentence makes one assertion, numbered (4).

Turning to the next paragraph, although long, doesn't the first sentence really make one assertion—that a bottle bill would solve the disgrace of this litter on the landscape? In the context of this argument, the material following the dash does not make an additional statement so much as explain what a bottle bill is. Hence we bracket this entire sentence and number it (5). The second sentence in this paragraph is a conditional. Recall that when conditional statements are asserted, neither the antecedent nor the consequent is asserted, but only the entire conditional as a whole. So in asserting

> If you give the people a monetary incentive to return the bottles, then they will.

we do not assert that you are giving this monetary incentive or that people will return the bottles. We are just saying that if one, then the other. Hence, the entire sentence expresses one constituent statement in the argument. It should be enclosed by one pair of brackets and given one number, here (6). The next statement is also a conditional, introduced by the coordinating conjunction "but." The next two sentences are straightforward. Look at the last. Doesn't this really reassert the first statement in this paragraph, (5)? Since it does, we assign (5) to it again. Our analysis so far looks like this:

① [Autumn comes,] and ② [the ubiquitous green of summer briefly explodes into autumn's warm golds and russets.] ① [Autumn comes,] and ③ [while the harvest of the summer fields is gathered, another crop—a repulsive one—is revealed by the receding roadside vegetation.] ④ [Covered by the summer's green, but now exposed to the recoiling senses, are countless littered beer bottles and soft drink cans.]

⑤ [There is a solution to this disgrace: A so-called "bottle bill"—a bill requiring beer and soft drinks be sold only in returnable bottles and requiring a refundable deposit on each bottle.] ⑥ [If you give people a monetary incentive to return the bottles, then they will.] But ⑦ [if people return the bottles, then they will not be discarded as litter.] But ⑧ [a monetary incentive is precisely what the bottle bill provides.] Hence ⑨ [the bottle bill would remove a major source of litter.] | Thus, | I repeat, (5) [a bottle bill would remove

this disgraceful blight on our landscape.]

What is the point of this argument? Isn't it that a bottle bill would be an effecitve measure to reduce unsightly litter, that is, (5)? Look at the sentences in the first paragraph. Although they may certainly reinforce our attitude that litter is a disgrace and stir up our desire to do something about it, in short, although they clearly contribute to the argument's persuasive force, do they say anything to justify this claim about the bottle bill? They may increase our interest in the bill as a solution to the problem, but in themselves they don't enter into the argument as premises or conclusions. Hence, in diagramming the argument, we can set them aside as background. In this example, Step IV is not trivial. Inspecting the second paragraph, no statement clearly appears as background material. Let's proceed then with the actual diagramming.

Since (5) appears as the main conclusion, we ask how (5) is supported. The conclusion indicator "thus" introducing (5)'s second occurrence suggests that the immediately preceding statement supports it, and surely (9) gives evidence for (5). So this subargument has the basic diagram shown in Figure 7.8.

Figure 7.8

Sentence (9) is introduced by a conclusion indicator. How is it defended? Look at (6), (7), and (8), the remaining statements to consider. Sentence (6) does not support (7), nor does (7) support (6). Think about what these statements say. Likewise (7) does not provide a reason for (8), nor (8) for (7). Nor does there seem to be support from (6) to (8) or (8) to (6). Do these statements support (9), and if so, how? Look at the reasoning: (6) says that if you give the people a monetary incentive to return the bottles, then they will, and (8) says that the bottle bill provides such an incentive. So with the bill, people return the bottles. But (7) says that if they return the bottles, then the bottles will not be discarded as litter. So with the bill, we don't get littered bottles. But the bottles are a major source of litter. Hence the bottle bill would remove that major source—but this is what (9) asserts. Hence (6), (7), and (8) all taken together, linked, support (9). Accordingly, we have Figure 7.9. It remains just to put these two diagrams together to represent the structure of the complete argument (see Figure 7.10).

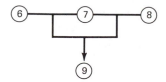

Figure 7.9

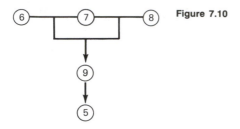

Figure 7.10

Points for Special Care

We have now presented our basic five-step procedure for determining the structure of arguments in natural language. Along the way we have called attention to certain points affecting the procedure—not counting modalities as parts of statements, distinguishing statements actually asserted from complete declarative sentences appearing in the passage, for example. A certain amount of sensitivity and intuition is necessary to get the analysis right. Let's conclude this section by explicitly discussing some of these issues.

Ordinarily, logical indicators are single words or short phrases. But consider the following argument:

> The current administration's foreign policy is a complete failure. You don't have to look far to see evidence of this: in the lack of confidence of our European allies, in the lack of progress on arms reduction with the Soviets, in our entanglements in wars of liberation.

How does the expression, "You don't have to look far to see evidence of this:" function? It certainly can stand by itself as a complete sentence. Should it be numbered as one of the statements constituting the argument? What is the point of the passage? Isn't it stated in the first sentence—the foreign policy has failed? How is this point established? Isn't the evidence presented in the list of problems and failures which concludes the argument? The arguer is really not interested so much in establishing that it is easy to find instances of failure as in signaling that the coming list is the evidence for the conclusion. Hence the entire sentence is a premise indicator and should be encircled. We must be prepared then to treat whole declarative sentences as logical indicators, and not to assign a number to each separate sentence. We shall return to this point shortly, when we discuss sensitivities in numbering statements.

In Chapter 1, we stressed that words that function as logical indicators in some contexts have different meanings in others. "Since" is perhaps the most obvious example here, being sometimes a premise indicator, sometimes a temporal indicator. Modal words can also have other meaings. The word "must" requires special care. Look again at statement (3) in our first example. We repeat it in context.

That   ①   [American parents are under increasing strain in bringing up children]　　(is shown by)　　②　　[the rapid and horrible rise in the

incidence of child abuse.]　　　Obviously　　③　　[the government must

provide substantial help to the family.]

As we have noted, when modalities are infixed in a statement, we need to paraphrase to get the modality out and identify properly the assertion being defended. The word "must" occurs in statement (3), yet we left it in the statement, and did not paraphrase (3) as

(3′) It must be the case that the government will provide substantial help to the family.

Should we have rephrased (3) this way to isolate the modality? This would be wrong. Besides expressing a modality, "must" can express notions of moral or legal necessity. Does our argument claim that assertion (1), that American parents are under increasing strain, guarantees that the government will provide substantial help to the family, that to the extent that we can be sure (1) is true, we can be sure that help, as a matter of fact, will be forthcoming? Doesn't it, rather, assert that because there is this strain, the government is somehow morally obligated to provide help to the family? "Must" in (3) expresses moral obligation. It is not a modality there, and so should be left alone, as part of (3), as we have left it.

Similarly, if I say

(a) You must repay that loan
　　or
(b) You must not tell a lie,

I am using "must" to express moral obligation. I am not saying that because something is true, we can be sure you will repay the loan or that you will not tell a lie. Rather I am saying that you are morally required to do something or not to do something. If I say

(c) You must stop at the red light,

I am again making a statement of obligation, although here it is legal obligation. I am not saying that given certain facts, we can be sure you will stop at the red light, but rather that you have a legal obligation to do so. The traffic laws require you to stop. Here again, "must" does not function as a modality, and we should not rephrase (c) to make it read that way. How do we tell when "must" functions as a modality or has some other meaning? Again, there is no escaping sensitivity here. We must consider carefully what is being said.

Sensitivity plays a role in determining just what are the component statements in a passage. Anyone who has followed our discussion so far can see that we do not mechanically assign numbers to separate declarative sentences. Some whole sentences may function as logical indicators. Logical indicator words, modalities, and coordinating conjunctions like "and" or "but" are left outside the brackets. In addition, expressions added just for rhetorical emphasis or flourish also should be left outside. "I repeat" was not counted part of (5) in the second argument presented. "I know that John will come." Often when we assert such statements, are we making a point about our knowledge or John's coming? If the latter, "I know that" is a rhetorical introduction. These expressions are not properly part of the statements constituting an argument. They should be left outside the square brackets delimiting the particular component statements of the passage.

Conditional statements require special care, since they are built up from complete declarative sentences. In Chapter 1, we pointed out that besides "if . . . , then" we may use "provided" and "only if" to form conditional statements. We may also use such expressions as "given that," "in case that," "assuming that," and "on condition that." Also, whether we say "If A, then B," or "B, if A," or "Assuming that A, B," or "B, on condition that A," it is all the same. We are asserting a conditional statement. These statements require special care because someone who asserts a conditional does not assert either of its components—at least not in the context of the conditional sentence. Should I say "If the economy remains strong, the incumbent will be reelected," am I asserting that the economy will remain strong? Am I asserting that the incumbent will be reelected? I am doing neither. I am making just one assertion that if the first happens, then so will the second. The entire sentence expresses one constituent assertion in the argument and so should be enclosed by one pair of brackets and given one number. The point is that we assign numbers to the separate assertions in an argument. Although the antecedents and consequents of conditional statements may be complete declarative sentences, they are not bracketed and assigned separate numbers.

Conditional statements are not the only ones which do not assert their components. What about the following?

Either a third party is not feasible or they have run the wrong candidate.

Does that sentence assert that a third party is not feasible? No. Does it assert that they have run the wrong candidate? No. So it would not be correct to separately bracket these components of the sentence and assign them distinct numbers as two constituents *of the argument*. Rather, the entire sentence would be one constituent. Such statements asserting alternatives are called *disjunctions*. Besides "or" and "either . . . , or," "unless" may also form disjunctions in English. "John will come unless his car breaks down." Is either component asserted here? However, in the following sentence

The current president has a winsome personality and he has made no serious errors in office.

we do have two distinct assertions, connected by "and." The statement is a *conjunction,* and by asserting a conjunction we assert each component. Here treating each as a separate component statement of the argument would be perfectly appropriate. This would hold true were "and" replaced by any other conjunction like "but," "however," "although," "even though" serving to show that two assertions were being made.

However, mentioning the word "and" only gives us another occasion to stress sensitivity to the meaning of what is said. In

Jim and Bill are cousins,

the word "and" occurs, but certainly we do not have two assertions here. We have one assertion that two persons are related as cousins. We cannot treat "and" mechanically. Sometimes paraphrasing is necessary to reveal what assertions are conjoined by "and":

Those on Social Security and those whose incomes are below $7,500 annually qualify for the subsidy.

Clearly this says that both those on Social Security qualify for the subsidy and those whose incomes are below $7,500 annually qualify for the subsidy. But notice that some paraphrasing was necessary to make this completely explicit. Again, we underscore the point: sensitivity to what is said is essential in determining just what the component statements of an argument are.

Not only may complete sentences not be asserted, phrases which are not complete declarative sentences may serve to make complete assertions. We saw this with statement (2) in our first example. "The rapid and horrible rise in the incidence of child abuse" is not a complete statement. Yet in the context of the argument, it makes a separate assertion. The argument about the administration's foreign policy being a complete failure highlights this possibility. None of the expressions, "in the lack of confidence of our European allies," "in the lack of progress on arms reductions with the Soviets," and "in our entanglements in wars of liberation," are complete sentences. Yet in the context of the argument, each serves to make a different complete statement. As with (2) in the first example, we can either assign such expressions separate numbers or paraphrase them as complete sentences and assign the numbers to those sentences.

As sensitivity to these factors should aid in correctly constructing argument diagrams, so practice in constructing diagrams should further cultivate these sensitivities. There should be two-way reinforcement here. We have now presented our basic procedure for analyzing arguments. In Chapters 8 and 11, we shall consider some further extensions of the diagramming technique. We defer discussing them now, since seeing the point of these extensions apart from the material of those chapters might be difficult.

Why do we diagram arguments? We want to get a picture of how the reasoning in a passage hangs together. We want to make perspicuous how the conclusion or conclusions are actually supported in a given piece of reasoning. We want to do this ultimately because we want to assess how good, how logically convincing, is this reasoning, and seeing how the reasoning hangs together is a proper first step. But how does argument diagramming help with argument evaluation? The next two chapters on argument evaluation should show the utility of the diagramming technique. However, there are some general remarks we can make relating diagrams to evaluation. We turn to these in the next section.

Summary

Let's restate the five steps in our procedure for determining the structure of arguments in natural language:

STEP I. Circle all logical indicators in the passage to be analyzed.

STEP II. Enclose all modalities in rectangles.

STEP III. Enclose the separate statements constituting the discourse in square brackets ([ ]) and number them with encircled numerals in the order in which they appear in the passage.

STEP IV. Decide which, if any, of the numbered statements are clearly background material, and so do not constitute part of the argument proper.

STEP V. Construct a tree diagram representing the structure of the argument.

Again we must stress how sensitivity is necessary if we are to assess argument structure correctly.

Exercise 7-I

Apply the five-step procedure to show the structure of each of the following arguments by means of tree diagrams.

Sample Answer

①   [The guidelines {issued by the Department of Health and Human Services concerning abortion and family planning clinics} are more accurately called a noose.] . . .   ②   [The department proposes to strangle with red tape 74 family planning clinics that also perform abortions—44 of them in hospitals.]

③ [Under the guidelines, family planning and abortion clinics may not share space, personnel, publications, supplies, entrances or exits.] (That means) ④ [a doctor working in one of those 74 clinics can prescribe a contraceptive but can't perform an abortion.] ⑤ [The same counselor can't advise the woman who wants to end a pregnancy and the woman who doesn't.] ⑥ [Two of everything, including doors.] ⑦ [Administrators of clinics faced with such restrictions will be swamped in construction, requisitions, personnel and cost.] . . .

—*The New York Times,* editorial, December 19, 1982. Copyright © 1982 by The New York Times Company. Reprinted by permission.

Only one logical indicator appears in this passage: "that means" in the fourth sentence. We circle that. Since there are no modalities, we proceed directly to identifying the component statements. This is very easy in this example, since each sentence constitutes a distinct statement, excluding the logical indicator from statement (4). Looking at the passage, there is a distinct air of controversiality about (1), suggesting it will be argued for. Doesn't (2) give evidence of why the guidelines are a noose? So we begin by diagramming this subargument (refer to Figure 7.1).

Figure 7.1

But isn't (2) itself controversial? We might expect reasons to appear in the next paragraph. The conclusion indicator "that means" suggests that (3) supports (4). Notice how (5) is parallel to (4). It draws out another consequence of (3). We could have inserted "It also means that" as a conclusion indicator to introduce (5). So (3) also supports (5). Look at (6). Don't (4) and (5) present examples of duplication as evidence for (6)? Finally doesn't (7) present a further consequence of (3)? Couldn't we introduce it by "it further means that"? So the diagram of paragraph 2 looks like that in Figure 7.11. But isn't this paragraph

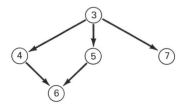

Figure 7.11

offered to support the first? Doesn't it offer documentation that the guidelines will strangle with red tape? Since (6) and (7) are the final conclusions of the second paragraph, we connect the two diagrams by having these statements converge on (2) (see Figure 7.12).

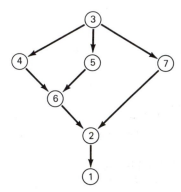

Figure 7.12

I. Since Congress is going on vacation tomorrow, the members cannot pass the legislation before they leave. Hence we may expect the president will be very angry.

II. Sex ed humanism style has been tried elsewhere and found devastating. We should not subject our children to this unsuccessful and undesirable program!—T.V. and C.V., *Sunday Star-Ledger* (Newark, N.J.), July 3, 1983.

III. I do not believe . . . that religious Americans want a theocracy as their form of government. Many, even of the strongest personal beliefs, would hold to the country's tradition of diversity in faith and separation of religion from government.—Anthony Lewis, *The New York Times,* May 24, 1981. Copyright © 1981 by The New York Times Company. Reprinted by permission.

IV. The National Urban League convention in New York has been a Presidential candidate's dream—an ideal place to woo the black vote. It was attended by 15,000 delegates, most of them black professionals. Small wonder that all the major contenders came and showered them with promises.—*The New York Times,* editorial, August 7, 1980. Copyright © 1980 by The New York Times Company. Reprinted by permission.

V. Whether you like his policies or not, Ronald Reagan is for real. He has a central core conviction that drives everything else that he does. He has one other endearing grace—he will listen to criticism.—Senator Howard Baker quoted by Carl T. Rowan, May 8, 1983. © by and permission of News America Syndicate.

VI. But even those who believe, as we do, that offshore oil should be exploited more rapidly need to be concerned about Mr. Watt's escalation. He would shift the focus of attention from small tracts to enormous areas of ocean. He would require environmental studies for the broad area, but in less detail than before. And only after a company had actually leased a tract would he study the drilling site to estimate the likely gains and risks—too late in many cases for withdrawal of the lease.—*The New York Times,* editorial, July 25, 1981. Copyright © 1981 by The New York Times Company. Reprinted by permission.

VII. America is sure to remain dependent on foreign oil for decades, and any prolonged interruption would do immense damage. That is why, five years ago, Congress authorized a billion-barrel emergency oil reserve, enough to replace six months of imports.—*The New York Times,* editorial, December 14, 1980. Copyright © 1980 by The New York Times Company. Reprinted by permission.

VIII. No jobholders are totally innocent when job discrimination is rampant, but these white layoff victims [white policemen and firemen in Boston, Mass., with more seniority than blacks or Hispanics who nevertheless in a budget crisis were laid off earlier to preserve affirmative action gains] come close. Neither the past hiring policies nor the current budget scarcities are of their making—nor have the minority hires done anything to deserve their last-in, first-out status.—*The New York Times,* editorial, March 26, 1983. Copyright © 1983 by The New York Times Company. Reprinted by permission.

IX. Obviously taxpayers should subsidize mass transit. Here are the facts: Train and bus commuters must pay in taxes the cost of building and maintaining roads they never use, and they must also pay considerably more for their commute than drivers do. It is not in the best interest of motorists to have 300,000 former mass transit riders joining them at rush hour, adding to the crowding and pollution on the roads they drive. And efficient train and bus systems, as well as good roads, are vital in getting people to their jobs (and persuading employers to stay and offer jobs) in our densely populated state.—L.M., *Sunday Star-Ledger* (Newark, N.J.), March 27, 1983.

X. Thousands of physicians, dentists, laboratories (often operating under kickback arrangements with doctors) are flagrantly milking Medicaid and Medicare of tens of billions of dollars every year. Hence there must be a crackdown.—Carl T. Rowan, December 5, 1982. © by and permission of News America Syndicate.

XI. The free market price of a barrel of oil . . . reflects only the price of finding another barrel to replace it. It does not include the political and military cost of depending on unreliable foreign suppliers. It does not include the impact of small increases in consumption on world prices. . . . Thus, in the absence of Government regulation—preferably, conservation-inducing taxes—the free market badly underestimates the real value of fuels.—*The New York Times,* editorial, December 21, 1981. Copyright © 1981 by The New York Times Company. Reprinted by permission.

XII. One other serious problem [in Jamaica] is inescapably domestic. This island nation of 2.5 million is not only the largest and most populous of the Caribbean's English-speaking territories; it has also become the most violent. Killings were incessant during the long campaign [for Prime Minister in 1980]. In one 24-day period, 104 murders were recorded. —*The New York Times,* editorial, November 5, 1980. Copyright © 1980 by The New York Times Company. Reprinted by permission.

XIII. The lack of media interest in science is mirrored by the disdain scientists hold for the media. Since budding scientists are rapidly channelled into specialized courses, there is little room in their education for philosophy, literature, humanities or history. Thus, few scientists ever give thought to the question of the cultural role of science or whether the practitioners of science bear any responsibility to the society that enables them to do science and which is so strikingly affected by applications from the pool of scientific knowledge. When most of the rewards of promotion, tenure, recognition and prizes are conferred by one's peer group, there is little need to communicate to a broader audience. Hence, popularizing science has generally been considered to be a vulgar activity indulged in by publicity hungry types or third-rate minds.—David Suzuki, "A Sorry Tale of Two Solitudes with Idiot Savants and Just Plain Idiots," *Toronto* (Canada) *Globe and Mail,* June 1977. Reprinted by permission of David Suzuki.

XIV. What a reservoir of special wisdom ex-Presidents must embody! Only thirty-nine men have served as President in our whole history, and the office is *sui generis.* "There is no experience you can get," John Kennedy used to say, "that can possibly prepare you adequately for the Presidency." Nothing but the experience of actual working responsibility can teach what the Presidency is finally about. Then, when this unique and costly education is completed and Presidents are finally beginning to master the job, we abruptly turn them out to pasture. Clearly, this is an act of folly, a tragic waste, a grave loss to the country. Hence, we should find some way to organize their hard-bought knowledge and draw on it through dark days to come.—Arthur M. Schlesinger, Jr., *Parade,* June 21, 1981.

XV. Ex-Presidents, like other old folk, tend to live in the past, preoccupied with the issues, remedies and self-justifications of another time. Their excursions into the unfamiliar present . . . are often the height of irrelevance. . . . In the private sector, when presidents retire from corporations or from universities, no one wants them offering advice. Hence, we should not succumb to the patriarchal illusion. After all, if our three living ex-Presidents are really all that wise, for example, they would surely have been better Presidents when they had the chance.—Arthur M. Schlesinger, Jr., *Parade,* June 21, 1981.[1]

XVI. Few experts believe that the availability of contraception has provided a significant incentive to have sex at a younger age. Why? Only an insignificant number of sexually active teenagers visit family-planning clinics before starting to have intercourse. Most adolescents still drift into, rather than decide to have, sex. Thus their first clinical visit often occurs when they suspect they are pregnant. All this shows that if family-planning programs deserve criticism, it is not because they aggressively peddle birth control to innocent virgins but because they are not diligent enough in finding sexually active teenagers in need of their services. —Frank F. Furstenberg, Jr., *The New York Times,* February 15, 1981. Copyright © 1981 by The New York Times Company. Reprinted by permission.

XVII. Sympathy for the truckers should not exceed to another of their demands: seeking to raise the speed limit from 55 to 65 mph. At a time of energy crisis, this borders on recklessness and arrogance. While a higher speed limit would save time and therefore money, it would also use more fuel. As evidence for this, consider that a Department of Transportation study, conducted with trucker volunteers last summer in Ohio, proved that trucks do *not* operate more efficiently at higher speeds than at 55 mph—as had been claimed.

It would also be totally unreasonable to allow truckers to operate at higher speeds than other road users. Furthermore, given the size of the rigs and their potential for horrendous mishaps, the best interests of road safety would not be served by raising the speed limit. Whatever progress the truckers gain on other fronts, they had better realize that they will have to keep on truckin' at 55 mph—just like the rest of us. —*Pittsburgh Post-Gazette,* editorial, June 13, 1979.[2]

XVIII. Ignore the calendar; it's still winter in Poland. The three months since General Jaruzelski partly lifted martial law have confirmed the cynicism of his maneuver. Jail conditions are harsher; new laws justify forced labor, and the universities have been purged with a crude "ideological verification" drive. To call this normality is a joke in the worst taste.— *The New York Times,* editorial, March 26, 1983. Copyright © 1983 by The New York Times Company. Reprinted by permission.

XIX. Surely any nation is in trouble when its morality reaches the low point currently found in the United States.

Richard Nixon, a disgraced President who was spared a prison sentence only by a disgraceful pardon from a Watergate-era crony, is actually welcomed as a resident of Saddle River [New Jersey], as if he were an honest man instead of a leech on the taxpayer.

Harrison Williams, a disgraced senator, fights his ouster from office not on the grounds that he did anything righteous but on the grounds that the FBI's conduct was worse than his own. And party flacks and people who have been helped by Williams rally to his defense against the Abscam sheiks like Iranians willing to die for the Ayatollah.

Meanwhile, Ronald Reagan is supported by a majority in the polls after cutting aid to the poor, the elderly, the handicapped, the unemployed, the schools, the minorities, the consumers and the environment so he can aid the oil companies, the airplane manufacturers, the tobacco growers, the teamsters and his stock-owning millionaire friends.

The reason for supporting Reagan is clearly egotism—most people seem to think that no matter how much Reagan hurts "other" people somehow he is going to help "them." It is total acceptance of the Reagan philosophy—ask, he says, are "you" better off than "you" were before? Don't consider others. Don't consider the nation, just think of yourself.

It is a sickness across the land.—R.W., *Sunday Star-Ledger* (Newark, N.J.), November 1, 1981.

XX. Florida has come to symbolize the hellish destruction wrought by the illegal drug trade in America.

The merchants of marijuana, cocaine, Quaaludes and heroin cover South Florida like the dew. They have put their deadly mark on almost every institution worth mentioning.

"I'm in banking" used to be a declaration of pride in this area. Now it leads people to whisper, "Oh, he's laundering money for the Mafia's drug peddlers."

Wars over "territorial rights" to sell drugs have produced such violence that law-abiding people who have lived in Miami and environs for generations are fleeing to Fort Lauderdale and much farther north, generally to discover that there is no hiding place.

Drugs have so escalated the incidents of violent crime that in Miami, armed policewomen and female FBI agents have to be escorted from their offices to their cars.

Drug trafficking in Florida has become a plague, corrupting everything in sight, making it a truism that no Soviet missile ever could do so much damage in America's high schools, colleges and other communities as does the cocaine from Bolivia and Peru, the marijuana from Colombia or the heroin from Iran and Pakistan.—Carl T. Rowan, October 18, 1981. © by and permission of News America Syndicate.

§7.2 ARGUMENT DIAGRAMS AND ARGUMENT EVALUATION

We have frequently stressed that there are three basic criteria for evaluating arguments: the premises must be true or well warranted, they must be relevant to the conclusion, and they must adequately support it. How does diagramming help in assessing whether an argument satisfies these criteria? How can we criticize an argument for having false or questionable premises unless we can first identify the premises? How can we assess whether the premises are relevant to the conclusion or how strongly they support it unless we can distinguish premises from conclusions? But argument diagrams make plain which statements function as premises and which function as conclusions.

Argument diagrams have a more intimate connection with argument evaluation than this, however. Suppose we recognize that one (or more) of the reasons offered for a conclusion is in itself questionable. The burden of proof lies with the respondent to argue for that statement. Should we charge the argument at this point with the fallacy of questionable premise? That could be hasty. We should first see whether that reason has been defended by further argument. We should diagram the argument to see whether one or more statements are offered to support this questionable assertion. This involves the ability to recognize serial structure at least. We look for statements defending the questionable premise, which in turn defends the conclusion.

Suppose a premise presents evidence for the conclusion which seems irrelevant. Are we justified in charging irrelevant reason at that point? Again, we should look at the argument diagram. Is the premise linked to a warrant explaining why it is relevant to the conclusion? If so, is the explanation satisfactory? Is there some unstated warrant which explains relevance and which the arguer has apparently assumed? How satisfactory is the argument when that warrant is linked to the premise? We need to answer such questions to judge the relevance of the data properly. The concept of linked structure pervades this discussion throughout.

Finally, to judge whether the premises support the conclusion with adequate weight or to determine just how strongly the premises support the conclusion, just how strong a modality is justified, we must determine what premises actually converge on that conclusion. We cannot ask about the weight of evidence until we determine just what that evidence is. But here again, this is manifestly displayed in argument diagrams. Hence, analyzing arguments through diagrams is an obvious first step in evaluating them.

In the last section of Chapter 2, we discussed evaluating arguments on the truth criterion, determining whether the argument involves the fallacy of false or questionable premise. The relevance and weight criteria remain. Of these two, the question of weight is more fundamental. The full discussion of relevance presupposes concepts developed in connection with weight. Accordingly, we turn to this criterion in the next chapter, and to relevance in Chapter 9.

FOR FURTHER READING

The procedure of analyzing arguments in natural language so that they may be diagrammed by the circle and arrow method is an adaptation to our account of argument structure of Stephen N. Thomas's procedure presented in *Practical Reasoning in Natural Language*, 2nd ed. (Englewood Cliffs, N.J.: Prentice-Hall,

Inc., 1981), pp. 57–81. The reader may find this interesting and useful collateral reading, remembering that Thomas does not treat modalities.

NOTES

[1]Both XIV and XV are from the same article, "Why Ex-Presidents Should Stay That Way." In Example XIV, Mr. Schlesinger presents an argument for one side of the question concerning whether ex-presidents should be given some special advisory role. In Example XV, he presents an argument for the other side, which is the one he favors.

[2]As in previous exercises, we owe several examples to the *Informal Logic Newsletter*. Both XIII and XVII appear in Vol. I, no. 4, July 1979.

8

ARGUMENT EVALUATION I— JUDGING THE WEIGHT OF THE EVIDENCE

How do we assess how strongly the premises support the conclusion? How do we tell whether the premises are strong enough to make the argument logically convincing? To put the question somewhat differently, what modality may we use to describe how strongly the premises support the conclusion? Or, if the arguer has used a modality, how do we know that this particular modality is justified? These are the questions we consider in this chapter. However, there is a preliminary issue we must address. Basically we may distinguish claiming the premises give complete, total support, support where the truth of the premises guarantees the truth of the conclusion, on the one hand, from less than complete support on the other. This distinction is crucial, for it leads to a central logical distinction, that between deductive and inductive arguments. Traditionally, this has been a watershed distinction in logic. Deductive and inductive arguments are evaluated by different standards and in different ways. Determining whether an argument is deductive or inductive is preliminary to weighing how strong a case it makes. Consequently we develop this distinction in the first section of the chapter. In Section 8.2, we present the basic concept behind appraising deductive arguments. In Section 8.3, we turn to inductive arguments. The remaining sections develop further aspects of evaluating inductive arguments.

§8.1 INDUCTION AND DEDUCTION

In Chapter 6 when introducing modalities, we illustrated how some make stronger claims than others. "Likely," "highly likely," "very highly likely," "morally certain," "necessarily"—each modality makes a stronger claim than the preceding. Look at "necessarily." If this is meant literally, what does it claim? If I say "Bill is Andy's uncle, so Andy is necessarily Bill's nephew," I am claiming that if the premise is true, then the conclusion is going to be true also—no ifs, ands, or buts. There is just no way, we are saying, for Bill to be Andy's uncle and Andy not be Bill's nephew. This is the strongest possible claim that we can make about how strongly the premises support the conclusion. They must not only give evidence for it, they necessitate it. "Must" also makes a claim this strong.

> If the man in the brown hat is Ben the Burglar, then that man is desperately wanted by the police. Now the man in the brown hat is in fact Ben the Burglar. Therefore that man must be desperately wanted by the police.

If our two premises are true, the conclusion is true also—that is what our modality claims—and rightly, as we shall see. An argument which involves such a modal claim—which claims that its premises necessitate its conclusion—or which should be evaluated as if it made such a claim is called a *deductive argument*. Hence, we may call such modalities deductive modalities.

When speaking of arguments throughout this chapter and the first two sections of the next, we are considering just simple arguments with one conclusion. It is quite possible, for example, that we could have a serial argument with a less than deductive modality qualifying the first arrow and a deductive modality qualifying the second. The presence of the deductive modality does not show that all connections are deductive or that the argument is deductive on the whole. We discuss overall argument evaluation, where there may be several conclusions, at the end of Chapter 9.

Since the presence of deductive modalities serves to indicate explicitly that we have deductive arguments, we could call them explicit deductive argument indicators. For future reference, let's list some of these modalities. We must add one note of caution, however. Since the deductive claim is so strong, sometimes these indicators really mean only that there is very strong evidence, not necessarily conclusive evidence. When we come to evaluating arguments, we should not take such explicit deductive claims quite literally. Again, there is no substitute for sensitivity in properly interpreting a passage.

Deductive Modalities—Explicit Deductive Argument Indicators

Expressions That Almost Always Indicate Deductive Arguments

it must be the case that   (must—infixed in conclusion)
it is necessarily the case that   (necessarily)
we may deduce that

Expressions that Frequently Indicate Deductive Arguments

it is certain that   (certainly)
this implies that   (implies)

this entails that	(entails)
this proves that	(proves)
it follows that	
consequently	

In general, expressions which involve necessity or certainty are deductive modalities.

Now look at such modalities as "presumably," "probably," "likely," "highly likely," "very highly likely," "morally certain." These expressions claim that the premises give some evidence, but only some evidence, for the conclusion, not that they unconditionally guarantee its truth. Some of these modalities claim strong evidence, but all claim less than total support. An argument which involves such a modal claim or which should be evaluated as if it made such a claim is an *inductive* argument. Hence we call such modalities inductive modalities—they serve to indicate explicitly that an argument is inductive.

Inductive Modalities—Explicit Inductive Argument Indicators

probably	apparently
likely	evidently
suggests	supports[1]
it seems	

One feature of our definition of inductive and deductive arguments may seem puzzling. Why didn't we opt for the neater definition, "An argument is deductive just in case it claims that its premises necessitate its conclusion," and analogously for defining inductive arguments? The problem is that not every argument contains a modality, as we well know. In the absence of a modality, what sense does it make to say that an argument makes the deductive or inductive claim? Now we could talk about making such claims implicitly. But this seems an artificial way of describing a basic fact. People do distinguish arguments lacking modalities as being deductive or inductive. They do it because they recognize that it is appropriate to apply deductive methods to evaluate some arguments, while it is appropriate to apply inductive methods to others.

How do we make such determinations? In some cases, it is intuitively obvious that some arguments satisfy the deductive claim, while others satisfy the inductive claim. Needless to say, our ability to intuit the obviousness of these cases grows with our study of deductive and inductive logic. But some arguments are obvious even to untutored intuitions. For example,

> All Pentax cameras are pieces of precision equipment. This camera is a Pentax. Therefore this camera is a piece of precision equipment.

Isn't it plain that if both premises were true, the conclusion would be true also? We can readily see that the degree of support the premises give the conclusion is that strong. Now consider:

(1) Jack had a sloppy joe, tossed salad, soup, ice cream, and a soft drink for lunch. He subsequently came down with food poisoning.

(2) Jim had a sloppy joe, corn on the cob, soup, a piece of cake, and beer. He came down with food poisoning.

(3) Jill had a sloppy joe, bean salad, cookies, and coffee. She came down with food poisoning.

(4) Jane had a sloppy joe, tossed salad, ice cream, and milk for lunch. She got food poisoning also.

(5) Sam had a sloppy joe, pickles, and beer. He came down with food poisoning.

(6) Barbara had a sloppy joe, tossed salad, fruit, and tea. She came down with food poisoning. So

(7) The problem was in the sloppy joes.

Don't the premises give a strong indictment of the sloppy joes—don't they give significant evidence for the conclusion? Notice that the premises do not guarantee that the problem is there. It could be that the sloppy joes were completely innocent. Our six friends all could have been munching on some exotic mushroom before lunch and *that* would have caused the food poisoning. But certainly the premises make a strong case for saying that the sloppy joes were the culprits. Plain common sense lets us see that this argument is inductive.

The absence of an explicit indicator may be a sign that we have a deductive argument. For example,

> Carla is the smartest student in the school. Some students have straight A averages. So Carla is a straight A student.

Isn't the conclusion asserted rather categorically? There is no qualification or hedging here, which an inductive modality would provide. (Notice that this is not a good deductive argument. Carla could be smart but lazy. Hence, although some students less able than she have straight A averages, she does not.)

However, perhaps the single most important factor besides modalities in deciding whether an argument is inductive or deductive is recognizing that it belongs to a certain family. There are inductive families—families of arguments appropriately evaluated by inductive means. Likewise there are deductive families. Recognizing that an argument belongs to one of those families allows us to classify it as inductive or deductive. We could, at this point, sketch the characteristic marks of these families. However, there is a close connection between recognizing the family to which an argument belongs and evaluating it. The distinguishing features of these families allow applying special evaluative techniques to determine how good are arguments in the family. Hence it makes far more sense to define these families specifically in connection with detailing these special evaluation procedures. We do this in Chapter 10 for inductive arguments and Chapter 11 for deductive.

At this point, we must stress that just because an argument makes the deductive claim does not mean it is a good deductive argument. It does not mean that the claim is true. Likewise, just because the inductive claim is made does not mean that it is justified. How do we assess whether these claims hold? As we said in introducing this chapter, the deduction/induction distinction is fundamental in logic because the methods of assessing these arguments are distinctly different. In the next section, we present the basic concept behind appraising the deductive claim. In the remaining sections, we look at fundamental procedures for evaluating inductive arguments.

Summary

A *deductive argument* either explicitly claims that its premises necessitate its conclusion or should be evaluated as if it made that claim. An *inductive argument* either claims that its premises give some evidence, although not conclusive evidence, for its conclusion or should be treated as if it made that claim. Deductive and inductive claims are explicitly made by deductive and inductive modalities. See lists on pages 226 and 227. In the absence of these indicators, various factors, principally membership in a certain family, may indicate whether the argument is inductive or deductive. We discuss inductive and deductive families in Chapters 10 and 11, respectively.

Exercise 8-I

State whether the following arguments are inductive or deductive and discuss why in each case. In particular, identify any deductive or inductive modalities.

1. The only footprints leading away from the house were a man's. Only two people could have been at the house when the murder was committed—Joanne and Franklin. Therefore, Franklin must be the murderer.

2. Over the past five years, Japanese automobile manufacturers have gained 20 percent of the American automobile market. If this trend continues, Japan will most likely take over from Detroit in supplying America's cars.

3. Although many heavy smokers do not get cancer, it is still likely that cancer is caused by smoking. For there is a high correlation between the number of cigarettes a person smokes and the chances of his or her getting cancer.

4. Some president of the United States was Catholic. Necessarily then some Catholic was president of the United States.

5. Harry bought a VW. John bought a VW. Jim bought a VW. Jack bought a VW. Mary bought a VW. Probably soon everyone will be owning a VW.

6. If Harry bought a new Subaru, then he was charged a hefty import tax, because anyone who buys a new imported car is charged a heavy import tax.

7. Alfred, Alonzo, and Rudolf are all in Room A. Also, they all reject

the proposed amendment. There are exactly five persons in Room A. Hence most of the individuals in Room A reject the proposed amendment.

8. Fifty percent of the observed times that die has been tossed, it has come up one. Hence we may expect that 50 percent of the times the die is tossed, it will come up one.

9. All mathematical logicians are frustrated mystics. All frustrated mystics are eccentrics. Therefore all mathematical logicians are eccentrics.

10. No speculative metaphysicians are good politicians. Plato was a great speculative metaphysician. Hence Plato was not a good politician.

11. I would hazard a guess that the marble head of a young black man in the Brooklyn Museum dates from the late Roman period. The absence of intense emotional expression together with only a slight turn of the head and summary treatment of the back of the head suggest a late date. The wide-open eyes and the asymmetrical facial features are often found in later Roman works.—Example in Sample LSAT.

12. John was dissatisfied with the stereo system he bought. So someone was dissatisfied with at least one of his purchases.

13. Both Joe and Steve ate a pinch of raw meat, and over the next several weeks they were sick in bed. Sam ate a whole hamburger of raw meat and ended up in the hospital in intensive care. Jim ate two raw meat hamburgers and within a few days died in agony. Hence something in that raw meat caused the illnesses.

14. Wheat costs $1.00 a bushel, but orders of 10 bushels or more receive a 10 percent discount. Hence the price of 9 bushels of wheat is the same as the price of 10 bushels.

15. Two of the most serious charges [against marijuana] are that marijuana reduces motivation and lowers testosterone (male hormone) levels. . . . A clinical sample of 41 pairs (users and nonusers) was selected and matched for age, education, marital status, tobacco and alcohol use and occupation. . . . The researchers were careful to test serum testosterone levels and could find no difference between users and nonusers. [Hence, we may expect that in the population at large there is no difference between users and nonusers, and the second of these charges at least is false.]—*Science News*, December 13, 1975.[2] Reprinted with permission from *Science News, The Weekly Newsmagazine of Science.* Copyright 1975 by Science Service, Inc.

§8.2 APPRAISING DEDUCTIVE ARGUMENTS—THE BASIC CONCEPT

Since a deductive argument claims that its premises necessitate its conclusion, that if the premises are all true, the conclusion must be true also, or should be evaluated as if it made this claim, when we appraise a deductive argument we want to know whether this claim is true. If the answer is yes, then the argument is *deductively valid* or just plain *valid*. Notice that validity is an all or nothing affair. Either the premises necessitate the conclusion or they don't. This means that either it is impossible for all the premises to be true and the conclusion false or such a situation is possible. Hence we cannot speak of one argument being more valid than another, or of an argument being somewhat valid, or strongly valid, or nearly valid. Hence when we test for validity, we are not testing for something there can be more or less of. Our test will be either positive or negative.

Not only is the concept of deductive validity central in evaluating arguments, it is intimately connected to several other logical notions, contradiction and consistency/inconsistency, which are central to our critical analytic vocabulary. Indeed we often hear charges that someone's statements were inconsistent or that certain persons had contradicted themselves. These are negative evaluations, but what do they mean? We shall develop this as we explore deductive validity.

How do we test arguments for deductive validity? To introduce our test, let's focus on these facts:

If a deductive argument is valid, then it is impossible for all its premises to be true and its conclusion false.

If a deductive argument is invalid, then it is possible for all its premises to be true and the conclusion false.

But what do we mean by "possible"? There are three standard meanings to distinguish. Today it is *technologically* possible to bounce radio and television signals off artificial satellites 22,500 miles in space. Satellite communication is a reality—we have the technology to make this possible. Before communication satellites, this was not technologically possible. However, the idea of doing so did not contradict any of the laws of physics, else such technologies could never be developed. Satellite communication, then, was *physically possible,* although not technologically possible. Today space travel outside the solar system for humans is not technologically possible, although in principle such technologies could be developed. So again such travel is physically possible. Whether it is physically possible to beam people to and from spaceships I do not know. But physicists are highly skeptical of the physical possibility of other science fiction notions. Is it possible to build a machine which will transport us backward or forward in time? Could anyone ever build a separator, so that one person could be split into two individuals? Such notions belong to the realm of fancy, not physical possibility. But notice that such notions are at least imaginable or conceivable. They are the stuff of science fiction literature. In this sense, they are still possible. This is the sense of "possible" which logicians use—logical possibility. A statement is *logically possible* just in case we can imagine or conceive it to be true. As long as we can conceive or imagine all the statements in a set being true together, then it is logically possible for all of them to be jointly true. Hence, when we ask whether an argument is valid, we are asking whether we can conceive or imagine the premises to be all true and the conclusion false. If we can, the argument is invalid. If we cannot—and the defect is not in our imagination—the argument is valid.

If we can imagine all the members of a set of statements true together, that set is *consistent*. If we cannot—and there is no problem with our imagination—the set is *inconsistent*. Is the following story consistent?

> The bomb had a long, slow-burning fuse which had just been lit. Quickly I snatched the device and hurled it overboard. I shuddered to think of what would have happened had I hesitated even for an instant. A few seconds more, and the explosion would have torn apart the entire ship.

Isn't there something wrong with this passage? According to the first sentence, it seems that the fuse has some time to burn, certainly more than a few seconds, before the bomb would go off. But according to the last sentence, the bomb would go off in just a few seconds. But can both these statements be true together?

> The fuse has some time to burn.
> The fuse does not have any time to burn.

Either one or the other will be true, not both. These two statements are *contradictories*: if one is true, the other is false, and if one is false, the other will be true. Given any statement, we can always form its contradictory by prefixing "it is not the case that."

> John went to the store.
> It is not the case that John went to the store; that is, John did not go to the store.

Can we ever imagine a contradictory pair of statements being true together? Can we imagine John both going to the store and not going to the store—on the same day, at the same time, to one and the same store? Can we imagine a fuse having some time to burn and not having some time to burn? Clearly we cannot, and this is no defect of our imagination. Contradictions are logically impossible, and we cannot imagine them true. Hence if in trying to imagine a set of statements true together we find we must imagine a contradiction to be true, we know we cannot do it—the set is inconsistent. As we shall see shortly, this has great importance for testing the validity or invalidity of arguments.

What about this passage?

> The sea is calm to-night.
> The tide is full, the moon lies fair
> Upon the straits;—on the French coast, the light
> Gleams, and is gone; the cliffs of England stand,

> Glimmering and vast, out in the tranquil bay.
> Come to the window, sweet is the night air!
> —Matthew Arnold, "Dover Beach"

Is there any inconsistency in Matthew Arnold's description of this scene? It's not hard to imagine all these statements being true together. The passage is consistent.

How may we relate this to appraising deductive arguments? These considerations yield a test procedure for determining whether or not an argument is deductively valid. We try to imagine that all the premises are true and the conclusion false or, what amounts to the same thing, we try to imagine the premises true together with the contradiction or negation of the conclusion, that these statements are all consistent. Three things can happen when we try to do this:

1. We may be successful. This shows that it is possible for the premises to be true and the conclusion false; the argument is invalid.

2. We may find that to imagine the premises and the negation of the conclusion all true, we have to imagine some contradiction true. Since this is impossible, it is impossible for the premises to be true and the conclusion false. The argument is deductively valid.

3. Our imaginations may conk out. This doesn't mean that the question of validity is undecidable for this argument. Other people may have more fertile imaginations. Ours may improve with practice. Perhaps just what conditions make the premises true and the conclusion false is unclear without further study of logic. Or the argument may have certain special features allowing us to make a determination. We return to this topic in Chapter 11.

Let's now apply this test to some specific arguments:

1. Professor Brown is a logic teacher.
   Professor Brown is a genius. So
   All logic teachers are geniuses.

Can we imagine the premises true while the conclusion is false? If it's false that all logic teachers are geniuses, then there's at least one logic teacher who isn't. Imagine Instructor Smith, who may be quite competent, even smart, but is not a genius. We can imagine Instructor Smith also teaching logic, while Professor Brown, the genius, also teaches logic. Hence we can imagine the premises true and the conclusion false, showing the argument invalid. What about the following?

2. If you study hard, then you'll pass the test.
   Myra passed the test. So
   She must have studied hard.

We can imagine an instructor designing a test which is comprehensive yet straightforward—no trick questions. If you apply yourself, you'll get a passing grade. We can also imagine a person, Myra, passing this test. But we can further imagine Myra being smart or already knowing the material and hardly studying for the test at all. So we can consistently affirm the premises and deny the conclusion. Hence the argument is invalid.

Now consider this argument:

3. Socrates was running quickly. Therefore
   Socrates was running.

Can I imagine Socrates running quickly but not running at all? Wouldn't I then have to imagine Socrates both running and not running, an outright contradiction? As long as I'm keeping the meaning of "running" the same, I can't imagine a situation where the premise is true and the conclusion false. The argument is valid.

4. This is a red balloon, so
   This balloon is colored.

Can I imagine a balloon being red yet not having any color at all? Wouldn't that be to imagine the balloon had a color and didn't have a color? Having to imagine a contradiction again shows the argument valid.

We have pointed out that on occasion we might find this test inconclusive because we do not understand the conditions under which the premises are true or the conclusion false. What exactly it means to deny the conclusion may be unclear. Perhaps the paradigm examples of deductive arguments are categorical syllogisms. We'll explain what these arguments are shortly. Although in many cases it is intuitively obvious that a categorical syllogism is valid or invalid, it may be quite helpful to review the circumstances under which their component premises are true or false. Let's conclude this section by defining these arguments and applying our test to them. This will reinforce our understanding of the test. What is a categorical syllogism? Here are three examples, all valid:

1. All axioms of geometry are hard things to understand.
   All hard things to understand give me a headache. Therefore
   All axioms of geometry give me a headache.
2. All horses are quadripeds.
   Some barnyard fowl are not quadripeds. Therefore
   Some barnyard fowl are not horses.
3. No English prime ministers are American politicians.
   Some American politicians are Democrats. Therefore
   Some Democrats are not English prime ministers.

By a *syllogism* we mean an argument with exactly two premises linked to support exactly one conclusion. A *categorical syllogism* is a syllogism where both premises and conclusion are categorical propositions. What is a categorical proposition?

There are four varieties of categorical propositions, all illustrated in our examples. Consider:

All horses are quadripeds.

This statement asserts that the entire class of horses is included in the class of quadripeds. It says that if anything is a horse, then it is also a quadriped. This relationship is graphically illustrated in Figure 8.1.

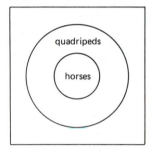

Figure 8.1

The horse circle's being completely included in the quadriped circle indicates that the class of horses is completely included in the class of quadripeds. We can see that an analogous claim is being made with the other statements beginning with "all." Each asserts that the class indicated by the subject term, the subject class, is completely included in the class indicated by the predicate term, the predicate class. Such propositions are called universal, affirmative categorical propositions, because the *entire* subject class is *affirmed* to be included in the predicate class.

No English prime ministers are American politicians.

claims that the class of English prime ministers is completely separate from the class of American politicians. There is no overlap between these two classes. This is represented by Figure 8.2.

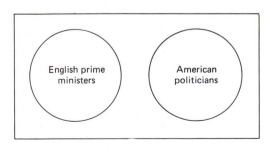

Figure 8.2

Any proposition asserting that one class is completely excluded from another is called a universal negative categorical proposition. The *entire* subject class is excluded from, *denied* to belong to the predicate class.

Some American politicians are Democrats.

asserts class inclusion, but only partial inclusion. It asserts that some members of the class of American politicians are included in the class of Democrats, but it does not make the stronger statement that all of them are. Diagrammatically, we can represent the proposition in Figure 8.3. The * indicates that there is an element in the overlap. Any proposition asserting partial inclusion of one class in another is a particular affirmative proposition. Only some *particular* members of the subject class are *affirmed* to belong to the predicate class.

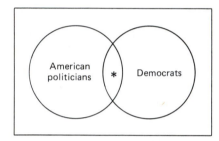

Figure 8.3

Finally,

Some barnyard fowl are not horses.

asserts that some members of the class of barnyard fowl are not members of the class of horses. It asserts class exclusion, although the exclusion is only partial. We can represent this relationship between classes with Figure 8.4. The * here indicates that there is an element in the barnyard fowl class which is not a member of the class of horses. A proposition which asserts the partial exclusion of one class from another is a particular negative categorical proposition. Some but only some *particular* members of the subject class are *denied* to belong to the predicate class.

Figure 8.4

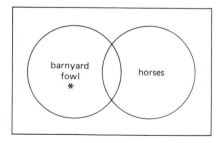

We may define a *categorical proposition* as a statement which asserts a relation between two classes, its subject class and predicate class. It asserts either that the subject class, in whole or in part, is included in the predicate class or that the subject class, in whole or in part, is excluded from the predicate class. Notice that each categorical proposition begins with the word "all," "no," or "some." These three expressions are called quantifiers. They indicate how much, specifically how much of the subject class, whether the whole or only a part, the proposition is concerned with. We shall meet other quantifiers in the next section, and shall have much more to say about them in connection with argument analysis and evaluation.

We have not only defined the four standard categorical propositions, but have also indicated what conditions obtain if they are true. But to apply our test to categorical syllogisms, we must also know under what conditions a categorical proposition is false. This question is logically interesting, because for each categorical proposition to be false, another categorical proposition will be true. In fact, this other categorical proposition will be the contradictory of the first. If "All horses are quadripeds" is false, then the entire class of horses is not included in the class of quadripeds. There is at least one horse which is not a quadriped. But in logic "some" means "at least one." So "Some horses are not quadripeds" is true. But if "All horses are quadripeds" is true, can there be even one horse which is not a quadriped? We could carry out this same reasoning for any pair of categorical propositions where one is a universal affirmative, the other a particular negative, and both have the same subject and the same predicate terms.

Now suppose "No English prime ministers are American politicians" is false. That means the class of English prime ministers and the class of American politicians are not completely separate, that there is some overlap, that at least one thing is in both. Hence "Some English prime ministers are American politicians" is true. However, if "No English prime ministers are American politicians" is true, can there be even one English prime minister who is an American politician? Clearly, under these circumstances "Some English prime ministers are American politicians" is false. Again this reasoning could be repeated for any pair of categorical propositions where one is universal negative and the other is particular affirmative, provided that the subject terms and predicate terms were the same in both.

What have we done at this point? We have paired up the four types of categorical propositions into two sets of contradictory pairs. Corresponding universal affirmative and particular negative propositions are contradictories, as are corresponding universal negative and particular affirmative propositions. Letting S and P be place holders for subject and predicate terms, these logical relations are frequently diagrammed this way, called *the square of opposition* (see Figure 8.5).

Let's now apply the validity test to our three syllogisms. Suppose it's true both that all axioms of geometry are hard things to understand and all hard things to understand give me a headache. Could it also be true that some axiom of geometry does not give me a headache? Suppose there were such an axiom.

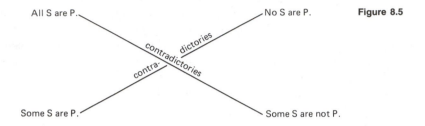

Figure 8.5

Then it would be hard to understand. So it would give me a headache. So this axiom both would and would not give me a headache. But that's an outright contradiction, which we can't imagine holding. Hence, it is not logically possible for the premises to be true and the conclusion false—the argument is deductively valid.

It's quite straightforward to apply our test to the other two syllogisms, for if "Some barnyard fowl are not horses" is false, then its contradictory, "All barnyard fowl are horses" is true. But if it's also true that "All horses are quadripeds," then isn't it true that "All barnyard fowl are quadripeds"? But that's the contradictory of the second premise, "Some barnyard fowl are not quadripeds," and we cannot imagine contradictions true. Again, if "Some Democrats are not English prime ministers" is false, its contradictory "All Democrats are English prime ministers" is true. But if we imagine that true together with "No English prime ministers are American politicians," we are imagining the class of Democrats completely included in the class of English prime ministers, which is completely excluded from the class of American politicians. So the class of Democrats and the class of American politicians are mutually exclusive, that is, "No American politicians are Democrats" is true. But that's the contradictory of the second premise. In both cases, in trying to imagine the premises true and the conclusion false, we are asked to imagine an outright contradiction. This shows these syllogisms deductively valid.

But what about the following syllogisms?

4. Some mystery stories are long.
   Some long things are boring. Therefore
   Some mystery stories are boring.
5. Some mediums are seducers.
   No wizards are mediums. Therefore
   Some wizards are not seducers.

Looking at the first, however we make precise the vague term "long," we can easily imagine there being long mystery stories. And at the same time we can easily imagine that at least one long thing, like a long logic lecture, is boring. But can't we also imagine a situation where all mystery writers really know their craft—none produce boring stories? The longer the story, the more gripping the tale. In that situation, the premises will be true and the conclusion false, showing the syllogism invalid.

What about the second example? A diagram may aid our imagination here. The contradictory of the conclusion is "All wizards are seducers." Let's represent that on analogy with "All horses are quadripeds" (see Figure 8.6).

Figure 8.6

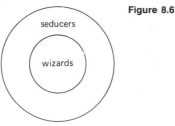

Can we add another circle to this diagram representing that the class of wizards is completely separate from the class of mediums? We certainly can. We can add a mediums circle either within the seducers circle, completely outside it, or partly overlapping, so long as no part of it overlaps the wizards circle. But we want to imagine also that some mediums are seducers. So we enter the mediums circle partially overlapping the seducers circle (but outside wizards completely) and enter a * to indicate there is at least one thing in this overlap (see Figure 8.7).

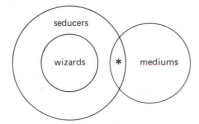

Figure 8.7

There we have it! We have imagined both premises and the contradictory of the conclusion true. The syllogism is invalid. As our discussion amply illustrates, knowing the contradictories of each categorical proposition helps greatly in applying our test. In principle, we can apply this test whenever the question of deductive validity arises. In practice, there are special methods, in some cases special adaptations of this test, for particular families of deductive arguments. Some of these we consider in Chapter 11.

Summary

An argument is *deductively valid* just in case its premises necessitate its conclusion, that is, just in case it is not logically possible for its premises to be true and its conclusion false. We cannot imagine such a situation. Otherwise it is *invalid.* Provided there is no problem with our imagination, a set of statements is *consistent* just in case we can imagine all its component statements being true together. Otherwise it is *inconsistent.* Two statements are *contradictories* just in case if one is true, the other is false, and if one is false, the other is true. We may test deductive arguments for validity by trying to imagine the premises true while the conclusion is false. If we can, the argument is invalid. If trying to imagine this requires our imagining a contradiction true, then the argument is valid.

A *syllogism* is an argument in which exactly two premises are linked to support exactly one conclusion. A *categorical syllogism* is a syllogism all of whose component statements are categorical propositions. A *categorical proposition* asserts that one class, in whole or in part, is either included in or excluded from another class. Being able to identify the contradictory of a categorical proposition helps greatly in applying the validity test to categorical syllogisms.

Exercise 8-II

Indicate whether each of the following sets of statements is consistent or inconsistent.

1. John walked across a bed of red hot burning coals. Yet he was not burned.

2. No college professors are stupid. Jones is a college professor. But he is stupid.

3. The plate came floating through the air, wobbling somewhat. As I watched it, I felt a force pulling me up off the bed and then setting me down on the floor.

4. At night, when I go to sleep, my body, the furniture in my room, the very walls cease to exist. In the morning, when I wake up again, they all pop back into existence.

5. Er had been dead for ten days when he stood up and began telling stories of remarkable visions.

6. Having been missing for almost a year, Ransom returned, telling stories of being kidnapped and taken on a space trip to Mars.

7. Ten couples came to the meeting. All ten became charter members of the club. This made nineteen charter members in all.

8. There is a round, square object on top of the university administration building.

9. Everyone who took the flight came away pleased and satisfied. Some said the service they received was the best ever on a plane. Three came away so disgruntled that they were threatening to sue the airline.

10. These two passages were written and published during the same year. The person who wrote the first passage was an accomplished writer, firmly

established in her craft, a real professional. The person who wrote the second was a sophomoric beginner. Yet the same person wrote both passages.

Exercise 8-III

A. Indicate whether each of the following arguments is deductively valid or invalid by applying the test developed in this section. Be prepared to discuss why you find each argument valid or invalid.

1. Alaska is one of the fifty states in the United States. So residents of Alaska are U.S. residents.

2. Jill told her psychoanalyst that she was afraid that a mad scientist was pursuing her with a laser gun. This means that Jill told her psychoanalyst something.

3. Aristotle is Greek. Aristotle is intelligent. Therefore all Greeks are intelligent.

4. Sherlock Holmes knows that Mr. Jefferson Hope is the murderer of Enoch Drebber and Joseph Stangerson. Therefore Jefferson Hope is the murderer of Enoch Drebber and Joseph Stangerson.

5. Everything true of Samuel Clemens is true of Mark Twain and vice versa. So Sam Clemens is Mark Twain, that is, Sam Clemens and Mark Twain are the same person.

6. This is a picture of the Empire State Building taken in the immediate vicinity of the skycraper. Therefore this picture was taken in New York City.

7. The Surgeon General has determined that cigarette smoking causes lung cancer, emphysema, and heart ailments. So cigarette smoking is harmful to one's health.

8. Cambridge is north of London. Edinburgh is north of Cambridge. So Edinburgh is north of London.

9. Logic courses are difficult but rewarding. Some logic courses are exciting. So some difficult things are exciting.

10. Philosophers and mathematicians are either precise or foggy-headed. Not all philosophers are foggy-headed. Therefore some mathematicians are foggy-headed.

B. Determine whether these categorical syllogisms are valid or invalid and why. In each case, indicate what is the contradictory of the conclusion.

1. Some students are good in logic, and some persons good in logic are proficient in mathematics. So some students are proficient in mathematics.

2. All aphrodisiacs are highly intoxicating. No bottles of beer are aphrodisiacs. Therefore no bottles of beer are highly intoxicating.

3. Some living things are not edible, because some plants are not edible and all plants are living things.

4. No subterranean vaults are aboveground. So some dangerous places are not subterranean vaults since some dangerous places are aboveground.

5. All things placed in safe containers are transportable, but some explosives are not placed in safe containers. So some transportable things are not explosives.

6. No nefarious activities are honorable. Some political policies are honorable. So some political policies are not nefarious activities.

7. All repressive things are illegal and some police activities are repressive. So some police activities are illegal.

8. No space weapons are stabilizing. All space weapons are expensive. Therefore no expensive things are stabilizing.

9. All aphrodisiacs are expensive, so some stalks of celery are not expensive, since some stalks of celery are not aphrodisiacs.

10. All churches are houses of worship. All synagogues are houses of worship. So some synagogues are churches.

§8.3 EVALUATING INDUCTIVE ARGUMENTS—FUNDAMENTAL PROCEDURES

Recall the inductive claim—the premises of an argument give some evidence, although not conclusive evidence, for the conclusion. If the premises are true, then we have some reason, in some cases a very strong reason, to believe the conclusion, although it is possible for the premises to be true and the conclusion false. We shall speak of inductive arguments as being inductively correct or incorrect. We reserve the validity/invalidity distinction for appraising deductive arguments exclusively. We do not speak of inductive arguments, even very strong ones, as being inductively valid. But just what does it mean to say that an argument is inductively correct?

What Do We Mean by *Prima Facie* Inductive Correctness?

There are two aspects to inductive correctness. Although the premises of a correct inductive argument do not guarantee, necessitate the conclusion, given that the premises are true, it must be more likely than not that the conclusion is true. That is, the conclusion must be true in most situations where the premises are true. Where this happens, we say that the argument is *prima facie inductively correct*. We are using *prima facie* as it is used in legal contexts. In law, *prima facie* evidence is sufficient to establish a point unless rebutted, unless counterevidence is presented. Counterconsiderations are crucial in making a final determination of inductive correctness. We'll turn to them shortly, after we further develop *prima facie* correctness. Where given all the conceivable or imaginable situations in which the premises are true, the conclusion is false in as many of them as it is true, or false in the majority, the argument is *inductively incorrect.* Here the premises either give as much evidence for the conclusion as they do for its contradictory or they more strongly support the contradictory.

How likely is the conclusion given the premises constitutes the *prima facie* weight of the argument. The more likely the conclusion, given the premises, the greater the percentage of situations in which it is true, the greater the *prima facie* weight. For *prima facie* inductive correctness, the weight must be better than 50 percent. Assessing the *prima facie* weight is the first aspect in determining inductive correctness. Let's illustrate doing this by looking at a class of inductive arguments—the statistical syllogisms—which roughly correspond to the categorical syllogisms we have just studied in the last section.

Imagine several urns in front of you, each containing a number of balls. Different urns have different colored balls, and not all the balls in a given urn are the same color. Suppose someone is picking balls out of these various urns and the next ball will come from Urn **1.** Suppose we are told that 100 percent of the balls in Urn **1** are blue. Then we can deduce that this next ball will be blue also.

> All (100 percent) of the balls in Urn **1** are blue.
> The next ball to be drawn is from Urn **1.** Therefore
> The next ball to be drawn is blue.

This is a valid deductive argument. But now suppose we are told that 90 percent of the balls in Urn **1** are blue. We cannot validly argue from this that the next ball will be blue. But the premises give strong support. If we were to number the balls in the urn, 90 percent of the arguments

> Ninety percent of the balls in Urn **1** are blue.
> n is a ball in Urn **1.** Therefore
> n is blue.

would have all true premises and true conclusion. If we knew that 80, 70, 60 percent were blue, we would still have positive support for our conclusion.

But suppose only 50 percent were blue. Would our premises give any more support to the conclusion that the next ball will be blue than they would to its denial—the next ball won't be blue? Suppose only 40 percent of the balls are blue or 30, 20, 10 percent. In these cases, don't we have stronger support for the claim that the next ball will *not* be blue than that it will be? The lower the percentage, the stronger the support for the denial of the conclusion. Hence, where the percentage of balls in Urn **1** which are blue is between 50+ and 99+ percent, the syllogism

> X percent of balls in Urn **1** are blue.
>
> The next ball to be drawn is from Urn **1.** Therefore
>
> The next ball to be drawn will be blue

is *prima facie* inductively correct. Whereas if the percentage of blue balls is 50 percent or less the argument is inductively incorrect. It should be pretty obvious why arguments of this pattern are called statistical syllogisms. We draw one conclusion from exactly two premises linked. Instead of the first premise being a categorical statement that "All A's are B's," we have a statistical statement that "X percent of A's are B's."

Assessing the *prima facie* weight of a statistical syllogism and judging how strongly a modality is justified are parallel and straightforward. If only 51 percent of the balls in Urn **1** were blue, an argument that the next ball drawn would be blue, although *prima facie* correct, would be very weak. Only a weak modality like "more probable than not" would be justified here. If we were in the 70 percent range, a modality like "probably" or "likely" would be justified. When we get into the 90 percent range, then our premises make the conclusion very likely, highly probable. And up towards 95+ percent, "almost certainly," "certainly," and similar modalities are justified. On the other hand, if 50 percent or less were blue, no positive modality would be justified. Not all statistical syllogisms will have a specific numerical percentage.

> Almost all A's are B's.
>
> Most A's are B's.
>
> More A's than not are B's.
>
> As many A's as not are B's.
>
> Many A's are B's.
>
> Few A's are B's.
>
> Almost no A's are B's.

Any such statement makes a claim about the percentage of A's which are B's and can serve as a first premise of a statistical syllogism. Like "all," "no," and "some," "most," "many," "few," "X percent" for any X, are quantifiers. The stronger the quantifier, the stronger the *prima facie* weight of the argument.

What Does It Mean to Rebut an Inductive Argument? How Can The *Prima Facie* Weight Be Undercut?

Let's go back to the situation where 90 percent of the balls in Urn **1** are blue and the next ball drawn will be from Urn **1.** Suppose we also knew that there were exactly 100 balls in Urn **1,** that they had been arranged neatly in ten rows, one on top of each other, ten balls to a row, that all the blue balls had been placed in the bottom nine rows, and that those balls which were some other color constituted the top row. Suppose we also knew that the person picking out balls from urns simply takes whatever ball comes first to hand. Whatever ball will be taken lies at the top of the urn. Given all this additional information, what would we think of the original argument

> Ninety percent of the balls in Urn **1** are blue.
> The next ball drawn is from Urn **1**. So
> The next ball drawn will be blue?

Given not just the premises but all the information, how much confidence may we have in the conclusion? Isn't it certain that the conclusion is false? Isn't the force of the statistical syllogism completely undercut?

This situation illustrates a very important point concerning how evaluating inductive arguments differs from appraising deductive arguments. In a valid deductive argument, we may expand the set of premises by adding in whatever statements we wish. The resulting argument will still be deductively valid. Let's see why. Suppose every statement in the expanded set is true. Then all the original premises are true, since they are all in the expanded set. So the conclusion has to be true. This holds true for any deductive argument. In testing it, we need look only at the premises and conclusion, not to any additional information.[3]

Inductive correctness, on the other hand, depends not just on the argument's having sufficient *prima facie* weight, but on its satisfying the requirement of total evidence. This is sometimes put by saying that the premises of an inductive argument must contain all the available relevant evidence.[4] We may say that an argument is inductively correct just in case it is *prima facie* inductively correct and satisfies the requirement of total evidence. Alternatively, we could introduce the concept of total weight as opposed to *prima facie* weight of the argument. The *total weight* of an argument is the likelihood of the conclusion given the premises and all available relevant counterevidence or rebutting evidence. We could then define an argument as inductively correct just when its total weight was greater than 50 percent. That is, the likelihood of the conclusion, given the premises and the available relevant counterevidence, is greater than 50 percent.

The requirement of total evidence poses a distinct problem for evaluating inductive arguments. For how can we assess whether an argument satisfies this requirement, how can we estimate the total weight, unless we already possess all the relevant available information? But surely we will not be in such a position for all arguments we encounter or even all the arguments we might want to evaluate. Need everyone know that all the balls in Urn **1** were arranged as we envisaged? Need we know all the factors impinging on some scientific claim or some issue of public policy? It would seem that in a number of cases, special expertise is required to determine just what information is relevant, just what questions need to be asked to discover the available relevant evidence or counterevidence. The requirement of total evidence presents us with an ideal in evaluating inductive arguments, an ideal we may not always be able to satisfy, given our present knowledge.

Just how, then, should we approach evaluating inductive arguments? First, we should realize that in some cases, determining the *prima facie* inductive correctness or *prima facie* weight is all that we can do. If we cannot assess the counterconsideration question, we may still be able to assess whether the argument is *prima facie* correct. Then we can put the burden of proof on any challenger to show that the total weight is less than the *prima facie* weight or that the argument is not inductively correct. But this leads to the next point. Should we possess rebutting evidence, should we know of counterconsiderations which undercut the *prima facie* weight of the argument, then we have every right to challenge the argument, to in effect ask the arguer why the premises make him so sure. Given the requirement of total evidence, it is perfectly proper to include these considerations in a preliminary assessment of the total weight of the argument or the total weight, given what we know.

We may respond in another way to the requirement of total evidence. This response is especially appropriate when the issue is not just how strongly the premises support the conclusion, but whether we should accept the conclusion, believe it. Given an argument to evaluate, we may seek to increase our knowledge by discovering counterconsiderations, rebutting evidence. One way to do this deserves special mention. Sometimes arguments are presented in the context of debate. One arguer seeks to defend a claim while the challenger advocates the opposite. Courtroom situations are typical here, with opposed attorneys arguing opposite sides of the issue. Here in effect we are presented with two arguments. Rhetoricians call such an exchange an adversarial situation.[5] Should some issue be particularly controversial or important to us, we may seek an adversarial situation before making up our minds whether or not to accept some claim about it.

Given an argument for some position presented in an adversarial situation, we would like to evaluate its total weight by asking how likely is the conclusion given both the premises and counterpremises, that is, the premises of both arguments. The problem is that premises and counterpremises need not be consistent with each other in an adversarial situation. Now there is nothing inconsistent in saying that 90 percent of the balls in Urn **1** are blue, the next ball drawn will come from Urn **1,** none of the balls in the top row of Urn **1** are blue, and the next ball will be drawn from the top row. We can imagine all four of these statements true together. The first two premises can be consistently combined with the latter two as counterpremises. The counterpremises do not show that the original premises are false, but rather undercut their *prima facie* weight. This is what we mean by rebutting evidence or counterevidence, information consistent with the premises which nonetheless undercuts their *prima facie* weight. Similarly, consider this adversarial situation:

ARGUMENT: Mrs. Wilson's probated will leaves her daughter Judith with only $1.00. Therefore, in effect, Judith will receive no share of her mother's estate.

COUNTERARGUMENT: Mrs. Wilson was mentally incompetent

when she made her will. Therefore the will is invalid and will be set aside. This means that Judith will receive some share in her mother's estate.

Again, premise and counterpremise are consistent.

However, in adversarial situations the challenger may attack an argument not by presenting rebutting conditions, but by attacking the premises themselves, claiming that they are false. For example, during the war in Vietnam, the Johnson administration argued that North Vietnam was committing aggression against South Vietnam. Their evidence for this claim included this premise:

> Under the terms of the Geneva Accords of 1956, South Vietnam and North Vietnam became independent states.

Critics of the war in Vietnam posed this counterpremise:

> South Vietnam and North Vietnam are really one country and were not divided by the Geneva Accords.[6]

Which side should we believe? For technical reasons,[7] we cannot ask how likely it is that North Vietnam was committing aggression against South Vietnam given both premise and counterpremise. Now it is conceivable that we have information which shows which of the two sides, the Johnson administration or their opponents, is correct on their point. We should then discount whichever statement is false. In the absence of such information, aren't both statements questionable? In assessing the weight of the argument, we should disregard both, basing our assessment just on the consistent premises and counterpremises, if any. However, in doing this we have gone beyond assessing the total weight of the argument. Two questions we must keep distinct are how strongly the premises support the conclusion—if the premises are true, how likely is the conclusion—from whether the premises are false or questionable. Questions of the truth or falsity of premises do not enter into determining *prima facie* or total weight. In the last section of Chapter 9, where we discuss overall generic argument evaluation, we shall see how to combine these two questions.

Our consideration of rebutting conditions leads directly to some further considerations on how we may argue for a claim. Careful arguers may take rebuttals into account in presenting their arguments. In the next section, we shall see how.

Summary

An argument is *prima facie inductively correct* if its conclusion is true in most situations where the premises are true. The likelihood of the conclusion given the premises is the *prima facie* weight of the argument. We may define being inductively correct two ways. To be *inductively correct* an argument must be *prima facie* correct and satisfy the requirement of total evidence—the premises must contain all available relevant evidence. Alternatively, we may define the *total weight* of an argument as the likelihood of the conclusion, given the premises and all available relevant rebutting evidence. Rebutting evidence is evidence consistent with the premises which undercuts the *prima facie* weight of the argument. An argument is inductively correct then when its total weight is greater than 50 percent.

Exercise 8-IV

Estimate the *prima facie* inductive weight of each of the following arguments. What sort of positive modality, if any, is appropriate in each case? Indicate whether or not an argument is *prima facie* inductively correct.

Sample Answer

By the year 1000 A.D., less than 5 percent of the inhabitants of Great Britain practiced tree worship. Wulfstan lived in Great Britain around 1000 A.D. So he did not practice tree worship.

Saying less than 5 percent of the inhabitants of Great Britain practiced tree worship in 1000 A.D. means that better than 95 percent did not. This is a very high percentage, way over 50 percent. Hence the *prima facie* weight of this argument is quite strong, and a modality such as "almost certainly" is justified. The argument is clearly *prima facie* inductively correct.

1.   In tossing a fair coin, the chances of getting a head or a tail are even, 50-50. The coin that has just been tossed is fair. So it will come up heads.

2.   Sixty percent of those voting in the last election cast their ballots for the president. Alice voted in the last election. So she voted for the president.

3.   Students usually find advanced symbolic logic the most difficult course they have taken. Maureen is registered for advanced symbolic logic. Consequently, we may expect that Maureen will find advanced symbolic logic the most difficult course she has taken.

4.   Fifty-one percent of Americans who voted in 1976 cast their ballots for Jimmy Carter. Jim voted in 1976. Therefore Jim voted for Mr. Carter.

5.   Ten percent of the students enrolled in State University have serious academic problems. Jack is a student at State University. So Jack has serious academic problems.

6.   Only ten percent of the students enrolled at State University have serious academic problems. Jack is a student at State University. So Jack does not have serious academic problems.

7.   Many times when people get dressed up, they are going to some big

social occasion. Jane is dressed to kill. Hence Jane is going to a big social occasion.

8. One-hundred-fifty of the two-hundred people residing in that town belong to the local Methodist Church. Jonathan lives in that town. So Jonathan belongs to the local Methodist Church.

9. Harry was born in Oklahoma City. So he is an American citizen.

10. John and Patty have never exchanged an unkind word in thirty years of marriage. So they have a stable and happy relationship.

Exercise 8-V

Each of the following arguments is accompanied by a counterargument. Indicate whether or not the argument is inductively correct in the light of the rebutting evidence presented in the counterargument. That is, how strong a case do we have for the conclusion given both the premises and the rebutting evidence? You may want to comment on the *prima facie* correctness of the argument and then on how this is affected by the rebutting evidence.

Sample Answer

a. A clinical sample of 41 pairs (of users and nonusers of marijuana) was selected and matched for age, education, marital status, and tobacco and alcohol use. The researchers were careful to test serum testosterone levels and could find no difference between users and nonusers. Hence, we may expect that in the population at large there is no difference between users and nonusers. So the serious charge that marijuana reduces testosterone (male hormone) levels is false.[8]

b. Marijuana does reduce testosterone levels, at least before age forty. A survey of 356 pairs, ranging in age from twenty to eighty-five, showed testosterone levels for persons under 40 who used marijuana to be distinctly lower. One-third of the pairs sampled were under forty. Like the clinical sample of forty-one pairs, they were matched for various factors which could affect the outcome, and all persons were screened for biological or health factors which could influence the result.

Given that forty-one but just forty-one pairs of users and nonusers were tested, does our premise give us better than 50-50 odds that in the population at large there is no difference between users and nonusers? Perhaps some users are resistant to the effects of marijuana for various reasons, and it was these users who were paired with nonusers in this particular clinical sample. It would seem that the conclusion need not be true in most situations where the premise is true. So it is questionable whether the *prima facie* weight of the premise is sufficient even for *prima facie* inductive correctness. In the light of the rebutting evidence, this argument is clearly not inductively correct. It would seem that in most situations where both premise and rebutting evidence were true, the conclusion would be false—marijuana would in fact have an effect on testosterone levels.

1. a. We should not raise the legal drinking age in this state from nineteen to twenty-one. When you are nineteen, you are old enough to vote, pay taxes, and serve in the army. If you commit a crime, you will be tried as an adult. So you're old enough to drink.

b. Forty percent of highway fatalities are due to drunk driving by people between the ages of nineteen and twenty-one. Sixty percent of serious but nonfatal traffic accidents are due to this same cause. All our neighboring states either have or will shortly raise the drinking age to twenty-one. We should raise the drinking age also.

2. a. Restoring the death penalty for first-degree murder will reduce the number of murders, which is growing at an alarming rate. Any criminal will think twice before pulling the trigger, if there is a death penalty.

b. The death penalty will not significantly decrease the number of murders. Many murders are crimes of passion, where the perpetrator thinks only of revenge and not of the consequences of the action for himself. Most other murders are committed by hardened criminals who either believe they can escape punishment or for whom threatened punishments have no deterrent effect.

3. a. Martin Luther King, Jr. was a fine man because, in spite of occasional arrogance, he was an unselfish and courageous worker for his fellowman.—Example cited by Carl Wellman, *Challenge and Response.*

b. Martin Luther King, Jr. may not be the saint many people think he is. There are stories that he was involved in extramarital affairs, and toward the end of his life his opposition to the war in Vietnam led to his investigation by the FBI.

4. a. Lead acetate should be banned as an ingredient in cosmetics. This substance is a known animal carcinogen. Furthermore, using any product containing lead incurs the risk of lead poisoning.

b. Regulators in Washington made an important decision last Friday. . . . It signals a surprising change in the way the Food and Drug Administration views substances that might cause cancer. For the first time in memory, the agency consciously—and we think reasonably—refused to ban the use of an animal carcinogen in a cosmetic. The substance is lead acetate. . . .

The F.D.A.'s restraint in this case is welcome. The amount of lead acetate that would be absorbed by humans from hair dyes is minuscule—only a half of one-millionth of a gram for each application. That is less than one percent of the lead that adults absorb from food, water and air every day. The chance that this amount of lead acetate would cause cancer is therefore very remote. Under a "worst case" risk analysis, the dyes would cause one cancer in five million cases of lifetime use. So the agency sensibly concluded that the animal studies proving lead acetate to be a carcinogen were not appropriate grounds for banning it in hair dyes.—*The New York Times,* editorial, November 9, 1980. Copyright © 1980 by The New York Times Company. Reprinted by permission.

§8.4 REBUTTALS AND COUNTERREBUTTALS

The requirement of total evidence has made plain the importance of rebutting evidence in evaluating inductive arguments. In some cases, once we have an inductive argument, we may be able to anticipate certain circumstances or conditions which would undercut the argument if they held. We may not know that they hold. What we do know is that if they did, the *prima facie* weight of the argument would be significantly undercut. For example, consider again Mrs. Wilson's will. There are a number of circumstances, besides mental incompetence, which may invalidate a will. In some states, disinheriting one's children or one's spouse may be illegal. A supervening will may be found. Even if we had no evidence that any of these conditions held, we do know that if any did, the argument that because Mrs. Wilson left her daughter Judith only $1.00, Judith in effect had no share in the estate would be seriously undercut.

Again, consider our argument from Chapter 6 that Jones is the best candidate to run for president next year. If it's true that Jones has consistently shown herself a very competent administrator, that she has more experience than any of her competitors, and that she is the best campaigner around, then we certainly have evidence for this claim. But Jones may have problems. Early in her life she may have acquired a criminal record; perhaps she is a member of a minority group subject to much prejudice. Perhaps she is divorcing her husband. Or perhaps her husband has been involved in shady business deals and people are questioning whether Jones herself was involved. Now these factors could constitute serious liabilities for any candidate for public office. Having liabilities, then, is the general excepting or rebutting condition we can foresee for the positive evidence that Jones is the best candidate. We call these excepting conditions *rebuttals*. Given the positive evidence for the conclusion, they are conditions which would undercut the force of the evidence.

Now it would be an overcautious arguer indeed who sought always to qualify his argument by listing all the rebuttals, especially if there were no evidence for these rebuttals, or if the evidence were only slight, nowhere near enough for an inductively correct argument that the rebuttal held. However, there are times when a careful arguer would want to acknowledge certain rebuttals. Suppose, given our knowledge of the world, that there was some question as to whether a rebuttal held. If we qualified how strongly we claimed our premises supported the conclusion by acknowledging this rebuttal, we would forestall a possible criticism of our reasoning. We are not claiming outright that our premises support the conclusion, but only that they support it with a certain weight if the rebuttal does not hold. Finding out that the rebuttal does hold does not affect that claim.

There is another reason for stating rebuttals. The possibility of a rebuttal raises a question about how adequately the premises support the conclusion. Hence, should we have evidence that a rebuttal does not hold, that should increase our confidence in the conclusion. It would be part of the evidence supporting it. We call statements presenting such evidence *counterrebuttals*. That is, counterrebuttals serve to rule out rebuttals, to show that certain rebutting conditions do not hold. We'll look at some specific examples shortly. But to include a counterrebuttal in an argument, we should somehow have to indicate what rebuttal it counters, giving us another reason for stating rebuttals.

Since careful arguers may incorporate both rebuttals and counterrebuttals in their arguments, we want to know how to diagram arguments with such elements. Rebuttals in effect refine or sharpen modalities. We say that the premises support the conclusion with the strength claimed, unless these rebutting conditions hold. This gives us a clue for representing rebuttals in argument diagrams. We list these rebuttals under the word "unless," enclose them in a box placed to the left of the modality, and connect the rebuttal box to the modality box by a horizontal line.

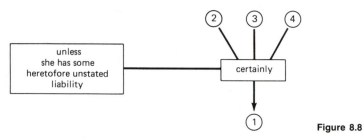

Figure 8.8

Figure 8.8 contains the diagram for our argument about Jones. We are letting (1) stand for the conclusion that Jones is the best candidate and (2), (3), and (4), respectively, for the premises that she is a consistently competent administrator, has the most expertise, and is best campaigner. Figure 8.9 shows what the Wilson will argument looks like, incorporating the rebuttals we have foreseen.

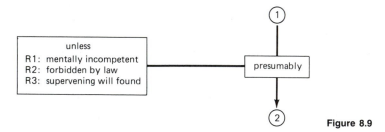

Figure 8.9

Statement (1) is the premise that the will leaves the daughter with only $1.00; (2) is the conclusion that the daughter has no inheritance from her mother. When several rebutting conditions are presented, we label them R1, R2, . . . , in the order they have been presented. We'll see the advantages of this shortly.

But now suppose that

(4) The witnesses who signed Mrs. Wilson's will, her lawyer, her doctor,

her nurse, and three close friends will all testify that she was in complete possession of her mental powers when she made the will.

Suppose also that

    (5) State law permits disinheriting children, and

    (6) An exhaustive search of Mrs. Wilson's papers by an investigator
hired by her daughter has produced no supervening will.

Conditions (4), (5), and (6) surely present strong evidence respectively that R1,
R2, R3 do not hold. They are counterrebuttals. Our example motivates how such
premises have a distinctly different function from premises we have already
seen. Clearly (1) is relevant to (2), and none of (4), (5), or (6) serves to explain
that relevance. So it would be inappropriate to link (4), (5), or (6) to (1). Would
an argument from (4), (5), or (6) to (2) make any sense without the rest of the
argument as context? Can I plausibly argue that many persons will testify that
Mrs. Wilson was mentally competent when she made her will; therefore her
daughter will have no inheritance from her mother? Does the premise, by itself,
support the conclusion? Figure 8.10 reflects their function.

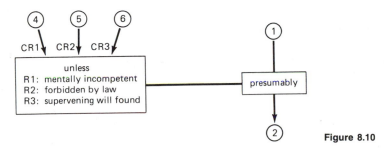

Figure 8.10

    The downward-directed arrows indicate that (4), (5), and (6) ultimately
give reasons for the conclusion (2), but they do it by ruling out rebuttals. The
labels CR1, CR2, CR3 indicate which rebuttal is being ruled out by which counterrebuttal. These labels are a distinct advantage in clarifying what our diagram
says. For it is quite possible that several counterrebuttals might be given for the
same rebuttal. Other rebuttals might be left uncountered. The first counterrebuttal stated might not counter the first stated rebuttal. The arrow connects
the counterrebuttal with the conclusion it supports. The label connects it with
the rebuttal it counters.

    Notice that counterrebuttals, although they have a distinctive role, are
nonetheless premises. Hence in working up an argument in natural language for
diagramming, we assign them numbers, just like the other statements constituting the argument. On the other hand, rebuttals modify modalities, and
modalities are not properly part of either premises or conclusions, as we have
stressed. Rebuttals, then, like modalities are part of the connecting material

between premises and conclusion. In working up arguments for diagramming that involve rebuttals, those rebuttals will be left outside of any brackets and not numbered.

Since counterrebuttals support the conclusion by showing that certain rebuttals do not hold, instead of directly supporting the conclusion, arguing by counterrebuttals constitutes a distinct argument strategy. This strategy is especially helpful when various alternatives to the conclusion are possible. For example, suppose someone argued that

> 5,000 laboratory rats were fed a diet rich in cockroaches. A significant number developed stomach cancer. Hence, the diet of roaches caused the stomach cancer.

Now certainly the premises give some evidence for the conclusion, but can we really place much confidence in that conclusion unless we know that competing explanations have been ruled out? Could the rats have been genetically predisposed to cancer? Could something else in the diet or in the environment be carcinogenic? We need to rule out these possibilities to establish the conclusion properly. Without ruling them out we can imagine these various situations where the premises are true and the conclusion false. But we may view these competing causal explanations as rebuttals and the arguments ruling them out as counterrebuttals. We shall return to this point again in Chapter 10 when we discuss appraising causal arguments. Similarly, suppose we have to choose between several alternative courses of action. Perhaps we have evidence favoring one choice. But to opt for that particular alternative on the basis of just that evidence might be rather hasty. We should argue against the other alternatives first. The competing alternatives are the rebuttals. The arguments against them present counterrebuttals.

Rebuttals and counterrebuttals may be more important for evaluating arguments than for diagramming them. We may find ourselves more often asking what rebuttals and counterrebuttals might be given than in seeing them included in arguments. Asking about rebuttals in particular can aid in estimating whether the conclusion is true in most situations where the premises are true. As we saw, considering rebuttals lets us imagine situations where the premises are true but the conclusion false. If, given the premises, there would seem to be at least as many situations in which some rebuttal is true as there would be situations where the conclusion is true, the argument is not inductively correct.

There are two aspects of evaluating inductive arguments we must still discuss. Since our presentation of both involves the notion of rebuttals, we have postponed them to this point. In the last section, we explicitly emphasized that deductive validity is an all or nothing affair. That inductive weight or strength is a matter of more or less has been implicit throughout our discussion of inductive correctness. Some inductive arguments may give more evidence for their conclusions than others. Hence we can not only judge arguments as inductively correct or not, but can *rank* inductive arguments as being more or less strong, as having more or less weight. Indeed this is another aspect of evaluating inductive arguments. Clearly as long as the premises are all true or plausible, the stronger the argument, the better, the more logically convincing, it is. In the next section, we present three principles for comparing the strength of inductive arguments. Finally, there are specific conditions under which an argument is inductively incorrect. We examine these in the last section of this chapter.

Summary

Rebuttals are excepting conditions. Given the positive evidence for the conclusion, if they held they would undercut the force of the argument. Besides mentioning rebuttals, some arguments may contain premises that specifically assert that certain rebuttals do not operate. These are *counterrebuttals*. In argument diagrams, rebuttals are listed in a box to the left of the modality they qualify, the two boxes connected by a horizontal line. Counterrebuttals are represented by encircled numbers, the numbers those statements are assigned in the argument, and their support of the conclusion by downward-directed arrows from these encircled numbers to the rebuttal box. Where more than one rebuttal is involved, we may label the rebuttals R1, R2, . . . , and the arrows CR1, CR2, . . . , to indicate which rebuttal is being countered.

Exercise 8-VI

A. Construct tree diagrams to represent the structure of the following arguments. Be sure to include the modalities and display the rebuttals according to the methods of this section.

1. In twenty-five years of marriage, John and Patty have never exchanged an unkind word. Presumably, unless they are unusually inhibited in expressing anger or their feelings for each other have grown completely cold, they have a stable and happy marriage.

2. The witness remained calm and cool under cross-examination. Evidently, unless he is a consummate liar, he was telling the truth.

3. Surely, unless there is some remarkable coincidence, Dee and Sam are brother and sister, for they both have the same shade of red hair.

4. The assailant admits that he fired the shot which wounded the president. His action was observed by many bystanders. The incident was recorded on videotape. Hence, certainly, unless the assailant is insane, he is guilty of the attempted assassination of the president.

5. Anne is one of Jack's sisters. All of Jack's sisters that I know have red hair. So presumably unless Anne has dyed her hair, or it has gone white, or she has lost her hair, Anne has red hair too.—Example in Stephen Toulmin, *The Uses of Argument.*

6. The proposal to send in military advisors would involve the United

States in a guerrilla war. But whenever in the past the United States has gotten involved in a guerilla war, it has suffered heavy losses. Hence, quite possibly, unless we are very clear about our goals, this proposal would entail heavy losses also.

7. Peterson is a Swede. But since the proportion of Roman Catholic Swedes is less than two percent, almost no Swedes are Roman Catholics. Hence, almost certainly, unless both his parents are Roman Catholics, Peterson is not a Roman Catholic.—Example in Stephen Toulmin, *The Uses of Argument.*

B. The following arguments all include both rebuttals and counterrebuttals. Again construct tree diagrams to represent their structure, showing the rebuttals and counterrebuttals by the methods developed in this section.

1. In twenty-five years of marriage, John and Patty have never exchanged an unkind word. Presumably, unless they are unusually inhibited in expressing anger or their feelings for each other have grown completely cold, they have a stable and happy marriage. But John and Patty have both always been demonstrative with their feelings in public.

2. The witness remained calm and cool under cross-examination. Evidently, unless he is a consummate liar, he was telling the truth. But character witnesses have testified that he is very truthful.

3. N.J. Transit should assign more conductors to its trains on holidays. For, evidently, unless they are saving money in the long run by using minimal crews on holidays, they are losing revenues by allowing passengers to travel free. But when fares go uncollected, they are losing far more than what they expect to save.—R.T.P., *Sunday Star-Ledger* (Newark, N.J.), December 5, 1982.

4. Last year we had forty children enrolled in our summer program. Hence unless the children were disappointed, we may expect that we shall have a good enrollment again this year. But the children were not disappointed with the program. We know this because many children told us how much they enjoyed the program, and many parents complimented us on our efforts.

5. Unless people were willing to move into bomb shelters when international tensions increased to a certain point and such shelters were absolutely impregnable, bomb shelters would provide no security or saving of life in a nuclear holocaust. We can be sure of this because people could not get to the shelters soon enough after learning that an attack had been launched. Furthermore economically feasible shelters cannot provide protection against the blast, heat, intense radiation, and mass fires that would probably occur in densely populated regions of the country.[9] But people in general are not going to move into bomb shelters until an attack is imminent, and absolutely impregnable shelters are impossible.

6. Since destroying someone's property is a wicked thing to do, John really did something wicked when he threw that baseball, breaking the picture window, unless he is only a child. But he is old enough to know better.[10]

7. The testimony of our moral tradition condemns extramarital sexual intercourse. Hence surely extramarital sexual intercourse is sinful, unless the traditional attitude was based on factors which no longer hold, such as the need to give children a secure social status, now circumvented by birth control measures supposedly. But we may easily overestimate the effectiveness of present birth-control methods, and furthermore jealousy is still a problem. In addition, intercourse brings with it emotional ties which are not easily broken.[11]

§8.5 COMPARING ARGUMENTS FOR INDUCTIVE STRENGTH

Three principles govern the comparative strength of arguments. The first and third, at least, have been implicit in our discussion of the last two sections. All three principles concern the *prima facie* strength or weight of inductive arguments. The first concerns the relation between the strength of the premises which directly support a conclusion (as opposed to the counterrebuttals) and the overall strength of the argument.

1. (DIRECT VARIATION PRINCIPLE) The stronger the premises with respect to the conclusion they directly support, the stronger the argument.

How may we strengthen the premises? There are two ways to do this. First, we may increase the number of premises—as long as the statements we add really are new premises, that is, they present evidence relevant to the conclusion and the evidence is new—not already contained in the original premises. For example, suppose someone argued that

(1) The *Star Wars* movies are good entertainment,

and gave as reasons

(2) The fantasy is genuinely enjoyable, and
(3) The plot is well contrived.

This is intuitively plausible. But if, in addition, we had

(4) The cinematography is stunning, and
(5) The musical scores are genuinely memorable,

we would have a stronger argument. Clearly, if all we knew were premises (2) and (3), it is possible the cinematography could be so terrible or the musical score so dreadful as to ruin the movies as entertainment. This may seem unlikely, but not inconceivable. Hence, there are fewer chances for the conclusion to be false, given (2)–(5), than given just (2) and (3), making the second argument stronger.

We should note, however, that the comparative strength of two arguments is not simply a function of how many premises are given to support the conclusion. Although certainly the second argument is stronger than the first, we are not warranted in saying that it is twice as strong as the first, just because it has twice as many premises. One premise may do far more to increase the likelihood of a conclusion than another. Knowing that the acting in the *Star Wars* movies is compelling might make the conclusion that they are good entertainment more likely than knowing the musical scores are genuinely memorable. Strength depends on how likely is the conclusion given the premises, not on how many individual pieces of information the premises contain.

But there is another way to increase the strength of premises. We can replace a premise by a stronger statement. But what does this mean? This question is important for both the first and second principles of argument strength, as we shall see shortly. It is also crucial for properly supplying suppressed premises, which we discuss in the next chapter. Although the concept of statement strength is easy to grasp, it sounds somewhat paradoxical at first. The strength of a statement is measured by how much it rules out. The stronger a statement, the more logically possible, imaginable situations it excludes or are incompatible with it. Let's look at an example:

The demise of slavery occurred sometime in the nineteenth century.

What does this statement exclude? It excludes the demise of slavery occurring before January 1, 1800, and after December 31, 1899. We may show this by representing time with an arrow and shading the two ends, that is, the times falling outside the nineteenth century (see Figure 8.11).

Figure 8.11

Suppose we modified our statement to read

The demise of slavery occurred sometime during the 1860s.

Intuitively this should seem a stronger statement. Does it exclude more? It certainly does, for to represent its information we must shade out all of the arrow except the interval between 1860 and 1870 (see Figure 8.12).

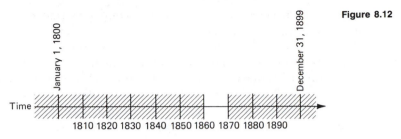

Figure 8.12

But we can be even more specific.

The demise of slavery occurred sometime during the 1860s but before 1865.

Here we shade out even more (see Figure 8.13).

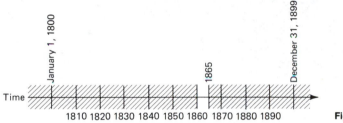

Figure 8.13

Finally, we can be most specific and indicate a particular date:

The demise of slavery occurred on January 1, 1863.

Here all the timeline is shaded except for one point (see Figure 8.14). As our statement becomes increasingly more specific, it becomes stronger. But as it becomes stronger, it rules out more possibilities for when the demise of slavery could have come.

Figure 8.14

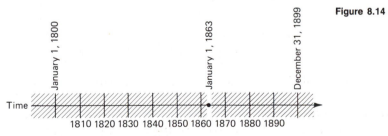

Now compare these two statements:

(1) All white human males are chauvinists.
(2) All white blue-collar human males are chauvinists.

Which is stronger? Which rules out more? The second says that every single white blue-collar human male is a chauvinist. It rules out there being a white blue-collar male who fails to be a chauvinist. It leaves open the possibility that some white male might not be a chauvinist, so long as he is not a blue-collar worker. But what about the first? That rules out the possibility of there being any white human male, blue collar or otherwise, who isn't a chauvinist. Now clearly, there are more white human males than white blue-collar human males. So (1) excludes more. We represent this nicely in Figure 8.15. Clearly the area ruled out by (1) is greater than the area ruled out by (2). So (1) is the stronger statement.

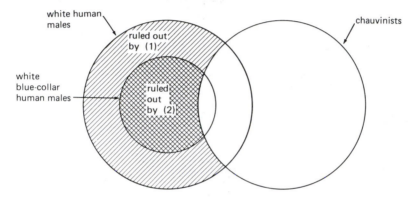

Figure 8.15

Another way to put this point is to say that the stronger a statement, the easier to show it false, or the greater possibility that it is false. There is a whole range of dates possible for the demise of slavery. To show that

The demise of slavery occurred sometime during the nineteenth century.

is false, all I need do is produce some date or some range of dates, outside the nineteenth century, when the demise of slavery occurred. But to show false that

The demise of slavery occurred sometime during the 1860s.

I could produce a date in the 1850s, 1840s, 1890s. I have many more dates to work with, many more possibilities, at least theoretically, for showing the statement false. Again, given what we have said, there are more possibilities for showing all white human males are chauvinists false than for showing all white blue-collar human males are chauvinists false.

We would like to say that the stronger the premises, the stronger the argument. But we must be careful here. One premise might be stronger than another, but the extra strength not be relevant to the conclusion of the argument. For example, contrast

> Most ducks mate in March.
> **d** is a duck. So
> **d** mates in March.

with

> Most ducks mate in March.
> **d** is a Mallard duck. So
> **d** mates in March.

The premises in the second argument are stronger, since the second premise gives more information, ruling out that **d** is anything but a Mallard. But is the second argument stronger than the first? Can we be more confident of the conclusion given the added information? Knowing that **d** is a Mallard would give us more confidence that **d** mates in March, if it were true, for example, that Mallard ducks *almost invariably* mate in March. But to get a stronger argument, we would have to include such information about Mallards in general. Also, consider these two statements:

(1) Exactly 80 percent of the balls in the urn are blue.
(2) Exactly 90 percent of the balls in the urn are blue.

Which statement is stronger? Which excludes more? Looking at the line in Figure 8.16, (1) rules out every point on the line except the one standing for 80 percent, while (2) excludes every point except 90 percent. It seems that (1) excludes equally as much as (2). But contrast these statistical syllogisms:

I. Exactly 80 percent of the balls in the urn are blue.
   n is a ball in the urn. So
   n is blue.
II. Exactly 90 percent of the balls in the urn are blue.
   n is a ball in the urn. So
   n is blue.

Isn't the second argument clearly stronger than the first? Doesn't it give its conclusion more support than the first? How can this be, if the premises are equally strong in each argument? The answer is that although the premises are

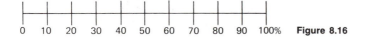

0   10   20   30   40   50   60   70   80   90   100%   **Figure 8.16**

equally strong, *relative to the conclusion,* the premises in the second argument are stronger. The second premise excludes more balls from being nonblue than the firt. When we are arguing that a particular ball is blue, that makes the second premise stronger. In general a premise or a set of premises is stronger relative to a conclusion just in case it rules out more chances for that conclusion to be false. Our example does illustrate that when we strengthen the premises with respect to the conclusion, we do get a stronger argument. A stronger modality is justified in II over I.

So far we have discussed strengthening premises. But we may strengthen conclusions also. What is the effect of strengthening the conclusion on the strength or weight of the argument? The second principle for comparative argument strength describes this connection, which may seem surprising at first. Yet the more we think about it, the more obvious and intuitive it becomes.

2. (INVERSE VARIATION PRINCIPLE) The stronger the conclusion, the weaker the argument.

Clearly the stronger the conclusion of an argument, the stronger the claim that statement makes, the stronger the premises needed to defend it adequately. The more the conclusion rules out, the more the premises shall have to rule out to plausibly support the conclusion. Put another way, should I have two arguments with exactly the same set of premises, but the conclusion of the second stronger than the conclusion of the first, the second would be a weaker argument. We would be justified in using only a weaker modality to describe how strongly the premises support the conclusion. For example, to defend my claim that the Yankees are going to win the World Series, I could cite such data as their winning the World Series in previous years, their playing against the same opponents, their performance earlier this season. But to justify claiming that they will win the World Series in five games, I would have to present much more data, if I could justify it at all. The data supporting my contention that the Yankees will win the World Series might constitute a plausible argument for it. But if I used that self-same data, not augmented, to support claiming that they will win in five games, my argument would be much weaker. Here is another example:

Suppose in a certain town there are two high schools, Northside and Southside, traditional rivals. Suppose for the last ten years, Northside has beaten Southside at the Thanksgiving Day game, by at least ten points on each occasion. Suppose the average margin of victory is fifteen points. Suppose we have the scores in front of us for each of the ten past years. Now if we claim that Northside will defeat Southside again this year, we shall have a ten-premise convergent argument to support our claim. If we claim that Northside will beat Southside by at least ten points, then although our conclusion will be stronger, our overall argument will be weaker. It will be weaker precisely because we are using the same premises, the same information, to support a stronger claim or conclusion. Now if we say that Northside will defeat Southside by fifteen points, we are making a stronger claim yet, and our argument is getting weaker. Suppose the most points by which Northside defeated Southside in this ten-game winning series was twenty-five. Then the conclusion that Northside will defeat Southside by close to twenty-five points is quite strong, and the argument for it based on our ten premises is very weak, certainly not inductively correct. Given these considerations, we see that if we strengthen the conclusion, we weaken the argument, while if we strengthen the premises with respect to the conclusion, we strengthen the argument.

Principle (2) is important, since the comparative ranking of arguments according to strength is important in both evaluating arguments and in composing and presenting arguments of our own. To point out that the premises of an argument better support a weaker conclusion or that if you want to support a particular conclusion, you better strengthen your argument by adding more or stronger premises is to provide a cogent criticism of the argument. Recognizing that we could strengthen our overall argument if we were defending a weaker conclusion, that if we are to give a plausible argument, we must either weaken our conclusion or strengthen our premises, could contribute significantly to our presenting logically convincing arguments.

The strength of counterevidence, the likelihood that a rebuttal operates, is another factor in assessing comparative argument strength. Sometimes to assess how strong a reason we have for a conclusion, to assess the extent that premise excludes the conclusion's being false, we should ask how likely it is that this reason be undercut. Consider the following argument:

(1) Charles acted wrongly in giving Sebastian that money because
(2) He helped an alcoholic to maintain his drinking problem and
(3) His action displeased Sebastian's family.

Which reason is better, which by itself gives us a stronger argument? Clearly, we want to say that (2) is a stronger reason than (3), but why? Given the ravages of alcoholism, how likely is it that sufficiently strong counterevidence holds which undercuts the argument that because Charles's giving money to Sebastian helped an alcoholic maintain his drinking problem, his action was wrong? This does not seem likely at all. By contrast, where we argue that because Charles's action displeased Sebastian's family, it was wrong, it would seem that the likelihood of finding counterevidence, of some rebutting condition intervening to undercut the argument would be much higher. Does someone's family always have his or her best interests at heart? Although we do not want to give offense and may agree that such actions are to be avoided, on occasion to do what is right for a person we may have to offend the family. In such cases our actions are not wrong, and the very circumstances serve as rebutting conditions to undercut the argument that because our action gave offense to the family, it was wrong.

We may sum all this up in a third principle for comparative argument strength:

3. The weaker the counterevidence, the less likely that some rebutting condition can be found which undercuts the argument, the stronger the argument.

We could also say that the stronger the counterrebuttals relative to showing some rebuttal does not hold, the stronger the argument.

Assessing the comparative strength of arguments is intimately bound up with another important logical skill: recognizing whether an additional statement would constitute a premise or a counterpremise for a given argument. If besides the premises, we knew that some additional statement was true, would that strengthen or weaken the case for the conclusion? If it strengthened the case, then that statement functions as a premise, and the case is stronger because we have this additional premise. If it weakens the case, then it functions as a counterpremise, and the case is weaker just because of this counterevidence. The principles we have developed in this section justify our judging the case stronger or weaker. Let's apply these principles now in an exercise which requires recognizing whether additional statements are premises or counterpremises.

Summary

For convenient reference, let's restate the three principles of comparative argument strength here.

1. (DIRECT VARIATION PRINCIPLE) The stronger the premises with respect to the conclusion they directly support, the stronger the argument.

2. (INVERSE VARIATION PRINCIPLE) The stronger the conclusion, the weaker the argument.

3. The weaker the counterevidence, the less likely that some rebutting condition can be found which undercuts the argument, the stronger the argument.

We may strengthen the premises directly supporting a conclusion either by giving more premises or by adopting stronger premises, as long as the strength is relevant to the conclusion. One statement is stronger than another when it excludes, rules out, more. A premise is stronger with respect to a conclusion when it excludes more chances for the conclusion to be false.

Exercise 8-VII

The three principles governing argument strength provide us with ways of deciding when one argument is stronger than another and with justifying our decision. Each of the following arguments is followed by a list of additional statements that could be true or of changes that could be made in the argument. In each case, indicate whether the addition or change would make the argument stronger (>) or weaker (<), and cite which principle concerning argument strength justifies your answer. You may, if you wish, construct additional argument diagrams to show what structural role the additional statements or material derived from them should play in the expanded argument.

Sample Answer

The president's proposal to build strategic defensive weapons in outer space which would "neutralize" Soviet offensive missiles is a good idea. It puts us in a strong bargaining position with the Soviets at the Geneva talks, and when built, the weapons will make nuclear war obsolete.

a. Many new jobs will be created by this program, helping the economy.

Clearly this statement gives us more evidence for the conclusion. It could function as an additional premise. So the answer is (>, 1).

b. Suppose the conclusion were changed to read: The president's proposal is the most important contribution to world peace in the past quarter century.

This statement is obviously stronger than the original conclusion, saying just that the proposal is a good idea. But the stronger the conclusion, the weaker the argument. So the answer is (<, 2).

c. This proposal involves technological problems which are impossible to solve without such heavy military expenditures that many other government programs would be hurt.

Surely this statement gives evidence that the proposal is *not* a good idea. It is a counterpremise, and if we knew it true, the strength of the argument would be diminished. So the answer is (<, 3).

1. The benefits which the Iranian hostages receive under existing laws are more than generous. They were paid their full salaries while in captivity—and exempt from income tax. In addition, the Government will pay their Iran-related medical expenses and college expenses incurred by their families while they were in captivity.[12]

a. Former hostages may also claim up to $40,000 for property losses in Iran.

b. The conclusion is changed to read: The benefits which the Iranian hostages receive under existing laws are adequate.

c. While they were in captivity, inflation jumped by 250 percent, yet government workers were given no increase in salary.

d. The second premise is changed to read: The government will pay the college expenses incurred by their families while they were in captivity (i.e., nothing is said about paying medical expenses).

e. Suppose the change in (d) were made. In addition, suppose the following is true: An independent panel of experts predicts that the cost of medical care for each hostage—physical and especially psychological—will average $250,000.

f. Each hostage may, if he or she chooses, retire at full salary on a government pension, adjustable for inflation.

2. U.S. relations with the Soviet Union are almost as bad as at the end of World War II. U.S. relations with mainland China are so strained that there is

fear the president could push a billion Chinese back into alliance with 270 million Russians. The Camp David peace process has deteriorated to the point of disappearing. Hence the president's foreign policy is a failure.

    a. We have an increasingly strained relationship with our northern neighbor Canada.

    b. Hardly another country in the hemisphere supports U.S. policy in Central America.

    c. NATO is in serious trouble.

    d. (a), (b), (c) are all true.

    e. The Soviet Union has committed many acts which have branded them as terrorists in the eyes of the world.

    f. Many of the factions in the Middle East among whom the administration must arbitrate are very radical and hard line.—Adapted from material by Carl T. Rowan, April 17, 1983. © by and permission of News America Syndicate.

    3. Con Ed failed to identify and correct the root cause of numerous leaks which eventually led to the flooding at the Indian Point nuclear plant last October. It coped poorly with the flooding once it occurred, and it failed to report the accident promptly to regulatory authorities. Clearly the blame for the accident lies primarily on Con Ed's management.[13]

    a. Suppose the conclusion were to read: the blame for the accident lies completely with Con Ed's management.

    b. It is practically impossible to cope with flooding in a nuclear power plant once it has occurred.

    c. The management made a number of misleading statements to investigators.

    d. Suppose the conclusion were to read: some blame for the accident lies with Con Ed's management.

    e. The leaks at the power plant were the responsibility of saboteurs.

    f. Con Ed's management did many things to hinder the investigation of the flooding at the Indian Point nuclear plant.

    4. The problem of violence on television has been overplayed. Although many concerned citizens fear that violence on television is harmful to young people, fewer than 10 percent of the nearly 2,000 junior high school students polled recently found television violence objectionable.—Adapted from an example in the Sample LSAT.

    a. The 2,000 young people polled were all from inner-city neighborhoods such as the South Bronx, Chicago, or the Watts area of Los Angeles.

    b. Suppose the premises were to read: 20,000 junior high school students were surveyed and fewer than 10 percent found the violence objectionable.

    c. Two thousand senior high school students were polled and less than 5 percent found the violence objectionable.

    d. Suppose the conclusion were to read: there is no problem of violence on television.

e. Television violence may have a harmful effect on young people without their being aware of it.

f. The junior high school students surveyed were randomly selected from all regions of the country and from all demographic areas within those regions.

5. I would hazard a guess that the marble head of a young black man in the Brooklyn Museum dates from the late Roman period. The absence of intense emotional expression together with only a slight turn of the head and summary treatment of the back of the head suggest a late date. The wide-open eyes and the asymmetrical facial features are often found in later Roman works.—Material in Sample LSAT.

a. Suppose the conclusion were to read: The marble head of a young black man in the Brooklyn Museum dates from between 200 and 210 A.D.

b. The style of late Roman artists has been copied by a number of contemporary artists in their work.

c. Suppose the second premise were to read: The wide-open eyes and the asymmetrical facial features are known only in later Roman works.

d. The representation of African blacks was popular with artists in the late Roman period.

e. Significant work in marble was done only in the late Roman period.

f. Art works having all these features were produced in Sicily 1,000 years before the late Roman period.

§8.6 THE FALLACY OF HASTY CONCLUSION

When an argument is so weak that it fails to create a presumption for the conclusion, given the total weight of the premises, we cannot be more than 50 percent sure that the conclusion is true, the argument is inductively incorrect. For a number of inductive arguments, at least, this can happen for one or more of three specific reasons. In such circumstances, we have the *fallacy of hasty conclusion*. Being able to recognize these situations facilitates identifying inductively incorrect arguments. The first reason for hasty conclusion is clearly related to the first and second principles for argument strength discussed in the last section. We can recognize something wrong with the argument either by seeing that the premises are too weak, the conclusion too strong, or both.

1. The premises give too little information to support the conclusion properly.

For example,

(1) Thomas Kean supported capital punishment in his campaign for governor of New Jersey and won.

(2) James Florio opposed capital punishment and lost the race.

(3) Ed Koch supported capital punishment and was reelected as mayor of New York City. Hence it looks like

(4) The majority of Americans favors capital punishment.

Clearly even if capital punishment was an issue in these races and so a vote for a candidate supporting capital punishment expressed approval of the death penalty, the premises give far too little information to justify the conclusion that a majority of Americans on the whole favor capital punishment. At best, the premises might show that a majority of those casting their ballots in New Jersey and New York City favor the death penalty. To support the conclusion properly, we should need information about other races where the candidates openly held positions on capital punishment and information gleaned from polls and public opinion surveys. If we had all this information and it supported the conclusion, then we might have a plausible argument. Under those circumstances, the conclusion would not be hasty. This argument is a classic example of hasty conclusion—we simply do not have the strength of information in the premises to establish even a presumption for the conclusion. We can readily relate why this example is logically deficient to the first two principles of comparative argument strength given in the last section. The premises themselves seem insufficient, since they contain too few reasons, and, given the strength of the conclusion, they are certainly too weak.

Because the premises deal just with New Jersey and New York City, and the conclusion makes a claim about all Americans, this argument illustrates the second way the hasty conclusion problem can arise. What is going on in the rest of New York state and in the other forty-eight states? To make a claim about the majority of Americans, our premises should give us information not just about one geographical region but about all those having a bearing on the conclusion. Capital punishment could be favored in one area but strongly opposed throughout the rest of the country. Where various sources or types of information have a bearing on the conclusion, unless the premises are representative of this variety, the conclusion is hasty. This is the second reason for the fallacy.

2. The premises give possibly nonrepresentative information. The data they present are drawn from too narrow a base, overlooking sources of relevant information which may yield contrary facts or considerations.

We could imagine arguments whose premises present an impressive amount of information and yet still commit the fallacy of hasty conclusion by overlooking relevant sources of facts. *Literary Digest* magazine's prediction in 1936 that Kansas Governor Alf Landon would defeat incumbent President Franklin D. Roosevelt is a classic example. *Literary Digest* took a sample poll, sending out about 10 million ballots. However, it derived the mailing list from lists of those who had telephones or owned automobiles. But 1936 was in the middle of the depression. Those who could afford telephones and automobiles were by no means representative of the American public on the whole. Although *Literary Digest* may have gotten enough information in the sense of sheer volume or amount, it was very biased and nonrepresentative. The prediction was also notoriously wrong. President Roosevelt won reelection in an historic landslide.

This second reason for the hasty conclusion fallacy is actually a special case of the third, and both are obviously related to the third principle for comparative argument strength. To point out that the premises are nonrepresentative is to present a rebuttal, and a serious one. If the information is nonrepresentative, there is a good chance of finding counterevidence. But there may be other rebuttals which significantly call the correctness of an inductive argument into question. To accept the conclusion before these rebuttals are countered is hasty. This leads to the third reason why the fallacy of hasty conclusion can occur.

3. The argument overlooks rebutting conditions which have a significant chance of being operative. It fails to present counterrebuttals where they are necessary.

Hence the fallacy of hasty conclusion may arise when too little information is presented in the premises to support the conclusion, relevant information or sources of information which might refute the conclusion are overlooked, or possible conditions which would rebut the premises supporting the conclusion have not been considered. In all these cases, we can say that the premises do not support the conclusion with sufficient strength. Although they may be relevant, they are not adequate to justify the conclusion. Recognizing these three conditions under which the fallacy of hasty conclusion may occur gives us grounds for saying the argument is inductively incorrect. We have just now alluded to the issue of relevance, which came up several times in the last section on comparative argument strength. It is time to say something directly about relevance, since it is one of the three conditions which must hold if an argument is logically convincing. We turn to this as the first item of business in the next chapter.

Exercise 8-VIII

Diagram each of the following arguments. Then discuss why the problem of hasty conclusion arises in each case.

Sample Answer

I have seen many times how marijuana and other opiates can relieve the suffering of those seriously ill and in significant pain. Therefore, narcotics should be made available to everyone.

We can fault this argument on all three grounds for hasty conclusion. First, the arguer is apparently basing the conclusion on his or her own experience. But can the experience of one person give us enough information to be confident that narcotics should be made available to everyone? So the premise gives too little information. Second, the seriously ill and those in significant pain are certainly not representative of the general population. Even if marijuana and other opiates can do them good, how much reason is that to believe they are good for all people? We can also ask how representative are marijuana and these other opiates of narcotics in general in their effects on humans? So the premise gives nonrepresentative information. Finally, it should not be hard to think of other rebutting conditions. Making narcotics available to everyone might significantly increase drug addiction and its toll on human life. On any of these grounds, we have hasty conclusion.

1. You won't let me go to the movies and you won't let me watch television. You never want me to have any fun.

2. Kennedy, Johnson, and Rockefeller were all wealthy. I guess you have to be wealthy in politics these days.

3. My program hasn't hurt anybody. No one has been thrown out in the snow to die.—Ronald Reagan.

4. I have to admit that I cannot fathom what happens during the course of the day to make a clean rest area in the morning deteriorate to something worthy of the condemnation of the board of health by twilight. Twice I went down to the (New Jersey) Shore for the day and twice I saw an exceptionally clean area become the horror comparable only to New York's Forty-second St. alleyway. I'm no perfectionist, but I'm appalled by the careless and slovenly attitude of people who use these areas.—L.H., *Sunday Star-Ledger* (Newark, N.J.), August 7, 1983.

5. Professor Piccard is more popular than Professor Frank. I know this because I heard several students talking in the cafeteria who said they liked Piccard more than Frank. That's why Piccard has more students in his section of critical thinking than Frank does.

6. For years now the strap has been banned in most of Metro's schools. Look at the result: Youngsters are more ill-mannered and more disrespectful of the rights of others than in the past. Our streets are less safe since counselling has replaced many forms of swift punishment for anti-social behavior.—B.A., Toronto, Canada.

7. Vasectomies are worthless as a method of male contraception. My friend's husband had a vasectomy and was supposed to be sterile. A few days after the operation, they had intercourse. Nine months later, my friend gave birth to a healthy young boy.

8. American society is permeated through and through with the greed of decadent capitalism. To see this, just look at the pandering on 42nd Street, the partying at Studio 54, and the life-style portrayed in "Dallas" on television.

9. I would like to say it for all time that the belief that the use of coloring books by children stifles their creativeness is a myth. I adored my coloring books when I was a child and went on to teach art myself for 25 years. I

see no reason for denying a child the opportunity to have pleasure with his crayons and coloring book.—F.J., Toronto, Canada.

10. The surest key to peace is for the United States to have military superiority over all other nations in the world. In the years after World War II, America had definite military superiority over any other nation. Yet America chose not to take one single step toward aggression, imperialism, or world domination. In all history, there is no record of any other nation holding such power in its hands and failing to use it to assert dominion over other nations and men. We proved that the peace and freedom of the world are safe when America has military superiority.—Phyllis Schlafly, "Nuclear Superiority Is the Key to Peace."

11. As a chemist, I take issue with the statement in "Double-Duty Heat Pump" that tanks of sodium sulfide (Na_2S) are completely safe for transport. Spilled Na_2S in contact with water containing even a bit of acid could generate considerable hydrogen sulfide, a fairly poisonous and extremely bad-smelling gas (rotten eggs). And various nasty oxides of sulfur could be generated if the accident involved a fire.—N.J.[14] Reprinted from *Popular Science* with permission © 1981, Times Mirror Magazines, Inc.

12. A 1979 survey reveals that between 1971 and 1979, the percentage of metropolitan-area teenagers who reported having at least one premarital pregnancy increased from 8.5 per cent to 16.2 per cent, while the percentage of these teens engaging in premarital intercourse increased from 30 per cent to 50 per cent.

Out-of-wedlock births to teenage mothers in the U.S. have increased from about 190,000 in 1970 to about 240,000 in 1978 (from about 22 per 1,000 unmarried teenage women to 27 per 1,000).

Premarital pregnancies increased from about 300,000 in 1970 to about 700,000 in 1978. Abortions increased from about 90,000 in 1970 to nearly 500,000 in 1978 among teenagers.

I conclude that the funding of national family planning programs during the past eight years has been a colossal failure because of the well-known high rates of contraceptive failure among teenage users.—J.S., *Sunday Star-Ledger* (Newark, N.J.), September 12, 1982.

13. Uncle Hushai was given to drink, even to drinking on the job. And as a railroad engineer, that was disastrous. You should see the pictures of some locomotives after he got through with them while he was under the influence. Aunt Ahithophela has quite a taste for the bottle too. And when she's been at her rum, you'd better stay clear of her, if you don't want to get hit over the head with an ashtray. Clearly the manufacture, distribution, and sale of all alcoholic beverages should be prohibited by law!

14. I am aware of how criminal the criminal justice system is. My brother was innocent and I know he was innocent because when the alleged crime of which he was convicted was committed, he was in Woodbridge with me and not in Newark. However, it took five years to get him out. Today's paper reports that it took eight years for another man to get justice, for the courts to recognize his

conviction was improper. Is it not criminal to keep a man in prison for almost half, if not two thirds of his sentence, before justice can be done?—D.R., *Sunday Star-Ledger* (Newark, N.J.), August 7, 1983.

15. Our society normally regulates a certain range of activities; it is illegal to perform these activities unless one has received prior permission to do so. . . . We require drivers to be licensed because driving an auto is an activity which is potentially harmful to others, safe performance of the activity requires a certain competence, and we have a moderately reliable procedure for determining that competence. We likewise license doctors, lawyers, and psychologists because they perform activities which can harm others. Obviously they must be proficient if they are to perform these activities properly, and we have moderately reliable procedures for determining proficiency. . . . Consequently, any activity that is potentially harmful to others and requires certain demonstrated competence for its safe performance, . . . [where] we also have a reliable procedure for determining whether someone has the requisite competence, . . . ought, all things considered, to be regulated.—Hugh LaFollette, "Licensing Parents," *Philosophy and Public Affairs*, Vol. IX, no. 2, 1980.[15]

Hint: Can we think of any rebutting conditions which should be countered here?

FOR FURTHER READING

Our basic test for evaluating deductive arguments is adapted from John Eric Nolt's *Informal Logic: Possible Worlds and Imagination* (New York: McGraw-Hill Book Company, 1984), pp. 54–59. Nolt adapts this test for inductive arguments on pp. 59–63 in a very interesting discussion. Chapters 1 and 2 of John Hoaglund's *Critical Thinking: An Introduction to Informal Logic* (Newport News, Va.: Vale Press, 1984) develop the notions of consistency and inconsistency, including a test for deciding whether passages are consistent. The concepts of inductive correctness, statistical syllogisms, and the requirement of total evidence are included in the induction chapter of Wesley C. Salmon's *Logic*, 3rd ed. (Englewood Cliffs, N.J.: Prentice-Hall, Inc., 1984). Nolt also discusses the requirement of total evidence along with kinds of probability on pp. 186–97 of *Informal Logic*. The idea of including rebuttals in argument diagrams is presented in Stephen Toulmin's account of "the layout of arguments" in Chapter 3 of *The Uses of Argument* (Cambridge: Cambridge University Press, 1958). In this discussion, Toulmin also suggests how premises may function as counterrebuttals.

NOTES

[1]Compare Monroe C. Beardsley, *Thinking Straight: Principles of Reasoning for Readers & Writers*, 4th ed. (Englewood Cliffs, N.J.: Prentice-Hall, Inc., 1975), p. 24.

[2]Example courtesy of the *Informal Logic Newsletter,* Vol. II, Supplement, June 1980.

[3]Some of you may have a question at this point. Suppose we added the statement, "All the balls in Urn **1** are white" to the premises "All the balls in Urn **1** are blue" and "The next ball to be drawn is from Urn **1.**" Would the expanded argument to the conclusion, "The next ball will be blue," be valid? Don't the premises entail that the next ball will be white— in which case the conclusion will be false? The premises do entail that, but look at the premises. They say that all the balls are blue, they are all white, and there is at least one ball in Urn **1.** So that ball is both blue and white—all over at the same time. Is this possible? The premises themselves are inconsistent. But if we look at our definition of a valid argument closely, we can see that should the premises be inconsistent, the argument will be valid. If the premises are inconsistent, that is, if it is impossible for all of them to be true together, is it possible for all of them to be true *and* the conclusion false? Clearly not, and so, by our definition, the argument is deductively valid.

[4]See Wesley C. Salmon, *Logic,* 3rd ed. (Englewood Cliffs, N.J.: Prentice-Hall, Inc., 1984), p. 97.

[5]See J. Michael Sproule, *Argument: Language and Its Influence* (New York: McGraw-Hill Book Company, 1980), pp. 86–87.

[6]The premise and counterpremise are taken from an account of this debate in ibid., p. 90.

[7]See note 3 above.

[8]Compare Example 15 in Exercise 8-I.

[9]This sentence is quoted almost verbatim from Jonathan Schell, *The Fate of the Earth* (New York: Alfred A. Knopf, 1982), p. 35.

[10]Compare Carl Wellman, *Challenge and Response* (Carbondale and Edwardsville: Southern Illinois University Press, 1971), p. 113.

[11]Compare Charles L. Stevenson, *Ethics and Language* (New Haven, Conn.: Yale University Press, 1944), pp. 123–24.

[12]Compare Example 14, Exercise 6-I.

[13]See Example VIII, Exercise 6-III.

[14]Examples 6 and 11 are adapted from material in Frank C. Carlone, Karol Dycha, and Leo Raffin, *An Informal Logic Workbook* (Windsor, Canada: 1981), pp. 40, 41, and 57.

[15]Example 9 was supplied by Dr. Trudy Govier in the *Informal Logic Newsletter,* Vol. IV, no. 3, July 1982. Dr. Govier also supplied Example 15 in the same issue, and Example 10 in Vol. V, no. 3, July 1983.

9

ARGUMENT EVALUATION II—RELEVANT PREMISES AND OVERALL EVALUATION

In the last chapter, we dealt with determining how strong a case an argument made for its conclusion. Is it deductively valid, inductively correct? What factors would make it stronger or weaker? When is an argument so weak that the premises, though relevant to the conclusion, do not even create a presumption for it? Now, even with an incorrect argument, the premises may make the conclusion more likely, even if only slightly. The premises may be inadequate, but they still give us some evidence we would not have otherwise. However, there are times when the premises do not make the conclusion more likely at all. This is because they are irrelevant to the conclusion. This directly affects whether the argument is logically convincing. Accordingly, we shall first discuss recognizing when premises are relevant or irrelevant.

Since a premise is put forward to support some conclusion, presumably those asserting a premise *think* it relevant to the conclusion. If we think the premise is irrelevant, this may be because the arguer is assuming some warrant which we are not. If the arguer is present, we can challenge him or her to explain the relevance. If the arguer produces a warrant, this may either show the premise relevant to the conclusion or help us show some mistake in the reasoning. The assumed warrant might have been false or questionable, or produce an invalid or incorrect argument when added as a premise. If the arguer is absent, the best way to proceed in analyzing and evaluating the argument may be to try to make that warrant explicit. This is the main issue in supplying suppressed premises, which we discuss in Section 9.2. At that point, we shall have considered separately three grounds for evaluating arguments—are the premises true or believable, are they relevant, how strongly do they support the conclusion? By and large, we have been asking these questions of simple arguments, where there is just one conclusion. Overall argument evaluation involves applying these questions together, not separately, to arguments which may be structurally complex. We end the chapter by examining these issues.

§9.1 THE FALLACY OF IRRELEVANT REASON

Clearly a premise cannot support a conclusion at all unless it is relevant to that conclusion. Hence an irrelevant premise constitutes a significant problem for an argument, just as serious as a false premise. Should all the premises be irrelevant, we have no case for the conclusion. Should several premises converge on the conclusion, the case devolves on those which are relevant. Frequently, recognizing that a premise is irrelevant is intuitively obvious. All we have to do is pay attention to what premise and conclusion literally say. Of course, the arguer may not want us to do this, especially if this is an emotional appeal. As we noted in Chapter 3, some emotional appeals are fallacious precisely because the premise is irrelevant.

> My client was abandoned by his parents at an early age. Left to the streets, he hardly ever had enough to eat or a chance for an education. All his life, he has never had a break. Can you now bring about the final chapter in this tale and find him guilty?

What an appeal to pity! But are the premises relevant to establishing that the defendant is not guilty? Not at all. Guilt or innocence should be determined by facts establishing whether a person actually committed the crime he is charged with and his mental competence at that time. And this information says nothing about that. If anything, the attorney's argument should backfire, for he has described the client as having a background which frequently leads to criminal behavior.

Let's look at another example:

> In 1981, House Speaker Thomas P. (Tip) O'Neill charged that President Reagan had "no concern, no regard, no care for the little men of America. . . . He doesn't associate himself with those types of people." Defending Reagan against this charge, Presidential advisor Edwin Meese replied that the President is "a man who came as a child from absolute poor circumstances" and achieved wealth by hard work.—Reported by Carl T. Rowan, June 14, 1981. © by and permission of News America Syndicate.

Let's look at how Meese is arguing explicitly. He is saying

1. The president is a man who came as a child from absolute poor circumstances and achieved wealth by hard work. Therefore

2. The president does have concern for the little man in America. He is interested in him.

Is the premise relevant to the conclusion? Does the premise, by itself, give us a reason for the conclusion? Now although some persons who escaped from poverty might be very concerned with the poor, hoping and endeavoring to see that they get the breaks that would lead them out of poverty also, this is by no means universal. Other persons might just turn their backs on their past, trying to forget that they were ever poor. There is a tremendous range of personal variation here. For (1) to create even a presumption for (2), we need a warrant explaining why (1) is relevant to (2). Such a statement must imply at least that persons who come from absolute poor circumstances and have achieved wealth by hard work tend, more often than not, to have concern for the little man. But given what we have just noted, isn't this statement at best questionable? Do we have any solid evidence for this warrant? But unless we can establish such a statement as this, the premise is irrelevant to the conclusion.

Although frequently we may recognize that a premise is irrelevant by inspection, there is a test we may apply to determine whether a premise is irrelevant or to defend why we think it not relevant. The test is interesting because it helps us to explain just what is involved in relevance and irrelevance. Suppose there has been a bank robbery. Suppose the vault is sealed by a combination lock and only ten bank employees know the combination. Suppose there are no signs that the lock has been picked or forced and that the vault is so well constructed that no one not knowing the combination could open the lock. Hence the culprit must be one or more of those bank employees who know the combination. Hence being one of the people with this knowledge arouses legitimate suspicion. It is a mark that the person is guilty. On the other hand, those who do not know the combination cannot be guilty, for we have established that whoever committed the crime, knew the combination. Hence the statement

(1) Stevens knows the combination.

is clearly relevant to

(2) Stevens is guilty.

For if (1) is true, then although we have far from sufficient reason to convict Stevens, we certainly have a reason to suspect he is guilty, while if (1) is false, then we know that Stevens is not guilty.

Compare this with the previous arguments. If anything, what the lawyer has said about his client is negatively relevant to establishing innocence. If the client has come from a cruel, deprived background, does that make it more likely that he is not guilty? If anything, it makes it more likely he *is* guilty. Suppose what the lawyer said is false—the client does not come from a poor, harsh, cruel background. Does that make it less likely that he is not guilty? Does that give us a reason to think him guilty? It is hard to see why. So the lawyer's premises are irrelevant to the conclusion. Similarly, we have already remarked that even if it is true that the president came from a poor background and achieved wealth by hard work, this does not increase the likelihood that he is concerned for the little man. Suppose it were false that the president came from a poor background. Does that decrease the likelihood that he is concerned with the little man? If we know that the president comes from a middle- or upper-class home, does that mean he does not care about the poor or the small individuals? Again, this is far from clear. Some of the greatest champions of the poor in public service have been individuals of significant inherited wealth, as were Franklin Roosevelt and John Kennedy.

This discussion suggests a criterion for assessing and explaining when a premise is relevant to a conclusion.

> If either the truth of the premise increases the likelihood that the conclusion will be true or the falsity of the premise increases the likelihood that the conclusion is false, or both, then the premise is relevant to the conclusion. If neither of these conditions holds, then the premise is not relevant.

Applying this criterion can give us good reason for judging a premise relevant or irrelevant. When one or more premises of an argument are irrelevant to the conclusion, we have the *fallacy of irrelevant reason.*

Given that irrelevant reason is such a significant flaw in an argument, how can irrelevant reason fallacies be persuasive? Answering this question is not only theoretically interesting, it may help us in spotting these fallacies. First, it may take paying attention to see that a premise is not relevant to the conclusion. Don't we have to think about Edwin Meese's argument for a moment to be aware that it is fallacious? But will an audience always be paying properly close attention? Second, the lawyer argument was an emotional appeal, and the emotions aroused by the argument may persuade the audience. One distinct way for this to happen signals a classic type of irrelevant reason fallacy. Suppose a state legislature is debating a bill providing support to higher education for the next two years. Suppose there is general support for higher education in the legislature. What is the question at issue? Is this bill being debated good or not? Suppose someone rises to support it, but says nothing about the particular bill itself, its advantages or drawbacks, but rather argues for higher education in general. Are these remarks relevant to the question? Is the commitment of some legislators to higher education in doubt? Although playing on the general support for higher education may arouse and confirm support for the bill, the lawmaker simply is not speaking to the issue. Again, care and attention may be necessary to distinguish arguing for a general principle from arguing for the merits of a particular application. But a number of irrelevant reason fallacies do just this—argue for the general principle when the question is about a particular case.

Finally, the truth of the premises may lull us into overlooking their irrelevance. Edwin Meese's statement about President Reagan's background is to be presumed true. But we should not let our recognition of the truth of a statement give it persuasive force to establish any conclusion whatsoever. Besides being true, a premise must be relevant to the conclusion if it is to contribute to the argument's cogency.

To summarize, if the premises of an argument are to support the conclusion adequately, they must be relevant to it. Frequently, we can intuitively recognize whether a premise is relevant. We can, however, test a premise for relevance by asking whether its being true increases the likelihood that the conclusion is true or its being false increases the likelihood that the conclusion is false. If either of these questions can be answered affirmatively, then the premise is relevant. If not, the premise is irrelevant. Just because a premise is true does not mean that it is relevant to the conclusion of an argument. These are two distinct, although interrelated, issues in argument evaluation, and one should not be confused with the other.

Exercise 9-I

Diagram each of the following arguments by the tree method and identify one irrelevant premise in each. Be prepared to discuss and defend why the premise is irrelevant.

1. Pornographic movies are not in any way morally objectionable. After all, the lust instinct allows for a great variety of sexual expression.

2. The secretary of a Democratic mayor of New York, speaking to a friend who had moved to New Jersey and was now a registered voter in that state: You should come to New York and vote for our mayor under your former name. It would be a big favor to me. Such things are done all the time and no one need know about it.—G.W., *Sunday Star-Ledger* (Newark, N.J.), November 22, 1981.

3. Our opponent would have lost anyway in the last election since he was unpopular. Hence our use of some dirty tricks in the campaign was really not that morally objectionable.

4. America is the wealthiest nation in the history of the world, so it is absurd to say that poverty is a problem for America.

5. Our nation is a democracy and is dedicated to the proposition that all persons are created equal. So our colleges and universities should admit every applicant, regardless of his or her economic or educational background.

6. Since smokers on the whole do not live as long as nonsmokers, they cost the taxpayers less in Social Security to support them at the end of their lives. But Social Security payments are the one principal payment that the government must make to senior citizens. Hence smokers cost the taxpayers less altogether, and so smoking should not be discouraged.[1]

7. I am inextricably opposed to the proposal that our organization discontinue its practice of giving Thanksgiving baskets and start a year-round distribution program of canned and packaged food. Why? This organization has always had a commitment to the poor. There are many starving people in the city who need help. Especially in this time of layoffs, inflation, and general economic hardship, this commitment must be maintained and strengthened. I for one cannot eat my Thanksgiving dinner in good conscience, knowing that there are others who are going without.

8. Genealogists have traced Ronald Reagan's family tree back to King Brian of Ireland. . . . What makes Reagan's heritage interesting is that his parents were married in a Roman Catholic ceremony, but his mother had been raised as a Protestant and saw to it that her children were also brought up as Protestants. Thus the new president is, in effect, a personal embodiment of the religious conflict that has torn Northern Ireland for centuries and underlies the bloody battle that has gripped the six northern counties of Ireland for the past decade.—Jack Anderson, November 30, 1980. Reprinted by permission of United Feature Syndicate, Inc.

9. You are totally wrong to predict a dip in business. That's playing with fire and doing a disservice to the country. Our prosperity is based on psychological foundations.—Dr. Ernest Dichter.

10. I want to argue that Third and Straight Street is exactly the right location for our new bridge. At each morning and evening rush hour, traffic in this city is unbearable. The bridge construction project would create many new jobs. With better access to the city, our downtown merchants would see better sales. Better traffic conditions in the city would encourage the construction of new dwelling units and the renovation of old ones, revitalizing our neighborhoods.

11. This country is founded on the principle of liberty and justice for all. That is enshrined in our pledge of allegiance. But currently the handicapped cannot travel from their homes to their places of work or recreation by public means, unlike the rest of the population. Clearly then we must install lifts on buses and ramps in subways to make public transportation available for all.

12. I was outraged to read in the *Star-Ledger* that 144 state employees have defaulted on their guaranteed student loans. The state has fulfilled its obligation by providing a sound education that has enabled these people to pursue careers in government—some in positions as important as deputy attorney general. Yet they demonstrate their gratitude to the government by reneging on loans which they promised in good faith to repay. Clearly people with such inconsiderate attitudes have no place in serving the people of this state.—G.F., *Sunday Star-Ledger* (Newark, N.J.), December 6, 1981.

13. We all know that Hitler was a fascist. In World War II, Hitler's military forces were defeated by the armed forces of the Soviet Union and the Western allies. These were nonfascist countries. Thus it was fascism that proved inferior.

14. Who is really protecting the rights of the working man? Certainly not Charles Marciante, president of the New Jersey AFL-CIO.

Point 1: In articles in the *Star-Ledger,* Marciante is reported to have received $55,000 as a "consultant" on a housing project. He also received $31,950 on a $1,000 investment in another housing project. He said he served as a "consultant" but had no real duties.

Point 2: Again from the *Star-Ledger,* Mr. Marciante bestowed a "Stink Tag to the Legislature," citing the voting records on 11 bills. Since five of the 11 bills did not involve labor issues, Mr. Marciante was unfair in his pronouncement. It is also ironic that as many Democrats were included on the "Stink" list as were Republicans.

Point 3: Mr. Marciante stressed that those legislators who were on his "Stink List" should make it up before the next election. What does he mean by "make it up"?

Point 4: Mr. Marciante has strongly opposed Senate bills on freedom of choice that permit workers the right to choose his or her own dentist, his or her own insurance representative, etc.—H.J., *Sunday Star-Ledger* (Newark, N.J.), February 27, 1983.

15. Recently I went to try to get a box of cheese the government is giving away. I was told I wasn't allowed to receive any. This is downright unfair!

What burns me up is the fact I put four years in the U.S. Air Force during World War II, and three of those years were spent overseas working on airplanes. I read in the papers where they gave boxes of cheese to several of the people who came here from Haiti. What did they ever do for this country, and why should they get things for free, when I never received a red cent for free, after working for 55 years?—W.H., *Sunday Star-Ledger* (Newark, N.J.), March 7, 1982.

§9.2 SUPPLYING SUPPRESSED PREMISES

In introducing this chapter, we pointed out that although someone may think the premises of his or her argument are relevant to the conclusion, this belief may be mistaken. The arguer has assumed a warrant which is false or questionable, or is not reasoning correctly from the warrant and the other premises. In the first section, we brought out how Edwin Meese's argument involved the fallacy of irrelevant reason by supplying the suppressed premise. By bringing this statement to light, we could see that it was obviously questionable and that it—or something like it—was assumed in Meese's argument to explain why the premise was relevant to the conclusion. Pinpointing the fallacy of irrelevant reason is a major motivation for supplying suppressed premises. If, in a given argument, it seems that each statement which would explain why a given premise is relevant to the conclusion is false or questionable, then we have grounds for saying that the premise is irrelevant. This can serve us admirably in exposing the logical faults of certain emotional appeals. Consider this abusive *ad hominem:*

Alphonso claims that conditions in Castro's Cuba are very repressive. But I would put no confidence in his testimony. Don't you know that he is a shameless transvestite who dances nightly in gay bars?

What's the assumed premise here? Isn't it that

> Transvestites—at any rate shameless ones who dance in gay bars—are totally untrustworthy.

But what evidence is there for that statement? By formulating the suppressed premise and seeing how questionable it is, we expose how the argument logically involves the fallacy of irrelevant reason.

Is our motivation for supplying suppressed premises always critical or negative—to show the argument fallacious? Not necessarily. We might supply suppressed premises to get a better picture of the reasoning—to understand better and so be in a better position to evaluate the argument. We may also supply suppressed premises to fend off argument criticism.

Consider this argument based on a famous example of Lewis Carroll:

> All kangaroos love to gaze at the moon. So it must be that all the animals I detest love to gaze at the moon.

The modality "must" signals that we have a deductive argument, but is this argument deductively valid? What does our test procedure from the last chapter tell us to do? Can we imagine a situation where the premise is true and the conclusion false? This seems easy. It just might be that all the kangaroos there are love to gaze at the moon. However, I might detest donkeys and elephants, which have no feelings about the moon at all, much less gazing on it. So conceivably the premise is true and the conclusion false. The argument is invalid. But isn't there something hasty about this criticism? Why would someone think the premise supported the conclusion unless he or she also believed that

> The animals that I detest are all of them kangaroos?

What happens when we link this statement to the premise? Is it possible for these two statements to be true and the conclusion false? By adding this premise which the argument strongly suggests is assumed anyway, we get a deductively valid argument. So we can readily defend our arguer against the charge of giving a deductively invalid argument. And shouldn't a challenger consider that a suppressed premise may very well be involved here before judging the argument invalid?

But how may we supply suppressed premises? How do we know which statement to add to the argument? This is one of the most difficult questions in the theory of logical thinking, one over which even the experts disagree. Although in certain cases, framing the suppressed premise is quite intuitive, developing a general method is no easy task. It's not hard to appreciate why this is difficult and why we must be very responsible here. How do we know what the arguer has assumed? Are we truly formulating his intentions and not putting words in his mouth? We met with this difficulty before in Chapter 5. How do we read between the lines—legitimate and necessary—without reading something into the passage?

Criteria for Suppressed Premises

Two criteria should guide us in formulating suppressed premises. First, since we are attributing these claims to an arguer, there should be grounds justifying that the arguer actually *used* the premise we supplied, or at least would accept it or recognize that it was in accord with his or her intentions. This is the *use criterion.* It licenses us to look at all the available evidence about an arguer in formulating the suppressed premise. Using this criterion, we might justify supplying some surprising premises. For suppose we know a person consistently reasons according to a fallacious pattern. Seeing that the manifestly stated premises and conclusion fall under this pattern, we can reconstruct the remaining premise.

But this circumstance is rather exceptional. Ordinarily, we are not going to know much about the arguer, other than that he or she put forward an argument with a logical gap. The best evidence we have that the arguer accepts the premise is that it fits this gap which needs plugging. But this leads us to the other criterion. The premises we supply should fill the gap. Once added to the argument, we should be able to see why the manifestly stated premises are relevant to the conclusion. This is the *need criterion,* and in general, in making out the suppressed premises, this will be primary. What we aim to develop in this section is a way of framing statements which fill the logical gap, which satisfy the need. However, the use criterion will play a role. For frequently, unless one suppressed premise is obviously suggested, we may be able to frame several that fill the gap, which serve to make the stated premises relevant to the conclusion. Although we may not be able to say which of these is *the* premise our arguer has assumed, there is a *range of acceptability* here. It may be fair to attribute some to an arguer but not others. Should the reconstructed argument be logically faulty, it's unfair to attribute the suppressed premise to the arguer, unless we have evidence that he or she actually used this particular premise, reasoned this way. In the absence of further evidence, the use criterion requires us to reject such candidates for suppressed premise. These are general and somewhat abstract considerations. We will make them concrete as we develop our method of supplying suppressed premises.

Enthymemes

How then do we decide how to fill a gap in the argument? Let's begin by looking at a class of cases which are very intuitive, and where we can concentrate almost exclusively on the question of need. In Chapter 8, we took categorical syllogisms as our paradigm in discussing deductive arguments. But categorical syllogisms are frequently stated with either one premise or the conclusion missing. Such an argument is called an *enthymeme,* and supplying suppressed premises for enthymemes is not only easy, from it we may formulate a more general method for filling gaps in arguments. Our example about kangaroos was an enthymeme.

Let's consider a few more.

All senators are politicians, so
All senators are amoral.

What's the tacitly assumed premise?

All politicians are amoral.

Recognizing this and that adding it produces an obviously valid deductive argument should be straightforward. Here is another example:

Hamilton was born in the eighteenth century, so
He is no longer living today.

It is easy to see that the premise to supply is

No one born in the eighteenth century is still living today.

Adding that premise gives us a valid deductive argument establishing the conclusion. Here is a final example:

No true conservative is poor, so
Some so-called conservatives are not true conservatives.

Here the premise,

Some so-called conservatives are poor.

is obviously assumed.

Although recognizing the suppressed premise in these enthymemes is quite intuitive, we must highlight two salient features of this process. First, look at these three enthymemes as stated. In each case, we need a connection between some concept used in the premise and a concept in the conclusion. In the first, we need some connection between being a politician and being amoral, in the second, between being born in the eighteenth century and being no longer alive today. In the last, we need a connection between being poor and being a so-called conservative. Notice that in each case, our suppressed premise established a connection between these two concepts. This is central to supplying suppressed premises. The warrant we supply must, in a very obvious way, connect one or more concepts in the premises with some concept in the conclusion. If a statement is proposed as a suppressed premise which fails in any obvious way to establish such a link, we have every right to challenge why that statement should be regarded as a suppressed premise.

To appreciate the second salient feature in supplying these suppressed premises, consider the enthymeme about the senators again. The premise we supplied was

All politicians are amoral.

Why would adding

Most politicians are amoral.

not be acceptable? It establishes a connection between being a politician and being amoral. It serves to show why being a politician is relevant to being amoral. It does a job a suppressed premise is supposed to do. But it does not seem the correct premise to add. Why? Look at the three premises we added. In each case, the resulting argument was deductively valid. In any of these cases, can you imagine the premises true and the conclusion false? But this seems appropriate, since enthymemes are incompletely stated categorical syllogisms—deductive arguments. But in

All senators are politicians.
Most politicians are amoral. So
All senators are amoral.

the premises do not establish the conclusion conclusively. Clearly the premises could be true and the conclusion false. This is not a valid deductive argument. Clearly any statement weaker than "Most politicians are amoral" would also be unacceptable.

Although we probably would not be tempted to add these weaker statements, it is worthwhile reflecting why not, and what this means for the general practice of supplying suppressed premises. What is an argument supposed to do? What does it claim? It claims that the premises support the conclusion. This means that if the claim is correct and the argument deductive, we should have a deductively valid argument. If the argument is inductive, then it should be inductively correct. When we reconstruct an argument by supplying suppressed premises, we presume that the argument as we are developing it is good, valid or correct as the case may be. Why do we assume this? We may call this the *principle of charity*.

Just as a criminal is presumed innocent until proven guilty, we presume an argument to be good until we can show otherwise. In reconstructing an argument, then, unless we have evidence to the contrary, we assume the suppressed premises *used* in the argument are strong enough to produce a cogent argument. Should our reconstructed argument be invalid or incorrect, the burden of proof is on us to show that this is actually the arguer's reasoning. If we have no such evidence, we should proceed according to the principle of charity to be faithful to the use criterion.

Again, we may draw an analogy with criminal procedure. We cannot get a conviction for wrongdoing if there is entrapment—if we force or lead a person into committing a crime he or she otherwise wouldn't. If a person is guilty of a crime, it must be one committed willingly and intentionally, not forced, cajoled, or enticed. Supplying suppressed premises provides an opportunity to entrap the arguer. By supplying a statement weaker than what is necessary to produce a cogent argument, we get an argument easy to criticize. But is this fair? By criticizing the reconstructed argument, do we really criticize the arguer's reasoning? Hence, barring contrary evidence, what is required to produce a cogent argument constitutes a lower limit on the strength of premises we can add.

Is there also an upper limit? Again the answer is yes, and we can justify this by similar considerations. Back to the argument about amoral senators. Suppose that instead of proposing

All politicians are amoral.

as the suppressed premise, someone proposed adding

All politicians and bureaucrats are amoral.

The resulting argument would be deductively valid—you can check this for yourself, could the premises be true and the conclusion false—but would this candidate be acceptable? I'm sure we feel not, but why not? First, the manifestly stated premise—All senators are politicians—says nothing about bureaucrats. There is no need to connect this concept to being amoral. But, second, which statement is stronger? Which is more questionable, if not downright false? Certainly, it is the second. To show that

All politicians are amoral.

is false, we must find at least one politician who is not amoral. But to show that

All politicians and bureaucrats are amoral.

is false, we need only find someone who is either a politician or a bureaucrat who fails to be amoral. And since the class of people who are either politicians or bureaucrats is larger than the class of just politicians, the chances of finding such a person are greater. Now employing a false or questionable premise is again a fallacy in an argument. Hence, unless there is evidence that our arguer actually has assumed a false or questionable premise, proceeding according to our principle of charity we should not attribute such a statement to our arguer. Hence, what we may plausibly say the arguer has used puts an upper bound on the strength of any premise we may supply.

So far, it looks like supplying a suppressed premise involves finding a statement which connects a premise concept with a conclusion concept, is strong enough to produce a valid or correct argument, and yet is not too strong to be false or questionable. But can all these factors always be satisfied together? The answer is clearly no. Just consider the irrelevant reason fallacies in the last section. Any warrant strong enough to produce a cogent argument would be false or questionable. But then we have identified a real fault in the reasoning. By pointing out that any warrant strong enough to link the manifestly stated premises properly to the conclusion is false or questionable, we have pointed to a problem in the original reasoning, not one we have invented to entrap the arguer.

Range of Acceptability

In our enthymemes so far, one statement appeared as the clear intuitive candidate for suppressed premise. This need not always be the case. However, where several competing warrants suggest themselves, our considerations on strength may let us eliminate some competitors, delimiting a range of acceptability. Within this range, some logicians might argue for one statement as being *the* correct premise to add, while others would favor a rival candidate. We are not going to worry about these controversies. As long as a premise is in the range of acceptability, we are not setting up the argument to be knocked down. If we find the argument fallacious, the fault is in the arguer's reasoning, not in our reconstruction.

Let's look at an example:

(1) Kentucky-bred Seattle Slew is a race horse. So
(2) He must be nervous.

Given the premise, what do we know about Seattle Slew? We know that he is a horse, a race horse, and was bred in Kentucky. The masculine pronoun in the conclusion also tells us that Seattle Slew is male. Our problem in finding a warrant is to find an appropriate statement which links one or more of these concepts to being nervous. There are quite a few possibilities here, since there are four concepts which singly or in combination might be connected with being nervous. Certain candidates, however, readily suggest themselves.

(a) All horses are nervous.
(b) All race horses are nervous.

(c) All race horses bred in Kentucky are nervous.

(d) All male race horses bred in Kentucky are nervous.

Since "male" does not appear in the premise, perhaps (d) does not readily suggest itself. Yet (d) is all that is logically needed to connect the premise and the conclusion properly. The modality "must" tips us off that the argument is deductive. Isn't the argument from premise (1) together with (d) to the conclusion (2) deductively valid?

Clearly (a) is stronger than (b), because (a) makes a statement about all horses, no matter what kind, while (b) confines itself just to race horses. Statement (c) is weaker than (b) and (d) is weaker yet. Are all four statements within the range of acceptability? Since we expect racehorses to be nervous, (b) and (c) are acceptable together with (d) (although "all" makes the claim rather strong), but are all horses, including those used for farming or recreational riding, nervous? Aren't many horses calm, docile creatures? Statement (a) is clearly outside the range of acceptability, and should not be added unless there is strong independent evidence that the arguer is actually using it. For our purposes, in evaluating the argument, it is appropriate to add any of the remaining candidates.

Let's apply this analysis to one other example:

(1) She's red-haired, so

(2) She's probably bad tempered.[2]

Here the inductive modality "probably" indicates that a quantifier like "most" rather than "all" will introduce the suppressed premise. There appear to be two candidates:

(a) Most red-haired persons are bad tempered.

(b) Most red-haired female persons are bad tempered.

We have to connect one or both of the concepts, being female and being red-haired, with being bad tempered. Certainly

Most females are bad tempered

besides not being suggested by the argument as manifestly stated, is highly questionable and outside the range of acceptability. But what about (a) and (b)? Statement (b) is the minimum necessary, but is there any reason to believe that red-haired females tend to be bad tempered as opposed to red-haired persons in general? Statements (a) and (b) are both acceptable.

Notice that in both these arguments we consulted the modality before framing the warrant. This raises a further issue concerning warrant strength. Clearly, inductive arguments do not need as strong a warrant as deductive arguments to be inductively correct. The strength of the argument's modality, whether it is deductive or inductive, affects the suppressed warrant's quantifier—the expression indicating how many—be it "all," "almost all," "most," "more than not." Deductive arguments ordinarily require strong quantifiers like "all." Not only are weaker quantifiers sufficient for inductive arguments, in many cases they may be all we can use to remain within the range of acceptability. Just replace "most" by "all" in (a) and (b). Aren't the statements

(a′) All red-haired persons are bad tempered.

(b′) All female red-haired persons are bad tempered.

highly questionable, if not downright false? Do (a′) and (b′) accord with the arguer's intentions?

A Four-Step Procedure

It remains to put all these considerations together in explicit directions for supplying suppressed premises. We present a four-step procedure. In cases where the suppressed premise is intuitively obvious, we need not mechanically go through this procedure. But should we want to justify why such a premise is appropriate, within the range of acceptability, we may appeal to these four steps.

STEP I. Identify what concept or concepts in the premises must be connected with some concept or concepts in the conclusion.

STEP II. Decide whether the argument is inductive or deductive.

STEP III. Formulate a warrant connecting premises and conclusion, suitable for inductive or deductive arguments, as the case may be.

STEP IV. Test the warrant:

(a) Is the warrant strong enough? Is the resulting argument valid if deductive, correct if inductive?

(b) Is the warrant not too strong? Is the statement false or questionable when a more plausible premise would suffice?

Should our proposed warrant pass these tests, it falls within the range of acceptability and so is appropriate.

Some Further Considerations

This then is our basic procedure for supplying suppressed warrants in arguments. We want to add a few elaborations. First, all the warrants we have added so far have been single statements, connecting concepts already present in the argument. But recall the argument from Chapter 6 which introduced the issue of relevance and linked structure:

Sam's car uses too much gas because it is a 1968 model.

We said that our respondent could explain relevance by adding that

> Cars made around 1968 are far less fuel efficient than later models.

But is there still, at least theoretically, a gap in this argument? Given the added premise, we can see why the car is less fuel efficient than later models, but why is that relevant to saying it uses too much gas? If challenged this way, our respondent could answer

> If a car is far less fuel efficient than some other model, it uses too much gas.

Surely our two added premises together explain why saying that Sam's car is a 1968 model is relevant to saying it uses too much gas. Jointly, do they constitute a warrant falling within the range of acceptability? Certainly they are strong enough. Adding both to the original premise produces a plausible argument for claiming that Sam's car uses too much gas. Are they too strong? Isn't the first statement common knowledge and the second obviously in accord with the arguer's intentions? So together these two statements do constitute an acceptable warrant. What this shows is that when a two-sentence warrant seems intuitively right, we may appeal to our procedure to examine critically whether our intuitions are right.

Notice that in this case, we brought in a new concept, being less fuel efficient than other models, not in the original argument. But notice also how we used the concept. We linked being a 1968 model car with using too much gas by means of this concept. This is quite different from the "All politicians and bureaucrats are amoral" warrant which we found objectionable earlier. There we had to link being a politician and being amoral—"bureaucrats" didn't contribute anything to this and actually constituted a liability. What this shows is that we can add new concepts in warrants, so long as the resulting warrant does the job it is supposed to do, explaining why the premise is relevant to the conclusion, and falls within the range of acceptability.

So far, all our supplied warrants have connected just one manifestly stated premise with the conclusion. But there are times when our warrant will explain the relevance of several statements taken together to the conclusion. Consider:

> (1) After being convicted of six brutal slayings, DB was sentenced to life in prison.
> (2) Upon conviction of killing his girlfriend, RT was put to death. This should show that
> (3) The punishment RT received was unfair.[3]

Intuitively, it is the two premises together which are relevant to the conclusion.
To explain this relevance, we would supply a warrant like

> If someone is put to death for killing his girlfriend while someone else is sentenced to life in prison for six brutal slayings, then the punishment the first received is unfair.

This illustrates how several manifestly stated premises together may be explained relevant to the conclusion. In diagramming the developed argument, we would link (1) and (2) to this supplied warrant.

Most of the time that we supply suppressed premises, we are looking for warrants to explain why the evidence, the data the premises give is relevant to the conclusion. This is not hard to understand. The evidence constitutes the grounds for accepting the conclusion. Why the evidence is relevant may be assumed understood, taken as obvious—which it may very well be—until some challenger asks for a warrant. Can the situation be reversed? Could an argument manifestly state a warrant and leave the data it explains relevant to the conclusion as understood? This is conceivable. In fact, we have an example of this in an earlier exercise:

> All logicians are mental cases. From this it follows that Bertrand Russell is a mental case and so also is Gottlob Frege.[4]

Clearly the argument presupposes that both Bertrand Russell and Gottlob Frege are logicians. Link that data statement with the manifestly stated premise, and we have a valid deductive argument.

Here is another example:

> The soul through all her being is immortal, for that which is ever in motion is immortal.—Plato, *Phaedrus*.

Clearly,

> that which is ever in motion is immortal

is a warrant. It explains why saying that something is ever in motion is relevant to claiming that it is immortal. But what is claimed to be ever in motion? Obviously the soul, although this is not stated explicitly. Adding that premise again produces a deductively valid argument. Just because both these examples concern deductive arguments does not mean that we cannot have inductive arguments with data premises missing. Consider:

> Dan probably has a really big concert coming up, for when he is nervous, it usually means that he has a performance.

Here we have an inductive argument. The obvious missing premise is

> Dan is (really) nervous.

After we formulate suppressed premises, be they warrants or evidence statements, how do we incorporate them into tree diagrams? To signal that *we* have formulated these statements rather than the original arguer, we assign them letters (a), (b), (c), rather than numbers. Once we do this, incorporating these letters into argument diagrams is completely straightforward. Our encircled letters will be linked to certain encircled numbers in diagramming the more developed structure.

Supplying suppressed premises is an art. Sensitivity and intuitive insight are necessary to reconstruct an argument appropriately and accurately. Yet it is not an art without principles, as our four-step procedure for formulating acceptable warrants illustrates. By making tacitly assumed premises manifest, we may get a more accurate and adequate picture of the reasoning going on in an argument. Thus we can understand better how a person is arguing for a position and be in a better position to evaluate the argument cogently.

Summary

We add premises when there is a logical gap in an argument, where there is a question why certain manifestly stated premises are relevant to the conclusion. Ordinarily, these premises will be warrants, although adding data is possible. When adding a premise, we should be able to justify saying that the arguer actually used that statement in his or her reasoning. Further, the added statement should fill the logical gap. Adding it should explain why manifestly stated premises are relevant to the conclusion. The premise must be strong enough to produce a cogent argument but not stronger than what the arguer would accept. Our four-step procedure gives guidelines for formulating such warrants.

STEP I. Identify what concept or concepts in the premises must be connected with some concept or concepts in the conclusion.

STEP II. Decide whether the argument is inductive or deductive.

STEP III. Formulate a warrant connecting premises and conclusion, suitable for inductive or deductive arguments, as the case may be.

STEP IV. Test the warrant:

(a) Is the warrant strong enough? Is the resulting argument valid if deductive, correct if inductive?

(b) Is the warrant not too strong? Is the statement false or questionable when a more plausible premise would suffice?

Exercise 9-II

In the following arguments, supply the needed missing premise.

1. All mammals are warm-blooded, so all whales are warm-blooded.
2. All brown things are colored, so some cows are colored.
3. No married persons are single, so no husbands are single.

4. No captive animals are really normal, so some lions are not really normal.

5. Jones is a homosexual, so he must be untrustworthy.

6. All college professors have doctorates, so all full-time members of the Hunter College faculty have doctorates.

7. All college professors have Ph.D.s, so Danny Daniels has a Ph.D.

8. No drunks should be on the road, so some drivers of automobiles should not be on the road.

9. No humpbacks are fish, for all humpbacks are whales.

10. No doctors promote this drug, for all promoters of this drug are quacks.

11. Some animals are not cats, because no dogs are cats.

12. Since all aristocrats are generous persons, all aristocrats are millionaires.

Exercise 9-III

For each of the following arguments, we may supply at least one suppressed premise. In each case, supply the missing premise or premises, referring to the four-step procedure to justify the appropriateness of the statements you formulate. Then, assigning these statements letters (a), (b), (c), . . . , construct a tree diagram to represent the more developed structure of the argument, including these added elements. If helpful, you may diagram the manifest structure of the argument first before supplying suppressed premises.

Sample Answer

Since enacting this measure will cause investors to lose the interest on their savings accounts, the ultimate consequence of passing this bill will be a decrease in total savings as funds are diverted into other assets. Therefore enacting the bill will reduce capital available for economic growth.

There are three statements in this passage, and clearly the first is a premise for the second, while the second is a premise for the third. To explain why the first statement is relevant to the second, we must connect causing investors to lose interest on their savings accounts with causing a decrease in total savings as funds are diverted into other assets. The second statement is asserted rather categorically. So we can construe the arguer as claiming that (2) follows deductively from (1). The statement

(a) Whenever investors stand to lose the interest on their savings accounts, they will divert their funds into other assets, decreasing total savings.

connects (1) to (2) with obvious proper strength.

To see why the second statement is relevant to the third, we must connect the concept of decreasing total savings as funds are diverted into other assets to reducing capital available for economic growth. Again, statement (3) is asserted categorically. So again, we are justified in recognizing a deductive connection. Clearly

> (b) Whenever there is a decrease in total savings, there is a decrease available in capital for economic growth.

properly connects (2) to (3). Numbering the component statements in the argument is straightforward. Hence we may diagram the developed structure of the argument as shown in Figure 9.1.

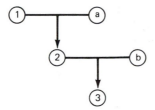

Figure 9.1

1. I just read the Surgeon General's report. Everything I like is bad for you! Now it seems that even smoking is a public health menace. It causes cancer.[5]

2. Raising the price of gasoline and home heating oil to get Americans to conserve fuel is pointless. Statistics show that when fuel prices are raised, Americans just grumble and pay. Hence higher prices will not reduce demand for fuel. But raising the price is really pointless, if higher fuel prices will not curb the demand for fuel.

3. The most valuable of all the soil invertebrates to man is probably the earthworm; these animals break down much of the plant debris reaching the soil and also turn over the soil and aerate it. Accordingly pesticide residues in soil that appreciably reduce the numbers of earthworms are a particularly serious matter.[6] (Just consider the argument to the final conclusion here.)

4. The testimony of our moral tradition condemns extramarital sexual intercourse. Hence surely extramarital sexual intercourse is sinful.

5. At a time of energy crisis, the proposal to raise the speed limit from 55 to 65 mph borders on recklessness and arrogance. While a higher speed limit would save time and therefore money, it would also use more fuel.

6. It is just plain common sense that children with serious diseases threatening the health of others should be excluded from the classroom. Hence we must exclude children with AIDS from the classroom.

7. Military actions are taken with some aim in mind. Surely, then, unless the adversary has gone insane, he will not launch a first strike that would in itself achieve nothing.—Jonathan Schell, *The Fate of the Earth*. © 1982. Published by Alfred A. Knopf, Inc.

8. Our not utilizing our ex-Presidents' rich fund of wisdom and expe-

rience is an act of folly, a tragic waste, a grave loss to the country. Hence, we should find some way to organize their hard-bought knowledge and draw on it through dark days to come.

9. To punish people merely for what they have done would be unjust, for the forbidden act might have been an accident for which the person who did it cannot be held to blame.—Barbara Wootton, *Crime and the Criminal Law.*

10. The majority of males who desert their wives and children cannot fulfill their natural role as protector and provider for their families because they cannot secure work. This is due to the fact that they lack training and employers use discriminatory hiring practices.

11. It is found difficult to rejoice and grieve in an intimate way with many people. For it may happen that one has at once to be happy with one friend and mourn with another. Hence it is difficult to be a friend to many people. (Just consider the argument to the final conclusion here.)

12. As a member of the World Federalists of Canada, I urge the Canadian government to play a more active role in solving the El Salvador crisis.

The governments of France, Mexico and many other countries have already condemned the military build-up and wanton killings, while West Germany has offered to mediate.[7]—B.J., Winnipeg, Canada.

13. The freedom of hospitals to gouge money out of these programs is illustrated by the fact that one institution will hit Uncle Sam for $3,000 to treat a heart attack patient while another will charge $9,000. Hospitals make shameful markups in the prices of pacemakers, pills and many other things.—Carl T. Rowan, December 5, 1982. © by and permission of News America Syndicate.

14. Legislation prohibiting handguns should not be passed. . . . The restrictions would leave the innocent defenseless against armed criminals. Prohibition did not eliminate drinking, only legal drinking.—*Sunday Star-Ledger* (Newark, N.J.), editorial, April 5, 1981.

15. Television journalism could be greatly enhanced if the three major networks adopt the suggestion of Roone Arledge, the president of ABC News. He wants all documentaries and special news programs removed from the prime-time ratings game. In Mr. Arledge's nutshell summary: "Serious news programs are a public service that rarely attracts a large audience, and they shouldn't have to compete with light-entertainment programming."—*The New York Times,* editorial, February 15, 1981. Copyright © 1981 by The New York Times Company. Reprinted by permission.

16. The Planning Commission scheduled the hearing on the Fox Hill apartment complex for 2:00 P.M. Wednesday. Most residents of Fox Hill work from nine to five, Mondays through Fridays. It looks like the Planning Commission does not want the residents of Fox Hill at the hearing.

17. This bill imposes on the mother and homemaker the financial obligation to pay for that home and all the expenses. It follows that it will force her to go into the job market to meet her obligations. Therefore the bill will obliterate the traditional family that has made this and other nations strong.

18. This is a country built on the concept of separation of church and state. If a person chooses to join a religion that does not advocate liberal causes, then it is that individual's private preference. The individual's freedom to pursue certain ideas is respected. So it does not seem right for a religious group to dictate its preference to the country that has allowed religions the freedom to flourish and develop.[8]—J.N., Warren, Mich.

19. Russia invades Afghanistan, Russia interferes in Poland, Russia dominates Czechoslavakia, Russia dominates Hungary, Russia dominates Romania, Russia dominates East Germany, Russia dominates Latvia, Lithuania and Estonia. Russia foments terrorism all over Central America. Russia has bases 90 miles from Florida. Russia keeps the terrorists alive in the Middle East.

The UN votes to boycott Israel because of the Golan. Anti-Semitism is alive and well at the UN.—S.B., *Sunday Star-Ledger* (Newark, N.J.), February 14, 1982.

20. The Iraqis need nuclear energy to produce electrical power as Eskimos need icemakers. (If you stumble in Iraq, you strike oil.)

The configuration of the nuclear plant ordered by the Iraqis from France was such as to permit it to go into the business of plutonium production. Their plant was cheaper to build than a conventional power reactor. Any plutonium the Iraqi plant produced could more conveniently have been withdrawn than from a conventional power reactor. In short, deductive scientific and logistical intelligence suggests that the Iraqis were indeed in the business of creating an A-bomb.

Also consider that on Oct. 4, 1980, Al Thawra, an official Baghdad newspaper said, "The Iranian people should not fear the Iraqi nuclear reactor, which is not intended to be used against Iran, but against the Zionist enemy." In addition, the state of Iraq and the State of Israel are technically "in a state of belligerency" with each other.[9]

§9.3 OVERALL ARGUMENT EVALUATION

We see argument evaluation involving three basic questions reflecting the three criteria of being logically convincing:

1. Are the premises true or believable?
2. How strong a case do they make for the conclusion?
3. Are they relevant to the conclusion?

Since these questions can be asked of any argument, deductive or inductive, they provide a method of generic argument evaluation. Up to this point, we have treated each of these questions separately. Overall argument evaluation involves applying all three questions to the same argument. In approaching an argument, we must be prepared to ask any or all of these three questions about it. We need not plod or be mechanical about this however. It might be obvious that the premises of an argument are all false or questionable. Pointing this out is enough to see that the argument is not logically convincing. In another, there is no problem with the premises being relevant to the conclusion. We need not worry about this criterion.

However, there is a systematic way of applying these three questions in overall generic argument evaluation. First, no matter how much *prima facie* weight a premise may lend to a conclusion, if we recognize the premise false or questionable, we don't accept it if we are thinking logically. Hence, checking to see which premises are true or believable and which are false or questionable is an obvious first step in making an evaluation. The real strength or real weight of the argument will rest just on the true or believable premises.

Similarly, no matter how persuasive a premise may appear, if it is irrelevant to the conclusion, it gives the conclusion no support. The real weight of the argument depends on the remaining premises. The next step, then, is to identify and discard any irrelevant premises. Notice that we may first be able to judge certain premises irrelevant after determining which premises are false or questionable. For we may identify a warrant as false or questionable. If, subsequently, we cannot find a plausible warrant, the data premise which the warrant allegedly explained relevant is irrelevant.

Having eliminated both false or questionable and irrelevant premises, we are now ready to determine just how strong a case the argument really makes for the conclusion. If the argument is deductive, we ask whether the remaining premises necessitate the conclusion. If it is inductive, by asking how likely is the conclusion, given the remaining premises, we assess the real *prima facie* weight of the argument. By asking how likely is the conclusion given the remaining premises and the available relevant counterevidence or rebutting evidence, we assess the real total weight of the argument. Provided that we have just a simple argument, one where there is exactly one conclusion, we can now say whether we have a good piece of reasoning. A valid deductive argument with true or believable premises establishes its conclusion as true or believable. If the real *prima facie* weight of an inductive argument makes the conclusion more likely than not, we have good *prima facie* reason to accept the conclusion. If again the conclusion is more likely than not, given the real total weight of the argument, why should we seriously doubt or reject the conclusion? With simple arguments, we can now say whether the reasoning is logically convincing or not.

But suppose an argument has several conclusions. From our study of argument structure, we know this happens when the argument involves either divergent or serial structure. Divergent structure essentially adds nothing new to our account of argument evaluation. Where one or more premises support several conclusions, we can evaluate the case they make for each conclusion, as if we had a separate argument each time. But suppose an argument involves serial structure, with one or perhaps a number of intermediate conclusions. There's a further consideration involved in evaluating arguments with such a structure. No matter how long is our series, there will be some premise or premises not defended by other statements. These are the basic premises of the argument. At the other end, there will be a final conclusion not used to support some further statement. The question is how logically convincing a case do the basic premises make for the final conclusion.

Let's assume we have the diagram of the argument—at least of its manifest structure—in front of us. To evaluate it, we proceed to evaluate each of the component simple subarguments our diagram reveals, working from the "top" down. In each case we apply our three generic questions. False or questionable premises, and irrelevant premises will be problems for the argument as a whole. But after we determine how strong each individual subargument is, whether it is deductively valid, inductively correct, or fallacious, there is still the issue—how strong is the overall case, the overall argument, from basic premises to conclusion? If each subargument is deductively valid, the answer is easy—the whole argument is deductively valid. This is not hard to appreciate. If the basic premises are true, so will be the first intermediate conclusions. But if they are true, so will be the statements following from them, down to the final conclusion.

But suppose our argument was composed of two subarguments—one inductively correct, the other deductively valid. Suppose its diagram looked like that in Figure 9.2.

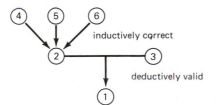

Figure 9.2

Would the overall argument be inductively correct or deductively valid? It would be inductively correct. If (4), (5), (6) are true, we have good, but not conclusive, reason to believe that (2) is true. If (2) and (3) are true, we do have conclusive reason to accept (1). So if (3), (4), (5), and (6) are all true, we have good, but not conclusive, reason to accept (1). This in effect is what we would expect. We would not expect a chain of arguments to be stronger than its weakest link.

Suppose our argument were composed of two inductively correct arguments. Would the argument itself be inductively correct? Would the overall strength be that of the weaker argument? Let's look at a chain of statistical syllogisms:

(1) Seventy percent of the cars in that garage are luxury cars.
(2) David's car is in that garage. So
(3) David's car is a luxury car. But
(4) Seventy percent of all luxury cars in that garage are Cadillacs. So
(5) David's car is a Cadillac.

Each subargument is inductively correct. The diagram is presented in Figure 9.3.

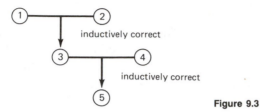

Figure 9.3

But if the three basic premises (1), (2), and (4) were all true, would it be more likely than not that David's car is a Cadillac? The percentage of Cadillacs in the garage is 70 percent of 70 percent, that is, $70\% \times 70\% = 49\%$. But given that information, the inference from David's car being in the garage to its being a Cadillac is not inductively correct.

When we have a series of inductively correct arguments, to estimate the overall strength of the argument, we must estimate the product of the strengths of each individual argument. In many cases, this will be just an estimate, since we shall have no precise numerical figure to rely on. For each argument, we are certain only to a given point x, where x percent is strictly greater than 50 percent but strictly less than 100 percent. But when we multiply two such percentages together, the product is always less than either percentage. So the overall strength of two inductive arguments in series will be less than the strength of either argument. Clearly the overall strength of an argument made up of a series of inductive arguments will be a function of the strength of each argument in the series and the length of the series as a whole. A series of a few distinctly strong inductive arguments may be inductively correct, but as we lengthen the series, the overall strength decreases.

Suppose one argument in a chain of inferences is inductively incorrect, is so weak as to be distinctly fallacious. Given what we have just said about series of inductively correct arguments, it's easy to see that overall the argument is fallacious. If the strength of the overall argument is the product of the strengths of the individual arguments, then if one of those arguments is fallacious, the overall strength will be weaker yet. We can sum up this discussion by saying that if an argument consists of a chain of arguments where each is deductively valid, then the entire argument is deductively valid. If there are one or more inductively correct arguments in the chain (but no incorrect arguments), then to estimate the overall strength of the argument, we estimate the product of the strengths of these arguments. Whether the overall argument is inductively correct or not we must judge on a case-by-case basis. Finally, if the chain contains a fallaciously weak argument, the overall argument is fallacious.

We have now presented a method for assessing the overall merits of an argument. We must determine whether the premises are true or believable, whether they are relevant to their conclusions, and the strength of each simple subargument. We must then estimate the overall strength of the argument. One issue remains.

Confronted with a long, extended argument, diagramming it and then completing an overall evaluation might prove a rather terrifying assignment. Suppose the argument contained thirty component statements with three major trains of reasoning converging on the final conclusion, each of these subarguments containing at least three sub-subarguments apiece. Where do we find the energy to produce this argument diagram, much less evaluate the argument? Could we ever meet such arguments in real life? Should we consider arguments sustained over several pages, or whole chapters in books, or whole books themselves, reasoning this complex is quite conceivable. What we need is some cutdown procedure in argument analysis which will let us get hold of a manageable unit to analyze and evaluate.

How Can We Effectively Approach Analyzing and Evaluating Extended, Complex Arguments?

Fortunately there are two ways of approaching extended arguments which simplify diagramming significantly. First, instead of treating the statement as the basic unit of the argument, we treat the paragraph. Hence, we assign distinct numbers to the separate paragraphs in the argument and then construct a tree diagram to display how they fit together to support the conclusion. Alternatively, we may seek for the topic sentences of the various paragraphs or subsections of the argument, assign numbers just to them, and see how they support the main conclusion or conclusions. If the argument at this level seems entirely implausible, if we can see that the entire argument just will not establish its conclusion or make a very good case for it, then we need not proceed further with the analysis. If, however, the argument as analyzed appears plausible at this point, we may then want to analyze each paragraph, seeing how the arguments they contain hang together and appraising them. Perhaps certain paragraphs will be more crucial than others to the argument. We may then choose to analyze and evaluate these subarguments first. If there is something significantly wrong with these parts of the argument, if, after analyzing and evaluating them, we see that the argument does not make its point, we need not go further.

But this leads to the other approach to analyzing extended arguments. An argument may have various final conclusions. Several of these may be main points of the argument. Others may be offered as interesting ancillary claims, but do not properly concern the main issue. Where we have several final conclusions, the argument involves divergent structure. We recognized earlier that we can treat a divergent argument as a collection of separate arguments, one for each final conclusion. We can ask of each of these arguments whether it is logically convincing. Whether one is cogent is a distinct issue from whether any of the others are. Consequently, unless there is some special reason, we can disregard the arguments for the ancillary points. Their correctness or lack of it is distinct from whether we have a logically convincing case for the main points. This simplifies our task in analyzing and evaluating the passage. Hence the first step in approaching an extended argument is to recognize the main point or main points of the argument.

Will the main points of an argument always be final points, conclusions not used to support further conclusions? This need not happen. To increase the interest of some main claim, someone might point out that it supports further secondary conclusions. Mathematicians often draw additional conclusions, called corollaries, from a main theorem. The thrust of the argument is not to establish these corollaries but, rather, the main theorem.

Since our main concern is with evaluating the reasoning just for these points, the second step is to select one of the main conclusions and determine what premises directly support it. We call this the case for that conclusion. That is, the case for the conclusion consists of all those premises which are one arrow away from the conclusion. It consists of the reasons which support the conclusion immediately, not through any intermediate conclusions. This situation is unaffected, should a modality interrupt the arrows. A modality is not an intermediate conclusion, and hence an arrow interrupted by a modal qualifier is still one arrow. At this point we should diagram the subargument we have recognized, proceeding according to the steps outlined in Chapter 7. When it comes to assigning numbers to statements, however, we need to identify and assign numbers just to the component statements of this subargument, not to all the statements in the passage. This in itself could significantly shorten our analysis.

There are two ways to proceed at this point. Which we pick we decide on a case-by-case basis, depending on our interests in the argument and what appears to be the most pressing issue. If this subargument is clearly fallacious, further analysis and evaluation of the overall argument for this main point seems pointless. Unless some portion of the argument used to support this main point has some special interest or value, we need not consider it. Evaluating the subargument to establish the fallacy would be the appropriate move. On the other hand, if certain premises appear questionable but are defended by further argument, we may want to analyze those arguments before doing any evaluation. Here again, our interest and sense of logical importance may guide our decision on which subarguments to examine. If a questionable premise lends significant total weight to the conclusion, we should be far more concerned with how it is defended than if it gives only a weak reason. After identifying and diagramming the case for a main conclusion, our next step then may be to identify and diagram the case for a questionable premise.

Of course, certain of the premises in these arguments to support some questionable premise may also be defended and the premises here again defended. In such instances, a further cutdown procedure is available. Suppose a given questionable premise is defended not just by two convergent premises but by two independent lines of reasoning. Suppose the structure looked like that in Figure 9.4.

We may want to subject just one of these chains of reasoning for (4) to evaluation, or perhaps consider one before the other. We may want to convince ourselves of the cogency of one line before entertaining the other. Hence, at this point, besides choosing to identify the case for (4) ((5) and (9) in our diagram), we may identify a complete chain of reasoning going back to the first or basic

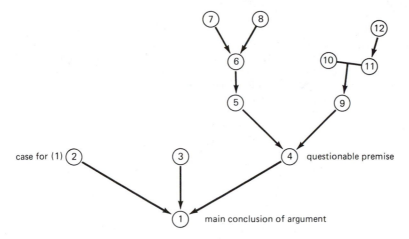

Figure 9.4

premises of the argument. The latter is identifying the entire *structural column* for the premise.[10] Two structural columns support (4) in our example. The first consists of (4) together with (5), (6), (7), and (8). The other consists of (4) together with (9), (10), (11), and (12). To find a structural column supporting a given statement, we identify one of the premises supporting that statement and then trace the support for that premise back to the basic premises of the argument.

Of course, we may want to identify just the case for some questionable premise and evaluate how cogent is that argument. The point is that once we have identified a case for a main point of the argument, we are confronted with various choices: either evaluate that subargument or continue analyzing the argument, either by identifying a case for a premise or a structural column. At each point when we complete a segment of the analysis, we can choose whether to evaluate the argument—or just a subargument—as analyzed or to continue the analysis further. After we complete our evaluation for one of the main points, we may then repeat this procedure for the others. Hence, in approaching an extended argument, we need not feel that we have to construct a tree diagram analyzing the entire structure first, and then evaluate the argument. We can proceed to select on a case-by-case basis just what is crucial, or most crucial, for each main point in an argument and confine our analysis and evaluation to those portions of the argument.

Exercise 9-IV

Construct tree diagrams for each of the following arguments. Then evaluate them according to the three critical questions we have developed. Where an argument consists of a chain of arguments, be sure to indicate the overall strength.

Sample Answer

A rating service executive denied responsibility for TV ills: "We're in the position of a reporter gathering and stating the news, that is, the ratings. Yet we're blamed for the kind of news we report. It's like blaming a garbage collector for gathering garbage that smells bad. Do you think people show poor taste in watching what are the most popular programs according to our ratings? Well, don't blame us—blame the TV audience."

He continued, "Are you going to change people's viewing habits by eliminating the rating services which only add up how many sets are tuned to what program? Those who criticize the ratings are refusing to face the real problem. They should apply their efforts to changing the programming structure instead of excoriating the mathematicians!"—Samm Sinclair Baker, *The Permissible Lie.*

Let's first work up this argument for diagramming:

① { [The rating services are not responsible for TV's ills.]
[A rating service executive denied responsibility for TV ills:]

② ["We're in the position of a reporter gathering and stating the

news, that is, the ratings.] ③ [Yet we're blamed for the kind of news

we report.] ④ [It's like blaming a garbage collector for gathering

garbage that smells bad.] ⑤ { [If you think the TV audience shows bad
[Do you think people show poor taste in

taste in watching what are the most popular programs according to our ratings,
watching what are the most popular programs according to our ratings? Well,

you should blame the TV audience.]
don't blame us—blame the TV audience."]

He continued, ⑥ { [You are not going to change people's viewing
["Are you going to change people's viewing

habits by eliminating the rating services which only add up how many sets are

tuned to what program(?)] ⑦ [Those who criticize the ratings are

refusing to face the real problem.] ⑧ [They should apply their

efforts to changing the programming structure instead of excoriating the mathe-

maticians!"]

Here is the tree diagram (see Figure 9.5). Premises (2), (4), and (6) essentially make the same point: (a) [The rating services are mere reporters on

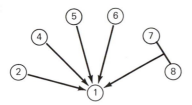

Figure 9.5

the popularity of various TV shows.] In each case, there is a suppressed premise: (b) [Reporters merely describe but are not responsible for the events they report.] The structure of this reasoning is presented in Figure 9.6.

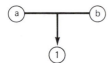

Figure 9.6

Clearly the linked premises are relevant to the conclusion, and the argument is deductively valid. Can we imagine the premises true and the conclusion false? But what about (a)? Are the rating services mere reporters? Although a reporter cannot cause or influence a past event just by describing it, can't rating services mold current popularity by announcing what shows are most popular? Remember the herd instinct underlying the bandwagon appeal. To maintain that the rating services are mere reporters, serving merely to describe, we need information that reporting the ratings does not influence popularity, and this is not given. So (a)—that is, (2), (4), (6)—is distinctly questionable.

A suppressed premise again explains why premise (5) is relevant to (1): (c) [If you should blame the TV audience, then the rating services are not responsible.] (See Figure 9.7.) Again we have relevant premises giving a deductively valid argument. Now certainly the TV audience bears some responsibility for what it watches. But in the light of what we have just said, doesn't (5) in effect beg the question? To maintain (5) doesn't the rating service executive have to show that the TV audience is *solely* to blame?

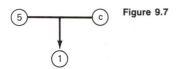

Figure 9.7

Premises (7) and (8) linked tell us that: (d) [The real problem is the programming structure.] And the ratings executive is apparently assuming that: (e) [If the real problem is the programming structure, the rating services bear no responsibility.] (See Figure 9.8.) Again the argument is deductively valid. But what about (e)? Although we are justified in attributing this premise to the ratings executive, is it really true that even if the main problem is the programming structure, the rating services bear no responsibility? A weaker premise would be more plausible, but then the argument would no longer be valid. So in all cases, we have false or questionable premise. In the light of all this, we do not have much of a case for the conclusion.

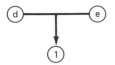

Figure 9.8

1. Never has the U.S. rejection of Russian proposals been so prompt. That must mean that their proposal is too close to a reasonable arrangement for comfort.—S.L.T., *Sunday Star-Ledger* (Newark, N.J.), January 2, 1983.

2. By buying up large quantities of tickets, the professional scalpers have been able to distort normal supply-demand ratios, create artificial shortages and increase the resale value of the tickets they had stocked up on. Therefore, everyone except the predators will be better off once the antiscalping controls are in effect.—*Sunday Star-Ledger* (Newark, N.J.), editorial, June 26, 1983.

3. Since Jack is so solicitous of his grandmother, he either expects to inherit something from her or hopes to get her to change her will. But Jack at present doesn't expect anything from his grandmother's will for he has seen a copy of it and it leaves him nothing. So Jack hopes to get his grandmother to change her will.

4. We should be concerned with the economic well-being of the Soviet Union. Why? If the Russians are permitted to make money, they will get to like it and eventually become capitalists. Which in turn will eliminate the Red menace and cancel the upcoming nuclear wipe-out.—C.L., *Sunday Star-Ledger* (Newark, N.J.), October 3, 1982.

5. Only two people could have been at the house when Harry was murdered—Joanne and Franklin. Hence, either Joanne or Franklin must be the murderer. But if Joanne was the murderer, then we would see her footprints leading away from the house. However, the only footprints leading away from the house were impressions of a man's shoe. So Joanne was not the murderer. Therefore Franklin was.

6. If the earth is in motion and a cannon is fired, shooting straight up (i.e., the cannon is pointed perpendicularly to the ground), then the path of the cannon ball will describe an arc, the ball landing some distance from the cannon. But this does not happen. The ball lands practically at the point where it was fired. Hence the earth is at rest.[11]

7. In the 1840s, the women in the First Maternity Division of the Vienna General Hospital were attended by medical students and doctors, who came to them right after performing autopsies, with only a superficial washing of hands. Hence these women were exposed to infectious material on the hands of the physicians and medical students. One physician cut his finger with an uncleaned scalpel used in performing an autopsy. Hence he was exposed to infectious material on the scalpel. In the First Maternity Division, there was an

alarmingly high mortality rate from puerperal or childbed fever. The physician died of an illness whose symptoms strongly resembled childbed fever. We know that the cause of the physician's death lay in the infectious material to which he was exposed by the scalpel cut. Therefore the cause of puerperal fever in the First Maternity Division lay in the infectious material on the hands of the medical students and doctors, who in effect were poisoning the women they were examining.[12]

8. Our way of life has been totally destroyed by greedy people and self-serving politicians.

First it was oil. We had to give up using our central heating system and switch to wood. Then the greed merchants concentrated on food, inflating retail prices while driving farm prices down. The government has aided and abetted these huge, rich corporations and has shown nothing but contempt for the farmer and consumer.

We have quit smoking because we can't afford the outrageous taxes imposed by Washington and Trenton.

The lawyers of this state are super-greedy and have a neat racket going. Through the courts, awards for damages are handed down which are three times too much. The lawyer then gets three times what he should. We, of course, pay three times what residents of other states pay for auto insurance.

Many of our legislators are lawyers, and in another moment of tender concern they raised the fines for traffic offenses. That kids may go hungry so parents can smoke, or pay for insurance, or pay for a fine, these rich people care not.—A.T.Z., *Sunday Star-Ledger* (Newark, N.J.), September 19, 1982.

9. Container Deposit Bill A-1753 . . . will recycle glass, cans and plastic containers by encouraging consumers to return containers for a five-cent refund.

Analyses of the effects of deposit legislation in states that have enacted such programs clearly show that substantial reductions in the amount of municipal solid waste (6–7 per cent), roadside container rubbish (85 per cent), and total litter (40–60 per cent), have been and can be achieved. Additionally, A-1753 has been drafted with specific provisions mandating that returnable containers be crushed and recycled (rather than washed and refilled) in order to protect the jobs of workers in New Jersey's glass industry. Instead, the bill as proposed will create a significant number of desperately needed minimum wage, low-skilled jobs to handle the returnables.

Our petitioning effort was so successful that in addition to receiving 300 signatures on the petitions, more than 500 letters were sent by individuals to their state legislators. We sensed a deep level of support from members of the law school community who represent diverse geographical, political and economic interests.

We urge all New Jerseyans to actively support this important bill.—Ellen Relkin and Roberta Yahr, co-chairwomen, Environmental Law Council, Rutgers School of Law, Newark, N.J., in *Sunday Star-Ledger* (Newark, N.J.), December 26, 1982.

10. The claim that President Reagan's economic policies hurt America's poor falls quite short of being true. Consider that for the month of February 1982 (the latest month for which figures are available at this time of writing) figures released by the Department of Labor show a price index rise at a three per cent annual rate. That is to be compared to a thirteen per cent rate of increase when Reagan took office. Hence, under Reagan the price index rise has decreased by ten per cent. Hence, purchasing power has increased by ten per cent. Now according to *Newsweek,* those earning $10,000 or less are hurting to the extent of $240 per person. In 1980, there were 40 million people earning less than $10,000 (using round figures). Hence, again using round figures, the Reagan Administration removed $10 billion from this sector of America. This sector spends $200 billion. Hence, the cash value of a ten per cent increase in purchasing power for this group is $20 billion. Therefore it would be pleasant, would it not, to read just once in a treatment of Reagan economics, or view just once on television, a story that said: "As of the month of February, Reagan's program has resulted in an increased purchasing power to the poor of a sum twice as large as that which they have given up in marginal benefits."—William Buckley, April 4, 1982.

11. I find it hard to believe that raising the drinking age from 19 to 21 will have any effect on the number of teenage traffic deaths. Teenagers will drink, no matter what the age is—I know, because I, unlike many, was a teenager once. It was always more fun before I turned 21. But there is a much more serious question involved here.

It is a question of fairness. Rights and responsibilities go hand in hand; you can't have one without the other. At 18, a young man or woman in New Jersey has all the responsibilities of an adult. He is tried in an adult court, and will be called upon to fight if there is a war. But he does not have the full rights of adulthood. He lives and works in our society without the privileges of it. Denying 18, 19, and 20 year olds the right to drink just increases the unfairness. Clearly, we should not raise the drinking age to 21.—B.R., *Sunday Star-Ledger* (Newark, N.J.), January 10, 1982.

12. For me, the indication that Italian terrorism is about to be defeated . . . is this: The terrorists are talking. . . .

[This] means first of all that they are not guided by any true political belief. Second, it indicates that they are feeling the ground eroded out from under their feet. . . .

Why do I say that they are not guided by a true political belief? . . . I was in jail under Fascism . . . for my political beliefs—I fought against Fascism—that is, against the Fascist dictatorship. Between imprisonment and exile, I lost 15 years of my youth. . . . At . . . three prisons I knew of only one person who requested a pardon. And he only did this because he was implored by his mother to petition for a pardon. And after he did this, not one person would look him in the face ever again. No one would speak to him anymore. He was banished. Thus, under Fascism, none of us talked.

That's because we were all volunteers in the struggle against Fascism. At the special tribunal very severe sentences were handed down. These 15- to 20-year sentences were no light matter. The prisoners responded to these sentences with shouts of their faith. . . .

[Thus] these were men of faith. And if today's terrorists are confessing . . . that means that they are not men of faith. They are not fighting for some higher and noble cause. Because otherwise, they wouldn't be talking!—Sandro Pertini, former president of Italy, *The New York Times,* April 3, 1982. Copyright © 1982 by The New York Times Company. Reprinted by permission.

13. I personally believe it to be totally unrealistic to expect public servants to abide by the letter and spirit of the Constitution for at least two reasons: (1) Public servants are ignorant of what provisions are in the Constitution, and furthermore, have a vested interest in perverting the Constitution to their own benefit and equally to the detriment of their sovereign masters. (2) Sovereign citizens are likewise ignorant of what provisions are in the Constitution, and, consequently, have no solid basis for exercising sound judgment in selecting public servants.—J.M.P., *Sunday Star-Ledger* (Newark, N.J.), April 3, 1983.

14. Recently a child was killed while playing in the leaves and a car burned up when the muffler set a pile of leaves on fire. Also a car overturned after skidding on wet leaves. Every fall there are incidents involving the loss of lives, injuries and destruction of property.

What is the solution to this problem? The state should repeal the law against the burning of leaves, which originated with the Department of Environmental Protection. Can the burning of leaves be more hazardous to us and our children than the accidents caused by the leaves? The DEP has offered no proof that the burning of leaves is hazardous to our health.

Leaf-burning would make our towns cleaner, safer and save taxpayers money. How much faith can we have in bureaucrats who make rulings that prevent these benefits? Sometimes I think DEP stands for Dumb Educated People.—R.E., *Sunday Star-Ledger* (Newark, N.J.), January 2, 1983.

15. I strongly urge that Family Living should be taught to all students. There is a tremendous need for family living education, especially at the junior and high school levels. It is a recognized fact that many parents do not teach their children about sexuality. In fact, I would estimate that about 50 per cent of the children in high school do not really understand the major functions of their sex system.

I myself received no education or formal instruction in family living until I was a college student. I feel by putting educated people in the position of teaching family living, students will be educated in this subject in an objective and unbiased way.

Students should be educated in every phase of family living, which will give students a good sense of their bodies. I feel it is essential to mandate family living.—R.G., *Sunday Star-Ledger* (Newark, N.J.), May 2, 1982.

FOR FURTHER READING

Our concept of generic argument evaluation is heavily indebted to Chapters 1 and 2 of Ralph H. Johnson and J. Anthony Blair's *Logical Self-Defense* (Toronto, Canada: McGraw-Hill Ryerson, 1977), where the fallacies of false or questionable premise, irrelevant reason, and hasty conclusion are singled out as basic. In particular, the criterion for assessing when a premise is relevant to a conclusion is due to them. We heartily recommend Sections 4 and 5 of Chapter 1 and all of Chapter 2 as collateral reading.

Irving M. Copi gives a basic presentation of enthymemes in *Introduction to Logic,* 6th ed. (New York: Macmillan Publishing Company, 1982), pp. 253–55. The distinction between needed and used assumptions in the issue of supplying suppressed premises is developed by Robert H. Ennis in "Identifying Implicit Assumptions," *Synthese,* 51 (1982), 61–86. The issue of supplying suppressed premises is also discussed in Karel Lambert and William Ulrich, *The Nature of Argument* (New York: Macmillan Publishing Company, 1980), pp. 57–60. For an account of adding suppressed premises with which we substantially agree, see Michael Scriven's *Reasoning* (New York: McGraw-Hill Book Company, 1976), ch. 4, Sect. 9, and ch. 6, Sect. 3.

Daniel Rothbart's article, "Toward a Structural Analysis of Extended Arguments," *Informal Logic Newsletter,* Vol. V, no. 2 (June 1983), 15–19, contains valuable insights for diagramming extended arguments and identifying useful portions for diagramming.

NOTES

[1] Adapted from an example supplied by R. W. Binkley in the *Informal Logic Newsletter,* Vol. II, Supplement, June 1980.

[2] This argument appears in Michael Scriven's *Reasoning* (New York: McGraw-Hill Book Company, 1976), pp. 81–82 and p. 166. Although we agree substantially with Scriven's account of supplying suppressed premises, we differ in detail. In particular, Scriven would opt for certain particular candidates in the range of acceptability.

[3] Example IX in Exercise 6-II.

[4] Example VIII in Exercise 6-II.

[5] Example adapted from Karel Lambert and William Ulrich, *The Nature of Argument* (New York: Macmillan Publishing Company, 1980).

[6] Example in Stephen N. Thomas, *Practical Reasoning in Natural Language* (Englewood Cliffs, N.J.: Prentice-Hall, Inc., 1973).

[7] This example appears in Frank C. Carlone, Karol Dycha, and Leo Raffin, *An Informal Logic Workbook* (Windsor, Canada: 1981), p. 21.

[8] This example is drawn from material in the *Informal Logic Newsletter,* Vol. II, Supplement, June 1980.

[9] Several examples have appeared in earlier exercises, where we were asked to display just the manifest structure. In some cases, we have reedited or paraphrased the material here. For convenience of reference, and to acknowledge again our sources, we indicate where each example occurs previously: Sample Answer in 6-I, Ex. IX; (4) in 8-VI-B, Ex. 7; (5) in 7-I, Ex. XVII; (8) in 7-I, Ex. XIV; (10) in 6-IV, Ex. XII; (11) in 6-IV, Sample Answer; (16) in 6-II, Ex. VII; (17) in 6-I, Ex. X; (20) in 6-IV, Ex. XIV.

[10]The notion of a structural column is due to Daniel Rothbart, "Toward a Structural Analysis of Extended Arguments," *Informal Logic Newsletter,* Vol. V, no. 2 (1983), 15–19.

[11]For a discussion of why this argument does not establish its conclusion, see I. Bernard Cohen's *The Birth of a New Physics* (Garden City, N.Y.: Anchor Books, 1960), ch. 1.

[12]This example is based on material in Carl G. Hempel, *Philosophy of Natural Science* (Englewood Cliffs,N.J.: Prentice-Hall, Inc., 1966), pp. 3–6, where we have a full account of how the physician Ignaz Semmelweis established the cause of the high rate of puerperal fever in the First Maternity Division.

10

EVALUATING INDUCTIVE ARGUMENTS

In developing generic argument evaluation, we have made few distinctions concerning specific types of arguments we can meet. So far we have distinguished deductive from inductive arguments and identified a special class of each—categorical syllogisms and statistical syllogisms. For inductive arguments especially, this generic approach is very appropriate. For there are a number of arguments which just claim to give evidence, good reasons for their conclusions, without being members of the three special inductive families we shall identify shortly. For example, in arguing for or against some proposed tax legislation, military program, or foreign policy, editorials will present various reasons to support their view. The claim is that the reasons are good although not conclusive reasons, their combined weight justifying accepting the conclusion. In weighing the strength of such arguments, we weigh their evidence against the counterevidence, ask whether enough reasons have been given, whether the evidence is representative or biased, or whether the argument fails to counter significant rebutting conditions. This, together with questions of the truth or plausibility of the premises and their relevance to the conclusion, constitute the logical tools needed to appraise whether arguments are logically convincing. Hence, these generic considerations will frequently be exactly what we should consider in evaluating arguments.

However, recognizing that certain inductive arguments belong to specific families allows us to sharpen up some of these generic questions, to ask more specific questions appropriate to these families. In particular, the first and third principles for comparing argument strength,

1. The stronger the premises with respect to the conclusion they directly support, the stronger the argument.

3. The weaker the counterevidence, the less likely that some rebutting condition can be found which undercuts the argument, the stronger the argument.

can be given special sharpened versions. We shall identify three inductive families: inductive generalizations, causal arguments, and arguments by analogy. After describing the characteristic marks of each family, we shall present the specific critical questions they raise. This shall occupy us in the first section of this chapter. Associated with each of these inductive families are certain fallacies, the inductive fallacies mentioned in Chapter 3. Being able to identify these fallacies is an extra and convenient tool in evaluating inductive arguments. We turn to this in Section 10.2.

§10.1 INDUCTIVE ARGUMENT FAMILIES

1. Inductive Generalizations

S_1 is a white swan.
S_2 is a white swan.

.

.

.

$S_{1,000,000}$ is a white swan. Therefore
All swans are white.

This is not only a paradigm inductive argument, but a paradigm inductive generalization. On the basis of examining 1 million swans and finding out that they all were white, the argument concludes that *all* swans are white. That is, on the basis of examining a sample of a certain class or population, here swans, a claim is made about the entire class. This is a very familiar type of inductive argument. We proceed from particular to general. Our premises make statements about the particular members of a class, and the conclusion makes a general statement about the entire class.

Inductive generalizations are of two types: categorical and statistical. Our example concluded that all swans were white. "All" is the distinguishing mark of a categorical inductive generalization. It concludes that all members of the class have the property in question. Statistical generalizations, on the other hand, claim that a certain percentage of the class displays a certain characteristic, based on the percentage of an observed sample which displayed the characteristic. This is the type of argument pollsters use to justify their conclusions about public opinion, attitudes, voter trends. For example, if George Gallup were to argue that

(1) Fifty-six percent of American voters will cast their ballots for the Democrats, because

(2) 56 percent of those polled said they would vote Democratic.

his argument would be a statistical inductive generalization. Again, we are going from particular to general. We have observed the particular members of a certain sample of the population and on that basis state a conclusion about the entire population. Only here, we do not find that all the particulars observed share some property, but only a percentage of them do. On that basis, we infer that in the entire population, that same percentage shares this property.

As with the white swan example, categorical inductive generalizations frequently proceed this way:

(1) e_1 is an A and a B.
(2) e_2 is an A and a B.

   .

   .

   .

(n) e_n is an A and a B. Therefore (probably)
($n + 1$) All A's are B's.

(Here A stands for the class some of whose members are being observed (e.g., swans), B for the property being checked (white), and $e_1, e_2, \ldots, e_n$ the particular examples observed (particular, individual swans out of the 1 million). n is some positive integer, say 1,000 or 1,000,000, numbering the last example observed.) Such arguments exhibit convergent structure, each premise concerning a particular instance contributing a little weight to the conclusion. Alternatively, the various premises may all be telescoped into one:

All A's observed so far have been B's.

This form is parallel to statistical generalization arguments, where we simply replace "all" by some percentage figure.

Inductive generalizations are such paradigm cases of induction that some logicians have proposed distinguishing inductive from deductive arguments by saying that the former draw general conclusions from particular premises, while the latter draw particular conclusions from general premises. But this is a gross oversimplification. How do we classify categorical syllogisms having all component statements general? How do we classify arguments like "On every particular day in the past, the sun has risen; so the sun will rise tomorrow"— which apparently reason from particulars to particulars? Besides leaving unanswered these questions, a mechanical application of this criterion will simply produce the wrong answers, for we can have inductive arguments with general premises and a particular conclusion, and we can have deductive arguments with particular premises and general conclusions. Consider:

> All red delicious apples have seeds. All yellow delicious apples have seeds. All Baldwin apples have seeds. All Rome beauty apples have seeds. All winesap apples have seeds. Therefore probably this apple has seeds also.

Although all the premises are general and the conclusion particular, this clearly is an inductive argument on two grounds. Besides the explicit inductive indicator "probably," common sense indicates that although the premises give evidence for the conclusion, they do not guarantee that it is true. Hence, although inductive generalizations move from particular premises to general conclusions, this is not the case for all inductive arguments.

On the other hand, consider:

> Socrates was the principal teacher of Plato. Socrates was executed on charges of impiety and corrupting the Athenian youth. Therefore anyone who is identical with the principal teacher of Plato was executed on charges of impiety and corrupting the Athenian youth.

Although the premises here are particular and the conclusion general, this is a deductive argument. Can we imagine the premises both true and the conclusion false? Hence, we can have deductive arguments which move from particular premises to general conclusions.

The first pattern for categorical inductive generalization, where a number of premises converge on the conclusion, suggests a way to sharpen the first principle of argument strength specifically for these arguments. For here, all the premises involved have a specific form. They say of some particular item that it is both an A and a B, some particular instance of the class A is also a B. Hence

1'. The more instances given in the premises, the stronger the argument, the greater the *prima facie* strength of the argument.

Of course, if we knew that some A was not a B, no matter how many premises we added to the argument, we would not increase its total weight. The force of the argument would be completely undercut.

Are there specific rebutting conditions which undercut the force of inductive generalizations? If so, we might incorporate them directly into the third principle for argument strength. Indeed, there are two types of considerations here, and we can get at them through two specific critical questions for inductive generalizations. These questions are closely related to the first two conditions for the hasty conclusion fallacy discussed in Chapter 8.

Notice that the premises of inductive generalization arguments, be they categorical or statistical, concern some sample of a class. We base our conclusion about the entire class on some sample. Our first critical question then is

(1) Is the sample large enough?[1]

Clearly, if there were a million members in class A and our sample concerned only five or ten A's, finding that all of them were also B's, the chances of finding some A which was not B would seem pretty good, and so we would have a bad argument here. Now clearly, in inductive generalization arguments, we are not confined to taking such small samples from such large classes. Presumably, we can take samples which are large enough, and we can advance and defend the claim that our sample is large enough as a counterrebuttal. To be cogent, such an argument would need to give us information about the total size of class A and how uniform we might expect A to be. For example, if we know that a certain ethnic population in a certain city has always voted in a block—how one person votes is how all vote—then even if we were to sample only five voters from this population, if all of them said they were supporting a certain candidate or issue, that could constitute a good argument that the entire population would do likewise—an argument which could be defended against the charge that its sample was too small.

This issue of homogeneity brings us to the second specific critical question for inductive generalizations:

(2) Is the sample varied enough?[2]

A sample must be representative. That is, the variety in the class being sampled must be mirrored, represented in the sample itself. Frequently, polls predicting the outcome of national elections are based on samples of less than 2,000 voters, yet these polls still provide good evidence for their predictions. This is because the diversity of the national population, geographic, ethnic, economic is mirrored in the sample. Pointing out, then, that class A is composed of various subgroups membership in which might be relevant to whether an item was a B or not, and that the sample observed contained representatives from all these subgroups in proportion to their number in the population, could be an effective counterrebuttal against the claim that the sample was not varied enough. Pointing out that a random sampling technique was used, giving each member of the population equal chance of being selected as a member of the observed sample, might also be an effective counterrebutting argument, especially when a sample is varied, but information as to how it is varied, that is how many relevant subclasses there are or the relative size of those subclasses in the population, is not available.

The sample's not being large enough or not being representative or varied enough are standard rebutting conditions for inductive generalizations. Let's incorporate this discussion into a version of the third criterion of argument strength, sharpened specifically for inductive generalizations:

3'. The less likely that some rebutting condition holds which undercuts the argument, in particular the larger and the more varied the sample with which the premises are concerned, the stronger the argument, the greater its total weight.

Principles 1' and 3', then, allow a sharper analysis of argument strength for inductive generalizations.

2. Causal Arguments

There are two types of causal arguments: arguments *to* causes and arguments *from* causes. An argument to a cause seeks to establish a causal claim as its conclusion. An argument from a cause uses some causal assertion as a premise. But what is a causal claim or causal assertion? More specifically, what does it mean to say two things are related as cause and effect? First, causal relations hold between two events or types of events, or conditions.

> Striking the match caused it to light.
> Billiard ball A's colliding with B caused B to move.
> Smoking causes lung cancer.
> The patients' fever caused their pallor.
> The dictator's madness caused him to order the executions.

The first two examples each relate two particular events, unique happenings at a specific time and place, the striking of a particular match with its lighting, the collision of two billiard balls with one's moving. The third example relates not particular events but types of events. The last two examples relate conditions. The fever and the pallor are not specific happenings at some particular time, but conditions that persist over some period of time. Likewise the dictator's madness did not happen at one specific point, although here the claim is that it caused a specific event, his ordering certain executions. Contrast this with the inductive generalizations just examined. We would not say that a thing's being a swan *caused* it to be white. Being a swan and being white are properties, not events or conditions, and we do not recognize the causal relation holding between properties.

Besides holding between events or conditions, whenever the cause/effect relation holds the cause temporally precedes the effect. Suppose we knew that a disease could not occur unless certain germs were present. Although there would be a regularity between contracting the disease and the presence of the germs, we would never say that people's contracting the disease caused the germs to be present. It is the other way around. The germs had to be there first.

But besides holding between events or conditions where the cause temporally precedes the effect, the cause/effect relation involves a regularity. However, the notion of cause is ambiguous, and there are several distinct, although related regularities a causal statement may involve. Consider our first causal assertion again: striking the match caused it to light. Now no matter how often I strike a match, no matter how hard I do it, if the match is soaking wet, it will not light. Being dry is causally necessary for a match's lighting. Accordingly, we say that A is a *causally necessary condition* for B just in case B cannot occur unless A occurs first. On the other hand, suppose we know that the match has been struck with sufficient force, that it is dry, that the tip has the proper amount of flammable material, and that oxygen is present. When all these conditions jointly occur, can the match fail to light? All of them together are sufficient to ignite the match. We say then that A is a *causally sufficient condition* for B just in case B must occur if A occurs. Frequently, we may speak of a number of conditions which are each necessary and jointly sufficient. A match will not light unless it has been heated to the proper temperature by striking or otherwise, it is dry, and oxygen is present. Each of these conditions is necessary. Together they are sufficient.

Now the word "cause" may be used in the sense of either necessary condition or sufficient condition. If I say that in the Middle Ages, many plagues were caused by total lack of sanitation, I mean that if sanitary procedures had been in effect, the plagues would not have happened. I am using "cause" in the sense of necessary condition. But if I say that lightning striking a dry forest in the absence of significant rain for the past six months caused the forest fire, I am using "cause" in the sense of sufficient condition applied to the lightning together with the dry forest.

But as ordinarily used, "cause" has a further sense—that of *catalytic condition*, the event or condition which, in the presence of other conditions normally occurring, produced the effect. In one sense, the catalyst is the trigger, the last factor we need to produce a sufficient condition. If I say "Striking a match causes it to light," I mean not that if I don't strike a match, it won't light— a match could light because it has been thrown into the fire or ignited by some other lit match—or that striking it all by itself causes it to light. Rather I mean that all things being equal—the match is dry, oxygen is present—it will light. The striking is the catalytic event. Adding it to the other conditions produces a sufficient condition.

The claim that A causes B in the sense of catalytic condition can be made with varying degrees of strength. I may mean that A together with generally prevalent conditions constitutes a sufficient condition for B, that if A + generally prevalent conditions occur, B must occur also. But I may mean something weaker. When I say that smoking causes lung cancer, do I mean that, all things being equal, those who light up will develop lung cancer or only that they are at significantly greater risk? Don't I mean that the chances of a smoker developing lung cancer are significantly greater than those of the nonsmoker and that it is the smoking which has increased this risk?

Necessary condition, sufficient condition, catalytic condition are three senses of "cause." Of these three, catalytic condition is perhaps the most common, widely used notion, and it is the notion we primarily will have in mind in what follows. Discussing the meaning of "cause" is necessary if we are to have a proper understanding of what a causal statement and so a causal argument is. Distinguishing these meanings of "cause" is necessary if we are to discuss causal arguments accurately.

How do we justify, argue for causal claims? Here again, we need to make a distinction. Some causal claims concern particular events:

> Jim's being thrown off his bicycle at 25 mph caused his broken finger.

Others concern causal generalizations:

> Sharp impacts cause broken bones.

But clearly, particular causal statements presuppose general causal claims. They state that this is an instance of a particular causal regularity. Establishing general causal claims, causal generalizations, is primary, and we are concerned with arguments to causes in this sense. The simplest arguments for causal generalizations are parallel to inductive generalization arguments. Where A and B are two types of events or conditions—like sustaining sharp impacts and incurring broken bones—from noting that in a number of particular instances, an A-type event is followed by a B-type event, we infer that A causes B. Where A_1, B_1, A_2, B_2, . . . , A_n, B_n stand for particular instances of these types, the following schemes describe this pattern of reasoning:

> (I) A_1 is followed by B_1.
> A_2 is followed by B_2.
>
>   .
>
>   .
>
>   .
>
> A_n is followed by B_n. Hence
>   A causes B.
> (II) Type A events or conditions have always been followed by Type B events or conditions. Hence
>   A causes B.

There can be a "statistical" version of this also:

> (III) B occurs significantly more often after A occurs than when A does not occur. Therefore
>   A causes B.

In a sense, these arguments go a step farther than inductive generalizations, asserting not just that A is always followed by B or followed by B in a certain percentage of cases, but that A causes B.

Now although such arguments present evidence directly supporting a causal generalization, if we are thinking logically about causes, they should seem incomplete. Suppose I observe a number of cases where someone eats a sloppy joe and subsequently gets sick. Clearly this gives me evidence for blaming the sloppy joes, but to be confident of this conclusion, shouldn't I rule out other possible explanations? How do I know that it was something in the sloppy joes which caused the food poisoning until I have eliminated other causal explanations? Although detailing the specific patterns of causal arguments which include eliminating, countering rival causal explanations is beyond the scope of this book,[3] we must keep in mind that these considerations are properly part of arguing for a cause. They are also intimately connected to evaluating causal arguments, as we shall see shortly.

As we said, we also may have arguments *from* causes, arguments which base their conclusions on some causal premise. Our discussion of the various senses of "cause" is very relevant to the question of evaluating such arguments. For suppose A causes B in the sense of A being a necessary condition for B. Then it is true that whenever something of type B occurs, something of type A occurs. So whether or not this claim is manifestly stated or taken as a suppressed premise, the argument that since B has occurred, A has occurred is deductive. Likewise, if A causes B in the sense that A is a sufficient condition for B, to argue from A's occurring to B's occurring is again to argue deductively. Hence we need not consider such arguments within the context of evaluating inductive arguments.

But if A is a catalytic condition for B, then knowing that A has occurred gives us a good, but not necessarily conclusive reason for asserting that B will occur. Just the information that A occurs does not tell us that all things are equal, that the other necessary conditions occur, and the connection between A and B may be statistical rather than categorical. So if I see a bomb with a lighted fuse and infer that shortly there will be an explosion, reasoning according to this pattern:

(1) A is a known cause of P.
(2) I am observing A occurring. Hence it is likely that
(3) P will occur (shortly),

I am arguing inductively. Similarly, if I conclude something about the cause of an event by observing certain effects, I am reasoning inductively. For example, suppose I hear a loud crash out in the street. I look out of the window and see two cars quite bashed in. I see the drivers getting out and other people running. In a few minutes the police arrive. I conclude that the two cars collided. From observing a number of effects a collision may have, I infer that one has occurred. Schematically, my reasoning displays this pattern:

(1) A is a known cause of P, Q, R, ...
(2) I am observing P, Q, R, . . . occurring. Hence probably
(3) A has occurred.

These are the two patterns of arguments from causes. We either argue from a cause to an effect or from an effect to a cause.

Having discussed the concept of cause and the general patterns of causal reasoning, how may we evaluate causal arguments? In the next section on inductive fallacies we shall identify how arguments from causes can be fallacious. For now, the question is how we may sharpen our principles of argument strength for arguments to causes. This is very straightforward. Clearly the first pattern for causal arguments is parallel to the first pattern for inductive generalizations. The premises offer instances of the causal connection. The more instances, the greater the *prima facie* strength of the argument. The first principle gets sharpened for causal arguments as it did for inductive generalizations.

Rival causal explanations to the one being argued for function as rebuttals. The instances are evidence that the conclusion is true unless, of course, they better support some rival explanation or that rival is more likely or known true. The greater the likelihood that one of these rebutting explanations holds, the weaker is the total strength of the argument. Similarly, the less likely that some rival hypothesis is the correct explanation, the stronger the argument. Clearly, given several rival explanations to the one being argued for, it should be possible to give counterrebuttals, if the basic argument is ultimately cogent. That is how evidence which rules out rival explanations functions, as counterrebuttals. Hence, for arguments to causes, there is a special and very important type of rebuttal, the rival causal claim. This merits being incorporated in a sharpened version of the third principle of argument strength:

3″. The less likely that some rebutting condition holds which undercuts the argument, in particular the less likely that some rival causal hypothesis holds, the stronger the argument.

In the next section, we shall develop how these sharpened versions of principle (3) are directly connected to identifying fallacies in inductive and causal generalization arguments.

3. Arguments by Analogy

This family of inductive arguments is perhaps the most interesting and important of the three inductive families presented in this chapter. In everyday contexts, arguments by analogy may be the most frequently encountered arguments belonging to a special family.[4] As with inductive and causal generalizations, we shall show how to sharpen the first and third principles of argument strength. However, we shall be able to sharpen both of these principles in two different ways. We shall also give a fourth criterion of argument strength specific to arguments by analogy. Hence, there are ultimately six criteria for assessing the strength of such arguments. But what is an argument by analogy? Consider:

(1) John, his brother Sam, and their parents smoked two packs of cigarettes a day since they were teenagers, ate a diet rich in fatty foods, never exercised.

(2) The parents and brother Sam all died prematurely of heart attacks. Therefore probably

(3) John will die prematurely of a heart attack also.

Here, four individuals are named and compared: a_1, Sam; a_2, the father; a_3, the mother; b, John. The properties on which they are compared are P_1, smoking two packs of cigarettes a day since being a teenager; P_2, eating a diet rich in fatty foods; P_3, never exercising; Q, dying prematurely of a heart attack. The argument, then, displays this pattern:

(1) a_1, a_2, a_3, b all have P_1, P_2, P_3.

(2) a_1, a_2, a_3 all have Q. Therefore probably

(3) b has Q also.

In general, of course, arguments by analogy may compare any number of items on any number of properties. The items compared can be of various sorts, individual persons, things, sets of things, events, actions. The general pattern of arguments by analogy looks like this:

(1) a_1, a_2, . . . , b all have P_1, P_2, ...

(2) a_1, a_2, . . . all have Q. Therefore probably

(3) b has Q also.

This type of reasoning occurs frequently in medical research. Why should the finding that laboratory rats when exposed to certain substances develop cancer have any implication for human health? Why should drug testing be done on animals when the ultimate question concerns human health? It is because rats and other animals resemble humans in certain respects. Their physiological systems are the same in these respects. Hence on the basis of this similarity, we infer, with some degree of probability, that if certain substances produce cancer in rats, then they will produce cancer in humans. If giving a drug to an animal produces a certain result, then a similar dosage given to humans should produce a similar result.

How may we evaluate the strength of arguments by analogy? It is important to remember that in everyday contexts, arguments involving analogical reasoning may not manifestly display the pattern just given. We may need to paraphrase to make them display this structure explicitly. However, making this paraphrase is an obvious first step in evaluation. We may also introduce some convenient terminology in this connection. We are comparing a_1, a_2, . . . on the one hand with item b on the other. Since b is the item the conclusion is about, since we are arguing about b, we call b the *target item*. Since we assert our conclusion on the basis of information about a_1, a_2, . . . , it is with reference to them that we draw our conclusion, we call a_1, a_2, . . . the *reference items*. Typically there will be several reference items and one target item, although there could be several target items or just one reference item. When paraphrased, the first premise states that reference items a_1, a_2, . . . share certain properties with target item b. Hence, a_1, a_2, . . . , b are similar in various respects. We shall call these the *similarities argued from*. The second premise states that a_1, a_2, . . . share some further property, and the conclusion says b has this property also. Hence the conclusion says that b is similar in some further respect to a_1, a_2, ... We call this the *similarity argued for*. Let's label our general pattern with these terms (see Figure 10.1).

reference items   similarities argued from

(1) a_1, a_2, . . . , b all have P_1, P_2, . . .

(2) a_1, a_2, . . . all have Q. Therefore, probably

(3)   b has Q also.

target   similarity
item   argued for

Figure 10.1

As with inductive and causal generalization arguments, the premises of arguments by analogy make statements about particular items. With both previous types of arguments, the more items mentioned in the premises, the stronger the argument, all things being equal. This is also true here for the reference items. Suppose that John and Sam had two sisters, Arlene and Sherry. Suppose that both these persons also had been two-pack-a-day smokers since they were teenagers, that they also ate fat-rich diets, and that they never exercised. Suppose also that both Arlene and Sherry died prematurely of heart attacks. Adding this information to the premises should clearly increase the *prima facie* strength of the argument. Hence, we can sharpen the first principle of argument strength as we have done before.

For arguments by analogy, there is a second way we can sharpen the first principle. Consider again just the four persons originally compared, John, Sam, and their parents. Suppose the first premise were expanded, comparing them not just on the properties mentioned, but also pointing out that all four persons had a type A personality and that all four engaged in stressful occupations. Type A personalities tend to be hard driving, demanding, impatient, tense, putting stress on others around them as well as on themselves. Clearly, if our premises contained this additional information, the case for the conclusion would be strengthened. But we have not strengthened the case by including more instances, but rather by increasing the number of similarities argued from, the number of respects in which John is compared with his brother Sam and their parents. Here are the two sharpened versions of the first principle of argument strength. To make them more memorable, we include descriptive labels.

1a. (NUMBER OF REFERENCE ITEMS PRESENTED)   The more reference items presented in the premises, the greater the *prima facie* strength of the argument. That is, where $a_1, a_2, \ldots, a_i, \ldots$ are compared with b, all being said to share some property or properties $P_1, P_2, \ldots$, the more a_i's, the stronger the argument.

1b. (NUMBER OF SIMILARITIES ARGUED FROM)   The more similarities argued from, the greater the *prima facie* strength of the argument. That is, where $a_1, a_2, \ldots$, b are said to share properties $P_1, P_2, \ldots, P_j \ldots$, the more P_j's, the stronger the argument.

Let's restate the second principle of argument strength here for convenience of reference.

2. (INVERSE VARIATION PRINCIPLE)   The stronger the conclusion, the weaker the argument.

There are two ways to sharpen the third principle. How might an argument by analogy be rebutted? Suppose that instead of John *sharing* the further properties of having type A personality and engaging in a stressful occupation with his brother and parents, John was *different,* disanalogous from these three persons in these respects. These would be relevant disanalogies between John and his brother and parents, relevant to whether John will die prematurely of a heart attack. Their mention would certainly weaken if not undercut the strength of the argument. As with inductive and causal generalizations, we can formulate a general rebuttal especially for arguments by analogy. Our premises create a presumption for the conclusion, unless there are sufficient relevant disanalogies between the reference items and the target item. Each assertion of a relevant disanalogy is evidence for this rebuttal and so weakens the argument. Hence, we may present this first sharpening of principle (3):

3a. (NUMBER OF RELEVANT DISANALOGIES)   The more relevant disanalogies, points of difference between the reference items and the target item, the weaker the argument. That is, where $a_1, a_2, \ldots$, are the items compared with b, said to share certain properties $P_1, P_2, \ldots$, with b, the more relevant disanalogies which hold between a_1, a_2, on the one hand, and b, on the other, the weaker the argument.

If producing relevant disanalogies tends to weaken or rebut arguments by analogy, producing reasons why such disanalogies do not hold or why they would be less likely to hold amounts to giving counterrebuttals. For arguments by analogy, there is one special way of doing this. Recall that with inductive generalization arguments, the more varied the sample referred to in the premises, the stronger the argument. If our sample of a certain class is representative or randomly chosen, and all members of the sample display some feature, the variety in the sample makes it less likely that this shared feature is peculiar to these instances and more likely that it holds in the class in general. The same principle holds for arguments by analogy. Suppose we interviewed 101 voters who all considered themselves middle class, all felt they were politically interested, that is, they followed political campaigns and voted regularly, and all were employed in steady jobs. Suppose 100 also said they were going to vote Democratic in the next election. By analogy, we would infer that the 101st person was going to do likewise. But suppose the 100 were all blue-collar workers and the 101st a white-collar worker. Occupation and its associated social class can have an influence on political preference, as can many other factors such as employment status, area of residence, religious affiliation, and family background. We have a relevant disanalogy, significantly weakening our argument. Now if our sample had been chosen to include representatives of a great variety of these factors, the possibility of such a rebutting condition would be greatly reduced, if not eliminated altogether. The more variety in the reference items, the less likely that some unstated similarity which they all share, but the target item does not, is the reason why the reference items all have Q, the similarity argued for. Hence the more varied the reference items compared, the stronger the argument. Statements pointing out the dissimilarities among a_1, a_2, . . . then constitute counterrebuttals strengthening the argument. The following principle expresses this:

3b. (VARIETY AMONG REFERENCE ITEMS)   The more varied the reference items, the more dissimilarities holding among them, the stronger the argument. That is, where a_1, a_2, . . . are the items compared with b, the more dissimilarities holding among a_1, a_2, . . . , the stronger the argument.

There remains yet the special criterion for assessing the strength of arguments by analogy, perhaps the most important criterion of all. Our discussion of relevant disanalogies suggests that the mere fact that b is different in some respect from a_1, a_2, . . . is not sufficient to constitute a rebuttal, that difference has to be relevant to whether b has Q or not. The last criterion concerns this issue of relevance. Consider the following argument:

> I've been thinking of buying a new car and I have picked out the one for me. Like my old car, it is fire engine red, with cream interior, has bucket seats, and a very sexy dashboard. My old car has gotten good gas mileage. So I expect the new one will also.

This argument is patently ridiculous, but why? It certainly fits the pattern of an argument by analogy. Two items, my old car and my proposed new one, are compared on various grounds. I then claim that my old car has some further property and conclude that the new one will also. The problem is that the points of comparison, being fire engine red, having cream interior, bucket seats, and a very sexy dashboard, have nothing to do with gas mileage. Possessing these other features is not in any obvious way relevant to the question of how much gas mileage a car will get. The argument fails to be logically convincing precisely because of this irrelevance. Contrast this argument with our previous examples of arguments by analogy. We recognize that cigarette smoking, fat-rich diets, lack of exercise as well as personality type and job stress are all relevant to whether someone will have a heart attack, because we know that all these are causal factors in heart disease. These examples illustrate their points nicely because the points of analogy are well-known causally relevant factors to the property being argued about. Hence, the following principle:

4. (RELEVANCE)   The similarities argued from must be relevant to the similarity argued for. That is, where an argument by analogy concludes that b has Q because $a_1, a_2, \ldots,$ b have $P_1, P_2, \ldots$ and $a_1, a_2, \ldots$ have Q, having $P_1, P_2, \ldots$ must be relevant to having Q.

This relevance principle has two applications in evaluating arguments by analogy. First, an argument which disregards this principle, where $P_1, P_2, \ldots$ are *not* relevant to Q, is obviously fallacious. It involves the fallacy of faulty analogy, which we shall discuss in detail in the next section. Second, we have seen how arguments by analogy can be strengthened or weakened by addition of further statements. Certain statements can function as additional premises either directly supporting the conclusion or acting as counterrebuttals, thus strengthening the argument. Other statements serve as evidence that a rebuttal holds, thus weakening the argument. Now it could be that a given further statement presents neither a premise nor a rebuttal. Its addition to the argument makes it neither stronger nor weaker. One instructive exercise in evaluating arguments by analogy is to assess whether the addition of a statement or some modification in the statements of the argument would make the result stronger or weaker. Keeping the relevance principle in mind, we may recognize that on some occasions, the strength will be left unchanged.

Summary

In this section, we have defined the three standard inductive families and discussed evaluating the members of these families. *Inductive generalizations* are of two types: categorical and statistical. In either case, a conclusion about an entire class is drawn from premises concerning an observed sample. Categorical inductive generalizations claim that all the members of the class have a certain property since all observed members do. Statistical inductive generalizations claim that a certain percentage of the entire class has a certain property because that percentage of the observed sample does. *Causal arguments* either seek to justify a causal claim or to use a causal connection to predict an effect from an observed cause or to infer a cause from an observed effect. The simplest arguments seeking to establish a causal claim argue that because one event or condition is always followed by a second; therefore, the first is the cause of the second. Since rival causal explanations function as rebuttals, causal arguments may, and in general should, include further counterrebutting premises ruling out such rivals. *Arguments by analogy* claim that where a number of items a_1, a_2, . . . , b share certain properties P_1, P_2, . . . and further that a_1, a_2, all share a property Q, then it is likely that b has Q also.

For each family, we have shown how to sharpen the first and third principles of argument strength. For both inductive generalizations and causal generalizations, the more instances given, the stronger the argument. For inductive generalizations, the larger and more varied the sample with which the premises are concerned, the less likely the argument may be rebutted, and so the stronger the argument. For causal generalizations, the less likely that a rival causal hypothesis holds, the stronger the argument. In effect, we have given six principles for evaluating arguments by analogy: number of reference items presented, number of similarities argued from, inverse strength of premises and conclusion, number of relevant disanalogies (rebuttals), variety among reference items (counterrebuttals), and relevance. By applying these various principles, we may assess the strength of these inductive arguments or at least may know what questions need to be answered before a proper assessment can be made.

Exercise 10-I

The following are the labels of the criteria for evaluating arguments by analogy:

(1a) NUMBER OF REFERENCE ITEMS PRESENTED
(1b) NUMBER OF SIMILARITIES ARGUED FROM
 (2) INVERSE VARIATION PRINCIPLE
(3a) NUMBER OF RELEVANT DISANALOGIES
(3b) VARIETY AMONG REFERENCE ITEMS
 (4) RELEVANCE

Each of the following arguments by analogy is followed by six additional statements. Some could be added to the argument. Others indicate changes in the argument. Paraphrase each argument according to the standard pattern for arguments by analogy and identify reference items, target item, similarities argued from, similarity argued for. Then for each of these additional statements, decide whether adding it to the argument or changing the argument as it suggests would make the resulting argument stronger (indicate by >), weaker (indicate by <), or leave the strength unchanged (indicate by —). In each case, indicate which criterion explains your decision.

1. The components for nuclear power plants are built by GE, Westinghouse, Chrysler, and other major companies, which also manufacture general consumer products, such as toasters, dryers, radios, cars, and so on. These general consumer products frequently break down. So we can be practically certain that nuclear power plants will break down also.

a. General consumer products are constructed by largely unskilled workers. These companies use highly skilled technicians to build components of nuclear reactors.

b. Suppose the conclusion read: Nuclear power plants will break down as frequently as general consumer products.

c. The workers who are employed in producing consumer products and those employed in producing parts for nuclear power plants have the same abilities and are subject to the same supervision; their work must pass the same standards of quality control; their materials come from the same companies.

d. These companies build parts for airplanes, space vehicles, and the military, and there are failures with all these products.

e. Large percentages of the stock in these companies are owned by mutual funds, pension plans, and such other organizations.

f. Some companies have strict policies of quality control. Others are lax. Yet all of them experience product failure.

2. Only 54 percent of the voters participated in the 1980 election, the lowest turnout for a presidential election in 32 years. . . . A complex of factors, ranging from the nature of the campaign to the weather on Election Day, contribute to the problem. But one simple change might help a lot: move Election Day to Sunday. . . .

Sweden, Austria, West Germany, Italy and France hold national elections on Sundays; in those countries, voter turnout is between 86 and 90 percent. . . . Moving election day to Sunday . . . would not elevate turnout to levels in European countries, but it would make some difference. . . .—*The New York Times,* editorial, August 21, 1982. Copyright © 1982 by The New York Times Company. Reprinted by permission.

a. Suppose the conclusion read: Moving election day to Sunday would raise voter turnout to levels comparable to European countries.

b. Australia, New Zealand, the Soviet Union, Zaire, Rhodesia, Albania, Brazil, and Mexico in addition hold elections on Sundays, and in all these countries the turnout is between 80 and 90 percent.

c. All these countries impose fines for not voting. No such fine is proposed for the United States.

d. Suppose (b) is added, along with the following statement: Sweden, Austria, West Germany, Italy, France, Australia, and New Zealand are Western-style democracies. The Soviet Union and Albania are communist countries. Zaire, Rhodesia, Brazil, and Mexico do not have the literacy rates to function as full-fledged democracies.

e. Like the United States, Sweden, Austria, West Germany, Italy, and France have long traditions of democratic government, high literacy rates, and general popular interest in political issues and candidates.

f. The citizens of Sweden, Austria, West Germany, Italy, and France, like the citizens of the United States, all speak Indo-European languages.

3. Jim has taken four philosophy courses and found them to be intellectually exciting and to have lasting educational value. Hence, he decides to take

another philosophy course, expecting that it will be equally exciting and valuable also.

a. Two of Jim's courses were in technical, analytic philosophy. The other two were very nontechnical, discussing questions about the meaning of life, death, and the universe.

b. The courses Jim took were philosophy of art, philosophy of literature, philosophy, politics and society, and existentialism. None required any use of technical symbols or anything like formal, mathematical reasoning. The course Jim has just signed up for is symbolic logic, cross-listed with the Mathematics Department.

c. The chairman of the Philosophy Department has just received a fellowship to complete a major research project.

d. Jim has taken eight philosophy courses and had the same positive feeling about all of them.

e. Jim concludes not that the course he is taking will be especially exciting and valuable but just that it will be worthwhile.

f. All four of Jim's previous courses were taught by the same professor, who is also scheduled to teach this one.

4. Professor Brown has attended the last five annual meetings of her professional association and has found them all to be boring wastes. Nonetheless, she plans to attend the meeting this year also, fully expecting it to be a boring waste.

a. The five previous meetings were the most boring, unstimulating, frustrating wastes of time Professor Brown has ever experienced.

b. Professor Brown has attended a number of other professional meetings in the past five years and found them to be boring wastes also.

c. Each of these past five meetings featured many papers around a selected main theme, which differed widely from year to year.

d. The previous five meetings were held in either New York, Boston, or Washington. This year's meeting will be held in Philadelphia.

e. Most of the papers at the previous meetings were not in Professor Brown's area of interest. This is true also of the papers at this year's meeting.

f. For the past five years, a certain political group antagonistic to Professor Brown has dominated the professional association, including the program committee. However, this year a new group, with which Professor Brown is in sympathy, has taken control of the association, including the program committee.

5. I recently started buying a certain brand of frozen cauliflower and broccoli mix. The outside of the package shows small chunks of cauliflower and broccoli flowerets. But inside the package were very large pieces of cauliflower and only stems and mashed pieces of broccoli. I have bought two packages now, and they have both been the same. I see my friend Joe has just bought a package. I think I'll give him a call in a few days. Possibly he will have the same problem.— Adapted from a letter to the consumer advocate column in the *Vancouver Sun*, April 1981.[5]

a. Besides the two packages I bought, a number of my friends have purchased this same brand of frozen cauliflower and broccoli mix. I know of 25 packages in all. In each case, there has been this problem.

b. The supermarket where I bought these packages was giving double value on coupons.

c. All the packages of this brand of frozen food sold in the supermarket where I bought my two packages and Joe bought his were processed at the same plant.

d. I have bought this brand's packages of many different types of frozen vegetables. In all cases, there was a distinct discrepancy between the picture on the package and its contents.

e. Suppose Joe has bought five packages and I conclude that he'll find this discrepancy between the contents and the packaging in all five.

f. I bought two packages several months ago after there had been labor unrest at the company. That was resolved several weeks ago and packages on sale now were produced after the settlement of the dispute.

Exercise 10-II

Part of the difficulty in evaluating inductive arguments depends on being able to recognize what rebutting conditions might undercut the force of the argument from the instances enumerated to the conclusion. It will frequently require background knowledge of the situation to formulate these conditions. However, for each of the argument families discussed in this section, we have suggested standard rebutting conditions. Indicate whether each of the following arguments is an inductive generalization, causal argument, or argument by analogy. Then frame a rebuttal for each argument.

1. I have asked ten people and all of them say they are voting for Ms. Julia Bream for shop steward. Hence I expect her to win.

2. Five thousand laboratory animals were fed a diet rich in cockroaches. A significant number developed stomach cancers. Hence, it was the diet of roaches which caused the stomach cancer.

3. Monkeys who have taken certain birth control hormones have produced malformed offspring. Hence, if humans should take this birth control hormone, they run a high risk of producing deformed offspring.

4. Each time Bill has asked Mary Alice to go to the movies with him, she has gone. Hence Mary Alice goes to the movies with Bill because he asks her.

5. My old Chevrolet gave me good gas mileage, seldom needed expensive repairs, and held up well in appearance over the years. Hence, I expect my new Chevrolet to do the same.

6. In all the cases I have observed where opium or opium derivatives have been used, the results have been beneficial. The drug has alleviated long-term pain. Hence I conclude that opium is always beneficial and should be made available to all.

7. It's great that Columbus police are rounding up so many drug pushers.

Unfortunately, the big money-making pushers aren't busted because they are protected by the law. These dealers happen to have MDs after their names.

My mother listened to their advice for years and now is addicted to pills in the worst way. Her habit is very costly, but it helps doctors play golf, take vacations and invest on the stock market.

Young people who see their parents taking pills are more inclined to pop sopors and downers. Then they are thrown in jail. Let's put the burden of guilt where it belongs.—D. McG., Columbus, Ohio.

8. For each of her five hourlies, June studied only a half-hour and subsequently failed the test. Hence it was her inadequate amount of studying which caused her to fail.

9. I have examined three balls from this urn and found them all to be blue. Hence all the balls in the urn are blue.

10. Ten men were sick in the hospital with high fever. The doctor prescribed the same medicine for all of them. The next day, all ten had died. Hence, it was the doctor's medicine which did them in.

11. On five different occasions, Professor Brown has excused students from attending class. Hence I wouldn't worry about missing one of her classes—surely whenever someone misses a class, she excuses them.

12. Inflation is the result of wage increases. Every time unions make a gain in wages, corporations raise the price of goods they produce to compensate themselves.—Paul Hellyer.[6]

13. In six cities, the phone company installed new glass and aluminum phone booths in busy bus or railroad stations. In each city, observations over a six-month period showed a significantly higher use of these phone booths than the old, drab structures they replaced. From this, the company concluded that the attractive appearance of the phone booths was responsible for the significantly increased patronage.

14. If a single cell, under appropriate conditions, becomes a man in the space of a few years, there can surely be no difficulty in understanding how, under appropriate conditions, a cell may, in the course of untold millions of years, give origin to the human race.—Herbert Spencer, *Principles of Biology*.

15. "Do you think," said Candide, "that men have always massacred each other, as they do today, that they have always been false, cozening, faithless, ungrateful, thieving, weak, inconstant, mean-spirited, envious, greedy, drunken, miserly, ambitious, bloody, slanderous, debauched, fanatic, hypocritical, and stupid?"

"Do you think," said Martin, "that hawks have always eaten pigeons when they could find them?"

"Of course I do," said Candide.

"Well," said Martin, "if hawks have always had the same character, why should you suppose that men have changed theirs?"—Voltaire, *Candide*.

§10.2 INDUCTIVE FALLACIES

In this section, we shall look at two types of inductive fallacies—patterns of inductive reasoning which may have persuasive force yet fail to be logically convincing: false or questionable cause and faulty analogy. Why don't we also consider faulty inductive generalizations? Our discussion of hasty conclusion in Chapter 8 is sufficient to identify faulty inductive generalizations. We have the fallacy of *hasty generalization* when the sample on which the generalization is based is either too small or nonrepresentative. We make a general statement about the entire class on the basis of too few examples for the size of the class being discussed or on the basis of nonrepresentative examples of that class. But these are just special cases of the first two grounds on which the fallacy of hasty conclusion can arise—the premises give too little information or possibly non-representative information, drawn from too narrow a base, overlooking relevant sources which may yield contrary facts or considerations. Negative answers to our critical questions—"Is the sample large enough?" and "Is the sample varied enough?"—show that we have a hasty conclusion argument here. Hence we need not specifically discuss the hasty generalization fallacy. There are several patterns of reasoning which could be classed as false or questionable cause. We begin with these.

False or Questionable Cause

Let us begin by saying that the fallacy of *false cause* occurs when what is not the cause of an event or condition is mistaken for the cause. Similarly, if a causal connection is asserted which is highly dubious, we have the fallacy of *questionable cause*. There are two general ways for this fallacy to occur in arguments. First, the causal claim may be the conclusion of the argument, and the premises simply do not provide adequate evidence to support the claim. In spite of the premises, the conclusion is not a credible causal statement. Second, the causal claim can be a false or highly questionable premise. We may identify three specific types of fallacious arguments to causes. Let's look at these first, and then consider how fallacious arguments from causes may occur.

1. Hasty Causal Conclusion. In the last section of Chapter 8, we said that an argument involved the fallacy of hasty conclusion if its premises gave too little information, nonrepresentative information, or failed to include needed counterrebuttals. The fallacy of *hasty causal conclusion* is just a special case of this, where we judge the argument too weak because it bases its conclusion on too few instances or fails to counter some rival causal explanation or some other rebutting condition. In particular, it may fail to counter the possibility that the alleged causal connection is a mere coincidence or just a statistical correlation. For example, many diseases have various symptoms. Hence we may find statistical correlations between the occurrence of one symptom and another. Yet we do not say that one symptom causes the other. Rather it is the underlying illness which causes both. If patients undergoing certain medical tests frequently suffer from both headaches and nausea, we don't say that either the headaches cause the nausea or the nausea the headaches. To conclude this just because the headaches and nausea occur together is fallacious, and it is easy to diagnose the fallacy. A hypothesis that some substance used in the test or some aspect of the procedure was the common cause of both symptoms has been overlooked.

This example illustrates how statistical correlations, although they may suggest causal connections, are not sufficient to establish them. Beware—people actually argue this way. A humorous example claims that when prices on the stockmarket go up, so do ladies' hemlines, and when the hemlines come down, so do the stock prices. This alleges a constant conjunction between two events. But if someone tried to manipulate stock prices by getting designers and manufacturers to raise or lower hemlines, that would involve blatantly fallacious causal reasoning.

Perhaps a good rule of thumb in identifying hasty causal conclusions is to ask whether alternative causal explanations readily suggest themselves. Consider the following example. At one time a question arose concerning why markedly fewer residents of El Paso, Texas, were in state mental hospitals than residents of Dallas. El Paso is one-third the size of Dallas. So we would expect roughly one-third as many patients. In actual fact, the number was one-seventh. Why the significantly lower percentage for El Paso? Here is an explanation offered by a University of Texas biochemist:

> El Paso's water is heavily laced with lithium, a tranquilizing chemical widely used in the treatment of manic depression and other psychiatric disorders. Dallas has low lithium levels because it draws its water from surface supplies. (So, the significantly higher levels of lithium cause the significantly lower rate of admissions to mental hospitals.)

Now this explanation is certainly worthy of investigation. But as an *argument*, the passage falls short on both the grounds of insufficient evidence and neglect of alternative hypotheses. At least one other hypothesis readily comes to mind. Isn't life less stressful in smaller cities and towns? Might this not account for fewer mental problems? Some background knowledge suggests another hypothesis. The nearest state mental hospital to El Paso is 350 miles away; to Dallas, only 35. Is Dallas's sheer proximity (or El Paso's lack of proximity) the reason for this discrepancy in number of patients in mental hospitals? Unless these are ruled out, we still have a hasty causal conclusion.

Notice also that only Dallas and El Paso are compared. Data about other cities with lithium levels comparable to El Paso and Dallas supporting that higher lithium levels are associated with lower rates of mental illness is necessary to establish even a statistical correlation.[7]

Here is another example:

> We have proof that marijuana causes violent behavior. In a murder trial in Alabama, the prosecution established that the defendant, previously a model

young man, had been smoking marijuana. He became inflamed—nay possessed—by overwhelming lust and slew a rival for his girlfriend's affections. This is not the only case like this. In New York, several young children were smoking marijuana. They went on a rampage, smashing everything in the apartment. In San Francisco, an arsonist torched several buildings—this after he became a regular marijuana user.

How may we criticize this argument? First, the evidence is not systematic but just anecdotal. The premises give too few instances. Representative samples of marijuana users and nonusers have not been compared to see if there is a significantly higher percentage of violent behavior among the users. If this were found, we would then have established a statistical correlation and would have grounds to suspect a causal connection. All we have here are a few examples, no systematic study, and so no established correlation between marijuana smoking and violent behavior. Second, this argument overlooks, fails to rule out alternative causal hypotheses. Was the young man jealous concerning his girlfriend? How strong were his feelings about her and could not that be the explanation of the violent behavior? What about the other cases alluded to? What about the young children in New York? Did they have known personality disorders? Had they been prone to violent behavior before? Had the arsonist in San Francisco been involved in similar crimes? Could he have had some clear motive for committing the crime? None of these rival hypotheses is even considered in this argument.

This example seems to argue that since the violent behavior followed the marijuana use, therefore using marijuana caused behaving violently. Arguments which proceed this way again are examples of hasty causal conclusion. But this pattern is so distinctive that it has been given a special name and deserves being treated as a special causal fallacy in its own right. As with some other logical concepts, the Latin name has remained current.

2. Post hoc.   Recall from our discussion of the meaning of "cause" that whenever we can truly say that one event A causes another B, A must temporally precede B. If a pile of sticks were already on fire when I tossed a lighted match onto the pile, I would not say that my tossing the lighted match caused the fire. The fire would have to start after the match was tossed for the causal claim to be true. Similarly, for one condition to cause another, the effect cannot precede the cause. If someone's being anemic causes pallor, the onset of his anemic condition should precede his being pale. If he became pale first, and then developed anemia, the cause of his pallor, at least before the time he developed anemia, would be something else. So the temporal precedence of cause to effect is necessary for the causal relation to hold. The *post hoc* causal fallacy occurs when the *mere* temporal precedence of one event to another is given as the reason why one caused the other.

Just because one event precedes another does not mean it had any causal effect on the other. My eating breakfast this morning has temporally preceded all sorts of events—people whom I do not know going to work, business transactions, crimes, parties—but my eating breakfast certainly caused none of these events. To argue that way would be to commit the *post hoc* fallacy. But such arguments do occur, and they can on occasion be rather persuasive. In the 1960 presidential campaign, John F. Kennedy is alleged to have said

> Vice-president Nixon visited Venezuela in 1959. Subsequently the government collapsed.

The conclusion is implicit here but quite obvious. Mr. Kennedy was suggesting that Vice-president Nixon or his visit was causally responsible for the government of Venezuela's collapse. His evidence is that Nixon's visit occurred before the government's collapse. That one event preceded another may suggest a causal connection, but it is not sufficient reason to justify claiming a causal connection. As we have seen, the causal claim could be patently false. *Post hoc* is an abbreviation of the Latin phrase *post hoc ergo propter hoc*—"after this therefore because of this"—temporal sequence means causal sequence, a principal example of faulty causal reasoning.

Some writers point out that this fallacy frequently occurs in justifying superstitious beliefs. If I use my birthdate to generate a number I pick for my Lotto ticket and subsequently win the jackpot, I may be tempted to claim that I have found my lucky number, that my picking this particular number caused me to win. But this is obviously *post hoc* reasoning. Writers of chain letters use this fallacy to play on fears and desires. The recipient is told that he will receive good luck in a few days if he sends the letter to ten or twenty others, but is warned that if he does not, disaster will occur. The letter may mention how some who participated in the chain met with good fortune, while those who broke it met with woe. Even if these claims are true (and surely these premises are questionable), claiming the existence of a causal relationship on their basis clearly involves the *post hoc* fallacy.

We may regard *post hoc* arguments as particularly flagrant examples of hasty causal conclusion. They base their conclusions frequently on just one or a few instances of one type of event following another and so fail to have enough instances to back up the conclusion. They fail to take account of rival causal explanations, and they fail to argue that we have more than a coincidence or correlation, where it is quite possible that is all we have. There is one other distinctive pattern of hasty causal conclusion which merits a special classification of its own. As we shall see, it involves a peculiar way of overlooking an alternative causal hypothesis, the correct one in this case.

3. *Reversing the Causal Order.* A classic example of this causal fallacy might go like this:

> Since wealthy, successful corporate executives frequently ride in chauffeured limousines, if you want to be a success in business, you should get a limousine and chauffeur.

This argument is absurd precisely because it reverses the causal line. Having the chauffeured limousines did not cause these corporate executives to be wealthy and successful. Rather, since they were wealthy, they could afford such luxuries as chauffeurs and limousines. The argument has the causal order switched, cause and effect reversed. This is obviously faulty causal reasoning. Although instances of this fallacy are frequently humorous, it can occur in serious contexts.

> Does belonging to the National Association of Female Executives really help? Only 9.7 percent of American working women earn over $15,000 a year—but 75 percent of NAFE members do. Only 0.8 percent of American working women earn over $25,000 a year—but 25 percent of NAFE members do. It looks like NAFE membership helps women advance their careers further, faster and easier than they otherwise would have.

Do our premises really support the conclusion that NAFE membership helps women advance their careers? The argument has gotten the causal order reversed. Presumably, being an executive is prerequisite for joining the NAFE. But achieving an executive position is a distinct mark of success. So it is not being in the NAFE which makes women successful; rather the success allows certain women to join the NAFE.

We have now surveyed the ways in which we can have faulty reasoning for causal conclusions. Now let's see how faulty reasoning *from* a causal statement can occur.

4. Questionable Causal Premise. Frequently, an argument which attempts to establish some causal claim is followed by another argument, using that causal claim as a premise. Such arguments are often for or against certain courses of action. We argue that one thing causes another, and on that basis argue that something ought to be done or avoided. But if the causal claim itself needs the support of an argument and that argument is faulty, in particular involves some type of hasty causal conclusion, then the causal claim is still questionable and the argument using it as a premise involves the questionable premise fallacy. For example, if someone argues

> The past three times that I have taken the express train to work, something unfortunate has happened that day. Surely taking the express is bad luck. So I shall avoid it.

not only does the first argument involve a hasty causal conclusion, but arguing further for a course of action—avoiding the express—on the basis of this flimsily supported causal claim is to reason on the basis of a questionable premise, a second fallacy. If a causal claim is not recognized as true or warranted by our background knowledge and is not properly supported by an argument, it is a questionable statement. Using it as a premise then is fallacious.

We have now surveyed the main ways in which causal arguments may be fallacious. Before discussing fallacies in analogical reasoning, we summarize our discussion here by indicating how we may argue that we have a fallacious causal argument (see Figure 10.2).

Figure 10.2 FALSE OR QUESTIONABLE CAUSE

The fallacy of false or questionable cause may arise either

1. when there is an argument *to* a causal conclusion *and*
   a. the premises give insufficient evidence or fail to counter some obvious rebuttal such as an alternative causal hypothesis or the possibility of a mere coincidence or correlation (hasty causal conclusion), or
   b. the argument claims that because A temporally precedes B, A causes B (*post hoc*), or
   c. the causal conclusion gets the causal order reversed, switching cause with effect (reversing the causal order),

or

2. when there is an argument *from* a causal claim *and* the causal claim is questionable, in particular because it is inadequately supported (questionable causal premise).

Faulty Analogy

In the first section of this chapter, we saw that there were six grounds for evaluating arguments by analogy. Of these, two are intimately connected with faulty analogical reasoning. Principle 3a points out that the more relevant disanalogies which hold between a_1, a_2, . . . , on the one hand, and b, on the other, the weaker the argument. Now where the conclusion says that b has property Q and these dissimilarities make it unlikely that b has Q even though b shares other properties P_1, P_2, . . . with a_1, a_2, . . . , then we have fallacious analogical reasoning. *Neglecting relevant disanalogies* is the first reason why we may have the faulty analogy fallacy. For example, the philosopher David Hume once wrote an essay arguing that suicide was permissible:

> It would be no crime in me to divert the Nile or Danube from its course, were I able to effect such purposes. Where then is the crime of turning a few ounces of blood from their natural channel?—"On Suicide."

Let's recast this argument into the standard form of arguments by analogy:

(1) Diverting the Nile or Danube (or other river) from its geologically established bed and diverting the blood from its biologically established channel are both instances of diverting a stream of liquid from its natural course.

(2) Diverting a river from its geologically established bed, if possible, is no crime. Therefore

(3) Diverting the blood from its biologically established channel is no crime either.

Now we might very well dispute the second premise. If I were able to redirect a river so that it flooded a city and drowned many of its inhabitants, that certainly would be a crime. But this just highlights a relevant disanalogy between diverting rivers ordinarily and opening veins. If I could divert rivers, I might be able to do so without harming life, limb, or property. But if I open my veins, I shall be destroying a human life—something very relevant to whether a crime is being committed. The two items are disanalogous, and this disanalogy is distinctly relevant to the question being argued: Is suicide a crime?

Here is another, and perhaps more subtle, example. In commenting on the campaign of Harold Washington, a black, for mayor of Chicago in 1983, the columnist William Safire saw the possibility of a double standard. Here is his argument:

> Rep. Washington won the Democratic nomination because the "white vote" was split between Mayor Jane Byrne and Richard Daley, and because he was able to turn out a really impressive "black vote." Hats are off to him for that. Citizens of Chicago who are black turned out mightily for one of their own, and blacks everywhere are understandably pleased.
>
> The double standard comes in when a possibility arises that whites may do the same thing. If it is laudatory for black voters to vote as a block for the black candidate, then logic dictates it should bother nobody that white voters are likely to vote as a block for the white candidate.
>
> But it bothers everybody, including the white candidate, who insists he wants no votes from racists. And racist is what such a voting pattern would be, of course: If words have meaning, voting on the basis of race is racist.
>
> Accordingly, we should either stop praising the black community of Chicago for uniting behind the black candidate, or stop complaining when whites show inclinations to do the same. Both actions are racist: praise or condemn both.— "Race in Chicago," *The New York Times*, March 24, 1983. Copyright © 1983 by The New York Times Company. Reprinted by permission.

We can recast this argument in two equivalent ways:

(1) Blacks voting for a candidate because he or she is black and whites voting for a candidate because he or she is white are both instances of a racial group voting for a candidate because the person is one of their own.

(2) We find blacks voting for a candidate of their own praiseworthy. So

(3) It should be praiseworthy, or at least morally acceptable, for whites to vote for a candidate of their own.

Alternatively,

(1) Blacks voting for a candidate because he or she is black and whites voting for a candidate because he or she is white are both instances of a racial group voting for a candidate because the person is one of their own.

(2) We find whites voting for a candidate because he or she is one of their own racist and so reprehensible. Hence

(3) We should find blacks voting for a candidate because he or she is black also racist and reprehensible.

Do we have a good argument here? Again, we may fault this argument from analogy for neglecting a relevant disanalogy. By longstanding tradition, blacks have been alienated from the American political process. When blacks vote to elect a black candidate, this alienation is being broken down in two ways. First, blacks are themselves participating in the electoral process. Second, should the black candidate be elected, this increases the proportion of blacks in elected public office, and so participating in the actual running of government. On the other hand, whites have always constituted the mainstream of American politics. Should whites vote for one of their own because he or she is white, this would be a vote to maintain the alienation of blacks and other minorities from the American political process. But isn't the question of whether an action increases or decreases alienation relevant to whether it is morally praiseworthy or blameworthy? The actions of blacks and whites are disanalogous in this respect, which is relevant to the conclusion. For neglecting this relevant disanalogy, we can again say we have faulty analogy here.

We illustrated how principle 4, the relevance principle, may help us pinpoint faulty analogical reasoning when we introduced it. Recall that for an analogical argument to be cogent, the similarities argued from must be relevant to the similarity argued for in the conclusion. P_1, P_2, . . . must be relevant to Q. So arguing that a new car will get good gas mileage because the old one did when both are similar in being fire engine red, having cream interior, bucket seats, and a very sexy dashboard involves faulty analogy. None of these features is relevant to gas mileage.

We can easily imagine situations where we can appeal to both these criteria, neglecting disanalogies and presenting irrelevant similarities, to explain why we have faulty analogy. In the foregoing example, besides recognizing that the similarities between the two cars are irrelevant, we might also know that my present car is a foreign compact, while the dealer's model is a luxury Cadillac. When the question is one of gas mileage, this is certainly a relevant disanalogy.

Some arguments by analogy are faulty because of a further problem with the relevance criterion. This is illustrated in the following example:

> The [Chicago] Bears advertised a professional football game but they don't play a very professional game. They make too many mistakes and don't live up to their advertising. *It's like* if Barry Manilow came on stage and suddenly got laryngitis and couldn't talk, I'd get a refund. If the Rolling Stones came to town without Mick Jaggar, that would be misrepresentation.—J.T.,[8] Rockford, Ill.

Our schema for arguments by analogy indicates that we spell out how our items are similar, in what respects they resemble each other, before we argue that they resemble each other in some further respect. But this may be left understood or at least not explicated in a given argument. For example, if we argue that because rats have developed tumors when fed high doses of some chemical, so will humans, we leave unstated those respects in which rats and humans are physiologically similar. The argument here is acceptable, because presumably respects in which rats and humans are analogous could be spelled out. But what about J.T.'s example? He has said the Bears's poor performance *is like* Barry Manilow or Mick Jaggar not appearing. But how is it like these possibilities and is the likeness relevant to whether J.T. should get his money back, presumably the conclusion he is arguing for?

Certainly in all these cases there is disappointment. But is being disappointed with a performance relevant to saying that one is entitled to a refund? When you buy a ticket, have you established a contract with the performer that he or she will give you a satisfying performance? If Barry Manilow or Mick Jaggar failed to appear for a scheduled concert, then the fans should get their money back, not because they were disappointed, but because the contract was not fulfilled—there was no promised performance. However, the Bears did live up to their end of the contract. They played the football game. So merely saying that two situations are like or similar may not be enough to establish that they are relevantly similar. In this case, spelling out the respects in which they were similar did not produce a similarity relevant to the conclusion. And the similarity which would be relevant to the conclusion, not fulfilling the contract, would be true of Barry Manilow and Mick Jaggar, but was not true of the Bears. Again, this argument in effect ignores the relevance criterion.

Our examples again illustrate that a helpful first step in evaluating arguments by analogy is to paraphrase them into standard form according to the basic pattern. Then we ask whether known disanalogies have been neglected or whether the similarities mentioned (or hinted at) in the first premise are not relevant to the similarity argued for in the conclusion. If either of these is the case, we have a fallacy of faulty analogy (see Figure 10.3).

Figure 10.3 FAULTY ANALOGY

We may argue that an argument from analogy involves the fallacy of faulty analogy by pointing out that either

1. there is some significant relevant disanalogy holding between the items mentioned just in the premises, a_1, a_2, . . . and the item argued about in the conclusion, b,

or

2. the similarities mentioned in the first premise, P_1, P_2, . . . are not relevant to the similarity Q argued for in the conclusion.

Both these defects may occur in the same argument. If the respects in which a_1, a_2, . . . and b are similar are not explicitly stated, it is possible that the similarities holding among all these items are not relevant to the similarity being argued for.

Exercise 10-III

Identify whether the fallacy of false or questionable cause or faulty analogy occurs in the following arguments. If there is a causal fallacy, state whether it is hasty causal conclusion, *post hoc,* reversing the causal order, or questionable causal premise. If an argument by analogy is faulty, be prepared to discuss whether this involves neglecting a relevant disanalogy or ignoring the relevance criterion.

1. University of Michigan medical researchers have discovered that highly educated people with low incomes catch cold more often than others, suggesting that susceptibility to colds might depend on one's frame of mind. Further, more people come down with colds on Monday than any other day.

Well, practically everybody thinks he is not being paid as much as his education calls for, and it's on Monday mornings when this feeling becomes most acute.

So obviously it's not a germ or virus that's causing all our colds but those cold-hearted people in the front office who never seem to realize how smart we are.—Adapted from an article that appeared in the *Oakland Press* (Pontiac, Mich.), April 16, 1974.

2. In the seventeenth century, people generally fell asleep after putting on sleeping caps. This must mean that those old sleeping caps had dormitive properties—they really put people to sleep.

3. Statistics show that students who get good grades study harder. So if you want me to study more, you should give me good grades.

4. It's not a germ or virus that's causing all our colds. It is those cold-hearted people in the front office who never seem to appreciate us or how smart we are. A cure for colds? One way would be to give everybody a raise and tell them to take Mondays off.—Adapted from an article that appeared in the *Oakland Press* (Pontiac, Mich.), April 16, 1974.

5. An attorney is always free to consult his law books. And a physician often looks up cases in medical texts. So students should be permitted to use their textbooks during examinations.—Adapted from an example in Copi, *Introduction to Logic,* 6th ed.

6. I saw on television that after Joe Namath used Brut aftershave, two attractive ladies threw themselves on him. I guess Brut is a good guarantee of success in the love life. Hence I'm going to use Brut before my big date on Saturday night. Any guy should!

7. A two-year-old child is not taught grammar before he speaks the language. So education students should not be taught education theory first and then given practical experience in the classroom.—H.E., Toronto, Canada.

8. When Roger Babson . . . became ill with tuberculosis, he returned to his home in Massachusetts rather than follow his doctor's advice to remain in the West. During the freezing winter he left the windows open, wore a coat with a heating pad in back, and had his secretary wear mittens and hit the typewriter keys with rubber hammers. Babson got well and attributed his cure to fresh air.—Martin Gardner, *Fads and Fallacies in the Name of Science.*

9. Whenever Senator Smith wins a debate, he has a glass of champagne. So if you want to start winning debates, you should start drinking champagne.

10. The proposals of the pro-nuclear freeze people are like Neville Chamberlain's attempted appeasement of the Nazis. Chamberlain let Hitler get away with murder, then when it was too late, he drew the line in Poland. By then Germany was too strong, we were too weak, and war was inevitable. Hence, unless we specifically draw the line somewhere, enacting a freeze will leave us so weak that the Soviets would risk war with us. We must never leave ourselves open to nuclear blackmail, and that is just where a nuclear freeze would take us.—G.T.M., *Sunday Star-Ledger* (Newark, N.J.), November 21, 1982.

11. I adored my coloring books when I was a child and went on to teach art myself for 25 years. Surely, my coloring books stimulated my artistic abilities.

12. At that time of his life, John was in the habit of smoking a pipe all day while reading. After a while, his eyes began to water. John concluded that the reading hurt his eyes.

13. The growing gay population is largely due to cannabis [marijuana]. Marijuana contains a female estrogen [a hormone] which is affecting male users. [So clearly the way to contain the gay problem is to ban marijuana by imposing strict penalties for its sale, possession, and use.]—V.S., British Columbia, Canada.

14. [Building further nuclear weapons will in no way make the world more secure and help to insure peace. Just ask yourself:] Would you feel more secure now if Toronto were armed? Are you less secure now that Toronto doesn't maintain an army in case Hamilton invades? We haven't ended conflict between individuals or cities, we've just found other ways of dealing with it.—J.S., Toronto, Canada.

15. Successful people are generally high paid. So if you want your teachers to be a success, you should pay them more.

16. Religious meddling is causing chaos in Iran; it has brought about the assassination of Anwar Sadat. Hence, any advice from the Catholic bishops, not only on the abortion issue but also on the issues of capital punishment, the living will, armaments, illegal aliens, public money for parochial schools, is dangerous and detrimental.—B.H.W. (adapted), Delaware, Ohio.

17. She could well be the most beautiful minister in the world but the thought has to cross your mind as you watch her and listen to her: Is it the medium or the message which attracts 3,000 people to her Sunday morning services at the California Theater?

I decided to put the Rev. Terry Cole-Whittaker's message to the test.

She had told us, during the meditation part of the service, to picture vividly in our minds whatever it is we desire and that, if we do that, we will discover that the picture will come to life.

Would the technique work on the tennis court?

I found myself an opponent I had beaten in practically every set of tennis we had ever played together. She had also heard Mrs. Cole-Whittaker expound her "visualization" theory at the Sunday service. She was anxious to try it out.

Before each serve—hers or mine—she would close her eyes and picture what she desired the score to be after the next point had been played.

For example, if the score was 40-30 my favor, she would form the picture "40-40" in her mind, which would mean she had won the next point. Then we would play the point.

Believe it or not—and I would not have believed it—she won the set, 6-3. . . .

There is a specialist in cancer therapy in California who combines conventional medical treatment with visualization by the patient.

This doctor—Dr. Carl Simonton—tells his patients they have a mind that is in charge of their body's cells. The body will do what you tell it to do, he says.

One of the techniques Simonton recommends to his patients is to form a picture in the mind of the healing process going on within their bodies. He told a 12-year-old boy to picture his white, healing corpuscles as cowboys attacking his tumor. The boy recovered.

Terry Cole-Whittaker, whose Church of Religious Science here has grown from a membership of 50 to 3,600 in five years, started practicing visualization in her freshman year of college.

"I wanted to be homecoming queen," she says, "but my hair had turned from blond to darker. I was overweight and not even close to being the prettiest in my class.

"So I worked on it. I did visualizations on being homecoming queen. I conjured up all the feelings, the emotions, the joy I would feel if I were picked. I lost 25 pounds and became a blonde again. I didn't understand a whole lot about the principles but they worked. I was chosen as homecoming queen."

At 41, she is still a startling beauty. A couple of years ago she finished third in the national Mrs. America contest. . . .

If people put her preaching into practice, they will "close the gap between potential and performance," she says.—George Plagenz, Scripps-Howard religion writer, November 21, 1981.[9] Reprinted by permission of Scripps Howard News Service.

FOR FURTHER READING

Inductive generalization arguments, arguments by analogy, and causal arguments are discussed very clearly in Merrilee H. Salmon's *Introduction to Logic and Critical Thinking* (New York: Harcourt Brace Jovanovich, Inc., 1984), chs. 3 and 4. These chapters provide excellent collateral reading for our discussion here. We have found her presentation of arguments by analogy and especially of inductive generalizations very helpful in developing our discussion. The six criteria for evaluating arguments by analogy are presented in Irving M. Copi's *Introduction to Logic,* 6th ed. (New York: Macmillan Publishing Company, 1982), ch. 11.

Excellent discussions of causal fallacies occur in Ralph H. Johnson and J. Anthony Blair's *Logical Self-Defense* (Toronto, Canada: McGraw-Hill Ryerson, 1977), pp. 82–94, and Merrilee H. Salmon's *Introduction to Logic and Critical Thinking,* pp. 115–20. The discussion in Johnson and Blair has been particularly helpful. Vincent E. Barry's *Invitation to Critical Thinking* (New York: Holt, Rinehart and Winston, 1984) contains a good roster of causal fallacies on pp. 217–19.

NOTES

[1]Compare Merrilee H. Salmon, *Introduction to Logic and Critical Thinking* (New York: Harcourt Brace Jovanovich, Inc., 1984), p. 57.

[2]Again compare ibid., p. 57.

[3]The English philosopher John Stuart Mill (1806–1873) identified five patterns of causal argument, which are called Mill's methods of experimental inquiry. In most cases, one effect of using these patterns is to rule out rival causal explanations. Mill's Methods are discussed in a number of elementary logic texts. See, for example, Irving M. Copi, *Introduction to Logic,* 6th ed. (New York: Macmillan Publishing Company, 1982), ch. 12, and Merrilee Salmon's text, ch. 4.

[4]Irving M. Copi speculates that arguments by analogy may be the most commonly used type of inductive argument. See *Introduction to Logic,* 6th ed., p. 389. Copi does not consider generic inductive arguments. Even so, his statement points to the significance of analogical reasoning.

[5]This material is presented in the Examples Supplement of the *Informal Logic Newsletter,* Vol. V, no. 3, July 1983.

[6]Example 7 appears in the Examples Supplement of the *Informal Logic Newsletter,* Vol. IV, no. 3, July 1982. Our thanks go to Charles Kielkopf of Ohio State University for submitting this material. Example 12 appears in the Examples Supplement of the *Informal Logic Newsletter,* Vol. V, July 1983. It is taken from a student newspaper report of a speech made by Mr. Hellyer, a former Canadian cabinet minister, at Wilfrid Laurier University. Our thanks to Christopher Tindale for submitting this example.

[7]This discussion is based on material in Ralph H. Johnson and J. Anthony Blair's *Logical Self-Defense* (Toronto, Canada: McGraw-Hill Ryerson, 1977), pp. 86–87. They credit *Time* with originally reporting the story.

[8]This example appears in the *Informal Logic Newsletter,* Vol. IV, no. 3, July 1982, italics ours.

[9]In this exercise, a number of examples are drawn from material in the Examples Supplements of the *Informal Logic Newsletter:* Vol. I, no. 4 [(1), (4), (7)]; Vol. II [(13)]; Vol. IV, no. 3 [(11, see 8-VIII, Ex. 9 for original version of this example), (14), (16), (17)]. We want to acknowledge our debt to the *Informal Logic Newsletter* for these examples and express thanks to those who contributed them.

11
APPRAISING DEDUCTIVE ARGUMENTS

As in the last chapter we distinguished three special families of inductive arguments, so we may distinguish three families of deductive arguments. The first has been familiar to us since early education: the family of mathematical arguments. Arguments involving arithmetical or other computation are deductive—they claim or we evaluate them as claiming that if the premises are true, so is the conclusion. For example,

> In shopping today, Anne spent $150 for a new suit, $45 for a pair of shoes, $25 for a new blouse, and $7.50 for three pair of stockings. She made no further purchases. Therefore she spent $227.50 in all.

This is a deductive argument. In appraising it, we add figures to see whether the premises necessitate saying that Anne spent $227.50 in all. If our computation verifies this amount and the computation is correct, can we imagine the premises true and the conclusion false?

Arguments involving mathematical reasoning as opposed to computation are also deductive. Proofs of theorems in high school geometry are deductive arguments and are perhaps some of the first examples of formal deductive reasoning that we encounter. From certain basic axioms, postulates, and definitions, other statements are shown to follow necessarily. The claim is always at least implicit that if the premises are true, so must be the conclusion. We cannot imagine the premises true and the conclusion false.

Clearly our ability to recognize that an argument is mathematical will increase with our study of mathematics and its various branches. But this leads us to a special problem. In determining whether or not a mathematical argument is valid, that its premises really do necessitate its conclusion, ordinarily special mathematical knowledge—be it of tables of computation, previously established mathematical theorems, or principles of mathematical procedure—is employed. This body of knowledge is not properly part of logic. Hence, in a book on logic, we cannot present means of appraisal specific to mathematical arguments, specific directions for imagining the premises of a mathematical argument true and its conclusion false. That is, in a logic book we cannot do for mathematical arguments anything analogous to what we did for the families of inductive arguments in the last chapter. We learn to appraise mathematical arguments as we learn mathematics. We mention this family of deductive arguments here for the sake of completeness. We want to be able to determine whether an argument is deductive or inductive, and recognizing that an argument is mathematical lets us correctly classify it as deductive.

There are two families of deductive arguments standardly considered in logic texts. For each, there are specific ways to formalize our imaginative test for logical validity. In Sections 11.1 and 11.2 we take up these families in turn, considering one special method of appraisal for each. Our discussion in Section 11.2 prepares us to consider arguments involving special strategies and requiring further techniques for proper diagramming. We consider these arguments and their special diagrams in Section 11.3.

§11.1 QUANTIFICATIONAL ARGUMENTS

In Chapter 8, we introduced a special paradigm class of deductive arguments— the categorical syllogisms. Recall that a categorical syllogism is an argument with exactly two premises and one conclusion, where the component statements are all categorical propositions. Recall also that a categorical proposition asserts a relation between two classes, that one, in whole or in part, is either included in or excluded from another. Thus

All horses are quadripeds.

asserts that the entire class of horses is included in the class of quadripeds, while

No English prime ministers are American politicians.

asserts that the class of English prime ministers is entirely excluded from the class of American politicians.

Some American politicians are Democrats.

asserts class inclusion but only partial inclusion, as

Some barnyard fowl are not horses.

asserts the partial exclusion of the class of barnyard fowl from the class of horses. Notice that the assertion of inclusion or exclusion and whether this be entire or partial is made by the expressions "all," "no," "some," "not." We pointed out in Chapter 8 that "all," "no," "some" are called *quantifiers*. To see how and why they should give their name to a whole family of deductive arguments, compare these two categorical syllogisms—the first comes from Chapter 8:

All axioms of geometry are hard things to understand.
All hard things to understand are things which give me a headache.
Therefore
All axioms of geometry are things which give me a headache.

All aphrodisiacs are love potions.
All love potions are beautiful things. Therefore
All aphrodisiacs are beautiful things.

Although the subject matter of these arguments is completely different, they have a very important logical similarity. Each component statement is a universal affirmative categorical proposition. Furthermore, if we replace both occurrences of "axioms of geometry" by "aphrodisiacs," similarly replace "things difficult to understand" by "love potions," and "things which give me a headache" by "beautiful things," we may transform the first argument into the second. In either case, we could represent the form of the argument this way:

All A are B.
All B are C.
All A are C.

It should not be difficult to convince ourselves that any argument with this form is deductively correct. For whatever classes A, B, and C may be, if "All A are C" is false, there is at least one thing which is A but not C. But should "All A are B" and "All B are C" be true, that thing will be C also. But it is impossible for something to be both C and not-C. This is a contradiction. Hence, for no argument of this form can we imagine the premises true and the conclusion false. Every argument instancing this form will be deductively valid.

What does the deductive validity of these arguments depend on? Not on the particular class terms appearing in the argument, for we saw that as long as we kept the same pattern of class terms and the same quantifier, we could vary the class terms at will, yet our arguments would be valid. Rather, we claim that the validity depends on the truth-conditions for statements beginning with "all" and the overall pattern of the argument. A statement of the form "All A are B" is true just in case every single thing which is an A is also a B. Should we vary the quantifier or the overall pattern of the argument, are we guaranteed of again having a deductively valid argument? Let's try replacing "all" by "some."

> Some A are B.
> <u>Some B are C.</u>
> Some A are C.

Can we imagine the conclusion of such an argument false while both premises are true? As we saw in Chapter 8, if "Some A are C" is false, "No A are C" is true. Let's imagine that A and C are two mutually exclusive classes, say, the class of plants and the class of animals. Can there be something common to A and some other class B, while something else is common to B and C? Let B be the class of things which live in the sea. But surely "Some plants are things which live in the sea" and "Some things which live in the sea are animals" are both true. So we can imagine an argument of this form with both premises true and conclusion false, an invalid argument.

What this shows is that the validity of categorical syllogisms depends essentially on the quantifiers they contain. We cannot replace quantifiers by other quantifiers in a valid argument and be assured that the argument will remain valid, the way we could with component class terms. Suppose we altered the overall pattern of our argument, keeping the quantifiers the same but switching the position of A, B, C; for example, suppose we transformed an argument of our form

> | All A are B. | | All A are B. |
> |---|---|---|
> | <u>All B are C.</u> | into | <u>All C are B.</u> |
> | All A are C. | | All C are A. |

There is a classic example of this pattern of reasoning whose invalidity is immediately apparent:

> All dogs are animals.
> All cats are animals. Therefore
> All cats are dogs.

We don't need our imaginations to see the invalidity of this argument. We *know* that the premises are true and the conclusion false.

In the next section, we shall meet with other particles—not quantifiers—and a family of arguments whose validity depends on the truth-conditions for these particles and the overall pattern of the argument. So what is specific to determining the validity of these categorical syllogisms we have just considered are the quantifiers. Now there is a whole family of arguments sharing this feature with categorical syllogisms—their validity depends essentially on the quantifiers. Hence, we call this family of arguments quantificational arguments. The quantifiers properly give their name to the whole family. Recognizing an argument as a quantificational argument lets us correctly classify it as deductive and appropriately test it for deductive validity.

We illustrated earlier that if a syllogism is valid, any other syllogism having that form—same quantifiers, same overall pattern—will be valid. Similarly, if a syllogism is invalid, its form is invalid, any other syllogism having that form will be invalid as a syllogism.[1] This explains the formal nature of syllogistic validity. Notice that if we know a syllogism has a valid form, we may judge it valid, even without applying our imaginative test, and similarly for invalidity.

This formal feature also gives us a new way to apply our imaginative test to show faulty syllogisms invalid. Instead of trying to imagine a situation where the conclusion of the given argument is false while the premises are true, if we can produce an argument of the same form where we can imagine the conclusion false and the premises true, we have shown the original argument invalid. Our new argument having the same form is called a *logical analogy* of the original. Remember that on occasion, when we try to apply our imaginative test, our imaginations may give out—we won't get an answer to whether the argument is valid or invalid. Trying to construct a logical analogy and applying our test to that analogy may be a way of getting out of this impasse. For example,

> All aphrodisiacs are beautiful things.
> All love potions are beautiful things. Therefore
> All love potions are aphrodisiacs.

It's not clear that we can imagine a situation where "All love potions are aphrodisiacs" is false. Aren't these terms synonymous? But we have already met with a logical analogy of this argument, our obviously invalid dogs–animals–cats example.

The problem with logical analogies is that they involve two imaginative exercises—we have to think up the logical analogy and then imagine its conclusion false while its premises are true to show our original argument invalid. The proper analogy which does the trick may escape our imaginations. This raises the question: Is there a set procedure yielding logical analogies which we may apply in investigating whether a categorical syllogism is valid or invalid? Indeed there is, and such a procedure is quite straightforward. Recall that when we introduced categorical propositions in Chapter 8, we illustrated the relation these propositions asserted between their subject and predicate classes by diagrams displaying various spatial relations between two circles. To illustrate "All horses are quadripeds," we drew two circles, labeled horses and quadripeds, with the horse circle completely within the quadriped circle (see Figure 8.1, p. 235). Anything within the horse circle, within that spatial region, is automatically within the quadriped circle. The diagram illustrates the claim the categorical proposition is making.

This shows that we can diagram categorical propositions, make pictorial representations of what they assert. Notice that once we have diagrammed a categorical proposition, we can read off from our diagram another categorical proposition, of the same form as the first, describing the diagram. "All objects within the horse circle are objects within the quadriped circle" obviously describes Figure 8.1. Should we be able to represent the premises of a categorical syllogism and the denial of its conclusion *on one diagram,* then we could read off a logical analogy of the original argument from the diagram with true premises and false conclusion, showing the argument invalid. We know the premises are true because they describe the diagram in front of us. The conclusion is false because its contradictory also describes the diagram.

The English logician John Venn (1834–1923) developed a specific way of diagramming categorical propositions and categorical syllogisms which allows this. If a categorical syllogism is invalid, we can diagram its premises and the negation of the conclusion. If it is valid, our attempt to construct such a diagram will be blocked. At one point, we shall be asked to diagram contradictory pieces of information. Attempting to construct such a diagram then constitutes a test of validity for categorical syllogisms—the Venn diagram test. If carried out properly, this test will give us a yes or no answer concerning whether a categorical syllogism is valid. What does it involve?

Venn Diagrams for Categorical Propositions

How may categorical propositions be pictured according to the Venn diagram technique? First, we represent regions of space, as we have done, by closed circles. Ordinarily we shall label the region within a closed circle by a letter, A, B, C, ... Our circle cuts the plane into two regions—everything within the circle and everything outside—everything which is A and everything which is not-A, which we label $\bar{A}$. (See Figure 11.1).

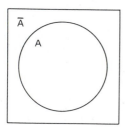

Figure 11.1

There are two very basic things we can say about a region: either there is some object in it—at least one thing—or there is nothing in the region—it is empty. As in Chapter 8, we diagram the claim that there is an object in a region by putting a * in that region (see Figure 11.2).

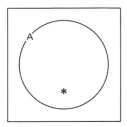

Figure 11.2

We diagram the claim that there are no objects in a particular region by shading that region out (see Figure 11.3). This says that region A is empty or there are no A's.

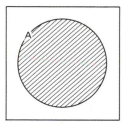

Figure 11.3

Since categorical propositions always involve two class terms, their diagrams will involve two circles. Unlike our diagrams in Chapter 8, our circles will always be drawn in this fixed pattern (see Figure 11.4).

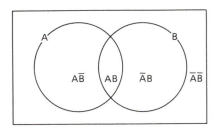

Figure 11.4

Given two regions of space, A and B, it is abstractly possible that an object be located either in their overlap AB; in A but outside B, in A$\overline{\text{B}}$; outside A but inside B, in $\overline{\text{A}}$B; or outside both, in $\overline{\text{A}}\overline{\text{B}}$. Our pattern represents these four possibilities.

Since there are four types of categorical propositions, we must consider how to diagram each: particular affirmative and particular negative propositions are diagrammed as in Chapter 8—we put a * in the appropriate region. To assert something of the form "Some A are B" is to assert that there is at least one thing which is both A and B, on the diagram that there is something in AB, the region where A and B overlap (see Figure 11.5).

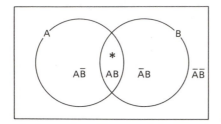

Figure 11.5

If the statement we assert is of the form "Some A are not B," we claim there is something which is A but fails to be B; there is something in A$\overline{\text{B}}$ (see Figure 11.6).

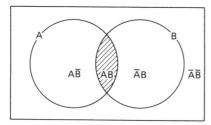

Figure 11.6

A universal negative categorical is of the form "No A are B," there is nothing which is both A and B. For our diagram, this means that the region AB is empty and must be shaded out (see Figure 11.7).

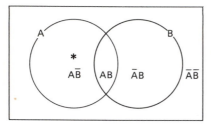

Figure 11.7

So far these diagrams have been completely intuitive. The universal affirmative categorical is slightly tricky—but only slightly. To assert something of the form "All A are B," we are asserting that everything which is A is also B. That is, there is nothing which is A and fails to be B. For diagramming purposes, this means that the region A$\overline{\text{B}}$ is empty (see Figure 11.8).

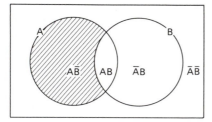

Figure 11.8

The trick is in seeing that "All A are B" involves the assertion that some class is empty and in identifying that class and the corresponding region. In these ways we can diagram any of our four types of categorical propositions.

Venn Diagram Test for Categorical Syllogisms

How can we diagram categorical syllogisms and use those diagrams to test for validity? To begin, let's notice that the categorical syllogisms we have examined so far have all shared certain further features besides having categorical propositions as their three component statements. Each syllogism involves exactly three class terms—each appearing twice. One term appears in each premise, while each of the other two terms appears in one premise and the conclusion. It is to such standard categorical syllogisms that we apply our Venn diagram test.[2] Now we can imagine syllogisms with only one or two terms or where the terms are not distributed over the various premises in the standard way. For example,

All A are A.
Some A are A.
No A are A.

But such syllogisms would be distinctly odd. Who, in real life, would ever argue according to the foregoing pattern? Should we ever encounter such a "syllogism," we trust our intuitive test to determine its validity or invalidity.

Much more interesting is the case where four terms occur in a syllogism. For example,

All cats are felines.
No dogs are fish. Therefore
No cats are fish.

Does the conclusion follow from the premises? Is this argument valid? Now it may strain our imaginations to try to picture a cat which is simultaneously a fish. But can we find a logical analogy of this argument? What is its form?

All A are B.
No C are D.
No A are D.

Does the following argument have the same form?

All mammals are animals.
No cats are dogs. Therefore
No mammals are dogs.

Clearly the form is the same, and both premises are true, the conclusion false. Hence any argument having this form is invalid. As a matter of fact, any categorical syllogism having four distinct component terms (or five or six) is invalid, no matter how those terms are arranged. Any such syllogism is said to commit the *fallacy of four terms*. Hence, should we recognize that a syllogism has more than three terms, we know it is invalid and need not apply any special test.

Thus we can turn our attention exclusively to syllogisms involving just three terms. Since we are working with three terms, we shall need three overlapping circles (see Figure 11.9). Ordinarily, we shall label each circle with one of the three class terms involved in the syllogism or with some letter or expression which abbreviates the term. Although which circle is labeled with which term is a matter of choice, one convenient way of matching terms with circles—one we shall follow in our discussion—is to label the upper left-hand circle with the subject term of the conclusion, the upper right-hand circle with the predicate term of the conclusion, and the lower circle with the term shared by both premises but not appearing in the conclusion.

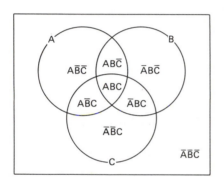

Figure 11.9

How do we represent categorical propositions on such diagrams? Consider "All A are B." Where we had just two circles, we shaded out the region $A\bar{B}$, the region of A's which fail to be B. We do the same thing again, only here the region $A\bar{B}$ is divided in two, part lying within C and part lying outside C, $A\bar{B}C$, $A\bar{B}\bar{C}$. But if the entire region $A\bar{B}$ is empty, then that part lying within C and that part lying outside C are both empty. If there is no object which is both A and not B, there is no object which is A, not-B, and C, nor is there any object which is A, not-B, and not-C. Hence, we shade out the entire $A\bar{B}$ region, $A\bar{B}C$ and $A\bar{B}\bar{C}$ (see

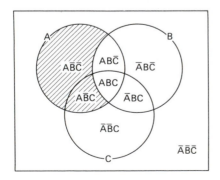

Figure 11.10

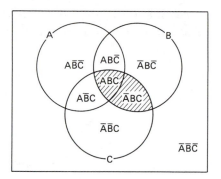

Figure 11.11

Figure 11.10). Similarly "No B are C" requires shading out two regions, ABC and ĀBC, that is, the entire BC region (see Figure 11.11).

To diagram "Some C are A," we have to indicate that the region where C and A overlap is not empty. But that region is divided into two parts, ABC and AB̄C. Where shall we put our *? Let's assume there is no antecedent information on the diagram. Then the information that there is something in the overlap of C and A does not tell us that this object either is in B or outside B. Should we put our * in the region ABC or AB̄C, we would be reading something in which wasn't there; we would be importing information into the diagram, information beyond the statement we seek to diagram. To avoid this, we put our * "on the fence," on the line separating ABC from AB̄C (see Figure 11.12).

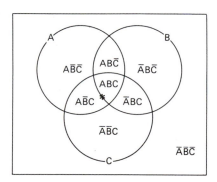

Figure 11.12

Suppose, on the contrary, that there is antecedent information on the diagram. Then that information may tell us either that the region ABC or the region AB̄C is empty, or both. If both, then we have a contradiction. We cannot diagram both that we have something in a region and that the region is empty. We shall say more about this shortly. However, if just one of ABC or AB̄C has already been shaded out, then we are quite correct in putting our * in the other region. If we know there is something in region CA = AC, and we know there is nothing in ABC, then this object must be in AB̄C. We might, for example, know there is nothing in ABC because one premise tells us that AB is empty (see

Figure 11.13). When we link, take the two statements together that "No A are B" and "Some C are A," we are not reading any information into our diagram by putting the * in A$\overline{\text{B}}$C.

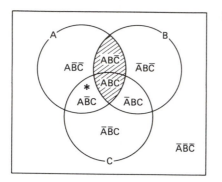

Figure 11.13

Finally, in diagramming statements of the form "Some C are not A," we proceed as with particular affirmative categorical propositions. We must diagram that there is some object which is inside C but outside A, that is, in C$\overline{\text{A}}$ = $\overline{\text{A}}$C. But is this object inside B or outside B? Is this object in $\overline{\text{A}}$BC or in $\overline{\text{A}}$$\overline{\text{B}}$C? Without antecedent information telling us that one or the other of these regions is empty, we cannot tell which, and so must put our * on the line separating these two regions (see Figure 11.14). On the other hand, should just one of $\overline{\text{A}}$BC or $\overline{\text{A}}$$\overline{\text{B}}$C have been antecedently shaded out, we should put * in the other.

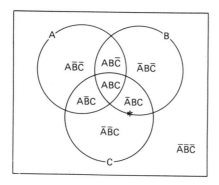

Figure 11.14

Clearly, it is possible to represent several categorical propositions together on one diagram. As we said, if we can picture both premises of a categorical syllogism and the denial of the conclusion on one Venn diagram, we have shown the syllogism invalid. However, if in attempting to do this, we find we must both shade out a region and put a * in it, our attempt is blocked. We cannot say that a given region of space is both empty and contains an object. This is downright contradictory information, and like being asked to imagine a contradiction true, this shows the syllogism valid. Let's see how the Venn diagram test works with actual examples:

No seahorses are horses.
Some dairy cows are not seahorses. Therefore
Some dairy cows are horses.

The contradictory of the conclusion is "No dairy cows are horses." Let's diagram that statement first (see Figure 11.15).

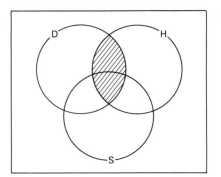

Figure 11.15

Let's next represent the first premise, adding its information to the diagram. We must represent the information that SH is empty. Half of that region is shaded out. We simply shade out the other half (see Figure 11.16).

Can we further diagram "Some dairy cows are not seahorses." We must add to our diagram the information that some object is inside D but outside S. Half of that region is shaded out, but not the other half. Hence we can add the information (see Figure 11.17). So our syllogism is invalid.

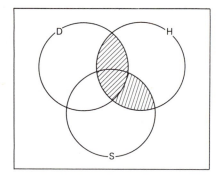

Figure 11.16

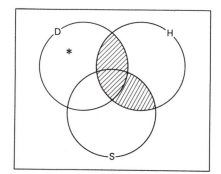

Figure 11.17

Let's test a second categorical syllogism:

All horses are quadripeds.
Some farm animals are horses. Therefore
Some farm animals are quadripeds.

The denial of the conclusion is "No farm animals are quadripeds." Let's diagram this statement first and then the first premise (see Figure 11.18). To diagram "Some farm animals are horses," we must put a * within the region where the F and H circles overlap. But that is impossible, for that region is entirely shaded out. So the argument is valid.

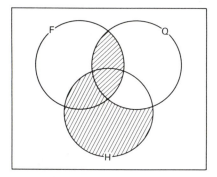

Figure 11.18

Notice that in both these examples, we proceeded to diagram universal categorical propositions before particulars. This is a convenient way to proceed. A universal categorical proposition identifies a certain definite region as empty. We are right in shading out both halves, both parts of that region, no matter what other statements we have to diagram. A particular categorical proposition indicates only that a * goes within a certain region, not in which half it is located. As we saw, to diagram such a statement rightly, we may have to put the * "on the fence." But suppose we did that and then found that one-half of the region was empty, because of another statement being diagrammed. Then we should have to move the * off the fence and into the region not shaded out. That's messy. It's far better to shade out regions first and then see where to place the *—if we can do this without contradiction—than to move *'s about which we have already placed on the diagram.

The Venn diagram test that we have just presented is a way of testing standard categorical syllogisms for validity. We cannot apply it to all quantificational arguments, because not all such arguments are standard categorical syllogisms. Besides the nonstandard syllogisms that we considered briefly before presenting the Venn diagram test, what other sorts of quantificational arguments are there?

Quantificational Arguments that Are Not Categorical Syllogisms

Some quantificational arguments involve categorical propositions, but are not syllogisms, since the conclusion is drawn either from a single premise or from three or more premises. In some cases, it is possible to use Venn diagrams to test the validity of such arguments, in particular for arguments called *sorites*. Here we have more than two premises, but these arguments can be recast as chains of syllogisms where from two of the original premises, we draw an intermediate conclusion. From that, together with another original premise, we draw a further conclusion, the process continuing until the intended conclusion is reached. Here is an example adapted from Lewis Carroll:

No kangaroos are suitable for pets.
All animals that love to gaze at the moon are suitable for pets.
All animals that prowl at night are animals that love to gaze at the moon.

So

No kangaroos are animals that prowl at night.

Clearly from the first two premises we may derive

No kangaroos are animals that love to gaze at the moon.

From that intermediate conclusion and the third premise we can derive the final conclusion. Obviously, we can check the validity of both syllogisms in our chain by Venn diagrams. However, for many quantificational arguments, Venn diagrams simply do not work to check validity properly because the component statements—at least some of them—are not categorical propositions.

Everyone who came to the party enjoyed it, so
if John came to the party, he enjoyed it.

Clearly the conclusion here is *not* a categorical proposition, nor is the premise in the following argument:

Alice was disappointed with the concert, so
someone was disappointed with the concert.

Not only do these last two examples differ from our previous cases in involving noncategorical statements, they differ in a more radical respect. Categorical propositions were composed of class terms. "Kangaroo," "animal," "person," "blue," "red," all designate classes of objects. But "comes to" is a relational term, indicating a relation which may hold between two things:

> Craig came to the auction.
>
> Death came to Socrates.
>
> Sue's brother came to the house.

We may represent class terms by circles, but how would we represent relations? Now consider the following argument:

> Since for any objects a and b, if a is less than b, b is not less than a, no object is less than itself.

How could we begin to apply a Venn diagram to such an argument? Is this argument valid? If the conclusion is false, then there is at least one object, call it a_0, which is less than itself. But what does the premise imply? It implies that if a_0 is less than a_0, then a_0 is not less than a_0. So a_0 both is and is not less than a_0—an outright contradiction. The argument is valid, but this cannot be established by Venn diagrams. Now many quantificational arguments involve relations. Indeed, in mathematics, physical science, law, discussions of kinship, and many other areas we encounter deductive reasoning involving quantifiers and relational concepts. Hence to evaluate quantificational arguments in general, we must go beyond Venn diagrams. Developing a formal method to do this, however, is beyond our scope here—it is the proper subject for a first course in symbolic logic.[3]

Although we shall not present a general method for assessing all quantificational arguments here, we can identify one fallacy connected with relational reasoning which we should be aware of. The following arguments should be intuitively valid:

> Somebody gave something away. So something was given away by somebody.

> Everyone heard all the news about John, so all the news about John was heard by everyone.

> Since there is a natural number less than or equal to all natural numbers (i.e., 0), for every natural number we can find one less than or equal to that number.

But what about the following argument?

> Since for every natural number, I can find a greater natural number, there is a greatest natural number, that is, a natural number greater than all natural numbers.

We don't need to use our imaginations, but just have a bit of basic mathematical knowledge to see that the premise here is true but the conclusion false. Given any natural number, I can always add one to it and get a greater number. But there is no greatest natural number.

This last argument illustrates a fallacious pattern of reasoning. We are arguing that because for every object A we can find some object or other B to which it bears a given relation, then there is some one particular object B to which all objects bear this relation. Here are some further examples:

Every child received a piece of candy. So there is a piece of candy which all children received.

Everyone voted (for some candidate or other). So some candidate received all the votes.

Imagining situations where the premise is true but the conclusion false should be easy here, and this should convince us that this pattern of argument is fallacious. The exchange of "every" for "all" in going from premise to conclusion gives this fallacy its name, the *fallacy of "every" and "all."* It is a common fallacy and can occur in serious contexts. For example, consider this philosophical argument for substance:

Since each change requires something constant and unchanging, there must be something that is constant throughout all change. This thing is substance.[4]

Even if it is true that in every change there must be something constant, does this mean there is some one thing which is constant throughout all changes?

We have pointed out that the words "all," "no," "some," "not" are essential to what categorical propositions assert. "All," "no," "some" are quantifiers, and we have been exploring their logic in this section. What about "not," which we seem to be neglecting? "Not" is not a quantifier. However, it is a logically important word, and it, together with certain other logically important words, can be used to determine the other family of deductive arguments studied in basic logic. We turn to that family in the next section.

Summary

The deductive validity of quantificational arguments depends on the truth conditions for the quantifiers, "all," "no," "some." Categorical syllogisms are a particular class of quantificational arguments. In showing categorical syllogisms invalid, we may extend the imaginative test presented in Chapter 8. If we can find a logical analogy of a categorical syllogism, an argument with exactly the same form—same quantifiers, same overall pattern of class terms—where we can imagine the premises true and the conclusion false, then the original argument is shown invalid. The Venn diagram test, representing categorical propositions on a system of circles, is a systematic way of finding such an analogy if there is one, or showing that such an analogy cannot be found. There are many quantificational arguments which are not categorical syllogisms and whose validity cannot be checked by Venn diagrams. In particular, we cannot check relational arguments this way. One notable fallacy here is the fallacy of "every" and "all." We cannot validly infer that because everything bears some relation R to some object or other, that there is an object to which all objects bear R.

Exercise 11-I

Construct Venn diagrams for the following categorical propositions. In constructing the diagram, use the first letter of the subject term to label the left-hand circle and the first letter of the predicate term to label the right-hand circle.

1. All horses are Shetlands.
2. No humans are angels.
3. Some cats are Persians.
4. Some birds are not swimmers.
5. Some kangaroos are not wild animals.
6. Some pelicans are residents of Antarctica.
7. All books in the collection are items which contain veiled symbols.
8. All mysterious investigations are vain things.
9. No mice are animals trapped inside.
10. Some jet planes are not good places to do metaphysics.
11. All veiled images are terrifying things.
12. Some additives are cancer-causing agents.
13. Some cancer-causing agents are additives.
14. No presidents of the United States are women.
15. No women are presidents of the United States.
16. All living things on Mars are organisms which can subsist on very little oxygen.
17. No cats are animals which find me attractive.
18. No even prime numbers greater than 2 are numbers divisible by 6.
19. All persons who are involved with the production or consumption of pornography are immoral individuals who are fostering the subjugation of women in this society.
20. No persons who are aware of the homeless in our cities and who do absolutely nothing about them are compassionate individuals with a social conscience.

Exercise 11-II

Determine whether the following syllogisms are valid or invalid by the Venn diagram test.

1. All omnivores are carnivores.
   All gorillas are omnivores. Therefore
   All gorillas are carnivores.

2. All cats are animals that love to stare at the moon.
   All kangaroos are animals that love to stare at the moon. Hence
   All kangaroos are cats.

3. No marathon runners are cigarette smokers.
   Some cigarette smokers are persons who will succumb to cancer.
   Hence
   Some marathon runners are not persons who will succumb to cancer.

4. No champion chess player is a resident of Manhattan.
   All champion chess players are citizens of the Soviet Union.
   Therefore
   No citizens of the Soviet Union are residents of Manhattan.

5. Some jet planes are conducive to meditation.
   All jet planes are good places to do metaphysics. Hence
   Some good places to do metaphysics are conducive to meditation.

6. No kangaroos are natives of Africa.
   Some kangaroos are not wild animals. Therefore
   Some wild animals are not natives of Africa.

7. All veiled images are terrifying things.
   Some terrifying things are not found in closets. Therefore
   Some things found in closets are not veiled images.

8. No mice are animals trapped inside.
   Some mice are not found in haystacks. Hence
   Some animals found in haystacks are animals trapped inside.

9. Some cancer-causing agents are not additives.
   All cancer-causing agents are chemicals. Therefore
   Some chemicals are not additives.

10. All Martians are people with green skin.
    All people with green skin are terrifying to look upon. Hence
    Some Martians are terrifying to look upon.

Be sure to determine which statement is the conclusion before applying the Venn diagram test to the following syllogisms.

11. Some basketball player is a football player. Consequently some basketball player is not a baseball player since no football players are baseball players.

12. Since some aristocrats are generous persons and all millionaires are generous persons, some aristocrats are millionaires.

13. Some animals are cats, because no dogs are cats and some animals are not dogs.

14. No lions are tigers, so some tigers are striped animals, since some striped animals are not lions.

15. All difficult assignments are bothersome, since all instances of great toil are bothersome and all difficult assignments are instances of great toil.

16. Because some merchants are unscrupulous, some men of character are not merchants, since no men of character are unscrupulous.

17. No houses are inexpensive things and some tents are inexpensive things. It follows that no tents are houses.

18. Some men are not politicians. Therefore some women are politicians, since no men are women.

19. Some squash players are not pros, because all masters tournament players are pros and some squash players are not masters tournament players.

20. All promoters are merchants. It follows that some swindlers are not promoters since no swindlers are merchants.

§11.2 TRUTH-FUNCTIONAL ARGUMENTS

In the last section, we saw that the validity of quantificational arguments depends essentially on the truth-conditions for the quantifiers and the overall pattern of the argument. Quantifiers are one type of logical word or logical particle. In this section, we shall study another type of logical particle, the truth-functional connective. The validity of another family of deductive arguments depends on the truth-conditions for these truth-functional connectives and the overall pattern of the argument. Hence we call this the family of truth-functional arguments. But what are these connectives and their truth conditions?

"Not," "And," "Or" and Their Truth-Conditions

We have already met one truth-functional connective—the expression "not" or "it is not the case that." Under what circumstances would the statement

The apples were not shipped in the refrigerator car.

be true? Clearly, the statement

The apples were shipped in the refrigerator car.

must be false. Should the second statement be true, the first will be false. Notice that the word "not" occurs in the middle of the sentence "The apples were not shipped in the refrigerator car." But we may paraphrase this as

It is not the case that the apples were shipped in the refrigerator car.

What is the point of this paraphrase? It is to highlight that the word "not" functions to build up a larger statement from a shorter one. That is what being a *connective* means. In the paraphrase, the statement "The apples were shipped in the refrigerator car" clearly appears as a component, the entire statement being built up from this component by prefixing "It is not the case that." Statements of the form

    not-P

or which may be paraphrased by such statements are called *negations*. Given this standard form for negations, we can conveniently summarize the truth-conditions for "not" in a table, called a *truth-table*. Whatever statement P may be, P will either be true or false. As we have seen, if P is true, not-P is false, and if P is false, not-P is true. Figure 11.19 displays this perspicuously.

P	not-P
T	F
F	T

Figure 11.19

    The connective "not" is called truth-functional because it *always* takes a true statement into a false and *always* takes a false into a true. In mathematics, a function always has a unique value. Adding 5 and 3 gives us 8 always, not just on Sundays, Tuesdays, and Thursdays, and something else other times. There is a unique value for $5 + 3$ and indeed for $x + y$, whatever numbers x and y may be. "Not" is a function in this mathematical sense. Whatever statement P may be, not-P has a unique truth-value.

    It may seem odd to talk of "not" as a connective. It does not seem to connect its component with anything. "Not" is unary; it builds a compound from a single component. The remaining truth-functional connectives are all binary, taking two component statements into a compound. Here it seems more obvious to call such particles connectives. The first binary connective is straightforward—the conjunction "and." Under what circumstances is the statement

    Mary sang and John played the piano.

true? Suppose both component statements—Mary sang—John played the piano—are true. Then the entire compound will be true. But suppose it's false that Mary sang. Can it be true both that she sang and John played the piano? Clearly not. Similarly, if it's false that John played the piano, it will be false that both Mary sang and he played the piano. And if both component statements are false, the conjunction will be false.

    We can summarize this also in a truth-table. Whatever the component conjuncts P, Q may be, either both P, Q will be true, P will be true but Q false, P false but Q true, or both will be false. In the first instance their conjunction will be true; in all the others, false. Figure 11.20 is the truth-table.

P	Q	P and Q
T	T	T
T	F	F
F	T	F
F	F	F

Figure 11.20

We must paraphrase some statements to see that they are conjunctions, but sensitivity is required here. We discussed conjunctions in Chapter 7, in connection with determining what statements a passage asserts. We pointed out that the statement

Rich and Jim are boys.

makes two assertions. It is a conjunction, correctly paraphrased as

Rich is a boy and Jim is a boy.

On the other hand,

Rich and Jim are cousins.

which on the surface has the same structure, is not a conjunction. It asserts that these two persons are related as cousins, not that one is a cousin and so is the other. Paraphrasing makes the conjunctive character of the first statement explicit; sensitivity tells us to paraphrase one statement but not another. Notice that a number of expressions are synonymous with "and" in English, at least in what they assert explicitly, although they may make certain additional suggestions. Expressions such as "but," "although," "however" all may be used to form conjunctions. "John came but he was tired" is true just in case John both came and was tired, although it suggests there is some contrast between the conjuncts. Similarly, the word "and" on occasion makes suggestions, in particular a suggestion of temporal succession or sequence. Suppose it is true that Jane got married last year. Suppose it is also true that last year she had a baby. Is the following statement true?

Last year Jane had a baby and got married.

If "and" functions just truth-functionally, the answer is yes. But "and" here suggests that Jane had the baby first and then she got married. We don't know whether that suggestion is true or false. However, fortunately to appraise truth-functional arguments for deductive validity, we may disregard all such suggestions.

Despite the various suggestions "and" together with its synonyms makes, it still has an unambiguous core meaning in ordinary language. The next connective—"or"—however is radically ambiguous in English. If we say

You may have ice cream or cake.

we don't expect the answer

I'll take both.

That's not the proper response. We are offering the person a choice, to have one or the other, not both. We are using "or" in its exclusive sense. On the other hand, suppose I said

Uncle Henry or Aunt Annie will come this afternoon.

and they both arrived—would that show my statement false? We might get a debate here. Those who deny that my statement would be shown false perceive that "or" has another sense in English, an inclusive sense. Here a statement of the form P or Q will be true just in case either P is true, Q is true, or both are true. Legal documents seek to remove this ambiguity by using the expression "and/or" to indicate the inclusive sense of "or."

The contract is valid and binding if Jones and/or his wife sign it.

This means that if just Jones affixes his signature to the contract, it is valid and binding. So, also, should just his wife sign it. And if they both sign it, again it will be valid and binding. It is this inclusive sense of "or" which is universally adopted by logicians. The truth-table gives the truth-conditions for this sense, and when "or" or an expression synonymous with it is met in ordinary English, it is interpreted as inclusive "or." Let's make the truth-conditions explicit in Figure 11.21.

P	Q	P or Q
T	T	T
T	F	T
F	T	T
F	F	F

Figure 11.21

Statements of the form P or Q are called *disjunctions* and the components *disjuncts*. There is one further connective we must examine, the conditional. We have met with conditional statements as early as Chapter 1. Before taking up this connective, however, we want to illustrate how our tables of truth-conditions for the three connectives given so far may be used to test arguments for validity. Here, the validity of the arguments we appraise will depend just on the truth-conditions of these three connectives and the overall pattern of the argument.

Truth-Table Test for Validity—the Disjunctive Syllogism

Contrast the following two arguments:

Either the apples were shipped in the refrigerator car or they have been ruined.
The apples were not shipped in the refrigerator car. Hence
They have been ruined.

Either the incumbent officeholder will win or the challenger will win.
The incumbent officeholder will not win. Hence
The challenger will win.

We have previously discussed categorical syllogisms as one type of deductive argument. These syllogisms just given are *disjunctive syllogisms,* because at least one premise is a disjunction. We may take this as defining disjunctive syllogisms.[5] As in the last section, we saw that distinct categorical syllogisms could share the same form, so these two disjunctive syllogisms obviously have the same form. Replace "the apples were shipped in the refrigerator car" by "the incumbent officeholder will win" and "they have been ruined" by "the challenger will win," and we transform the first argument into the second. We can display the common form of these two arguments this way:

P or Q
not-P
Q

It is well to stop at this point and be clear about what has been substituted for what in going from the first to the second argument. Negations, conjunctions, disjunctions are all *compound* statements. By this we mean that they contain other complete statements as components. In our examples so far, the component statements have been *simple*; that is, they have not contained other complete statements as components. "The apples were shipped in the refrigerator car." "The apples were ruined." "The incumbent officeholder will win." "The challenger will win." Do these statements contain other complete statements as components, the way the first premises of our disjunctive syllogism contain them as components? Can you exhibit any such components? We cannot, and that shows that these four statements are simple. As our discussion in the last paragraph shows, we transformed one argument into another by replacing simple statements by simple statements. The contrast between simple and compound statements is fundamental in truth-functional logic, and we shall see its importance in testing arguments shortly. Simple statements in effect are the basic building blocks out of which all other truth-functional compounds are built by means of truth-functional connectives. Once we build a compound out of simple components, for example,

> Socrates was the teacher of Plato and Plato was the teacher of Aristotle.

we may construct larger compounds, with that given compound as component.

> Either Aristotle was an Egyptian philosopher, or both Socrates was the teacher of Plato and Plato was the teacher of Aristotle.

We may continue to build on further. Theoretically, we may continue this indefinitely. Also, it is theoretically possible for such compound statements to appear as premises or conclusions in truth-functional deductive arguments. But no matter how many or how complex the component statements of a truth-functional argument, we may always identify the simple statements out of which they were compounded, the ultimate building blocks of the argument.

What does this have to do with appraising deductive arguments for validity? According to our basic test, we try to imagine the premises of an argument true and the conclusion false. With categorical syllogisms, we saw that we could apply this test to logical analogies of the original argument, and the Venn diagram test gave us a standard way of constructing such analogies. The *truth-table test* does the same thing for truth-functional arguments. What does this test involve? We first identify the simple component statements in the argument, and abbreviate them by the letters P, Q, R, S, ... Then we display the form of the argument by replacing the simple components by their abbreviations, as we have just done for the two disjunctive syllogisms. Next, for convenience, we write out the form on one horizontal line, underlined, with the conclusion separated from the premises by a vertical bar (see Figure 11.22).

Figure 11.22

No matter how difficult it may be for us to imagine the constituent statements of such arguments true or false, we can certainly imagine all of the simple components true together. And we can imagine all simple components but one true, that one false. And for each simple component, we can imagine that it is the sole false component. Likewise we can imagine all but two simple components true, all but three, and so on, down to the possibility of all component statements false. But the truth or falsity of the premises and conclusion is a function of the truth or falsity of these simple components. Imagining the premises true and the conclusion false, then, means imagining (or better constructing) one of these possible combinations of truth-values where on that combination, the premises will all be true and the conclusion false. Since no statement can be both true and false, being asked to imagine such a situation is being asked to imagine a contradiction. To find a combination of truth-values making the argument invalid, we ask on what combinations the conclusion will be false, and then see if all the premises will be true on any of these combinations. If for every combination of truth-values which makes the conclusion false, we are asked to imagine some simple statement both true and false to make all the premises true, this shows we cannot imagine the premises true and conclusion false—we have a valid argument. As we construct a particular combination of truth-values, we enter the value of the simple components under those components and then compute and indicate the value of our compounds. Let's apply this to our example.

The only combinations of truth-values where the conclusion will be false are those where Q is false. Let's enter F under Q (see Figure 11.23). The only way not-P can be true, according to our truth-table for "not," is for P to be false. So we enter F under P and indicate that not-P is true (see Figure 11.24). But for the statement P or Q to be true, according to our truth-table for "or," at least one of P, Q must be true. So to make P or Q true, we must make P true where we have already made it false. But that's impossible. That's asking us to imagine P both true and false—a contradiction. Thus our test shows, what we should intuitively perceive, that this form, and our original arguments are valid.

P or Q	not-P	Q
F		F

Figure 11.23

Figure 11.24

P or Q	not-P	Q
F F	_F_ ‿ T	F

What about the following disjunctive syllogism?

For our vacation this summer, we shall go either to the mountains or to the seashore. We are going to the mountains for our summer vacation. Therefore we are not going to the seashore.

The form of this argument is

P or Q
P
———
not-Q

Is this argument valid? Let's apply our test (see Figure 11.25).

P or Q	P	not-Q

Figure 11.25

Is there a combination of truth-values which will make both premises true and the conclusion false? Since not-Q is to be false, by our truth-table for "not," Q must be true. So we enter T under Q (see Figure 11.26). Since P must be true, we enter T under P directly (see Figure 11.27).

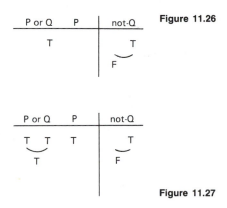

Figure 11.26

Figure 11.27

But now what have we done? We have constructed a combination of truth-values on which both premises are true and the conclusion false. This shows the form and so the argument invalid. We can apply our imaginative test to get the same results as our truth-table test here. We can imagine splitting our vacation between the mountains and the seashore. Hence the fact that we are definitely going one place does not rule out that we shall go to the other. Notice how similar are the two forms of disjunctive syllogism we have examined so far. In Chapter 3—in connection with introducing the fallacies—we said that some formal fallacies, fallacious deductive arguments, are persuasive because their forms closely resemble valid patterns of reasoning. Here we have a concrete example. It practically goes without saying that the form

> P or Q
> Q
> ---
> not-P

is also invalid. But obviously, it closely resembles this form:

> P or Q
> not-Q
> ---
> P

and, given our argument to show that the form of the first two disjunctive syllogisms is valid, it should be easy to see this form valid also. Hence, we must determine the form of a deductive argument carefully if we are to appraise the reasoning properly.

So far, we have not seen the connective "and" occur in any of our arguments. Let's look at one example where it does:

Peter will buy a Datsun, and either Jim will buy a Datsun or he will buy a VW.

It's not the case that both Sharon and Jim will buy Datsuns. Therefore Peter will buy a Datsun and Jim will buy a VW.

What are the simple statements out of which this argument is built?

P — Peter will buy a Datsun.
Q — Jim will buy a Datsun.
R — Jim will buy a VW.
S — Sharon will buy a Datsun.

What is the form of the argument?

P and (Q or R)
not-(S and Q)
P and R

Here we introduce parentheses to do the punctuating "either" and "both" do in ordinary language. Such punctuation is necessary if we are to avoid statements whose truth-conditions are ambiguous. Is this argument valid? Can we find a combination of truth-values on which the premises will come out true and the conclusion false? Unlike our previous arguments where there was just one way to make the conclusion false, since the conclusion here is a conjunction, there are three ways for it to turn out false according to the truth-table. P could be true and R false, P false and R true, or both false. But if we consider the combinations where P is false, then the first premise will be false also because, as our truth-table shows, any conjunction with a false conjunct is false (see Figure 11.28). So P must be true and R false (see Figure 11.29).

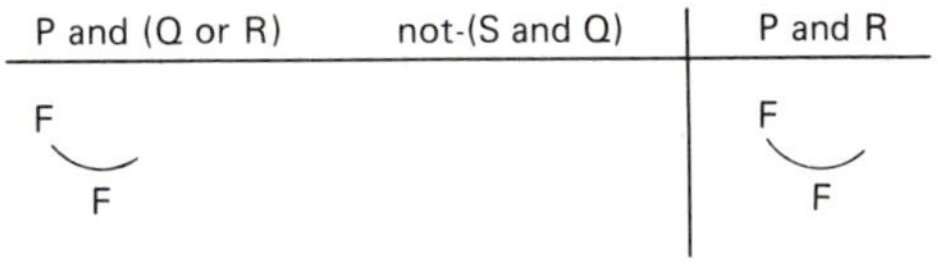

Figure 11.28

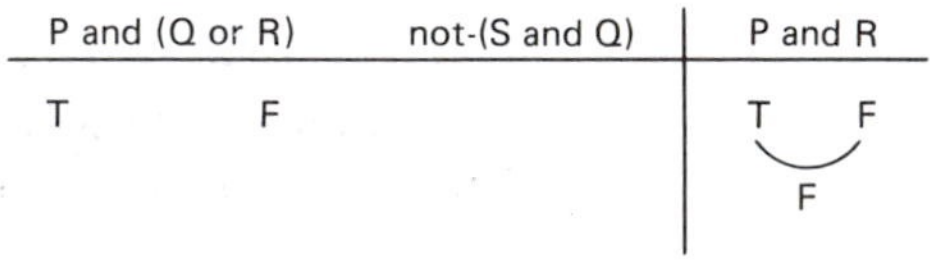

Figure 11.29

For the first premise to be true, both conjuncts must be true, according to the truth-table for "and." P is true. We know that R is false. According to the truth-table for "or," then, Q must be true for the disjunction Q or R to be true (see Figure 11.30).

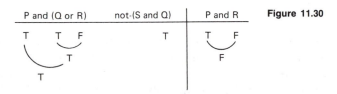

Figure 11.30

Turning to the second premise, for a negation to be true, its component must be false. So the conjunction S and Q must be false. If Q is true, then according to the table for "and," S must be false for the conjunction to be false (see Figure 11.31). But now what have we done? We have constructed a combination of truth-values on which the premises are true and the conclusion false. The argument is shown to be invalid.

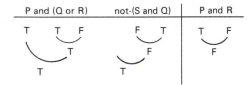

Figure 11.31

We can give one further tip on procedure for the truth-table test illustrated by our discussion. There is just one way to make a simple statement P true or false, as there is just one way to make not-P true or false. There is just one way for a conjunction to be true or a disjunction false. But there are three ways to make a disjunction true or a conjunction false. Suppose a conclusion is a conjunction, and so we want it false. We can begin by considering one of the three combinations. But we have no guarantee that the other statements will have the necessary truth-values on that combination. It is much better to start with statements or components of statements where we have no choice, where just one truth-value will be appropriate, and see whether we can find values for the other simple statements on which all the premises are true and the conclusion false.

Why does the truth-table test do for truth-functional arguments what the Venn diagram test does for categorical syllogisms? Remember that if a Venn diagram shows a categorical syllogism invalid, we can read off from the diagram an invalidating logical analogy. If the truth-table test shows an argument to be invalid, we have a combination of truth-values on which the premises are true and the conclusion false. But clearly if, for example, P, Q, S are true and R false on this combination, we can imagine three true simple statements and one false. Replacing P, Q, S by the true statements and R by the false in our argument form, we get an invalidating logical analogy of the original argument.

Truth-Conditions for the Conditional

There is one connective left to discuss, the conditional. Recall from Chapter 1 that a conditional is any statement of the form

If P, then Q.

P, the statement constituting the if-clause, is called the *antecedent* of the conditional. Q, the then-clause statement, is called the *consequent*. Conditionals are problematic. In ordinary language, many of them are not truth-functional. To see this, suppose that both "Ben the Burglar robbed the store" and "The police will find the merchandise at his shack" are false. What about the conditional

> If Ben the burglar robbed the store, then the police will find the merchandise at his shack.

Is that statement true? We can imagine not only that Ben the Burglar is a thief, but a rather stupid one. He's well known to the police—he gets caught so easily. When he steals something, he keeps it in his shack before disposing of it. Under these circumstances, it seems that if Ben did rob the store, the merchandise would be in his shack for the police to find. The conditional is true. But consider,

> If the moon is made of green cheese, then 2 + 2 = 5.

Both statements are false, but is the conditional true? Many will say no, because there is no connection between antecedent and consequent, as there is in the Ben the Burglar example. But we recognize the two component statements—the moon is made of green cheese—2 + 2 = 5—as both false. This shows that at least in some senses, the conditional is not truth-functional. In one case, two falses are taken into a true, in the other into a false. We don't have a function here.

Some authors see the conditional as having various senses.[6] However, there is one thing on which all various senses agree—the conditional will be false if the antecedent is true and the consequent false. Suppose Uncle Henry is at home, but the porch light is not on, then the conditional

> If Uncle Henry is home, then the porch light is on.

is clearly false. Suppose Aunt Annie has forgotten to add her secret ingredient, but her pie is nonetheless a success. Then the conditional

> If Aunt Annie has forgotten to add her secret ingredient, then her pie will not be a success.

will be false. At least in the case where the antecedent is true and the consequent false, the conditional will have a single value—false. So we may present one line of the truth-table (see Figure 11.32).

P	Q	If P, then Q.
T	F	F

Figure 11.32

Fortunately, in checking several basic forms of arguing, this is all we need. However, there will be times when we need to imagine P, Q having other values than P true and Q false. What should be the value of the conditional in these cases? Notice that with the Ben the Burglar example, we could have a conditional true with P, Q both false. Suppose it's false that Ben the Burglar robbed the store, but it's true that the police will find the merchandise at his shack. Someone else put it there in an attempt to frame Ben. But given what we have said about Ben, isn't the conditional

> If Ben the Burglar robbed the store, then the police will find the merchandise at the shack.

still true? Now suppose Aunt Annie has added her secret ingredient, and this makes her pie so good that there is no competition. It will get first prize at the fair. Then the conditional

> If Aunt Annie adds her secret ingredient, then her pie will get first prize at the fair.

is true, and both antecedent and consequent are true. What this shows is that for the other three conceivable combinations of truth-values—antecedent and consequent both true; antecedent false, consequent true; antecedent, consequent both false—there are conditionals which are true. This motivates introducing a special, completely truth-functional sense of the conditional called the *material conditional* or *material implication*. In this sense, the conditional If P, then Q is true just in case we don't have P true and Q false. We can present its truth conditions in a truth-table (see Figure 11.33).

P	Q	If P, then Q.
T	T	T
T	F	F
F	T	T
F	F	T

Figure 11.33

As the truth-functional "and" discounts any temporal or other suggestions a conjunctive expression may make, so the material conditional discounts any assertion of some connection between the antecedent and consequent. The material conditional is completely truth-functional. Given a possible combination of truth values, there will be associated one unique value of the entire conditional, given by the truth-table. This sense of the conditional, however, is logically very important. In appraising arguments for validity which involve conditionals, we interpret the conditional this way and count the argument valid or invalid depending on whether or not it is impossible to imagine a combination of truth values on which the premises are all true and the conclusion false.

Hypothetical Syllogisms

There are a number of patterns of reasoning involving conditionals which frequently recur. Some are valid; others invalid. Let's identify these patterns of reasoning and apply our truth-table test to see why they are cogent or fallacious. Categorical statements are also called hypotheticals. Logicians have identified and given special names to various types of hypothetical syllogisms. If all three component statements of a syllogism are hypotheticals, the argument is a pure hypothetical syllogism. For example,

> If Jack is out in the motor boat, then he'll enjoy cruising around.
> If Jack enjoys cruising around, then he'll run out of gas. Therefore
> If Jack is out in the motor boat, then he'll run out of gas.

Is this argument valid? First, what is its form?

$$\frac{\begin{array}{l} \text{If P, then Q} \\ \text{If Q, then R} \end{array}}{\text{If P, then R}}$$

Can we imagine a combination of truth-values on which the premises are both true and the conclusion false? According to our truth-table for the conditional, if the conclusion is false, P must be true and R false. Let's enter those values in our truth-table (see Figure 11.34).

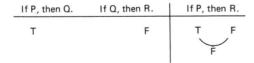

Figure 11.34

Given that P is true, our truth-table shows that Q also must be true, if the first premise is to be true. But what about the second premise? For that to be true, since R is false, Q must be false. So Q must be both true and false. Impossible. So this pattern is valid, and every argument sharing this form is valid also. But is every pure hypothetical syllogism valid?

If Allison has insomnia, then she will take sleeping pills.

If Allison has a drug dependency, then she will take sleeping pills. Therefore

If Allison has insomnia, then she has a drug dependency.

The form is

> If P, then Q
> If R, then Q
> ———————
> If P, then R

Can we imagine a combination of truth-values which shows arguments of this form invalid? Again P must be true, R false. But suppose Q is true. The first premise will have true antecedent and consequent. The second premise will have false antecedent, true consequent. Both will be true according to our truth-table for the conditional (see Figure 11.35). The argument is invalid.

If P, then Q.	If R, then Q.	If P, then R.
T T	F T	T F
T	T	F

Figure 11.35

Pure hypothetical syllogisms may be contrasted with *mixed hypothetical syllogisms,* where at least one component statement is *not* a conditional. Two pairs of mixed hypothetical syllogisms have particular logical interest. The first member of each pair is valid; the second, although it closely resembles the first, is invalid. Here's an illustration of the first pair:

Valid

A. If the bull is let loose in the china shop, then there will be a terrible disaster.
The bull will be let loose in the china shop. Therefore
There will be a terrible disaster.

Invalid

B. If the bull is let loose in the china shop, then there will be a terrible disaster.
There will be a terrible disaster.
Therefore,
The bull will be let loose in the china shop.

What are the contrasting logical forms of these arguments?

Valid

A. If P, then Q
   P
   ———
   Q

Invalid

B. If P, then Q
   Q
   ———
   P

Form A is called *modus ponens*. In Latin, *modus* means "way" or "method"; *ponens* is derived from *ponere* meaning "to affirm." *Modus ponens* then means "method of affirmation." The conditional premise asserts that if one thing, P, is the case, so is something else, Q. But that P is the case is *affirmed* as the second premise, and Q is drawn as the conclusion. Why is *modus ponens* valid? To find an invalidating combination of truth-values, Q must be false and P true. But then to make the first premise true, we must either imagine P simultaneously false or Q true; that is, we must imagine a contradiction.

Form B is called the *fallacy of affirming the consequent*. Why are arguments of this form invalid? Can we imagine a combination of truth values making the premises true and the conclusion false? Indeed we can! P must be false and Q true, but then, according to our truth-table for the conditional, the first premise is also true (see Figure 11.36).

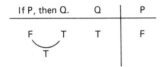

Figure 11.36

The second pair of mixed hypothetical syllogisms is illustrated by these examples:

Valid	*Invalid*
A. If John buys stock in Consolidated Illusionists, then he will be buying a risky investment. John will not buy a risky investment. Therefore He will not buy stock in Consolidated Illusionists.	B. If John buys stock in Consolidated Illusionists, then he will be buying a risky investment. John will not buy stock in Consolidated Illusionists. Therefore He will not buy a risky investment (i.e., there's no risky investment he'll buy).

Here are the contrasting forms of these arguments:

Valid	*Invalid*
A. If P, then Q	B. If P, then Q
not-Q	not-P
not-P	not-Q

Form A is called *modus tollens*. Again we go back to the Latin. The term *tollere* means "to deny." The name means "method of denial." The hypothetical premise claims that if one thing, P, is the case, so is something else, Q. But the other premise *denies* that Q is the case. From this we conclude that P is not true either. It should be easy to see why arguments of the form *modus tollens* are valid. To make not-P false, P must be true, and to make not-Q true, Q must be false. But then the first premise is false. To make it true, either P must also be false or Q true, a contradiction.

But what about arguments displaying form B? This form is called the *fallacy of denying the antecedent*. Why is it fallacious or invalid? We can readily imagine an invalidating combination of truth values. Q must be true and P false. But, then, according to our truth-table for the conditional, the first premise is true (see Figure 11.37).

If P, then Q.	not-P	not-Q
F T	F	T
T	T	F

Figure 11.37

In examining these hypothetical syllogisms, we have not only illustrated again how our truth-table test works to appraise truth-functional arguments, but also how closely fallacious argument forms resemble valid ones. This again underscores how we must be careful in determining the form of arguments if we are to appraise them properly. We have now surveyed the principal forms of disjunctive and hypothetical syllogisms. By remembering these forms, we can readily appraise whether a number of deductive arguments are valid or invalid. Our truth-table test, however, can be applied to any truth-functional argument.[7]

One issue remains. Now that we have looked at negations, conjunctions, disjunctions, conditionals, and their truth-conditions, how may we argue that such statements are true? We may, of course, as in all arguments we have seen so far, seek premises which directly support our claim. However, for conditionals and negations, there are special strategies. Although not all arguments employing these strategies need be deductive arguments, many of them will be. It is important to consider these strategies, since diagramming them requires extending the techniques developed in Chapter 6. We turn to this in the next section.

Summary

We have presented in truth-tables the truth-conditions for four truth-functional connectives: negation, conjunction, disjunction, and the conditional. With these truth-tables at hand, we can readily determine the truth or falsity of statements built up by these connectives, once we know the truth or falsity of their components. A statement which has no other complete statements as components is simple; one which does is compound. Given a truth-functional argument, an argument whose validity depends on the truth-conditions of the truth-functional connectives and the overall pattern of the argument, we may identify the simple statements out of which it is built. If we can imagine a combination of truth values on which all the premises are true and the conclusion false, then the argument is invalid. If attempting to do this requires us to imagine a statement both true and false, then the argument is valid. This is the truth-table test.

Exercise 11-III

Determine whether arguments displaying the following forms are valid or invalid by applying the truth-table test.

1. P or (if Q, then R)
   Q and not-R
   ―――――――――――
   P

2. If P, then (Q or R)
   not-Q
   ―――――――――――
   not-P

3. If P, then Q
   If R, then S
   P and R
   ―――――――――――
   Q and S

4. If P, then Q
   If R, then S
   P and Q
   ―――――――――――
   R and S

5. If P, then R
   If Q, then R
   P or Q
   ―――――――――――
   R

Exercise 11-IV

Using the letters P, Q, R, . . . to represent simple statements, display the forms of the following arguments. Then in each case, determine whether the argument is valid or invalid. Indicate if the argument is an instance of *modus ponens, modus tollens,* fallacy of affirming the consequent, fallacy of denying the antecedent. Otherwise use the truth-table test to appraise the argument. Note that in a number of examples, the conclusion is not stated last. Be sure to determine which statement is the conclusion in determining the form of the argument.

1. If John is the father of Joe, then Joe was born after 1946. John is the father of Joe. Hence Joe was born after 1946.

2. If the price of gas goes up, then I shall have to drive less. I'm not going to have to drive less. Hence the price of gas isn't going to go up.

3. John received a letter. If John has gotten the appointment, then he has received a letter. Hence John has gotten the appointment.

4. Mary is not feeling cold. If Mary is feeling cold, then she will put on a sweater. Thus Mary is not going to put on a sweater.

5. Oil prices will go up or gas prices will go up. Oil prices will go up. It follows that gas prices will not go up.

6. If oil prices rise, then inflation will rise. If inflation rises, then the administration's unpopularity will grow. Hence if oil prices rise, then the administration's unpopularity will grow.

7. David has just solved an outstanding mathematical problem. Now if David has just solved an outstanding mathematical problem, Alonzo will be pleased. Hence Alonzo will be pleased.

8. Rudolf is very unhappy. Now either Alfred has not been silent about his theological views or Rudolf is happy. So Alfred has not been silent about his theological views.

9. Mr. Roper will go to Washington and he will be besieged by lobbyists. Hence Mr. Roper will be besieged by lobbyists or he is an honest politician.

10. Either the United States won't go to the Olympics or the Soviet Union won't go to the Olympics. So it's not the case that both the United States and the Soviet Union will go to the Olympics.

11. If the president chooses someone other than the current vice-president as his running mate, then there will be quite a flap in the party. Also, if the president chooses someone other than the current vice-president as his running mate, then his chances of winning will improve. Therefore if there is quite a flap in the party, the president's chances of winning will improve.

12. If Kenneth sells his car, then Barbara will be unhappy. Kenneth is going to sell his car. Hence he is moving to Washington.

13. If Elinor discourses on company policy, then Harry will be mad. Also, if Jim discourses on company policy, Harry will be mad. Hence if Elinor discourses on company policy, Jim will discourse on company policy.

14. If a Republican and a Democrat discuss their political views, then there will be an acrimonious debate. If the opposing presidential candidates have a debate, then a Republican and a Democrat will discuss their political views. Hence if there is an acrimonious debate, then the opposing presidential candidates will have a debate.

15. If the recession gets much worse, then Mr. Roper will go to Washington. If Mr. Roper goes to Washington, then he will learn many things. Hence the recession will get much worse.

16. If Myra goes to Japan, then she will take many photographs. But Myra's camera is broken, since she will not take many photographs.

17. It's not the case that the siege engine isn't broken. So it must be broken.

18. If Captain Smith sells his boat, then there will be one less ship in the fishing fleet. If the price of gasoline goes up, Captain Smith will sell his boat. Hence if there is one less ship in the fishing fleet, the price of gasoline is going up.

19. If fluctuations in the price of gold indicate the amount of terror people feel, then the price of silver will jump dramatically. This is because if fluctuations in the price of gold indicate the amount of terror people feel, then the price will skyrocket over the next six months. But if the price of gold skyrockets over the next six months, then the price of silver will jump drastically also.

20. Tomorrow never comes. For if tomorrow comes, then it is today. But tomorrow is never today.

§11.3 ARGUMENT STRATEGY

Conditional Argument Strategy

Consider the conditional:

If John gets the promotion, then he'll get married.

How could we try to convince someone of this statement other than by presenting premises which directly support it? First, what do we mean by direct support? Think of our tree diagrams. The arrows so far all point downward to conclusions; if one statement supports another, we can trace a path via these arrows from the supporting statement down to the supported statement. If the path does not pass through any rebuttal, but just through intermediate conclusions and modalities, if any, it should be obvious to see that the path goes directly from the premise to the conclusion. The argument exhibits *direct argument strategy*. When some premises serve as counterrebuttals while others give direct evidence, we may say we have *direct strategy with counterrebuttals*. So all our diagrams so far have been for arguments exhibiting direct strategy. Now we might give such a direct argument for our conditional. But more likely, we would proceed this way: we would assume, *for the sake of argument,* that John does get the promotion. We would then try to argue from this assumption and other information which we could use as premises to the claim that John will get married. If this argument were successful, then since on assumption that John got the promotion, we showed he would get married, we would conclude that we had shown true the conditional statement that if John gets the promotion, then he will get married.

Clearly if upon assuming the antecedent of a conditional, we could *deduce* the consequent, produce a series of deductively correct arguments with the antecedent as a basic premise in the first argument and the consequent as the final conclusion, we would have deductively strong justification for the conditional. Why? Remember that in a valid deductive argument, if the premises are true, so must be the conclusion. So, given that the other premises used in our argument are true, if the antecedent is also true, so is the consequent. But that is precisely the conditional we wanted to establish. By means of this reasoning we have given a deductively valid argument for it. Similarly, if upon assuming the antecedent, we have a correct inductive argument for the consequent, then we have inductively good reason to assert that if the antecedent is true, so is the consequent.

How do these arguments differ from all that we have seen so far? To assert a premise in an argument with direct strategy is to assert that statement as true. But when we assert, for the sake of argument, that the antecedent of a conditional is true, do we claim that the statement is true outright, or are we just treating it as true, regarding it as true provisionally for the purpose of argument? If I say "Suppose something is true," am I claiming that this is true? Clearly not. I'm only asking for a provisional assumption. We know that if a premise directly supporting a conclusion is false, we have a real problem with the argument—the fallacy of false premise. But suppose our provisional assumption proved false? Suppose John isn't going to get the promotion. Would we charge the argument with false premise? Since we never claimed the statement was true, this would be inappropriate. Even if our assumed premise is false, we can still validly deduce statements from it. If we have validly deduced the consequent from the antecedent, the falsity of the antecedent does not affect the deductive correctness of the argument. Remember that a deductive argument is valid just in case *if* the premises are true, the conclusion must be true. This does not claim that the premises are true. Similarly, if a premise of an inductive argument is false, this does not mean the argument fails to be inductively correct. If the premise were true, it still could be more likely than not that the conclusion would be true. But—and we shall develop this more shortly—in arguing for a conditional by assuming the antecedent and reasoning to the consequent, we are presenting this whole argument as the reason for the conditional, not the assumed premise.

Let's see how this procedure would go. We frequently indicate that we are assuming a premise by such expressions as "suppose" or "assume." The beginning of our argument might look like this:

> Let us assume that John does get the promotion. Then he will have enough income to support a wife. But if John has enough income to support a wife, then he will get married. Hence he'll get married.

Preparing this argument for diagramming, we have

(Let us assume that) ① [John does get the promotion.]

(Then) ② [he will have enough income to support a wife.] But

③ [if John has enough income to support a wife, then he will get

married.] (Hence) ④ [he'll get married.]

The structure of the argument so far looks like that in Figure 11.38.

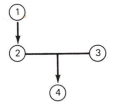

Figure 11.38

But having assumed (1), we have shown that (4) follows or is supported; we have justification for asserting that *if* (1) is true, then so is (4), if John gets the promotion, then he'll get married. But this is precisely the conditional we wanted to establish. Let's number it as (5). How do we show that the *argument* from (1) to (4) supports (5)? We enclose the argument from (1) to (4) in a box on both sides and below, with a downward-directed arrow from the lower line to (5). Notice that the status of (1) is radically different from (3). Statement (1) is a provisional assumption. Statement (3) is a basic premise. Should (3) be false or questionable, we would have the fallacy of false or questionable premise. We indicate that (1) is a provisional assumption, but (3) is not by drawing a line at the top of the box over (1) but not over (3). The entire diagram looks like that in Figure 11.39.

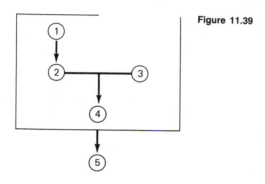

Figure 11.39

Frequently, when people first encounter conditional argument strategy, they find it rather magical. Why were we allowed just to assume that John does get a raise? Why did we assume *that* (and not something else)? Can we just assume anything? But if we can assume anything, then why not assume what you are trying to prove and be done with argument? Something must be wrong here. Let's go back. We assumed that John will get the promotion because we wanted to show that if he gets the promotion, then he will marry. Knowing what our conclusion was that we were trying to establish, knowing that it was a conditional, and identifying the antecedent of that conditional explains why we assumed that particular statement. Notice that we did not assume the entire conditional, but just the antecedent. So we are not assuming what we are trying to prove; we are not committing the fallacy of begging the question. Our procedure is legitimate, because we have specifically acknowledged the provisional character of our assumption and have ended with a final conclusion which does not depend on the truth of that provisional assumption. Our diagram displays this by putting the argument from (1) to (4) in a box and putting a line over (1).

In an argument using conditional strategy, it is possible that all the initial premises are provisional assumptions. In that case, we may simply draw a line across the entire top of the box to indicate that the case for the conditional conclusion is based on the deductive or inductive correctness of the argument inside the box, not on the statements themselves or their truth.[8] On the other hand, the conditional argument may have several provisional assumptions together with several basic premises on which the truth of the conclusion depends. In that case, we draw the top line over all the provisional assumptions, but not over any of the other basic premises.

The Strategy of Reduction To Absurdity

Consideration of conditional arguments leads directly to the next strategy, *reduction to absurdity*, also frequently referred to by its Latin name, *reductio ad absurdum*. In conditional arguments, our goal was to establish some conditional statement as conclusion. In reduction to absurdity arguments, the goal is to show some negation, to show that it is not the case that some statement holds. This is done by assuming provisionally that the statement is true, that it does hold, and reasoning to a statement which is recognized as false. The argument then points out that this consequence is false and concludes that the provisional assumption is false. That is, it concludes to the negation of the provisional assumption, what the argument wanted to show in the first place.

It is not hard to see an intimate connection between this strategy and the valid *modus tollens* argument form presented in the last section. Let not-P represent the negation we are trying to establish. Then our provisional assumption will be P. Let Q be the false statement we reason to from P. Then our argument in effect establishes the conditional, If P, then Q, using conditional argument strategy. But then our argument points out that Q is false, that is, not-Q, and concludes via *modus tollens* to not-P. Let's look at a concrete example:

> Jones clearly is not the murderer, for suppose that he did commit the murder. Then since the coroner's autopsy shows that the victim died between 8:00 and 9:00 P.M. of a gunshot wound which would kill immediately, and the victim was in his apartment in New York City, Jones was in New York at that time. But this is impossible, since witnesses will testify that Jones was in San Francisco at 10:00 P.M. (Eastern time) (7:00 P.M. Pacific time) on the same day. So Jones is not guilty of the deed.

How did this argument proceed? After stating the negation it sought to prove, it assumed the opposite. From this and from other information known about the situation, it derived a conclusion for which there was significant evidence to show it false. After presenting this evidence, the argument ended by viewing its original claim as being established.

How should we diagram this argument? First, let's prepare it for diagramming:

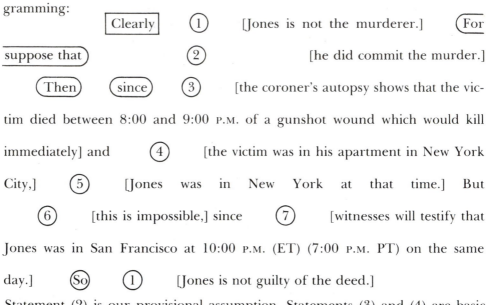

Statement (2) is our provisional assumption. Statements (3) and (4) are basic premises. All three are linked to derive (5). As with conditional argument strategy, this part of the argument should be enclosed in a box. At the top of the box we draw a line over (2) but not over (3) or (4), to indicate that (2) is a provisional assumption (see Figure 11.40).

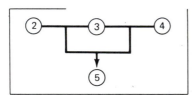

Figure 11.40

Since the argument proceeds to show (1), its final conclusion, by showing that (5) follows from (2) and showing that (5) is false, the claim that (5) is false, that is, (6), should be linked with the boxed argument to support the final conclusion (see Figure 11.41). All that remains is to represent (7) in the diagram. It is a reason for (6) as the premise indicator clearly shows. All we need do is add (7) circled with an arrow down to (6) to our previous diagram.

Figure 11.41

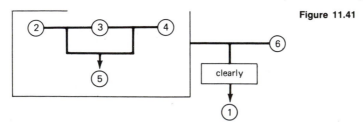

Why is this called the strategy of reduction to absurdity? When we have derived a conclusion Q from our provisional assumption and have further claimed that conclusion false, we in effect have a contradiction; better anyone still accepting the provisional assumption would be forced to believe a contradiction. But this is something absurd. Our provisional assumption has been reduced to absurdity, and so we are justified in denying it. Conditional and reduction to absurdity strategies are rather specialized. However, we can meet with such arguments in everyday contexts. Without extending our diagramming technique, it would be rather confusing trying to ascertain the structure of such arguments. Having considered conditionals and negations in the last section, it was appropriate to take up this topic here.

Exercise 11-V

Construct diagrams for each of the following arguments according to the circle and arrow method as supplemented by the techniques of this section. Indicate in each case which strategy is being used.

1. We claim that if the Federal Reserve Board increases the money supply, then the stock market will rally. For suppose the Federal Reserve Board increases the money supply. Then there will be more money in the economy. Hence competition for money will not be as fierce, and so banks will lower the rate of interest charged for loans. But if we have lower interest rates, businessmen and other investors will take out more loans. As a consequence, business will be good. But if business is good, then the stock market will rally. Hence the stock market will rally.

2. Consider the theory that whether an action is right or wrong depends entirely upon the amount of happiness or unhappiness it brings into existence. Suppose this theory is true. What is the consequence? We can imagine that I could bring about a world in which millions would be kept permanently happy simply by consigning a certain lost soul on the far-off edge of things to a life of lonely torture. On this theory, that action would be right. But it is clearly not right. It is an act of injustice. Hence making the rightness or wrongness of an action depend on the amount of happiness it brings about is an inadequate and inaccurate moral theory.—Adapted from material in Carl Wellman, *Challenge and Response.*

3. If there is no other way to defend our citizens from unjust Soviet aggression than the threat of the bomb, then the bishops' document [the pastoral letter on nuclear weapons issued by the Roman Catholic House of Bishops in May 1983] puts the American government in the position of being morally wrong no matter what it does. How may we see this? Suppose it is true that there is no other way to defend our citizens from unjust Soviet aggression than the threat of the bomb. Now on the one hand we have the moral stricture against the use of the atom bomb under any circumstances. Yet on the other hand we are told that it is "obligatory" for a government to defend its citizens "from unjust aggression." So the government cannot use the bomb, and yet it must use the

bomb or at least the threat of it—which means it must be able to use the bomb. So no matter what the government does, it is morally wrong.—Adapted from material in a William F. Buckley editorial, May 8, 1983.

4. Suppose, as classical theism claims, that there is an all-powerful god and that this god is also all benevolent. Now we know that evil exists. Therefore this god does not prevent evil from existing. But since this god is all benevolent, he does not will that this evil exist. But if this god is all powerful, if he does not will something to exist, he prevents it from existing. Hence this god is not all-powerful. But nothing can be all-powerful and not all-powerful. Hence the god of classical theism does not exist.

5. If the Giants are first, then the Braves will be fourth. How may we see this? Suppose the Giants are first. Now we know that if the Giants are first, then the Cards will be third. So, on our supposition, the Cards are third. Now if the Cards are third, then if the Dodgers are second, the Braves will be fourth. In fact, the Dodgers will be second. So the Braves will be fourth.—Adapted from an example in Patrick Suppes, *Introduction to Logic*.

6. Suppose that by a subscription of the rich the eighteen pence or two shillings, which men earn now, were made up to five shillings. It might be imagined, perhaps, that they would then be able to live comfortably and have a piece of meat every day for their dinner. But this would be a very false conclusion. The transfer of three additional shillings a day to each laborer would not increase the quantity of meat in the country. There is not at present enough for all to have a moderate share. What would then be the consequence? The competition among the buyers in the market of meat would rapidly raise the price from eight pence or nine pence to two or three shillings in the pound, and the commodity would not be divided among many more than it is at present.—Thomas Malthus. (Hint: Malthus's final conclusion is left unstated. How would you formulate it?)

7. Rev. Jerry Falwell, leader of the Moral Majority, has spread a lot of hatred in the name of religion. But he now carries meanness to a new low as he goes about declaring that the terrible disease AIDS (acquired immune deficiency syndrome) is a plague that God is using to punish homosexuals.

Let's assume that AIDS is a form of divine retribution. It is true that homosexual males are the primary victims of AIDS, a baffling disease that cripples the body's ability to ward off infections, cancers and other afflictions. Of the 1,676 cases of AIDS recorded by the Center for Disease Control in Atlanta through June 27, 1,185—or 70.7 percent—involved homosexuals.

But there have been 394 cases of AIDS involving intravenous users of drugs, Haitian immigrants and hemophiliacs—victims who were not gay. Is God punishing these groups?

The disease control center reports that all the homosexual AIDS victims are male, which raises a question for Falwell: Is God being selective in imposing his "plague" because he hates male homosexuals more than gay women?

Then there is the question why God hasn't cursed homosexuals with equal vengeance in all the world. While our disease control center was recording

1,676 cases, including 650 deaths, Italy was reporting only two cases of AIDS, Japan only one, Mexico two and the United Kingdom six. Does Falwell think that God hates American gays more than those in England, Italy, or countries like the Soviet Union and China, which haven't mentioned the disease?

It is irresponsible—no, it is blasphemous—for a self-styled man of religion to finger God as the purveyor of the fear, the suffering, the dying that is involved in this outbreak of AIDS.—Carl T. Rowan, July 10, 1983. © by and permission of News America Syndicate. (Hint: Key elements in this argument are the rhetorical questions. They indicate suppressed premises and conclusions. Does Rowan expect them to be answered "yes" or "no" by his audience? Does he implicitly conclude that on Falwell's assumptions, Rev. Falwell must conclude the opposite?)

8. Much of the nation continues to wallow in guilt over the outrageously racist internment of 120,000 West Coast Japanese Americans during World War II. A U.S. commission has told Congress that it ought to allocate some $1.5 billion to pay $20,000 to each of the 60,000 Japanese Americans who have survived what the commission calls a "grave injustice."

However, there are sound grounds to question this proposal. Suppose we grant we should pay 60,000 Japanese Americans $20,000 each. That is, suppose Congress wants to go on a guilt trip and use its budget to ease America's conscience. Then it will find that at least three groups are in line ahead of the Japanese for compensation in the name of justice.

America is a picnic for citizens of Japanese descent, compared with the millions of Indians (Native Americans, I'm supposed to say!)

It has taken four decades for Americans to admit officially that we committed a grievous offense against the humanity of Japanese Americans. But we have been spitting on American Indians for more than 30 decades. We still have most of them in unofficial internment, hidden away in their misery in the most wretched backwoods of America.

Anyone for giving every injured Indian $20,000?

Then there are the Haitians who fled their miserable country seeking freedom in the United States, only to find imprisonment in the Krome Avenue Detention Center in Florida, and similar places.

I saw the dehumanizing conditions under which the Haitians lived until the U.S. federal courts declared that this government was behaving abominably toward some pitiable people.

Anyone for giving $20,000 to every abused Haitian?

Black Americans have been interned in the ditches, the kitchens, the cotton fields, the ghettos, the jailhouses of America for as long as this country has existed. Anyone in favor of the federal government giving $20,000 to every black American as compensation?

Yet is it fair to give compensation to one group and not another? Clearly, this proposal is very questionable.—Carl T. Rowan, June 26, 1983. © by and permission of News America Syndicate. (Hint: What is Rowan's implicit conclusion about the consequences of the commission's proposal? What elements in the passage support this conclusion? What is the role of the rhetorical questions?)

FOR FURTHER READING

The concept of logical analogy and the formal nature of syllogistic argument are discussed in Irving M. Copi's *Introduction to Logic,* 6th ed. (New York: Macmillan Publishing Company, 1982), pp. 214–16. Copi discusses why Venn diagrams work for testing syllogistic validity on pp. 223–25, and we are indebted to his discussion. Indeed, having taught Venn diagrams from Copi's text on a number of occasions, we have had his whole discussion, presented on pp. 202–08 and pp. 217–23, in the back of our minds when composing our account of the Venn diagram test. Copi discusses sorites on pp. 258–61 and one premise inferences on pp. 185–98. He considers asyllogistic inferences on pp. 378–82. His discussion of disjunctive and hypothetical syllogisms occurs on pp. 261–64. On pp. 268–72 he discusses the dilemma, a special kind of argument involving disjunction. Chapter 8 gives a basic discussion of truth-functional logic.

In *Logic,* 3rd ed. (Englewood Cliffs, N.J.: Prentice-Hall, Inc., 1984), Wesley C. Salmon discusses relational arguments and the fallacy of "every" and "all" on pp. 73–85. The boxing method to display the structure of arguments using the conditional argument or reduction to absurdity strategies is taken from Stephen N. Thomas's *Practical Reasoning in Natural Language,* 2nd ed. (Englewood Cliffs, N.J.: Prentice-Hall, Inc., 1981), pp. 155–58.

NOTES

[1]Note that we say invalid as a syllogism, not invalid outright. It is possible that an argument instancing an invalid syllogistic form can be deductively valid, but this is because the argument possesses further features—further form or structure—which makes it valid. Deductive arguments can be instances of many different forms, some invalid while others are valid. However, for our purposes in this section, we need not consider such possible further structure. If an argument instances an invalid syllogistic form, we count it invalid.

[2]Some texts actually build these features into the definition of a categorical syllogism.

[3]The consistency tree method does for quantificational arguments in general what our Venn diagram test did for categorical syllogisms. It gives us a formal way of tracing out the consequences of trying to imagine the premises true and the conclusion false. The test first appeared in a text in Richard Jeffrey's *Formal Logic: Its Scope and Limits* (New York: McGraw-Hill Book Company, 1967). It is presented also in Howard Kahane's *Logic and Philosophy: A Modern Introduction,* 4th ed. (Belmont, Calif.: Wadsworth Publishing Company, 1982), pp. 347–63, and Hugues Leblanc and William A. Wisdom's *Deductive Logic,* 2nd ed. (Boston: Allyn & Bacon, Inc., 1976).

[4]See Wesley C. Salmon, *Logic,* 3rd ed. (Englewood-Cliffs, N.J.: Prentice-Hall, Inc., 1984), p. 84.

[5]Technically this definition should be amended to handle certain complex syllogisms. But we need not consider such refinements at this point.

[6]See Irving M. Copi, *Introduction to Logic,* 6th ed. (New York: Macmillan Publishing Company, 1982), pp. 290–91.

[7]Standard treatments of basic truth-functional logic include another connective, the biconditional "if and only if." However, as its name suggests, a biconditional statement "P if and only if Q" can be treated as a conjunction of conditionals, "If P, then Q and If Q, then P." Hence, its logic requires nothing new, and we leave consideration of this connective specifically to courses and texts in formal logic.

[8]Compare Stephen N. Thomas, *Practical Reasoning in Natural Language,* 2nd ed. (Englewood Cliffs, N.J.: Prentice-Hall, Inc., 1981), p. 157.

INDEX